Balaguer and the Dominican Military

ALSO BY BRIAN J. BOSCH

The Salvadoran Officer Corps and the
Final Offensive of 1981 (McFarland, 1999)

Balaguer and the Dominican Military

*Presidential Control of
the Factional Officer Corps
in the 1960s and 1970s*

BRIAN J. BOSCH

McFarland & Company, Inc., Publishers
Jefferson, North Carolina, and London

LIBRARY OF CONGRESS CATALOGUING-IN-PUBLICATION DATA

Bosch, Brian J.
    Balaguer and the Dominican military : presidential
control of the factional officer corps in the 1960s and
1970s / Brian J. Bosch.
     p.   cm.
    Includes bibliographical references and index.

    ISBN-13: 978-0-7864-3072-7
    softcover : 50# alkaline paper ∞

    1. Dominican Republic—Armed Forces—Officers—
History—20th century.   2. Balaguer, Joaquín, 1906–2002.
3. Dominican Republic—Armed Forces—History—20th
century.   4. Dominican Republic—Politics and government
—1961–   I. Title.
UB415.D65B67   2007
972.9305'4—dc22   2007010964

British Library cataloguing data are available

Cover photograph: Dominican Armed Forces color guard at
the 1st Brigade, 1973

Manufactured in the United States of America

McFarland & Company, Inc., Publishers
  Box 611, Jefferson, North Carolina 28640
  www.mcfarlandpub.com

For my wife, Polly, who shared my three and one half years in Santo Domingo, who provided me with guidance on literary composition, and who was first editor of this manuscript.

Contents

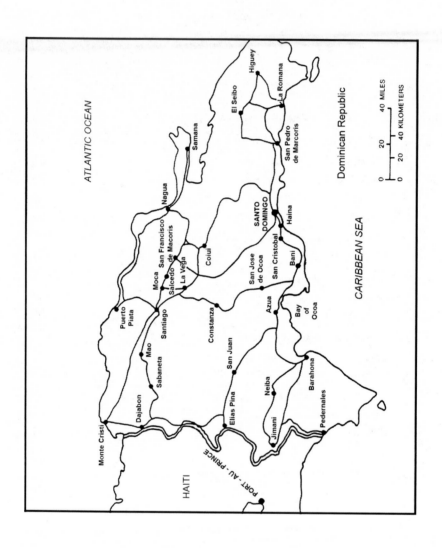

Preface

In 1961, the dictatorship of Generalissimo Rafael Trujillo in the Dominican Republic collapsed after thirty-one years. With the disappearance of the Trujillo regime, the country descended into a period of national turmoil and political instability. At that critical time, the military establishment could have been a stabilizing transitional force; instead, the officer corps contributed to the chaos that enveloped the Dominican Republic by engaging in internecine factionalism. The height of the turbulence was reached in 1965 when a catastrophic civil war engulfed Santo Domingo. It was a conflagration that could be extinguished only by the intervention of foreign troops in which the United States played the lead role. A multinational effort allowed presidential elections to take place in June 1966, resulting in the installation of Doctor Joaquín Balaguer in the presidency. This meek-looking scholar and poet proved to be a skillful politico-military *caudillo*. Through manipulation, he brought the various virulent officer corps factions to heel, and by the mid–1970s, he had successfully consolidated his control over the Armed Forces establishment.

President Balaguer faced military threats both from outside and from within his government. In 1971, he neutralized the external danger from ultra-right retired General Wessin y Wessin by staging a counter-coup, and in 1973 he eliminated the threat from left wing former Colonel Caamaño by defeating Caamaño's Cuba-based guerrilla expedition. Internally, Balaguer demonstrated his uncanny ability to prevail over the officer corps, principally by manipulating the rivalry of the factions of Generals Nivar and Pérez y Pérez, the two most powerful military leaders in the country. In the presence of strong men, a master puppeteer subtly but skillfully was pulling the strings. No officer, or clique of officers, was able to dominate the mild-mannered, but iron-willed, diminutive civilian president.

I was a personal observer of many of these events. In describing what occurred in the Dominican Republic, I have utilized three major sources. The first was the broad range of military and politico-military information that I absorbed while serving as the army attaché in the U.S.

1

Embassy, Dominican Republic, during 1971–1974. As with American military attaches worldwide, my basic task was to provide the U.S. government with a description of the host country's military capabilities. This routine requirement centered on the organization, equipment, and operational proficiency of the Dominican ground forces. (The two principal users of this category of reporting were the Defense Intelligence Agency in Washington, D.C., and the U.S. Southern Command, headquartered in the former Panama Canal Zone.) Ordinary Dominican order of battle, however, was not the highest priority for the majority of U.S. government agencies. That priority was politico-military affairs. After the 1965 intervention of American troops in Santo Domingo, the embassy's Defense Attaché Office devoted the majority of its effort to tracking the politics of the Dominican military establishment. This mission was intensified because Washington had assumed an active role in stabilizing the Dominican Republic. (The main consumers of this type of message traffic were the American ambassador, various national-level civilian departments and agencies in Washington, and, in the Department of Defense, the policy apparatus of the Pentagon and politico-military analysts in the Defense Intelligence Agency.)

The second major source for this project was the political reporting filed by the U.S. ambassador in Santo Domingo. These messages usually were disseminated as Department of State "telegrams" and "airgrams." State Department records for the years 1963–1973 have undergone an official security review, and, subsequently, large quantities of documents from the U.S. Embassy, Santo Domingo, were declassified. This correspondence was transferred to the National Archives, providing researchers with access to American embassy reporting on the Dominican Republic.

The third important source for this work was the collective body of "intelligence information reports" (IRs) dispatched by the Defense Attaché Office, Santo Domingo, concerning the Cuba-based guerrilla incursion into the Dominican Republic in 1973. Most of those reports were radio-transmitted messages. Beginning in November 1998, I submitted numerous Freedom of Information Act requests to the Defense Intelligence Agency for the release of select documents on the subject. From these declassified IRs, it was possible to reconstruct the Armed Forces' counterinsurgency campaign, which, after the 1965 civil war, was the most important Dominican military action in the second half of the 20th century.

In addition to these three unique general sources, information was gained through secondary works, the press, and military journals. Biographies and histories were the best means to acquire an understanding of the Trujillo era. Newspapers presented a day-to-day account of the Balaguer years; the two prominent Santo Domingo dailies, *Listín Diario* and *El Caribe*, were the most reliable papers in the country. Equally important was the radio reporting from Dominican, as well as from other foreign, news stations. The U.S. Foreign Broadcast Information Service gathered and published this valuable historical data in its *Daily Report: Latin America*. Among the journals utilized, the Dominican *Revista de las Fuerzas Armadas* was the most useful for background information.

Finally, recent interviews with various U.S. military officers who served in the Dominican Republic in the 1960s and early 1970s gave the author significant additional insights into the nature of the Armed Forces. (Their names are listed at the end of the bibliography.) Special mention should be made of retired U.S. Army Lieutenant Colonel Mario A. Burdick, who, from 1998 to 2002, held numerous lengthy discussions with me concerning the politics of the Dominican officer corps.

I

The Foundations of
the Officer Corps

The Dominican officer corps of the 1960s and 1970s was a direct out-growth of the U.S. Marine occupation of 1916–1924 and the thirty-one year Trujillo dictatorship. The Marines provided the military institution with a superficial structure while the Generalissimo wove in elements derived from traditional Hispano-Caribbean political practices and his own unique style of governing.

U.S. OCCUPATION

When the U.S. Marine Corps arrived in the Dominican Republic approximately one year prior to America's entrance into World War I, it discovered practically no indigenous military establishment. The Dominican army was in reality a series of armed bands under the leadership of various chieftains. One objective of the U.S. occupation was to attempt the modernization of Dominican public institutions; therefore, positive steps were taken to create a security force. The result was the establishment of the National Guard in April 1917 and the disarming of the numerous irregular units in the interior of the country. To maintain peace in the rural areas, the National Guard located small interlocking posts throughout the countryside.[1] This modernizing process took place under the direct command of U.S. Marine officers; thus Americans led the transition from provincial *cacique* rule to a national security organization. The next phase necessary in the development of long-term stability was to establish a native officer corps to replace the Americans when the occupation was terminated. A major step in this process was taken when an officer training school was opened in Haina with the intention of establishing at least minimum military standards (the course was only four months in duration) for the new Dominican officer corps.[2] From as early as 1917, however, a problem for professionalism in the fledgling organization was noted. When the U.S. Marines began recruit-

5

ment for their officer program, they quickly discovered that the sons of
the socially prominent families of the country would have no association
with occupation-sponsored projects.[3] In an underdeveloped nation such
as the Dominican Republic, this ostracism of the new *Escuela Militar de
Haina,* as it was called, resulted in the exclusion of the only sector of
society with an acceptable educational background. Consequently, only
Dominicans with substandard preparation were inducted as cadets. One
such man was former petty thief and sugar cane field supervisor Rafael
Leonidas Trujillo Molina. The future Generalissimo had approximately
six years of formal education before he was enrolled as a cadet in Haina[4];
his colleagues were of the same stamp.

THE TRUJILLO DICTATORSHIP

When the U.S. Marines departed the Dominican Republic in 1924,
the constabulary which they left behind fell under the influence of the
men whom the Americans had trained and commissioned as officers.
The most resourceful of these officers was the then Lieutenant Colonel
Trujillo. In 1930 his natural leadership, organizational skill, and ruthlessness propelled him from commandant of the Dominican military force
to the presidency of the country. He inherited the constabulary of the
U.S. Marines, and he nurtured it for the 31 years of his rule; his small,
dispersed, but centrally controlled units maintained political domination
of the Dominican Republic. To exert his power through the National
Army, as it was termed by 1928, Trujillo adopted a military policy well
suited to his background and temperament: The main virtue of the
Dominican officer was to be loyalty. This trait, at the expense of intelligence and professional skill, was considered the most prized. Officers
who were blindly loyal to *"El Jefe,"* as Trujillo was called, were to climb
up the promotional ladder fast. In contrast, members of the officer corps
who displayed too much interest in their profession (or in any subject
that required certain intellectual accomplishments) were immediately
suspect. Mental aptitude to Trujillo suggested a possible interest in affairs
that could detract from the all-important characteristic of loyalty and
thus endanger the highly personalized regime of the dictator. The subsequent additions of air, sea and police services did not change the situation. The new National Police became the mirror image of the
National Army. It was a military counterbalance in the countryside, not
a modern police force as seen in more developed nations. The Navy
received numerous ships, but few troop units to endanger the political
balance of power. The advent of aviation in the Army was controlled
more directly; the handful of pilots in the new *Aviación Militar Domini-*

cana was given to Trujillo's older son Rafael "Ramfis" Trujillo. Throughout, Trujillo carefully selected his Army commanders. Once they were appointed, Trujillo would not allow them to work through a chain of command, for he wished to maintain their loyalty to his person alone. These officers continued to be drawn from the same social class that had provided the dictator. They usually attended a basic parade ground course similar to that of Haina, but never anything more. The Dominican Republic had no advanced military school, and Trujillo frowned on officers leaving the island to attend institutions of higher learning. A functioning General Staff was never created. Thus, with careful calculation, professionalism was kept divorced from the Dominican Armed Forces.[5]

In the last years of Trujillo's regime, the Generalissimo was required to make some unavoidable changes in his policy as a result of external affairs. Caribbean politics had changed to the extent that there were numerous countries eager to destroy the Trujillo regime. These nations expressed this desire by openly assisting exile groups in the preparation of military invasions.[6] The result was that Trujillo was required to purchase armaments abroad (they were mainly of Spanish, French, or Swedish manufacture). The appearance in the late 1950s of new, more sophisticated equipment in the Dominican Armed Forces meant the need for officers with at least a fundamental modern military education. The problem was solved in two ways: The newly equipped armor and artillery units were all made a part of Ramfis' air force, and a military academy was created in the same service to train young officers so that they could lead the new formations. Eventually, all these elements were concentrated into an air force organization located close to the capital at San Isidro; on June 9, 1959, it was designated the *Centro de Enseñanza de las Fuerzas Amadas, 5 de Junio* (CEFA-Armed Forces Training Center, 5th of June; June 5th was Ramfis' birthday).[7] Despite the creation of the CEFA, the old dictator still continued to give key commands only to reliable, under-educated non-professionals.

On May 30, 1961, Trujillo was assassinated, and power in the Dominican Republic was temporarily passed to Ramfis. Dr. Joaquín Balaguer, *El Jefe's* figurehead civilian president, remained at his post without any authority. The Armed Forces swore allegiance to Ramfis[8]; however, he was unable to govern. By November 1961, the era of Trujillo was over.

II

The Officer Corps and Factionalism

The history of military officers in the Dominican Republic has been one of internal partisan conflict. This factionalism can be traced back to the earliest days of colonial Santo Domingo and would continue for 400 years except when the country was under foreign domination or authoritarian single-man rule. Beginning with the period when the Columbus family governed the island, the route to success was to attach oneself to a leader in Santo Domingo. Followers would remain loyal as long as they thought their patron was in the ascendance. If a particular clique's chief were to be eclipsed, a different leader would be sought out and new alliances would be formed. At any given time, the strong man who had the largest number of adherents was the most admired; prestige went to the patron whose faction was the most powerful.[1]

The Trujillo years would see factionalism brought under rigid control. The dictator maintained complete dominance over his officers; no group was allowed to exist which was in any way independent of the Generalissimo. Trujillo's techniques were as follows:

He exercised absolute personal authority over the military to include promotions, retirements, organization, and funding.

He never allowed an officer to remain in command long enough for that individual to build a following.

He provided the means for his officers to be satisfied with their status by using corruption and special privileges, and by playing to their sense of pride and esprit.

He appointed family members and cronies to key posts despite their lack of qualifications.[2]

With the death of Trujillo and the exile of his family in 1961, the Dominican Republic descended into political chaos. From January 1, 1962, to the inauguration of Joaquín Balaguer as constitutional president on July 1, 1966, there were eight governments (not including the rebel "Constitutionalist" government of 1965):

January 1, 1962–January 16, 1962—Council of State
January 16, 1962–January 18, 1962—Civilian-Military Junta
January 18, 1962–February 27, 1963—Council of State
February 27, 1963–September 25, 1963—Constitutional presidency of
  Juan Bosch
September 26, 1963–April 25, 1965—Triumvirate (principal leader: Don-
  ald Reid Cabral)
April 27, 1965–May 7, 1965—Military Junta
May 7, 1965–August 30, 1965—Government of National Reconstruction
September 3, 1965–July 1,1966—Provisional presidency of Héctor García
  Godoy[3]

Eight years before the first Council of State assumed responsibility for governing the Dominican Republic and the conflict among the officer corps' factions began, Balaguer was a witness to a routine annual ceremony which reflected the nature of military life during the dictatorship. The January 21, 1954, event was the passing in review before the Trujillo family of a mixed regiment of all the services in honor of the Virgin of Altagracia in Higuey. Balaguer was present with the papal nuncio in his official capacity as Dominican minister for foreign affairs and worship. Balaguer could not have known that the major factional leaders of the first half of the 1960s were all present in that regiment as lieutenants. Army First Lieutenant Neit Nivar Seijas, the future head of the San Cristóbal Group, marched with the Presidential Guard. Air force First Lieutenant Elías Wessin y Wessin commanded an infantry company of the *Aviación Militar Dominicana* (AMD); from 1962 to 1965 he would be the director of the powerful CEFA. With him was AMD Second Lieutenant Miguel Angel Hernándo Ramírez who would be the leader of the Constitutionalist officers. And with the naval infantry was *Alférez de Navío* Francisco Alberto Caamaño Deñó, the 1965 successor to Hernándo, and, eventually, the president of the rebel Constitutionalist government.[4]

Eight years after the parade in Higuey, the officer corps lurched out of control. The vacuum left by the disappearance of the Trujillo family could not be filled by a strong civilian government, and no military individual had the strength to take the place of the Generalissimo. The officer corps had no tradition of participating in well-defined politico-military movements based on either ideology, professionalism, or generational competition. The examples of the idealistic "*Tenentes*" of 1922 in Brazil, of the professionally-oriented "*Puros*" of pre-Castro Cuba, or of the young officer "*Juventud Militar*" movement during 1948–1979 in El Salvador[5] were completely outside the experience of the Dominican military establishment. Its history was either internecine factionalism or submission to a dictator. In the mid–1960s, cliques were in the process of forming, but they were not firm or binding. Five combinations were evident, but not permanent—they were the CEFA officers, the San Cristóbal Group, the Constitutionalist officers, the San Isidro Group, and the Navy's officers. What may appear to be a coherent grouping along service lines is deceptive, however. Dominican officers changed service often and loyalty to individuals predominated over support to a branch of the military. With these realities in mind, it is still possible to identify five cliques which were major players in the Dominican Republic prior to Balaguer's 1966 assumption of the presidency.

CEFA Officers

From the outset, CEFA officers considered themselves members of an elite corps. One account of their organization's origin as an exclusive unit was that President Trujillo modeled his air force on the *Luftwaffe* on the recommendation of Otto Winterer, a former World War II German air force major. Trujillo was reportedly advised to combine aviation, armor, artillery, infantry and airborne under one loyal commander as had been done in Hermann Goering's branch of the *Wehrmacht*.[6] Although this story is unconfirmed, there is no doubt that if a modern ground force was needed in the Dominican Republic, the German structure under Trujillo's son Ramfis would have appealed politically to the dictator. The buildup of officers and equipment for such a force began adjacent to the San Isidro Air Base in the mid–1950s and crested in the last years of that decade.

The new armored battalion was the most salient element of the expanded AMD. It was the only unit in the country to possess tanks. The battalion first absorbed the older U.S.-made M3A1 Stuart light tanks as well as the M-16 armored personnel carriers ("half-tracks") from the Army. Twenty-five Swedish-made L-60D Landsverk light tanks with a 37mm gun and ten Lynx Landsverk armored cars with a 20mm gun were subsequently purchased abroad.[7] On September 14, 1959, the most impressive acquisition was presented to the Dominican public. Twenty French-made 14 ton AMX-13 tanks with a 75mm gun were paraded under the command of Trujillo's younger son, CEFA First Lieutenant Rhadamés Trujillo. The AMX-13s were publicized as *gigantes de hierro* or "iron giants."[8] After the Trujillo family was forced out of the Dominican Republic in 1961, the tank battalion, renamed the Armored Battalion, *27 de Febrero*, was the CEFA's principal means of exercising leverage in national politics.

Further modernization took place with the purchase of twelve Spanish-made 105/26 Reinosa howitzers. This 105mm towed gun was called the *Cañon Naval Reinosa*. They formed the main armament of a new CEFA artillery battalion designated in 1961 the Artillery Group, *General Gregorio Luperón*. The Army continued to maintain some World War I-type Schneider, Krupp, and St. Chamond 75mm guns and small caliber mortars, but Spanish-made 120mm ECIA mortars, as well as Swedish-made 105mm Bofors recoilless rifles and 20mm Hispano Suiza antiaircraft guns, were integrated into the CEFA's artillery.[9]

The CEFA combined arms structure was completed with the creation of an infantry battalion, eventually named the Infantry Battalion, *Enriquillo,* and with the founding in 1960 of the Dominican Republic's first airborne company.[10] These units were provided the modern Spanish-made 7.62mm CETME assault rifle.

Special privileges were associated with CEFA officers from the beginning of CEFA's existence, starting with its first director. On January 4, 1958, Major Luís José León Estévez, an AMD crony of Ramfis, married Trujillo's daughter Angelita. Three months later León was promoted to lieutenant colonel and in February 1959 to colonel. In early 1959, he was given command of the newly forming CEFA. He remained the director of CEFA, under the personal orders of Ramfis, until the Trujillo family was driven into exile.[11] Afterwards, although León was gone, the entire CEFA infrastructure continued to exist intact.

Among the CEFA officers who remained were some of the most promising professionals in the Dominican Armed Forces. Two exceptions, however, were the new director, Colonel Wessin y Wessin, and his armor unit leader Colonel Perdomo Rosario. Elías Wessin y Wessin was a dim, artless infantry officer with only a modest military and civilian education. After completing an eighteen-month cadet course, he was commissioned on January 1, 1948, a second lieutenant in the Army. On January 31, 1953, he transferred to the AMD infantry where he was assigned to rifle and weapons companies until 1958. In that year, Major Wessin y Wessin was appointed an instructor at the Military Academy. On April 24, 1959, he was designated the director of the school with the temporary rank of lieutenant colonel; but, only four months later, he was returned, as a major, to line duty in the AMD. The routine nature of Wessin's career changed rapidly, however, after the May 1961 assassination of the Generalissimo. Because of the political vacuum created by the events of that year, Wessin found opportunities normally open only to members of the Trujillo family. On November 24, 1961, newly promoted Colonel Wessin y Wessin, the son of immigrants, assumed the former post of Trujillo's son-in-law—the directorship of the CEFA. A mediocre officer with only limited professional training and with no experience as a senior commander became the head of his country's most powerful military organization.[12]

The officer who ranked second to Wessin in the CEFA was equally unimpressive professionally. Elio Osiris Perdomo Rosario also had transferred to the AMD from the Army in 1953, and became associated with the Dominican Republic's tanks. Under Wessin he had an almost unbroken tour as commander of the CEFA's Armored Battalion. (The only break was a six month stint as the quartermaster general of the CEFA—a gift from Wessin so Perdomo could augment his salary by pocketing a percentage of government supply funds.) This uncomplicated, sociable officer was mainly identified with sports rather than with military matters. He managed the tank unit's baseball team and eventually became a leader in the overall Armed Forces sports program. In the 1970s, when newspapers continually published pictures of him throwing a baseball, he was the subject of derision by the officers who were more oriented toward a military career.[13]

Despite the questionable personal examples of these two senior ground commanders, the CEFA became the starting point for the Dominican Republic's most serious professionals. This small group of junior and mid-level officers would form the vanguard of the move toward professionalism in the Armed Forces of the 1970s. An early concentration of these officers was found in the 1958 faculty of the Military Academy, *Batalla de las Carreras*, eventually to be a part of the CEFA. They were Captain Manuel Antonio Cuervo Gómez, First Lieutenant Pedro Medrano Ubiera, and Second Lieutenants Ramiro Matos González, Téofilo Ramón Romero Pumarol, Héctor Valenzuela Alcantara, and Jesús Manuel Porfirio Mota Henríquez.[14] All would remain career CEFA officers and two, Cuervo Gómez and Medrano, would command the CEFA's armor and artillery units respectively in the early 1960s. Of special interest was the fact that they were among the first group of Dominicans to receive staff college training. In addition, other more junior CEFA officers would be the recipients of such training: Luís García Recio and Alfredo Balcácer Vega of CEFA infantry, Jaime Núñez Cosme of CEFA armor, and Franco Benoit Liriano of CEFA artillery were examples. By 1972, approximately one half of all Army, Navy, and Air Force graduates of a general staff course were ex-CEFA officers.[15]

Two extraordinary CEFA officers who do not fall into the categories described above were Salvador Lluberes Montás and Juan René Beauchamps Javier. Both of these action-oriented officers progressed at a rate faster than expected—they became generals when their contemporaries were attending staff college. Before their elevation to flag rank, Beauchamps Javier was the CEFA's infantry commander and Lluberes Montás was the leader of the country's airborne unit which was initially organized in the CEFA.

From the first Council of State to the beginning of the 1965 civil war,

CEFA officers exercised an inordinate amount of power in the Dominican Republic. Brigadier General Wessin (he was promoted after his September 25, 1963, overthrow of President Juan Bosch) was sought after by civilian politicians because the CEFA had become the nation's final political arbiter.[16] Although Wessin's officers continued to wear Air Force uniforms, in April 1964 they began the practice of using the acronym "CEFA" with their rank, thereby openly becoming a separate service from the Army, Navy, and Air Force. That year, the preparation of the Armed Forces budget for 1965 cited entries for the three traditional branches, plus an allocation for a fourth co-equal organization—the CEFA. The general public became aware of the CEFA's new status when the press released Armed Forces communiqués signed by the three service chiefs and Wessin, and revealed that the CEFA was providing President Reid Cabral with a personal security escort. (CEFA officers already controlled all the tanks on the National Palace grounds.)[17] Under his immediate command, Wessin had a total of 59 armored vehicles and approximately 2,000 troops concentrated less than 15 kilometers from the capital.[18] Only the Duarte Bridge over the Ozama River stood between him and the center of government. Thus, when the Constitutionalist revolt against the regime began on April 24, 1965, CEFA officers psychologically as well as militarily were in a position to control events. By the 27th, however, the aura of belonging to an elite corps had dimmed decidedly. Although Wessin's personal indecisiveness was the major reason for the CEFA's inability to quell the rebellion, the military performance of the CEFA's armor and infantry officers was the immediate cause of Wessin's failure.

Colonel Ramiro Matos González in 1971 explained that a simple error at the tactical level resulted in the chain of events that ended with the necessity for U.S. military intervention on April 28th. CEFA units from San Isidro crossed the Duarte Bridge on the 27th. The lead tanks, however, moved faster than the infantry could follow; consequently, the armor arrived on the opposite side of the river unprotected. Initially, the rebels, who were mostly civilians, were stunned and ready to flee when they abruptly faced the tanks. This situation rapidly changed, however, when a small group of braver insurgents attacked the AMX-13s with Molotov cocktails. With no CEFA infantry available, the tankers were overwhelmed and the crowd realized they had more power than expected. From that point on, the rebels set up a determined defense around the wavering CEFA bridgehead on the Santo Domingo side of the river, which led to the collapse of the armored force. The once potent CEFA withdrew to the San Isidro bank of the Ozama; its officers would never recover.[19]

Although CEFA units participated in the remainder of the civil war, their officers were overshadowed by other loyalist Dominican leaders.

Propaganda written by rebel officers singled out CEFA members as part of an anti-democratic cabal. Colonel Medrano and Major Romero Pumarol were denounced as Wessin's "intellectual advisers," Colonel Perdomo Rosario was identified as the commander of the tanks which had fought the people near the Duarte Bridge, and Major Valenzuela and Captain García Recio were accused of treachery.[20] Peace negotiations required that Wessin give up his command and temporarily leave the Dominican Republic, steps that Wessin refused to accept. On September 4th, provisional president Héctor García Godoy abolished the CEFA and on the following day he re-designated it the 4th Brigade, an Army unit at San Isidro. Wessin still refused to depart, so, under U.S. military escort, on September 9th, he was forced to turn over his command to Colonel Perdomo, to retire, and to fly out of San Isidro Air Base into exile.[21]

The 4th Brigade retained armor and artillery units into 1966 (first under the command of Colonel Perdomo, then under Lieutenant Colonel Beauchamps Javier), but in September 1966 President Balaguer began the dismemberment of the brigade's combat power.[22] Former CEFA officers were dispersed throughout the Armed Forces. Cuervo Gómez went abroad for advanced study; Medrano worked with American advisers on the reorganization of the Army; Matos González remained in the Air Force as part of the base security system; Romero Pumarol taught in the staff course at the U.S. Army School of the Americas; Valenzuela and García Recio became General Staff officers in Army headquarters; and Núñez Cosme, Balcácer Vega, and Benoit, like other ex-CEFA junior officers, found homes in the U.S. Army-advised Schools Command. Three major CEFA figures—Perdomo, Beauchamps, and Lluberes Montás—were able to convince President Balaguer that they would be loyal to the new regime; consequently, they were fit into his balance-of-power scheme. Although Wessin remained in exile, numerous rumors continued in the late 1960s that he was in contact with his former officers for the purpose of overthrowing the government. And there does exist evidence that some CEFA men—of lesser ability than those cited above—did harbor thoughts of returning to the forefront of Dominican military affairs. This fact continued to cause suspicion against ex-CEFA officers throughout the 1970s.

SAN CRISTÓBAL GROUP

The "San Cristóbal Group" was initially a designation used for a small circle of senior and mid-level officers who advocated the return of Joaquín Balaguer to the presidency. Eventually, the term became synonymous with hard-line *Trujillista* Army officers who not only opposed moderate and left-wing civilian politicians, but also the Air Force and CEFA cliques located at San Isidro. Some members of the San Cristóbal Group had been active conspirators since 1962. They had participated in forming the Civilian-Military Junta of January 16, 1962, and in overthrowing President Bosch on September 25, 1963, but it was in the plotting against the government of Donald Reid Cabral in 1964 that San Cristóbal officers as a group gained the most notoriety. In 1964, the usage of its name (derived from Trujillo's birthplace in San Cristóbal) became widespread.[23]

Membership in the San Cristóbal Group was never officially recorded nor was the faction ever formally founded. It was merely a loose grouping of officers—usually in the ranks of lieutenant colonel, colonel, and brigadier general—which changed composition periodically. An overview of the San Cristóbal Group before July 1966 clearly reveals, however, that one officer—Neit Nivar Seijas—was continuously singled out as a member, and that he was the principal architect and operational director of the clique's anti-government activities.[24] Among the Army generals identified as sympathetic to the faction were Félix Hermedia Jr., Renato Hungría Morell, and Salvador Montás Guerrero. Of these, only General Montás would play any overt role that would suggest that he was a San Cristóbal officer. The colonels associated with the coterie, in addition to Nivar Seijas, were Braulio Alvarez Sánchez, Rafael Leger Báez, Marcos Rivera Cuesta, Manuel Pagán Montás, Rafael Nivar Ledesma, Francisco Coradín Benesario and Marcos Antonio Jorge Moreno. Lieutenant Colonels identified as San Cristóbal officers were José Manuel Pérez Aponte, Julio Soto Echavarría, Enrique Casado Saladín, Maximiliano Ruiz Batista, José Ramón Féliz de la Mota and Rafael de Jesús Checo.[25] Suspected collaborators were Carlos Jáquez Olivero and José Napoleón Pimentel Boves.[26]

These colonels and lieutenant colonels shared the same experiences during the first phases of their military careers. All had either attended the *Escuela de Cadetes del Ejército* or had been commissioned directly from the ranks. (The Cadet School provided a two-year high school-level course. Four of the San Cristóbal Group officers were from the first class in 1943.) After this basic training (if they received any preparation at all), they were assigned to constabulary duty in the interior of the country. There they remained in rural outposts as lieutenants and captains. These assignments would continue past the rank of captain unless family connections opened doors for them in the capital, as was the case with Braulio Alvarez Sánchez, the son of Trujillo's boyhood friend and long-time confidant Virgilio "Don Cucho" Alvarez Piña. From 1952 to 1957, Alvarez Sánchez was stationed as a captain in El Seibo, San Pedro de Macorís, La Romana, Santiago, Pedernales, and San Juan de la Maguana, but after he was promoted on May 1, 1957, Major Alvarez Sánchez was appointed adjutant to the Army's inspector general.[27] Regardless of whether the young officers who later would make up the San Cristóbal Group remained in rural assignments or were moved to the capital, their career progression called for no further military education and only the rare opportunity to be associated with any military maneuver element larger than the size of a rifle company.

The more politically active San Cristóbal officers, such as Nivar Seijas and Alvarez Sánchez, also had in common their enemies. The three civilian governments, from the second Council of State of 1962–1963 to the Triumvirate of 1963–1965, wanted the country rid of the pro-Balaguer conspirators. On this matter, the civilian leaders and Wessin were in full agreement, and Wessin, in turn, had the support of CEFA officers. Since the San Cristóbal Group had neither the concentration of troops nor the tanks and artillery of the CEFA, the Army faction was at a distinct disadvantage.

San Cristóbal weakness became abundantly clear in October 1964. During the autumn, plotting to overthrow Reid Cabral's Triumvirate government had reached a high point, causing the President to realize that neutralization of the Balaguer supporters was essential. With Wessin backing him, Reid Cabral, on October 1st, removed Nivar from his command of the *16 de Agosto* Military Camp, then located in Villa Duarte east of the Ozama River. The following day Alvarez Sánchez was dismissed as sub-chief of staff of the Army and transferred to Washington, D.C. The purge of other San Cristóbal Group activists and sympathizers followed. In the case of Nivar, reducing his power was not sufficient. He had become such a threat to the President and to Wessin, that on January 27, 1965, he was retired involuntarily, and, on April 12, 1965, he was forced into exile.[28] San Cristóbal officers groused, but Wessin's tanks made their complaints useless.

On April 24, 1965, the pro-Bosch revolt against Reid Cabral began without San Cristóbal Group involvement. The only effective unit in the hands of a member was the *Ramón Matías Mella* battalion, stationed in San Cristóbal approximately 30 kilometers west of the capital. The commander, promoted to lieutenant colonel 23 days earlier, was José Manuel Pérez Aponte. His battalion received orders on the 24th from the President to proceed to Santo Domingo with the mission of defending the National Palace. General Montás assumed command of the battalion and other scattered troops west of the capital on April 25th and began his march east. His progress was slow, however; on the 27th he was within the city limits of Santo Domingo, but there Montás held back his units reportedly to avoid providing any assistance to Wessin and the CEFA who were approaching the city from the east.[29]

As with CEFA officers, the San Cristóbal Group gained no prestige or political advantage from the civil war of 1965. Nivar Seijas would claim in later years that if he had been in the Dominican Republic on the 24th of April, he would never have allowed the situation to have deteriorated as it did, thus making U.S. intervention on the 28th unnecessary. The soundness of this boast is highly doubtful. The San Cristóbal Group had not controlled militarily powerful units; its influence was felt only in the widely dispersed Army constabulary detachments and posts in the countryside.

In the 1970s, veteran San Cristóbal Group officers still would not forsake the old *Trujillista* Army constabulary system. For example, in 1972, Rafael de Jesús Checo, by then a brigadier general and head of the Army, explained this view in private. He remarked that in the U.S. Army an officer became a specialist such as a tanker, an artilleryman, or an engineer, and devoted most of his life to that one field. In the Dominican Army, officers had contact with the people in villages and towns throughout the country. They had to learn how to be able to deal with issues involving farming, sanitation, schools, labor unions, crime, and the clergy. The population looked to the Dominican Army officer to resolve these types of problems and more. To be successful, he remarked, the Dominican lieutenant would need experience gained by serving in the countryside, not by classroom instruction similar to what the U.S. military educational system provided.[30] It was foreign to General Checo that there were some areas where an Army officer should not interfere. He did understand (but did not state), however, that Dominican Army officers could best control the political life of a community by involving themselves with the daily activities of that community.

When Nivar Seijas was reintegrated into the Armed Forces after Balaguer's successful electoral campaign of 1966, he revealed a heightened interest in massing military strength for political purposes as his enemy Wessin had exploited the CEFA. The term "San Cristóbal Group" was no longer used but a successor existed in the form of the Nivar clique. Nivar cast a wide net after 1966. He attempted to improve on the old CEFA and San Cristóbal Group by simultaneously controlling a concentrated combined arms brigade adjacent to the capital and having allies among commanders throughout the nation.

CONSTITUTIONALIST OFFICERS

There is a widespread view that the Constitutionalist officers who initiated and fought in the 1965 civil war were the best educated and most progressive professionals of the Dominican Armed Forces. In fact, this is an overstatement. The leading Constitutionalist officers came from a broad range of military organizations and backgrounds, and had varied attitudes concerning the politics of the day. They became corporately identified as Constitutionalists after the events of 1965 placed them forever in that category. While some of their non-Constitutionalist colleagues in the CEFA and the San Cristóbal Group would move in and out of different cliques over the years, the Constitutionalists were branded as such for the remainder of their lives. This situation was the case even with the very few who returned to the Armed Forces in the early 1970s.

The Constitutionalist rebellion began when two Army units west of the capital—the *Juan Pablo Duarte* and *Francisco del Rosario Sánchez* battalions—rose up against the Triumvirate government of Donald Reid Cabral on April 24, 1965. Constitutionalist spokesmen maintained that the purpose of the revolt was the return of constitutional President Juan Bosch, hence the term "constitutionalist." This initial force of approximately 1,000 troops[31] was augmented in the following days with other Army units from within Santo Domingo and from the light artillery element at *Libertad* Military Camp, with sailors and frogmen from *Las Calderas* Naval Base, and with a small number of Air Force and National Police officers. The total is estimated to be less than 3,000.[32] A September 2, 1965, rebel government document lists 49 officers above the rank of first lieutenant from the Army, Air Force, Navy, CEFA, and National Police who were members of the Constitutionalist armed forces.[33] Among them, the most prominent militarily during the civil war were Colonel Francisco Alberto Caamaño Deñó, *Capitán de Fragata* (commander) Manuel Ramón Montes Arache, and Captain Héctor Lachapelle Díaz.

Caamaño began his career in the Navy. In 1952, he was reassigned from the line to the naval infantry and, two years later, he received training in fundamentals from the U. S. Marine Corps. On January 2, 1959, Caamaño, a naval infantry captain, was transferred to the Army where he was designated commander of the company guarding La Victoria penitentiary. During 1960, he was moved to the CEFA. In all these branches of the service, he was a member of the shooting team. After the death of Trujillo, he was transferred once again—this time to the National Police. Caamaño never had the benefit of advanced schooling such as a staff college course. He was taken into custody on January 13, 1965, for plotting against the chief of the National Police. Five days later President Reid Cabral appointed him consul in Kingston, Jamaica, a position Colonel Caamaño refused to accept. He was then transferred to the Air Force without assignment. After the revolt began, he first became Constitutionalist minister of the interior, then, on April 27th, minister of the armed forces, and, on May 24th, president until September 3rd.[34]

Former U.S. Ambassador to the Dominican Republic John Bartlow Martin was of the opinion that Caamaño was basically an opportunist. This, plus revenge, probably were the reasons he joined the Constitutionalists. Caamaño was an enemy of Wessin and he blamed President Reid Cabral for his 1965 problems. The Ambassador further commented that Caamaño had not supported Juan Bosch when he was president and that he had not opposed the coup against Bosch.[35] Also, there exists no evidence that Caamaño was in league with those officers who had planned the April 1965 pro-Bosch uprising.

After Caamaño, the Constitutionalist who made the most significant impact on the civil war was the naval officer Montes Arache. He had had a career similar to Caamaño in the naval infantry; except, unlike Caamaño, he had a reputation for bold exploits. It was alleged that in the 1950s he had participated in one of Trujillo's assassination attempts against Rómulo Betancourt, the Venezuelan democratic politician. In the early 1960s, Montes Arache became the commander of the Navy's frogmen, a group with probably the best individual training in the Armed Forces. Although Montes Arache was respected as a small unit leader, he had neither the experience nor the formal preparation for higher command. His motivation for joining the Constitutionalists appears to have been his friendship with former naval infantryman Caamaño and his dislike of Wessin and Reid Cabral.[36] Even a supporter of his admits that Montes Arache "... did not have the slightest interest..." in the Constitutionalist cause when he joined the movement.[37] When Caamaño became provisional president, Montes Arache followed him as minister of the armed forces.

Although Captain Héctor Lachapelle Díaz, as operations director, G-3, of the Constitutionalist military staff was subordinate to a chief of staff, he was credited by observers to have been third in importance after Caamaño and Montes Arache among the rebel leaders. He had a relatively short pre-rebellion career—from when he was commissioned in April 1959 to when he was cashiered in October 1963 by Wessin, he had been almost exclusively in the CEFA. There is no question that he had innate ability (he rose to be a rebel lieutenant colonel and he became a major force within the Constitutionalist army); however, he had been an officer for too short a period before his dismissal to have deserved being considered one of the Dominican Republic's leading professional officers of the 1960s. Unlike Caamaño and Montes Arache, Lachapelle joined the pro-Bosch coup plotting early.[38] Years later, in exile, he would explain that he did so for other than leftist ideological reasons. When he was finally allowed to return to the active Army in December 1972 by President Balaguer, the most frequently heard explanation for his reintegration was that he had provided a valuable, but undisclosed, service for the government.[39]

Ironically, the rebel officer who came the closest to the idealized description of the Constitutionalist officer (professional and progressive) only participated eight days in the civil war. Lieutenant Colonel Miguel Angel Hernándo Ramírez spent the 1950s in the AMD infantry. After the end of the Trujillo regime, he transferred to the Army and, as a lieutenant colonel, was in the first group of Dominicans to graduate from a U.S. Army staff college course. On his return to Santo Domingo in December 1963, he taught other officers general staff procedures and became the G-3 (plans and training) of the Dominican Army.[40] Hernándo Ramírez appears to have been genuinely concerned that the legitimacy of constitutionality had been violated by the overthrow of Juan Bosch in September 1963, although he is known to have had little sympathy for the former president as an individual.[41] In the end of 1964, he began planning for the return of Bosch through a coup d'état. When the revolt began on April 24th, he assumed the role of rebel military leader. He was the first minister of the armed forces in the provisional government; however, on the 27th he took asylum in the Ecuadorian Embassy. On the 12th of June, he rejoined the Constitutionalist army, but five days later he was wounded. Hernándo Ramírez regained his health in July; however, reportedly disillusioned with the leftist nature of the movement he had helped start, Hernándo Ramírez began a self-imposed exile.[42]

Other key Constitutionalists fell far short of the so-called "professional and progressive" label portrayed by pro-Bosch publicists. Lieutenant Colonels Pedro Alvarez Holguín and Giovanni Gutiérrez Ramírez—two Army commanders who led the rebellion on April 24th—were not aggrieved believers in Constitutionalist principles, but were opposed to President Reid Cabral and Wessin because the colonels were *Balagueristas*. Colonel Emilio Ludovino Fernández, a former CEFA lawyer, and Lieutenant Colonel Vinicio Fernández Pérez, an early plotter who had backed out, were opportunists who joined the movement when they thought it would succeed and were the first to leave it when it began to falter.[43] Major Manuel Núñez Nogueras, a CEFA officer who had been cashiered in September 1964 for anti-government activity, was seeking his return to the officer corps.[44] A last example was that of Army Captain Mario Peña Taveras who had intrigued with dissident enlisted men in Army headquarters independent of the main Constitutionalist conspiracy. Thirteen of his collaborators received commissions by the rebel government as a reward for their support during the coup. Peña Taveras was known to have links with Marxist groups.[45]

In May 1965, the Constitutionalist military effort began to change its character from a conventional ground force organization into an urban guerrilla front. After the U.S. intervention, the Constitutionalist units, led by career officers, were marginalized in favor of civilian revolutionary *comandos* headed by insurgent chiefs. With this backdrop of a growing threat from the radical left, continuous negotiations were under-way to end the civil war and to set up a workable government. The Inter-American Peace Force (IAPF), made up of U.S. and Latin American troops, exerted pressure on the negotiators when necessary. On August 31, 1965, the Act of Dominican Reconciliation and the Institutional Act were signed providing an end to hostilities and the establishment of a provisional government to be led by Héctor García Godoy. Article 8 of the reconciliation document called for the reintegration of rebel troops into the Armed Forces; on September 27th, Law Number 21 was promulgated with the details of how this was to be accomplished. Political realities and further organized violence between Caamaño's men and loyalist units prevented the implementation of the law in the full spirit of the agreement, however. In mid–October 1965, Constitutionalist troops were herded into the *27 de Febrero* Military Camp; the exits to the installation were guarded by the IAPF.[46] Their principal officers were nominally returned to the regular Armed Forces, but they were assigned abroad as military attaches in January 1966. Among them, Caamaño was sent to Great Britain, Montes Arache to Canada, Lachapelle Díaz to Bel-gium, Hernándo Ramírez to Ecuador, Alvarez Holguín to France, Núñez Nogueras to West Germany, and Peña Taveras to Chile.[47] During the remainder of the 1960s, overseas assignments were changed, placing Constitutionalists in different embassies, or positions were even invented such as "military advisor to the Dominican delegate to the United Nations" in New York City, but no Constitutionalist leader was allowed to come into contact with the Armed Forces at home. Their names were not entered in the officers register or *escalafón*, but were part of a spe-cial *escalafón* which was not disseminated. Promotion for them in the early 1970s was out of the question.[48]

Although some of these officers were undoubtedly talented, their exile did not create a marked personnel gap in the officer corps. Their absence was not seriously noted even among the small number of pro-fessionally oriented officers. It must be remembered that of the thirteen graduates of the new staff college program for the Dominican Republic in 1963 and 1964, only four had been Constitutionalists. (They were Hernándo Ramírez, Alvarez Holguín, Juan María Lora Fernández , and Eladio Ramírez.[49])

SAN ISIDRO GROUP

The term "San Isidro Group" was popularly used in the Dominican Republic to refer to the opponents of the San Cristóbal Group. It was a designation that was adopted after the 1964 coining of the "San Cristóbal Group" label and was most utilized during the 1965 civil war. To Dominicans, the expression "San Isidro Group" referred to the Air Force and CEFA officers at the San Isidro installations as if they all belonged to the same organization. In actuality, there was a clear dividing line between the pilots, technicians, and ground defense officers at the air base and the CEFA leaders in their adjacent barracks.

When Ramfis in 1952 was given the *Aviación Militar Dominicana* for his 23rd birthday, he placed an umbrella of protection over the country's pilots, and his father increased the size of the air arm in an extraordinary manner. In the 1950s, the AMD was flying a total of 240 aircraft. Among them were U.S.-made B-17 "Flying Fortresses," B-25 "Mitchells," B-26 "Invaders," PBY-5A "Catalinas," P-51 " Mustangs," P-47 "Thunderbolts," and C-46 and C-47 transports. Trujillo also purchased British-made De Havilland Mark I "Vampire" jets and French-made Alouette II and III helicopters.[50] For a Caribbean country, this display of air power was unprecedented. The Dominican people, in the 1952 inaugural parade, observed B-17 and B-25 bombers overhead and two years later, in the Armed Forces Day air review, they saw the spectacle of forty-four "Mustang" fighters and "Thunderbolt" fighter-bombers, formed in squadrons, flying over Santo Domingo. (Most of the senior pilots of the 1960s and 1970s were young lieutenants in those P-51s and P-47s.)[51] It was no wonder that the Generalissimo reportedly boasted that he could destroy Havana in three hours.[52]

By the technological nature of their work, the pilots were exposed to a broader set of experiences, to include foreign training, than their ground force counterparts. This overseas training usually was in the United States. Pilots were normally required to learn English at Lackland Air Force Base in Texas. Consequently, because of their early and extensive contact with the U.S. Air Force, Dominican aviators generally were pro-American. They were still obligated, however, to pander to the Trujillo family, and especially to the whims of Ramfis, if they expected advancement. A good example of what Ramfis emphasized in an officer was demonstrated in the rapid rise of Second Lieutenant Guarién Cabrera Ariza. Without being promoted to first lieutenant, Cabrera Ariza became a captain in 1954. On July 27, 1956, he was appointed *ayudante personal* to Ramfis; by 1961 he was a full colonel. The pilot's qualifications were that he played polo with Ramfis.[53]

With the end of the Trujillo era, the newly named *Fuerza Aérea Dominicana* (FAD) faced a military as well as a political period of uncertainty. Their equipment was aging fast and the United States was not willing to subsidize a foreign air arm which had a tradition of and a preference for flying aircraft such as B-17s. During the internecine political strife from 1962 to 1965, the pilots had few means to exert pressure on governments or politicians. In contrast, the CEFA had gone its own way and had become the final authority in most domestic confrontations before April 24, 1965. The air base at San Isidro would make its presence felt from an unexpected quarter, however.

When the CEFA was organized in 1959, it did not absorb all of the AMD's ground units. The infantry that was retained became base security squadrons, air police, and the *Grupo de Anti-guerrillas*. These units in the early 1960s were located at FAD headquarters at the San Isidro Air Base, and at the air bases in Santiago and Barahona (the *Coronel Piloto Juan Antonio Minaya Fernández* and the *Capitán Piloto Rafael Dávila Quesada* installations, respectively). On August 1, 1963, the *Grupo de Anti-guerrillas* and the CEFA's parachutist company were merged into the airborne Special Forces Group of the Air Force. The new organization's commander was Major Lluberes Montás. Although the general commanding the Air Force did not have the firepower of the CEFA, he could utilize troops armed with 120mm, 81mm, and 60mm mortars, 50 caliber and 30 caliber machine guns, and 3.5 inch rocket launchers.[54*]

The revolt of April 24, 1965, found the CEFA and the FAD on the same side; however, they were separate organizations under two different commanders. Brigadier General Juan de los Santos Céspedes, a pilot, led the Air Force, while Wessin y Wessin, as stated above, was in charge of the CEFA. To outsiders they and their officers were all members of the San Isidro Group, but there was considerable strain between the two generals.

One characteristic that de los Santos and Wessin shared was irresoluteness. The Air Force leader was reluctant to order his aircraft to strafe the rebels and Wessin used the excuse that he could not send his tanks forward without close air support. The issue was resolved abruptly when Lieutenant Colonel Beauchamps Javier of the CEFA and Major Lluberes Montás of the FAD, on their own initiative and armed, confronted the chief of the Air Force and demanded boldly, but unwisely, that he order air strikes against the rebel-held National Palace. De los Santos acquiesced, and, on April 25th, four P-51 "Mustangs" began the first of several air assaults against the capital.[55] These attacks (and a naval bombardment) were the most counterproductive acts of the civil war. In addition to being militarily useless, high civilian casualties turned an

---

*Officers of both the Air Force ground units and the CEFA continued to wear the same curious Trujillista garb during parades and ceremonies. Their uniform was a dark service tunic, cream-colored jodhpurs, dark brown riding boots, a Sam Browne belt (model 1912), and saber. All this was topped off with a German-style gray helmet acquired from Franco's Spanish Army. (See Dominican Republic, Aviación Militar Dominicana, Reglamento de Uniformes. Ciudad Trujillo: Roques Román, C por A, n.d., p. 11)

originally apathetic public against the San Isidro officers and were effectively exploited in left-wing propaganda.

On May 24th, a list of pilots' names was read continuously on the radio denouncing them as "enemies of the country" because they had "bombed the Dominican civilian population." Among those officers were the following pilots who would lead aviation in the 1960s and 1970s:

Juan Folch Pérez—a future FAD chief
Alfredo Imbert McGregor—a future FAD chief
Mario Imbert McGregor—a future FAD sub-chief and head of Armed Forces
Ismael Román Carbuccia—a future FAD sub-chief
Renato Malagón Montesano—a future FAD chief
Joaquín Nadal Lluberes—a future director, operations, FAD
Juan Manuel Ortega Piñeyro—a future FAD sub-chief
Octavio Jorge Pichardo—a future FAD sub-chief
Marino Polanco Tovar—a future chief, Air Command[56]

The combination of the loss of Ramfis' patronage, the physical deterioration of the air fleet, and the poor showing in the civil war left the San Isidro pilots demoralized as well as politically impotent. The officers who gained the most after the debacle of 1965 were a small group of FAD infantrymen. First among these was Major Salvador "Chinino" Lluberes Montás. He had completed the academy in 1954 and was commissioned a second lieutenant in the AMD infantry. He was the honor graduate of a San Isidro basic infantry course given in 1957. Three years later, after successfully completing the Spanish *Escuela Militar de Paracaidistas,* First Lieutenant Lluberes Montás founded and organized the nation's only airborne unit with his three fellow Dominican graduates from Spain (José Isidoro Martínez González, José Rosario Espinal, and Freddy Franco Díaz). They would become the nucleus of the new Special Forces of the FAD and would hold real power in the so-called San Isidro Group. On September 6, 1967, thirteen years after being commissioned an AMD second lieutenant, Lluberes Montás was appointed the head of the Air Force; on the same day, he was promoted from lieutenant colonel to brigadier general.[57] He was only 34. During the years that followed, U.S. military observers would remark in disbelief that the most dynamic officer in the Dominican Air Force was not a pilot but an infantryman.

If General Lluberes Montás was the most prominent officer in the Air Force to come out of San Isidro after the civil war, Enrique Pérez y Pérez would become the most prominent officer in the entire Armed Forces to have had an association with the San Isidro Group. Unlike most Air Force infantry officers, Pérez y Pérez had not spent the formative years of his career in the *Aviación Militar Dominicana.* In fact, because of his race (black), it would have been highly unlikely that Ramfis would have allowed Pérez y Pérez to have been a field grade officer in his organization. This bigotry was far less the rule in the Trujillo-era Army where Pérez y Pérez had completed his first eleven years as an officer. Pérez y Pérez's Army assignments prior to 1962 were unexceptional—cadet school, platoon leader, company commander—but he had one qualification that was extremely rare for line officers. He was a university graduate. On November 30, 1962, Pérez y Pérez transferred to the post-Ramfis Air Force as a lieutenant colonel. Prior to the outbreak of the civil war, he served on the air staff at San Isidro where he gained a reputation for hard work and solid management. The subject that most absorbed his attention was counterguerrilla operations. When the April 24, 1965, revolt began, he had been a FAD colonel for two years and was considered a highly knowledgeable staff officer. Pérez y Pérez's subsequent appointment as commander of the Base Defense Command at San Isidro placed all the Air Force's ground units under his direction. By the end of the year, he was in command of *Fortaleza Ozama*, the traditional location for controlling all forces in the capital.[58] In addition to providing steady leadership during those chaotic days, Pérez y Pérez also impressed the U.S. military operating in the Dominican Republic. In Pérez y Pérez, American Army officers saw characteristics which were admired in their own service: He exercised strict self-discipline, he never lost control of his emotions, he lived unostentatiously, he placed duty above personal interests, and he was physically fit. What was not obvious at the time was that he was absolutely ruthless in accomplishing his objectives.

A complete portrait of Pérez y Pérez's character may not have been clear in 1966, but there is little doubt that he was the ideal compromise choice to lead either the post-war Army or Armed Forces. On February 4, 1966, he was nominated as one of three Army colonels to be minister of the armed forces.[59] Provisional President García Godoy selected Pérez y Pérez. Seven days later he took office as a temporary brigadier general[60]; in the following month, he was designated the only major general on active duty in the country.[61] After Joaquín Balaguer won the June 1, 1966, elections for president, he surprised Dominicans (and shocked the old *Balaguerista* San Cristóbal Group), by retaining Pérez y Pérez as his armed forces minister. Although he had been in the Air Force for only a little over three years, many Dominicans categorized Pérez y Pérez as a member of the San Isidro Group. A further oversimplification of Santo Domingo's military politics was the explanation heard in the late 1960s that the San Isidro Group had changed its name to the Pérez y Pérez group.

NAVAL OFFICERS

As with the Air Force at San Isidro, the Navy during the Trujillo regime had a materiel strength far exceeding what would be expected of any country in the Caribbean Basin. Ordinary Dominicans were witnesses to this power when a total of 32 warships passed in review on Independence Day 1952.[62] The complete fleet included two destroyers, four frigates, five corvettes, three patrol vessels, and numerous coastal surveillance and auxiliary craft. During the Trujillo dictatorship, naval officers sailed the high seas in the following ships:

Destroyers—former British HMS *Fame* and HMS *Hotspur*
Frigates—former American USS *Knoxville*, USS *Pueblo*, and USS *Natchez*, and British HMS *Carlplace*
Corvettes—former Canadian HMCS *Lachute*, HMCS *Louisbourg*, HMCS *Peterborough*, HMCS *Belleville*, and HMCS *Riviere du Ioup*
Patrol vessels—former American Coast Guard Class B cutters USCGC *Icarus*, USCGC *Thetis*, and USCGC *Galatea*[63]

(Many of these ships would receive Dominican names more than once. For example, HMS *Carlplace* became the *Presidente Trujillo* following its acquisition by the Dominican Navy, and then, after the dictatorship fell, it was renamed the *Mella*.)

The Dominican Navy not only had sufficient officers to deploy these ships, but also to man a naval infantry ("marine corps") brigade, an underwater demolition unit, a port captaincy organization down to the smallest coastal havens (e.g., Azua, Samaná, Sánchez), a naval base structure that included three principal installations located at Santo Domingo, Las Calderas, and Haina, and a guard post system which had a coast watcher mission.

The story of Dominican naval officers from the end of the Trujillo era in 1961 to the early 1970s is an account of the steady decline in those officers' involvement with the maritime profession. Political strife and civil war played a part in the downward trend, but the main cause was simply the deterioration of the Trujillo fleet. With fewer and fewer seaworthy ships in the inventory, naval officers found themselves without maritime functions. Related activities such as the naval infantry and the underwater demolition unit had been eliminated. (In 1959, Trujillo broke up his "marine corps" for political reasons,[64] and in 1965 the *Comando de Hombres Ranas*—frogmen—was abolished[65] because it had fought on the side of the Constitutionalists.)

The evolution of the Navy into a non-seagoing force became more evident each day. A small group of younger officers were assigned to the patrol craft, but the mid-level and senior personnel rotated from

Navy headquarters to the naval bases to the port captaincies. The Navy became more famous for its sports car rallies, parties on the frigate *Mella*, and business transactions using naval auxiliary vessels to haul cargo, than for its role as a military service. Naval officers were more readily accepted in educated civilian circles than officers in any other branch of the Armed Forces, but their domestic political leverage was minimal. Since the Navy's leaders could not field a ground force with any firepower, the Navy had no ability to influence events decisively in the Dominican Republic. Naval officers, however, were able, on occasion, to make their presence felt not through physical strength, but through the political and administrative capacity of individual flag officers. These commodores could not stand up to the CEFA, the Army, the Air Force infantry, or even the National Police, but they were skilled enough to be considered among the players in Dominican military politics.

The three most prominent post-Trujillo flag officers were Francisco Rivera Caminero, Ramón Emilio Jiménez, Jr., and Francisco Amiama Castillo. They all graduated from the Dominican *Escuela Naval* and received foreign training over the years. Rivera Caminero's highest military education was the Inter-American Defense College late in his career. Jiménez studied at the *Escuela Superior Naval* staff college in Peru and, much later, at the U.S. Navy's war college at Newport, Rhode Island. Amiama Castillo served on the Spanish naval training ship *Juan Sebastián Elcano*, and afterward, attended the Peruvian naval staff college.[66]

They experienced the same level of important staff assignments; but, while Rivera Caminero and Amiama Castillo had commanded ships, Jiménez never was a captain of a vessel. All had served as naval attaches in Dominican embassies abroad; however, Rivera Caminero's two tours in Washington were under duress. (Jiménez had been assigned to Lima and London, Amiama Castillo to Havana and Washington.)[67] The three were considered intelligent and professionally competent as junior and mid-level officers.

Rivera Caminero was the first to become head of the Navy. After only twelve years of active duty (his last assignment was captain of the destroyer *Duarte*, the Dominican flagship), he assumed command of the naval service on January 21, 1962, as an acting commodore. He lasted only six months during that politically turbulent period. Rivera Caminero returned to the post on August 19, 1964, once again as a commodore, and remained through the opening of the civil war. It was on April 27, 1965, that he gave the now infamous order for the Navy to bombard the capital, which was militarily a failure, and provided a windfall for left-wing propaganda.[68] One week later he was appointed minister of the armed forces in the anti-Constitutionalist Government of National

Reconstruction. One of the compromises made during the peace negotiations called for his temporary departure from the Dominican Republic; on February 11, 1966, therefore, he began his second tour in
Washington in the reduced rank of captain.

When Rivera Caminero moved from the Navy to the Armed Forces
post on May 6, 1965, his deputy Jiménez took command of the naval service. Where Rivera Caminero had had an irregular and strife-ridden
career since 1962, Jiménez would experience a steady ascendancy up to
retirement. As with non-pilot Lluberes Montás and the Air Force, outsiders would question how it was possible that the most successful officer
in the Navy had never been a captain of a ship. He remained leader of
the Navy through the provisional presidency of García Godoy and was
retained by President Balaguer. (Jiménez's father, a noted author, had
been a personal friend of Balaguer.) In the president's second elected
term, on July 12, 1971, Jiménez was appointed secretary of state of the
armed forces and was promoted to rear admiral. In June 1975, Balaguer
designated Jiménez foreign minister. He remained at that post after Balaguer lost the 1978 elections until January 1980 when he retired as a vice
admiral.[69]

Some were of the opinion that Amiama Castillo was the most professional of the three. Although the youngest, his initial advancement
was the most rapid. As a *capitán de corbeta* (lieutenant commander), he
was appointed on February 5, 1958, deputy chief of the Navy—a position
usually filled by an officer two grades higher. The fall of the Trujillos,
however, brought problems for him from an unexpected quarter.
Amiama Castillo was not connected to the Trujillo family, but he was
related to one of the assassins of the dictator. In the chaotic politics of
the 1960s, Amiama Castillo was pushed by his family for the top Navy
post. President Balaguer, however, refused to allow Amiama Castillo to
command any organization. On August 21, 1970, he was appointed sub-
secretary of the armed forces for navy as a commodore; although the
job carried no authority, he did make a valuable contribution behind
the scenes by assisting in the formulation of plans and policy.[70] He
remained in that same position until Balaguer left office in 1978. It was
only then that he finally led the Navy.

The political views of Rivera Caminero, Jiménez, and Amiama
Castillo were essentially the same—they were rightists who believed in a
democracy which did not advocate too large an opening for the left. To
Dominican leftists, Rivera Caminero was considered the most dangerous because he was thought to have persecuted Socialists and Communists—a natural assumption if one remembers that he was the Armed
Forces chief during the 1965 revolt.[71] Amiama Castillo was a more closed-
mouthed rightist than Rivera Caminero. Few Americans would have

known that he was an admirer of Spain's Francisco Franco.[72] Jimenez was the least identified as right wing. He fully appreciated the value in avoiding sharp-edged statements to the wrong audience. Jiménez always gave the outward impression of being a moderate, willing to go along with the most reasonable approach.

These naval officers all had been exposed to the United States and were intelligent enough to recognize how to gain the most from Washington. They were skilled political leaders, but within the realm of Dominican military politics they brought no real power to the table. Although there were cliques in the Navy, they mattered little to the Armed Forces as a whole. For example, in the early 1960s Jiménez and Amiama Castillo were considered protégés of Rivera Caminero,[73] and in the early 1970s Jiménez and Rivera Caminero were in separate naval cliques, but in the entire military establishment they were little more than wordmen. The Navy had no force that could affect the internal politico-military balance; even though naval officers made individual contributions, they were marginalized when the issue demanded raw power.

III

The Officer Corps and Balaguer

There are many causes for the political disintegration of a nation after the passing of a tyranny such as the Trujillo era. In the case of the Dominican Republic, its officer corps contributed to that disintegration rather than assisting in the transition to a better form of governance. The factionalism and corruption within the military establishment had become so excessive after 1961 that the officer corps was unable to furnish the desperately needed stability that its type of institution would have been expected to provide in a time of crisis. The 1965 intervention of foreign troops was only a temporary measure in bringing the Dominican Armed Forces under control. It would be a most unlikely figure who would ultimately dominate the officer corps. He was Joaquín Balaguer— a meek-looking intellectual who had none of the traits commonly associated with the archetypical Latin American *caudillo*. He was educated in Europe, he became a recognized poet and scholar, and he was a long time civil servant more accustomed to polite diplomacy than to playing the role of a leader on horseback. Balaguer had been the puppet president of the country when Trujillo was assassinated; after exile and a subsequent electoral campaign, he was sworn in on July 1, 1966, as the legitimately elected president of the republic. It was then that he began the process to bring the officer corps to heel. Soon pundits would say that he had learned well from *El Jefe;* by the time his control of the military was fully consolidated in 1971, the wags in the Dominican Republic would amusingly remark that, in actuality, it was Balaguer who had secretly taught Trujillo everything the dictator had known.

Since Balaguer neither had the personal charisma nor the raw power to command the Armed Forces to obey him, he needed to devise a different technique to curb the officer corps. His principal means of exercising his authority was to pit individuals and the various factions of the Armed Forces against each other, thereby denying any person or group the strength to challenge Balaguer himself. Other methods used by the President were to deploy military units in such a manner that a

30

physical balance was always maintained, to prevent professional officers from gaining authority or influence, to use corruption to buy loyalty, and to keep quietly alive the emotional linkage which the officer corps retained with the Trujillo regime.

MANIPULATION OF INDIVIDUALS AND FACTIONS

Balaguer's success in dividing the officer corps against itself and having the various fragments beholden to him alone was based on a well thought out scheme. First, he would not deal with the outer edges of the political spectrum—at least not during his 1966–1970 term. Wessin y Wessin on the right and Caamaño on the left were kept outside Balaguer's system. Second, he found exploiting individuals and factions far easier than dealing with units or branches of the service. Third, he always understood the motivation and needs of his targets.[1] The officers would accept his manipulation as long as he never failed to live up to his unspoken pledge that he would give members of the Armed Forces the type of life style and government that made them feel secure.[2]

Pitting individuals and cliques against each other was a full time project for Balaguer. There was his open technique of making personnel appointments without warning. For example, individuals would learn that they had been sacked or reassigned during a routine radio news broadcast. On occasion, a transfer would be leaked and then Balaguer would not follow through with the posting. Some would state that Balaguer purposefully started the rumor so that he could do the opposite. Balaguer would also use this method to reshuffle groups of commanders—a faction could be in a favorable position one day and the next they would be powerless and in decline. These types of actions kept senior officers publicly off balance.[3]

Beneath the surface was the more insidious practice of revealing to an officer how his enemy was plotting against him. One way among many in which this was accomplished was by silently handing an intelligence report to the subject of the report so that the recipient would know who had denounced him.[4]

Generals and colonels would be pleased with their president if they fared well; however, they would blame their adversaries, not Balaguer, if their fortunes took a downward turn. Through it all, the officers knew that if they remained loyal to Balaguer he would not allow a hostile clan to damage permanently their own group.

The end product of the Balaguer method was a subservient officer corps. If an individual or faction were to grow too strong, thus threatening the internal equilibrium of the military establishment, or more serious, the undisputed authority of the president, Balaguer would not have to suppress the errant officer or clique personally. He would merely induce another officer, clan, or combination of clans to deal with the potentially dangerous issue.

When Balaguer returned to the presidency in July 1966, he faced a multitude of officer factions that could have challenged his ability to exercise his constitutional mandate as commander in chief. There were no shortage of problems he could expect from groups such as ex-CEFA members in the 4th Brigade, Air Force parachutists and infantrymen, and disgruntled pilots and naval service personnel. Even his own supporters in the Army's old San Cristóbal Group would be a thorn in his side because they expected the most powerful and lucrative assignments in payment for their time out of favor. Balaguer would manipulate these groupings with dexterity. What was evident to him from the outset was that in the various cliques, there were two leaders who stood out in strength, and in the intensity in which they despised each other. One was Neit Nivar Seijas of the ex-San Cristóbal Group and the other was Enrique Pérez y Pérez, the nominal heir to the San Isidro Group. It was clear to the new president that he would have the most to gain by keeping these two officers and their followers perpetually at each other's throats.[5]

BALANCE AMONG UNITS

Integral to Balaguer's skillful manipulation of individuals and factions was his maintenance of a balance among Armed Forces and National Police units. Although military life had never been a part of his personal experience, he appreciated how Trujillo had successfully offset organizational power for many years, and, most of all, Balaguer did not wish a repetition of 1962–1965 when the CEFA alone dictated the politics of the entire nation. Other lessons drawn from Wessin y Wessin's CEFA and the subsequent events of the 1965 civil war were that the control of the capital and the distribution of armored vehicles were of primary importance while the military in the interior was a secondary priority. Balaguer's main objectives, consequently, were that no unit should dominate Santo Domingo and no individual or command should have a monopoly of the armor. He implemented this policy during his 1966–1970 term by stationing units around and within the capital. (Please see following page.)

In addition, in the Santo Domingo area there were aviation and naval personnel, Army logistics organizations, and National Policemen, but they had no serious impact on the balance of power.

Unit	Location
3rd Battalion, *Ramón Matías Mella*, Army	San Cristóbal (30 km west of the capital)
2nd Battalion, *Francisco del Rosario Sánchez*, Army	*16 de Agosto* Military Camp (25 km NW of the capital)
Artillery Battalion, Army	Artillery Military Camp (7 km NW of the capital)
Duarte Department, National Police (infantry battalion-type unit)	Duarte Camp, Santo Domingo
1st Battalion, *Juan Pablo Duarte*, Army	*Fortaleza Ozama*, Santo Domingo
1st and 2nd Military Police Companies, Army	Military Police barracks, Santo Domingo
Presidential Guard Battalion, Army (light infantry unit)	National Palace grounds, Santo Domingo
Special Forces Group, Air Force	San Isidro Air Base (15 km east of capital)
Base Defense Command, Air Force	San Isidro Air Base[6]

Aircraft and ships had proven woefully inadequate in the urban struggle of 1965; while troop-carrying helicopters could have made a difference, they did not exist in sufficient numbers at the time. In contrast, the hardware that received the most attention was the armored vehicles. In the post-1965 Dominican Republic, they became the chess pieces which most reflected intramural strength. Even though their operational value was greatly diminished (some of the World War II American equipment could barely move), the number of vehicles a commander controlled had political significance.

Balaguer desired to dismantle the strike force of the 4th Brigade soon after his inauguration. It was essential for him to begin the process as quickly as possible because of the necessity to weaken the former CEFA before the Inter-American Peace Force departed the country; he needed the foreign troops to back him if ex-*Wessinista* officers attempted to obstruct his orders.[7] The 4th Brigade's infantry battalion, the *Enriquillo*, needed no presidential attention because it already was practically nonexistent. Therefore, Balaguer's purge started with the artillery. On September 5th, he announced that the Artillery Group, *General Gregorio Luperón*, was disbanded. Even before the President's announcement was delivered, the transfer of artillery pieces was underway from San Isidro to garrisons in the interior such as those located in Santiago and San Juan de la Maguana, and to the Army's old artillery camp outside Santo Domingo.[8] This was followed by the vital redistribution of Dominican armor. At a measured pace, Balaguer methodically began the movement of armored vehicles from San Isidro to different sites in the country. The result was that the armor was diffused among six commanders in the vicinity of the capital and at installations in La Vega, Santiago, San Juan de la Maguana, and Barahona. In October 1969, the President sent the remainder of the San Isidro armored vehicles to the border area at Neiba and Dajabón ostensibly to reinforce the Dominican Army in response to reports of political unrest in Haiti.[9] Thus, in the beginning of 1971, all 68 tanks and other armored vehicles of the Dominican Armed Forces were dispersed throughout the country in 13 different garrisons. At San Isidro, where CEFA power had threatened its opponents from 1962 to 1965, there would eventually only remain two "half track" armored personnel carriers, and they were assigned to the air base rather than to the Army.[10]

PROFESSIONALISM DISCOURAGED

Balaguer held a deep distrust of an officer corps that had an institutional identity and could function autonomously of the presidency. The incidents of political intervention on the part of the quasi-professional CEFA were ample proof to him that educated military leaders who could mold a cohesive modern organization would be potential threats to his future control of the state. Thus, when Balaguer began his first post-Trujillo term, he embarked on a clear policy of discouraging professionalism in the Armed Forces.

From Balaguer's inauguration through 1972 he appointed twenty general/flag officers. Only five could be considered qualified professionals. He gave key commands to officers who were personally loyal to him. The greater majority of them were old *Trujillistas* with no military education other than the Haina-type introductory course. He eliminated officers from the Armed Forces, no matter how professionally oriented they were, if there was a possibility of their political unreliability. This elimination program was extended to cashiering officers for no other fault than unfortunate family ties. Balaguer was wary of officers who had been trained in foreign staff colleges and senior service schools. In 1971 only two officers who had graduated from the U.S. Army's staff college course commanded battalion-size or larger units in the Army. Yet similar posts were held by four officers who had failed that course. There was no general staff college training in the Dominican Republic at that time; however, U.S. advisers from 1966 had established basic, middle, and advanced courses beneath that level. Even that rudimentary military education was eyed with suspicion by the President. In 1972, only five cadets from the Military Academy, *Batalla de las Carreras*, were commissioned as officers in the Army. During the same year, approximately 60 enlisted men were designated second lieutenants without the benefit even of an officer candidate school.[11]

Illustrative of Balaguer's attitude toward professionalism was the secretary of state of the armed forces he appointed to succeed General Pérez y Pérez. (Balaguer reestablished that Trujillo-era title for his minister of the armed forces in November 1966.) After more than four years, Pérez y Pérez's transfer from his cabinet position was anticipated. What was not expected by observers or by the small circle of mid-career professionals was the August 18, 1970, selection of Joaquín Méndez Lara to lead the military establishment. The new major general had entered the Army at the age of 21 as a private thirty years before, four years later he was promoted to corporal, and on August 17, 1944, he was commissioned without benefit of a cadet course. His first officer assignment was duty with Trujillo's bodyguards. For the remainder of his career in the Army, he never attended a military school at any level.[12]

The fate of two Dominican staff college students in 1967 is also very telling. On March 3rd, Colonels Rafael Valdez Hilario and Pedro Medrano Ubiera departed Santo Domingo together to attend the U.S. Army's 40-week command and staff course. Valdez Hilario's background had been mainly in the constabulary Army stationed in the interior. In contrast, Medrano had been a tank instructor, an operations planner, the director of the Military Academy, and the commander of the Artillery Group in the CEFA. Valdez Hilario was unable to complete the staff course and was sent home early. Medrano was the only Dominican officer to graduate in 1967. Far from being in disgrace, Valdez Hilario, in the following three years, was appointed a brigade commander, then subsecretary of state of the armed forces with promotion to brigadier general, and on April 15, 1970, head of the Army with the title of chief of staff. After Medrano's return, he became the Army's G-3 (plans and training). In that position, he worked closely with U.S. military advisers on the modernization of his service. Much to the disappointment of the Americans, however, he did not remain in the post for a full tour. In 1969, he was sent out of the country as the delegate to the Inter-American Defense Board in Washington, D.C., where he remained until 1973.[13] His career, in effect, had been terminated. These occurrences were not merely Balaguer's favoring of a *Trujillista*-type officer over a former CEFA member. It was also a clear directive to the officer corps that professionalism would not be a quality highly prized in the Dominican Armed Forces.

A comparable message was also sent in the cases of Carlos Jáquez Olivero and Eladio Marmolejos Abréu of the Army and Air Force, respectively. Lieutenant Colonel Jáquez had followed the traditional Army career in the interior with most of his assignments in the northern Cibao Valley. Through his command of the constabulary-style 9th Battalion, *General Santiago Rodríguez*, located in Mao, the capital of Valverde province, he became, in 1969, Balaguer's political chieftain for the region. Newly promoted Colonel Jáquez's activities were so blatant during the 1970 presidential campaign that the electoral control commission, on April 27, 1970, recommended his transfer from the battalion. That year Jáquez faced a second threat to his command: The 9th Battalion had been chosen by the American Embassy and the Dominican government to be organized and equipped as a tactical maneuver unit as had the 1st, 2nd, and 3rd Battalions in the capital area after the civil war. A problem for the U.S. advisers was that Jáquez had never been trained to be a modern infantry commander. In turn, despite the electoral control commission and the American advisers, the President wanted to keep Jáquez in Valverde province for obvious political reasons. The solution was the assignment of Lieutenant Colonel Mélido González Pérez, a 1966 graduate of the U.S. Army's staff college course, to command the battalion; Jáquez would become the commander of Fort *General Benito Monción* where the headquarters of the battalion was located. Through hard work, González Pérez transformed the 9th Battalion into a combat-prepared tactical unit. In 1971, he was considered the best infantry battalion commander in the Dominican Army; however, only U.S. personnel dealt with him in that capacity. To the Dominican Armed Forces and the public, Colonel Jáquez was still commander of the 9th Battalion. When the President officially visited the battalion on August 14, 1971, military and civilian press releases stated that Balaguer was welcomed by the 9th Battalion commander, Colonel Jáquez. González Pérez , the officer who had created the new battalion, was nowhere to be seen. Subsequently, Jáquez was promoted to brigadier general (but not moved from Mao) while González Pérez's career remained in the shadows.[14]

When Balaguer visited the 9th Battalion in August 1971, a member of his coterie was Brigadier General Eladio Marmolejos Abréu, the commander of San Isidro Air Base. Marmolejos and Jáquez were the same type of officer although they were in separate services. It was assumed that Air Force officers would be more technically oriented than their Army counterparts, but this was not the case with Marmolejos. His main qualification was that his intense loyalty to Trujillo had been transferred to Balaguer. On April 29, 1944, he had joined the National Police as a private. Marmolejos subsequently moved to the Army, then to the air arm where he became a sergeant. He remained an enlisted man for almost thirteen years. Marmolejos was designated a second lieutenant in the *Aviación Militar Dominicana* on January 22, 1957; on June 5th he graduated from the only full course he ever attended throughout his career. In a basic AMD infantry program, he finished 21st in a class of 23. (Second Lieutenant Lluberes Montás was the honor graduate.) Marmolejos' lack of military education was not an impediment to his advancement in Balaguer's Air Force, however. In August 1966, when Marmolejos was stationed at the air base in Barahona, he was accused of detaining members of Juan Bosch's legal opposition party. The politicians were released on Balaguer's orders and Marmolejos was soon rewarded by being promoted to full colonel after only ten years as an officer. On January 23, 1967, he was appointed to a post especially created for him: commander of the San Isidro Air Base. Six months later he was promoted to brigadier general. His principal duty at the air base was to inform Balaguer if any political mischief was being hatched presumably by former CEFA members such as General Lluberes Montás or by the aviators and base security personnel of the Air Force. He spent the majority of his time traveling with the president on political swings through the country—a fact that was observed with disdain by the young officers who were attempting to modernize Dominican military aviation.[15]

There were many more examples of Balaguer's efforts to discourage professionalism in the Armed Forces, but nothing more emphatically revealed his contempt for the Dominican officer corps than the President's promoting his barber to major, elevating his chauffeur to lieutenant colonel, and retaining on active duty Trujillo's old boot black as a first lieutenant.[16]

LOYALTY THROUGH CORRUPTION

Corruption involving Dominican officers existed throughout the country's history. It had been reduced under the U.S. Marine occupation,[17] but was reintroduced, though "regulated," during the Trujillo period.[18] From the death of Trujillo to the 1965 civil war, it was excessive and out of control.[19] After July 1, 1966, Balaguer brought a form of Trujillo-type order back to military peculation, with the exception that Balaguer was disinterested personally in material gain and there was no extended family to keep content as *El Jefe* had to do with his numerous relatives.

At the lowest level of the Armed Forces during the Trujillo era, it was expected that commanders would skim off mess funds. A common practice was to release troops early on weekends and holidays so that money for absent soldiers' meals could be pocketed. The best position after the commander in a military unit such as a rifle company was the mess officer. Becoming the *oficial de mesa* was considered such a privilege in the 1950s that the assignment to be a ship's mess officer was announced formally throughout the Armed Forces along with appointment of the vessel's captain.[20] Another custom from the Trujillo regime was the assignment of the *intendente general* of one of the services. The quartermaster general post was so lucrative that the dictator would not allow any individual to hold the job for more than half a year. During that period, an automatic 10% of funds was retained by the *intendente general*. At the end of six months, the position was filled by another officer who had been singled out for reward by *El Jefe*. This policy and the mess officer tradition were both followed during Balaguer's administration. They were so engrained in the daily life of the officers that these practices were talked about freely by them and their families to outsiders as if this form of graft was part of the monthly paycheck.

Further up the organizational hierarchy, corruption became more diverse. Personnel officers (S-1s) sold assignments, intelligence officers (S-2s) had access to special contingency funds, and logistics officers (S-4s) could rake off *pesos* for fuel and other expendables. The one position usually sought after in professional armies, the operations officer (S-3), was of little value in the Dominican military because it was difficult to convert it into a paying concern.[21]

The services also had their unique benefits. The Air Force could fly in duty free foreign goods to San Isidro Air Base for resale. Round trips by transport aircraft to Puerto Rico were a common and profitable occurrence. In the case of the Navy, assignment to the port captaincy of Santo Domingo or to one of the larger coastal towns was a guarantee that the naval officer's salary would be augmented by commercial shippers. The Army had two specialized units that were always lucrative: the Engineer Battalion and the Transportation Battalion. The engineers devoted almost all of their time to building houses and roads as part of the Armed Forces civic action program. From these projects, there were numerous opportunities to make money from the purchase of construction materials. The advantage to being in the Transportation Battalion came from siphoning off a percentage of the funds allocated for maintenance, fuels, and spare parts for the Army's large truck fleet.[22]

It was at the national level, however, that Balaguer truly allowed the Armed Forces to become a business. He bought the military leaders' personal loyalty by giving them access to the nation's economy. Important to understanding Balaguer's relationship with his generals was that the graft he made available to them mainly did not derive from the military sector. A basic policy of the President was to avoid, where at all possible, the funding for major equipment. If the United States wanted to assist the Dominican Armed Forces with modernization, he had no objection, but he refused to buy new sophisticated aircraft, ships, or armor. Instead, he satisfied his senior officers' greed by allowing them to participate in the country's civilian projects where they could make substantial amounts of money. With these gains, the generals and commodores were willing to control their aspirations for jet aircraft, modern destroyers, or expensive tanks. The president, thus, had secured both their loyalty and their disinterest in pressing for large government expenditures on armaments.

The military had a wide range of opportunities to make their fortunes. Controlling contracts and involving themselves in major government public works such as the construction of highways, bridges, dams, and tourist hotels were but a few. Kickbacks from those efforts were not the only means in which the generals and commodores enriched themselves. They became key players in entire projects. An example was the illegal importation of cane cutters from Haiti for the nation's sugar harvest. One Dominican general handled this process for the country directly with counterpart Haitian officers. Inserting themselves in the government's financial activities with the consent of the President was merely the first phase for a few of the more enterprising generals. In the case of Neit Nivar Seijas, he expanded his interests by acquiring legitimate businesses in the private sector. By the end of Balaguer's 1966–1970 term, Nivar owned or was part owner of a radio station, a racetrack, and numerous properties.[23]

The rapid accumulation of wealth by the generals was quickly apparent to soldiers and civilians alike. New large homes were built in the most expensive section of the capital, modest automobiles were exchanged for large, black sedans (Ford LTDs were the fad), and imported uniforms and accouterments (such as Italian boots and Mexican gold pistol grips) became commonplace. Bodyguards with submachine guns, retainers, and advisers surrounded the new millionaires; this projected an image that was a cross between a renaissance prince and a mafia boss. Upper class civilians were quick to remark that the generals did not deserve such riches because of their low social status and lack of education. To the enlisted men it was much simpler. These officers were flaunting the wealth that had been acquired on the backs of the soldiers who were detailed to be their servants, laborers, farm hands, and guards at no expense to the generals.

There were honest officers in positions of responsibility at the time but they were a small group. Two such officers were Army Colonel Manuel Antonio Cuervo Gómez and Air Force Colonel Ramiro Matos González. The former commanded the Army's Artillery Battalion and the latter was the head of the Air Force's North Command in Santiago. They were recognized as accomplished men who were devoted to the military profession, but the average junior officer could readily see that the road to success was not in following them, but in belonging to the entourage of a general like Nivar. The general's supporters in the officer corps benefited with promotions and extra income while Nivar's enemies were falling by the wayside. From the President's point of view, both types of officers had their value, but it was clear to Balaguer that, over-all, there was more to be gained by controlling generals like Nivar through corruption than by devoting too much energy in satisfying the professional needs of two admirable colonels like Cuervo Gómez and Matos González.

LINKS TO THE TRUJILLO PAST

Balaguer was fully aware that the officer corps had been deeply affected by the Trujillo era. In the late 1960s and early 1970s, it was unusual to hear any criticism of the dictator from military men. Even the exceedingly small number of well-educated officers in the institution would speak favorably of him. Their typical comments would be that Trujillo had been responsible for the development of the Domini-can Republic as a modern state. In guarded terms, they would explain how Trujillo had transformed their country from a nineteenth century backwater into a twentieth century nation. The less educated officers, usually with the aid of alcohol, would, on occasion, be more blunt, how-ever. Even though Trujillo's favorite merengue *San Cristóbal* was banned, they would order musicians to play it loudly. Tales about *El Jefe's* prowess were commonly heard at such times. When, in 1971, Trujillo's close friend and Haina classmate retired Lieutenant General Fausto Caamaño (known by some as the "butcher") visited the *16 de Agosto* Military Camp, he was swamped by young lieutenants who wanted to hear stories about the dictator. Once a year, on May 30th, a mass was given for the Gener-alissimo, and, after Ramfis died on December 28, 1969, a similar mass was said for the son. Officers, such as General Marmolejos, would attend despite the adverse publicity that they knew would follow. Also, it was no secret that General Nivar, in defiance of the official prohibition of displaying Trujillo's image, had an oil portrait of the dictator in full uniform, to include a plumed bicorne cocked hat, prominently exhib-ited in his residence. Balaguer could not afford to ignore these emo-tions.

The approach Balaguer followed in exploiting the attitude of the officer corps toward Trujillo was extremely low key but effective. First, he never denigrated the dictator in the presence of military men. Sec-ond, he allowed *Trujillista* military customs and ceremonies to continue as long as the Trujillo family name was not publicly involved. And, third, in the beginning of his second elected term, he quietly brought back on active duty a small number of Trujillo-era officers, who had been exiled in 1961, to demonstrate to the military establishment that he shared the same feelings as the officer corps concerning Trujillo.

Balaguer refused to rehabilitate the odious thugs and cronies who were associated with the more brutal aspects of the Trujillo regime. Though some of the officers he selected had questionable reputations, they, by and large, were acceptable to enough Dominicans so that outbursts from the press could be avoided. Also, he kept the group very small because he did not want officers already serving to worry that their jobs were in danger.

The first former *Trujillista* general to receive a military post was Guarionex Estrella Sahdalá; on July 12, 1971, he was returned to active status as a brigadier general and appointed commander of the 2nd Brigade in Santiago, the second city of the Dominican Republic. He had served almost continuously for ten years in the dictator's Corps of Military Aides—in the last three years of Trujillo's life he had been the Corps' chief as a general officer. An extenuating factor which made his return more palatable to the public was that his brother Salvador had been part of the assassination plot against Trujillo and was executed by Ramfis.[24] Consequently, the general had been cashiered in 1961 not because he was a *Trujillista*, but because he was related to one of the assassins.

In 1971, the most urbane and articulate officer to regain active status was appointed an Army lieutenant colonel almost in secret. Roberto Oscar Figueroa Carrión had trained as a cadet in Argentina and was one of the most promising members of Ramfis' ground forces. When the brightest young officers in the Armed Forces were concentrated in the faculty of the Military Academy, he was first the sub-director then the director of that institution.[25] From that assignment, Lieutenant Colonel Figueroa Carrión was appointed the personal aide-de-camp to Trujillo. His next position was the main reason he was banished from the country. Only a short period before the dictator's assassination, newly promoted Colonel Figueroa Carrión was made the director general of the SIM (military intelligence service) in an attempt to improve the image of that notorious organization. He had no opportunity to practice public relations, however, because he almost immediately was immersed in the investigation of the assassination, one of the most infamous episodes in the Trujillo family's history.[26] Figueroa Carrión spent almost ten years in exile before Balaguer reinstated him, ostensibly as a civilian instructor at the Military Academy. For approximately two years, he was stationed out of the public eye at the *16 de Agosto* Military Camp. It was only in 1973, when he was designated the commander of the Army battalion in Barahona, that it became widely known that he was on active duty; by that late date there was little negative reaction.[27]

Another officer who had belonged to the exceptional faculty of the Military Academy under Figueroa Carrión was First Lieutenant Julio

César Ramos Troncoso.[28] Unlike his fellow instructors, he would not become a part of the CEFA officers faction nor a member of the professional nucleus of the Armed Forces. His close association with the Trujillo brothers, Ramfis and Rhadamés, and brother-in-law León Estévez, at San Isidro (he was considered an *hombre de confianza* or "man of trust" to them[29]) marked him for exile just months after he was promoted to major. Ten years later, Balaguer reintegrated him at the Military Academy as an Army captain. Throughout the 1970–1974 term, Ramos Troncoso studiously kept his distance from the public.

Beginning in 1969, a retired Army brigadier general began to participate in activities open to the press with the President. In April 1972, César Augusto Oliva García was appointed director general of immigration, although he continued in military retirement status. The significance of his return was that Oliva García had been Trujillo's chief of National Police in 1953–1954 and director general of the Security Service in 1956 and again in 1958. Anti-Trujillo activists had called him a "notorious hatchet man."[30] Although Oliva García was more visible than Figueroa Carrión or Ramos Troncoso, thereby representing a clear link with the Trujillo past, his early 1970s governmental work was divorced from the Armed Forces.

In contrast, the reappearance of Major General Santos Mélido Marte Pichardo was a highly charged event. The former secretary of state of the armed forces had begun his 40-year military career with Trujillo; together they had attended the Haina school run by the U.S. Marines. During four decades, he had been in every arm of the institution. After aviation training in the United States, he became, in 1933, the Dominican Republic's fourth military pilot.[31] Among his assignments, he was commander of the Presidential Guard, sub-chief of the Army, sub-chief of the Navy, commander of the naval infantry ("marine corps") brigade, chief of staff of the Army, and finally head of the Armed Forces. Two months after the death of Trujillo, Marte Pichardo retired. In mid–1971, Balaguer appointed him chief of presidential security at the age of 72, and, at the end of the year, put him in charge of the *Comedores Económicos,* a government-run program to provide meals for the needy.[32] (The graft potential of the latter position caused people to humorously remark that the old general had been given the ultimate mess officer job in the country.) Although Marte Pichardo did not have control of troops, he was considered to have access to Balaguer, and his son Captain Rafael Mélido Marte Hoffiz was given command of an independent motorized unit with mounted machine guns to act as security for the President and to perform special tasks for him.[33] The return of Marte Pichardo was probably the most significant appointment Balaguer made in demonstrating his unspoken commitment to the Trujillo past. Although Balaguer may have gained a certain amount of advice from the veteran general, Marte Pichardo's main value to the president, insofar as the officer corps was concerned, was that Balaguer had refused to turn his back on the roots of the military institution.

IV

A Military View of
the Armed Forces

On November 26, 1964, a Dominican military delegation arrived in El Salvador for an orientation on civic action programs—an effort which the United States was endorsing throughout Latin America. A major segment of the seven-day visit was a series of Salvadoran briefings and follow-on discussions concerning El Salvador's General Staff and Armed Forces educational system.[1] Although both countries were agricultural, exceedingly small in geographic area, and with similar size populations, there were stark differences in their military institutions.

On November 27th, after a courtesy call on the reform-minded president of El Salvador, Colonel Julio Adalberto Rivera, the Dominicans received their first briefing—the history, organization, and operations of the Salvadoran Armed Forces General Staff.[2] In the beginning of the twentieth century, a Chilean military mission which had been influenced by Prussian advisers established the foundations of the Salvadoran Army. The Chileans stressed the importance of a general staff and a strong military educational system.[3] With their assistance, the first General Staff in El Salvador was formed on January 5, 1912.[4] In contrast, the Dominican Armed Forces had never possessed a functioning general staff and only recently had begun, reluctantly, to experiment with the concept.

The second conference was at the *Escuela de Comando y Estado Mayor* on November 30th where the Dominicans received a briefing on general staff training. They were told that the Salvadoran students received instruction to prepare officers for duty on the General Staff. Their program included technical military subjects, history, geography, law, and economics. Graduates were granted the *Diplomado de Estado Mayor* or "DEM" certification. Further advanced course work was provided to select Salvadoran officers who then received the title of *Profesor Militar* in a specialty such as logistics, intelligence, or military history.[5] El Salvador's first general staff course was given from April 1936 to October 1937.[6] Conversely, the Dominican military institution, as of 1964, had never had a general staff college course in its country.

On the same day, the Dominican delegates received an orientation on *the Escuela de Armas y Servicios*, founded in January 1955, where they were exposed to educational programs for company grade and non-commissioned officers. The briefer, Major Arturo Armando Molina (a future president of El Salvador), explained that Salvadoran lieutenants first received training in a basic infantry or artillery course; later in their careers they attended an advanced course at the same school.[7] In the Dominican Republic, at the time of the El Salvador visit, no plan was in effect to establish a military educational system.

The day before departure, the Dominicans visited the *Escuela Militar,* El Salvador's military academy. Its predecessor organization had been founded in 1868, and it had evolved into its present configuration by 1927.[8] Dominican cadets had not been put through a program similar to the *Escuela Militar* until the founding of the Military Academy, *Batalla de las Carreras*, with the aid of Spanish Army officers, in September 1956.[9]

Other than from formal, protocol-driven speeches, it is not known how Brigadier General Renato Hungría Morell, the head of the Dominican delegation (and former chief of staff of the Army), reacted to the Salvadoran presentations. It is known, however, that he was a good example of the typical Dominican senior officer. After the short Haina-type cadet course, Hungría Morell was commissioned on January 1, 1945, a second lieutenant in the Army. From that date to his trip to El Salvador, he had not had any additional military or civilian schooling.[10] John Bartlow Martin, the U.S. Ambassador to the Dominican Republic in 1963, wrote that he "... had never suspected [General Hungría Morell] of harboring an idea ..."[11] Possibly, therefore, the Dominican delegation chief may not have fully appreciated how deficient Dominican officers were in 1964 compared to their Latin American counterparts such as the officer corps of El Salvador.

Organizations, however, can be more impressive on a briefing chart than in reality, and El Salvador's military institutions were no exception, but when that country went to war with Honduras in 1969, the Salvadorans, by most accounts, out-performed the Hondurans. This success was attributed to El Salvador's aggressive officer corps and its General Staff planning for rapid mobilization and for task force organization. The record for the Dominican Armed Forces in the 1965 civil war was the opposite.

THE AMERICAN LEGACY AND THE AGREEMENT OF 1962

Whereas the foundation of the Salvadoran Army was Prussian/Chilean, the roots of the Dominican Armed Forces were decidedly American. The U.S. Marine occupation had left a visible mark on the Dominican military, and, since Trujillo felt strongly about his relationship with the Corps,[12] no attempt was made within the institution to erase the evidence of the Marines' former presence in the Dominican Republic. This legacy was apparent in fundamentals, such as unit organization, uniforms, and drill and ceremonies, and in curious, smaller ways. For example, in the latter case, the Armed Forces used convoluted, English language-derived military terms such as "*wapons*" (from "weapons carrier"),[13] "*yip*" (from "jeep"),[14] and "*hangares*" (from "hangars").[15] Dominican soldiers repeated Marine slang so that eventually it became part of the vernacular. The American words "chow" (food) and "rum" became "*chao*" and "*romo*" (even though the Spanish translation of "rum" is "*ron*"). And the common U.S. expression "full colonel"—to differentiate a colonel from a lieutenant colonel—was used by the Dominican Army in a different form: "*coronel ful.*" Other reminders were that an orderly room of a 1970s Dominican rifle company looked the same as it did when it had been set up by the U.S. Marine Corps, and the communications wire linking posts along the Haitian border was the original wire laid by the Marines in 1916–1924.

In the late 1950s, Washington began a policy of distancing itself from the dictator's increasingly repressive regime. A major step in this course of action took place in 1958 when the U.S. government stopped providing the Dominican Republic with arms.[16] The Generalissimo acted that year as well. As a result of Ramfis' failure to receive a diploma because he had attended but not successfully completed the U.S. Army Command and General Staff College course at Fort Leavenworth, Kansas, an offended Trujillo withdrew the Dominican cadets and young officers studying in the United States.[17]* In February 1960, the U.S. Military Assistance Advisory Group (MAAG) in Santo Domingo closed. American military advisers would not serve in the Dominican Republic again until after the assassination of Trujillo.[18]

In effect, the American legacy was mainly a Marine Corps legacy; the Marines contributed in shaping the lives of Dominican "regimental duty" officers, but they made little impact on national-level command and general staff matters. In addition, American advisers from all services were not able to establish in the Dominican Republic a lasting professional military educational system, which had been an essential part of U.S. Army career development between the world wars and after. The bilateral Military Assistance Agreement of 1962 would be the first modest move in that direction.

*El Jefe *struck back at Washington in peculiar ways: He ordered the Dominican Armed Forces to remove the "RD" (*República Dominicana*) *lapel insignia from their uniforms because the "RD" was a copy of the "US" on U.S. Army service jackets. Not content with this measure, he also had the "RD" defaced on photographs taken before his order.*

The March 8, 1962, accord provided the framework for a new relationship between the Armed Forces of the United States and the Dominican Republic. From that broad document, agreements were drawn up concerning various military assistance programs for the Dominicans. Included was training for officers and enlisted men in U.S. military schools. A highlight of that arrangement was a systematic means for the Dominican officer corps to receive general staff instruction. Beginning in 1963, a select group of Dominican officers would attend the 40 week Command and Staff Course at the U.S. Army School of the Americas in the Panama Canal Zone.[19] It was understood that this staff college training would be the capstone of the officer corps' military education.

During the same month that the agreement was signed, the MAAG reopened in Santo Domingo with five members. The size of the United States advisory effort would fluctuate depending on the changing political situation. In 1963, the MAAG was increased to 45 to demonstrate support for President Juan Bosch. His overthrow caused a termination of assistance; however, in 1964, the MAAG opened again with 13 members. The following year it was increased to 26 personnel, but the 1965 civil war disrupted normal MAAG operations; over 23,000 U.S. troops intervened in the Dominican Republic.[20]

Despite these variations, command and staff students were sent to the School of the Americas almost every year. From 1963 to the end of 1972, a total of 30 graduated.[21] Unfortunately, during the first years of the program, suspicious senior Dominican officers were opposed to using young staff college graduates in the new, functional, MAAG-promoted General Staff.[22] Notwithstanding this resistance to change, the Army was provided with a capability heretofore never seen in the history of the Dominican Republic—within the officer corps there was a nucleus, albeit small, of general staff-trained professionals.

THE NEW ARMY

In July 1969, the Dominican Army completed its reorganization along U.S. guidelines.[23] The Army adopted its new structure through a lengthy process at two levels. In the beginning of 1966, work began to create the 1st Brigade as an immediate means of providing security for the capital area. The following year, American and Dominican officers started the two year project to modernize the organization of the entire ground force.

Beginning in 1962, elements of three infantry battalions—the *Juan Pablo Duarte*, the *Francisco del Rosario Sánchez*, and the *Ramón Matías Mella* —had received counterinsurgency training from U.S. advisers and mobile training teams.[24] The 1965 civil war had left these units inoperable, however. With the approach of the June 1, 1966, presidential elections, U.S. Embassy officials and the Dominican provisional president realized that security in Santo Domingo would be essential. The National Police was not prepared for the task; therefore, both governments agreed that an Army brigade of three light infantry battalions must be organized and trained to maintain stability during the electoral period.[25] The missions of the new U.S. Military Assistance Program (MAP)-supported brigade were to back up the police, to guard polling places in order to guarantee free and orderly elections, and, if necessary, to provide small units to operate in the countryside. The brigade's battalions were to be the reconstituted *Duarte*, *Sanchez*, and *Mella* cited above; they were designated the 1st, the 2nd, and the 3rd, respectively. Accelerated training and delivery of equipment were to be undertaken by the U.S. Armed Forces. The target date for completion was May 1, 1966.[26]

On May 7th, the American Embassy dispatched an evaluation of the new 1st Brigade to Washington stating that by June 1st the readiness of the three battalions would be "fair," and that 90% of their equipment would be in the Dominican Republic. It was added that seven of the brigade's nine rifle companies had completed training in counterguerrilla operations, riot control, and small unit tactics. It was projected that all rifle companies of the 1st Brigade would complete these phases of training by June 1st. For the election period, the 1st and 2nd Battalions would be deployed in the capital, and the 3rd Battalion would be stationed in San Cristóbal as brigade reserve.[27]

The initial training was done at the company level by instructors from the U.S. intervention forces already in the Dominican Republic. Subsequently, advisers were assigned temporarily to the MAAG for the purpose of continuing the training. Finally, in the summer of 1966, U.S. permanent advisers in the MAAG took over responsibility for the preparedness of the 1st Brigade. An U.S. Army field grade officer was appointed adviser to the Dominican brigade commander and each of the three battalions also received full-time advisers.[28]

After the elections, the 1st Brigade was based in three locations: The headquarters of the brigade and the 1st Battalion were billeted at *Fortaleza Ozama* in Santo Domingo; the 2nd Battalion was eventually quartered at the new *16 de Agosto* Military Camp, located 25 kilometers northwest of the capital; and the 3rd Battalion was stationed in San Cristóbal, 30 kilometers west of Santo Domingo. These three battalions were equipped with sufficient weapons, communications gear, and transportation to make them the most effective in the nation.

The 1966 creation of the U.S. MAP-supported 1st Brigade resolved the immediate problem of security during the electoral period. Also, the three battalions filled the vacuum produced when the Inter-American Peace Force departed the Dominican Republic. The next order of business for the American advisers was the modernization of the entire Dominican Army. The chief of the Army Section of the MAAG, Lieutenant Colonel William C. Camper, was one of the principal planners at that time. He and his American and Dominican colleagues had to take into account requirements for geographic defense and for disaster relief. Consequently, in addition to traditional military missions, the Army would need to provide support services at the national level. The structure that the MAAG proposed, therefore, resembled an U.S. infantry division with a broader logistics capability.[29]

The American Army in the 1960s used the terms "combat support" and "combat service support" to describe the two types of units which provided support to the combat forces in a division. It was from a variation of that terminology that the Dominican Army's major organizational designations were derived. The new Army's command group and staff also followed the U.S. model; they were patterned on the headquarters of an American division.

By 1969, the Army was organized into four infantry brigades (the "combat forces"), a Combat Support Command (*Comando de Apoyo de Combate*), and a Combat Service Support Command (*Comando de Apoyo de Servicio de Combate*). The brigades consisted of from two to five battalions. The Combat Support Command included one battalion each of armor, artillery, and engineers. And the Combat Service Support Command was made up of a communications battalion, a transportation battalion, an ordnance battalion, and a quartermaster company. In addition to those organizations, separate military police and medical companies and a presidential guard unit existed. The headquarters of the Army was divided into a general and a special staff. In July of that year, the 4th Brigade was disbanded and the Schools Command was founded. It would include the Military Academy and three subordinate schools.

Both U.S. doctrine and Dominican tradition were merged, in various degrees, in the actual functioning of the new organizations. At the headquarters of the Army, the commander of the institution continued to carry the title of "chief of staff" as had been the custom during the Trujillo regime. He had a general staff consisting of a G-1 (personnel), a G-2 (intelligence), a G-3 (plans and training), a G-4 (logistics), and a G-5 (civil affairs), and a 15 member special staff. The general staff had a coordinating role while the special staff had the responsibility to assist the chief of staff in specialized areas such as communications, transportation, ordnance, and medical.

The brigades were to consist of a combination of tactical and constabulary battalions. The Americans placed little value in the latter type of unit, but the Dominicans insisted on retaining the battalions, companies, detachments, and posts that spread like a net across the countryside. The U.S. government would eventually commit itself to providing the Army with a total of five MAP-supported tactical light infantry battalions.

Armor, artillery, and engineers in the Combat Support Command, according to the overall plan, were to be attached to the infantry battalions as needed. This process was followed insofar as armored vehicles and guns were concerned (if internal military politics permitted), but, in the case of the engineers, there were other overriding considerations. The Engineer Battalion became a MAP-supported unit which meant it received extensive heavy equipment. Consequently, the battalion devoted its full time to the construction of roads, bridges, and buildings. The U.S. Embassy was enthusiastic about the engineers' civic action programs and the Dominicans saw more gain for their interests in having a "construction" battalion rather than a "combat engineer" unit.

The activities of the Combat Service Support Command adhered more to the unit's name than the functions of the Combat Support Command. As the major Army logistics organization, it was reasonable that the Combat Service Support Command would have subordinated to it the Transportation, Communications, and Ordnance Battalions (the first two were MAP-supported) and the Quartermaster Company. But, by following that logic, the Engineer Battalion, more appropriately, should also have been included in that Command. What was not logical to the Americans, but most sensible for the Dominicans, was the assignment, in 1970, of a new Military Police Battalion to the headquarters of the Combat Service Support Command at *Fortaleza Ozama*. Its mission was not to assist the Army's logistics effort, but to operate from *Fortaleza Ozama* as a show of force in Santo Domingo. The reason for this departure from U.S. Army doctrine involved President Balaguer's balance of power policy and the Dominicans' historical imperative to project military authority in the capital from *Fortaleza Ozama*. Despite these anomalies, the daily logistics needs of the Army were met by the Combat Service Support Command in a manner that was, to some extent, an improvement from the Trujillo era.

Although the Schools Command had no parallel in the American Army's infantry division, it was, nevertheless, organized almost completely in accordance with U.S. military thinking. (The only exception was the Military Academy which continued to retain some Spanish Army influence left over from its founding in 1956.) The three subordinate schools set up by American advisers were patterned after the U.S. Army's centralized training programs. The Officers School provided the equivalent levels of instruction seen at Fort Benning, Georgia. The Recruits

School (*Escuela de Tropas*) was a copy of basic combat training (BCT) given at U.S. Army Training Centers from Fort Jackson, South Carolina, to Fort Ord, California. And the Specialists School curriculum was based on advanced individual training (AIT) for enlisted men held, at the time, in U.S. Army institutions such as the signal school at Fort Monmouth, New Jersey, and the intelligence school at Fort Holabird, Maryland. The CEFA had conducted recruit training and had provided some specialization instruction for enlisted personnel, but no military educational system had ever been available for officers in the Dominican Republic before the founding of the Officers School.

CREATION OF A MILITARY EDUCATIONAL SYSTEM

On October 8, 1966, the Dominican Army formally began its program to provide the officer corps with a building block system of military education. The first major step was the inauguration of the *Escuela para Oficiales* or Officers School on April 1, 1967. It was in that new institution that second lieutenants would begin their four phase career development by attending a basic infantry course. Subsequently, they would return to the Officers School for the *curso medio* of infantry, then later, the *comando y plana mayor* course which was command and staff instruction at the battalion and brigade level. The last phase was to be an in-country general staff course; however, it was not projected to be offered until 1968.[30]

From the outset, Dominican planning for an officer's military education was undertaken in conjunction with U.S. Army advisers. American influence was exerted not only in the curriculum, but also in the selection of Dominicans to serve at the Officers School. The first director was Lieutenant Colonel Pompeyo Ruiz Serrano and the sub-director was Major Jesús Manuel Porfirio Mota Henríquez; both were graduates of the 1963 Command and Staff Course at the U.S. Army School of the Americas.[31] Appointed to the faculty were Lieutenant Colonel Téofilo Ramón Romero Pumarol (the chief of studies), Major Héctor Valenzuela Alcantara, and Captains Franco Benoit Liriano and Ramón Rodríguez Landestoy. The School adjutant was Captain Porfirio Alejandro Díaz and the logistics officer was Captain Aris Burgos Villa.[32] Romero Pumarol and Valenzuela Alcantara were also alumni of the staff college in the Canal Zone (class of 1966), and the remainder of the officers would attend and graduate from that course in the early 1970s. (Six of those staff and faculty members were ex-CEFA men.)

For a combination of reasons, many senior Dominican officers were cool, if not completely opposed, to the educational reforms proposed at the Officers School. An expected reaction was that the older generation questioned the practical need for the courses. They had reached the ranks of colonel or general without classroom instruction; therefore, they could not understand why the younger officers would require that type of formal schooling after receiving their commissions. More to the core of the problem, however, was the view that success in the Armed Forces should be based on loyalty to superiors rather than on completion of advanced studies. These obstacles were surmounted by the presence and, at times, intercession of the U.S. advisers. But advice did not originate from one side only. On occasion, American impatience with the obstructionism of the older officers was mollified by Dominican diplomacy. The chief of the Army Section of the MAAG, Lieutenant Colonel Camper, remarked that Colonel Medrano, the Dominican G-3, had advised him that it was advantageous to move slowly in order to gain acceptance for the reforms. Colonel Medrano explained that "it was like having a glass of muddy water and slowly pouring clean water into it. Eventually, it would clear up."[33]

Despite the lack of enthusiasm toward the Officers School from the senior sector of the Army, the program took hold. The first *promoción* or graduating class consisted of 11 officers in the *comando y plana mayor* course, 8 in the *curso medio* of infantry, and 11 in the basic infantry course. In 1968, the second *promoción* included 11, 14, and 8 officers in each course respectively, plus 24 officers who received instruction in intelligence and counterintelligence. In 1968, while the third *promoción* was underway, the Officers School revealed that it was planning to augment the courses with general staff studies, counterinsurgency training for officers, and a wide range of specialist training for enlisted men.[34] At the graduation ceremony of the third *promoción* on December 12, 1968, it was announced that the goal of the Officers School was to raise its status to that of a general staff college.[35]

The chief of the Army Section of the MAAG and Colonel Medrano utilized the success of the Officers School as a basis to establish a far broader training institution. They envisioned a major command at San Isidro made up of the Officers School, the Military Academy, a training center for recruits, and one for enlisted specialists. These four entities would be managed by a centralized staff and faculty. The structure devised to orchestrate the various functions was as sophisticated as could be found in any small defense establishment. The results of their planning was the Schools Command. In July 1969, the new organization took over the 4th Brigade buildings at San Isidro. In the same month, it graduated the fourth *promoción* made up of 9 officers from the *comando y plana mayor* course, 10 from the *curso medio* of infantry, and 7 from the basic infantry course, and 10 officers successfully completed intelligence and counterintelligence instruction. Additionally, enlisted graduates from the new Specialists School were honored. The concept of a military educational system for officers and the necessity for cadet and enlisted training were amalgamated into the organization of the Schools Command.[36]

It had been the hope of the MAAG that Colonel Medrano would be appointed the director of the new command, but, as Lieutenant Colonel Camper has written: "Colonel Medrano was one of the first casualties of our plans." Disgruntled senior officers were pleased when President Balaguer assigned Medrano outside the country.[37] In his place, Colonel Salvador Escarramán Mejía received the appointment as director of the Schools Command. He was a good compromise choice politically for the position. Although he had not taken a staff college course under U.S. Army auspices, he had graduated from an artillery school in Spain and from the 1963 class at the Inter-American Defense College in Washington, D.C. After his return from the United States, he had conducted two short orientation courses on staff procedures in 1963 and 1964.[38] This instruction was sponsored by the MAAG. Important to the senior Army officers (and to President Balaguer) was that Colonel Escarramán was not a product of the CEFA, as was Colonel Medrano, and was not associated with the reformers in the Armed Forces.

Colonel Escarramán would remain at the Schools Command for approximately three years; this was a period in which step by step progression in the educational system for officers took root. By mid–1971, total graduates of the key courses at the Officers School were as follows:

Comando y plana mayor—60
Curso medio de infantería—79
Curso basico de infantería—60

In addition to Army officers, the Navy, the Air Force, the National Police, and the Panamanian military had all sent students to the Officers School.[39] This surge in officer training appears even more remarkable when the number of Dominican officers who graduated from the U.S. Army's School of the Americas in 1962 through 1971 is added. A total of 303 officers successfully completed courses in subjects as diverse as civic action, preventative maintenance, and communications in the Panama Canal Zone.[40]

Quietly dropped was the subject of a general staff college or course in the Dominican Republic. In 1967 and 1968, this idea continually surfaced, but afterwards it received scarce attention, and by President Balaguer's second elected term, it was dead. In 1971, it was clear that the last phase of officer training within the Dominican Republic was the nine-month *comando y plana mayor* course at the Officers School. The apex of the Dominican military educational system remained, however, the 40 week Command and Staff Course at the School of the Americas in the Panama Canal Zone.

DIMINISHED ROLES FOR THE
AIR FORCE AND NAVY

While the forward thinking officers of the Dominican Army were content thanks to modernization and reform, the pilots and infantrymen of the Air Force were demoralized. By the time President Balaguer was inaugurated on July 1, 1966, Dominican combat aircraft had been reduced to one B-25 and six B-26 bombers, 30 Vampire jets, and 28 P-51 fighters. One and one half years later, all the bombers had been scrapped and 12 Vampires and 25 P-51s of limited effectiveness remained.[41]

Since the end of the civil war, the Air Force had been requesting help from the MAAG to repair at least the aging P-51 aircraft. The questionable Dominican rationale was that the P-51s would be ideal for tactical operations against any guerrilla activity. In 1967, the U.S. position was that in return for rehabilitating the usable P-51s, the Air Force should divest itself of the Vampires, close the air bases in Santiago and Barahona, and eliminate the excessive infantry troops from the Air Force. American reasoning was that the FAD should concentrate on being an efficient flying force only.[42] These conditions were disturbing to the FAD for various reasons. The air bases in Santiago and Barahona provided the Air Force with a politico-military role in the north and in the south of the country up to the Haitian border (the San Isidro Air Base projected FAD strength in the capital and in the east), the Vampires gave the pilots jets to fly, and the loss of air infantry meant the emasculation of the FAD in the overall balance of power within the Dominican Republic. Also, it must be remembered that as of September 6, 1967, the chief of staff of the Air Force was General Lluberes Montás, an infantryman, not a pilot. It could not be expected that that officer would be sympathetic to eliminating or reducing ground combat forces in the FAD.

After much negotiating, agreement was reached. The FAD would keep the Vampires, but they would not be part of the U.S. aid package; the air base at Barahona would close, but not the installation in Santiago; and the Air Force would reduce its personnel strength from 3,854 to 3,000 by August 1971. In return for those concessions, the U.S. government would provide Military Assistance Program (MAP)-support for fourteen P-51 fighters. (The remainder were not considered airworthy.) This project, called "Peace Hawk," would involve the overhaul of the P-

51 engines, the complete rebuilding of their air frames, and the delivery of spare parts for 5,000 flying hours. There would be no financial cost to the Dominican Republic.[43] A memorandum of understanding between the two governments was signed on August 12, 1968, stipulating the conditions.[44]

Although the FAD was temporarily rejuvenated by the rehabilitation of the P-51s, and General Lluberes Montás did not move hastily to reduce the size of his ground troops, the Air Force was not able to regain its position of strength in the Armed Forces. President Balaguer refused to spend sufficient Dominican money for the FAD to have adequate fuel and spare parts. This austere budget for the Air Force greatly reduced flying time, which affected the helicopters, transports, and trainers, as well as the combat aircraft.[45] The Air Force's Special Forces Group and Base Defense Command infantrymen were ignored by the U.S. government; therefore, while the Army eventually received MAP-support for five tactical infantry battalions, the FAD ground elements were locked in time as Trujillo-regime, leftover units.

As with the Air Force, the United States would not support a Dominican Navy that in any way reached the scale of Trujillo's fleet. In the 1960s, American naval advisers attempted to interest the Navy in acquiring practical vessels such as patrol boats and tugs, but this policy was not well received among the maritime officers. Some headway was evident when, in 1964, President Reid Cabral advocated selling the two destroyers and five corvettes for scrap so the Dominican Republic could purchase patrol craft.[46] Three years later, the Navy assured the U.S. Embassy that it was planning to dispose of one frigate and three corvettes.[47] While many naval officers continued to cling to their vision of a blue water fleet, the MAAG attempted to push the Navy in the opposite direction.

Washington provided the Dominican Navy with one former U.S. motor gunboat (PGM 77) in 1966 and with three 85-foot Sewart patrol boats in 1967 and 1968 to perform the functions of *guardacostas*. The vessels were designated the *Betelgeuse,* the *Bellatrix,* the *Proción,* and the *Capella,* respectively.[48] Also, the MAAG emphasized the need for the Dominicans to complete construction of the U.S.-funded synchrolift dry dock at *Las Calderas* Naval Base. In February 1972, the U.S. Navy transferred a tugboat to the Dominican Navy. (A second tug would follow later in the year.)[49] Despite these clear actions by the American Navy signifying an interest in supporting only a modest coastal naval service for the Dominican Republic, Santo Domingo sent a diplomatic note to Washington on June 29, 1972, requesting a cost-free destroyer escort and other vessels to replace two frigates and a corvette which were inoperable.[50] On July 14th, U.S. Ambassador Francis Meloy dispatched a message to the Department of State explaining "... that the Dominican Navy does

not currently command sufficient funds, repair facilities, or spare parts
to maintain its present force and that any increase in that force would
... severely overtax its current limited capabilities...."[51] The Dominican
request for the destroyer escort was turned down. Two days before the
Ambassador's message was sent, however, he personally turned over
another Sewart boat already in the pipe line to the Dominican Navy. (It
was christened the *Aldebarán*.) In his speech at the ceremony, he stressed
that the Sewart boat would be of great assistance in protecting the country's coasts.[52]

MILITARY-STYLE UNITS
IN THE NATIONAL POLICE

An assessment of the Dominican Armed Forces would not be complete without commenting on two National Police organizations which
were military in character: the *Departamento Duarte* and the *Departamento
de Operaciones Especiales*. Both units had in common their similarity to
Army light infantry, their non-involvement in traditional police work,
and their heritage of being founded by the U.S. government. But that
is where the similarities ceased.

In May 1962, two Los Angeles Police Department detectives were sent
to Santo Domingo to organize a much-needed riot control squad in the
National Police. U.S. Ambassador Martin had urgently requested this
assistance when he met with President Kennedy in the White House in
the end of April. Part of the equipment given to the Dominican policemen were white helmets—thus the unit was known as the *Cascos Blancos*
(its official designation was *Fuerza de Choque*).[53] The formation grew to
approximately 500 men; it was stationed at *Fortaleza Ozama* where the
Dominican government believed it could best control disturbances in
the capital. In the opening days of the 1965 civil war, the *Cascos Blancos*
were attacked by Caamaño's rebels (he had been a police major in the
unit during 1962), and, by April 30th, *Fortaleza Ozama* was captured.[54]
Many of the *Cascos Blancos* were slaughtered as they tried to escape across
the Ozama River to the rear of the colonial fortress.[55]

After the civil war, the riot police were reconstituted into the Duarte
Department. Its members were armed with rifles and wore combat boots
and black helmets; consequently, they were called the *Cascos Negros*. The
Duarte Department numbered 450 and was quartered in the Duarte
Camp situated in the western sector of Santo Domingo. The unit was
within easy traveling distance (six blocks) of the Autonomous University of Santo Domingo where it was periodically dispatched to control
student demonstrations. (On September 8, 1972, when the youths started

pelting the Duarte Department troops with rocks, the policemen drove up in a stone-filled truck and began hurling their own rocks at the students. Photographs of this incident were on newspaper front pages the next day.[56]) During parades, it was common for Dominicans to see the *Cascos Negros* marching as infantry with the Armed Forces.

In contrast to the Duarte Department, the *Departamento de Operaciones Especiales* was rarely seen by the public. This organization (known as the DSO in the American Embassy) was formed on December 2, 1965,[57] as a rural counterinsurgency force. Its headquarters and training camp were on a farm near Manoguayabo west of Santo Domingo. Initially, it was organized into 15 rapid reaction teams with the mission to collect information and to operate against guerrilla groups in the countryside. The DSO was totally supported by the U.S. Agency for International Development's Public Safety program. By 1971, this elite organization numbered 185 highly motivated policemen in camouflage uniforms.[58] Its American Public Safety adviser had extensive experience as a law enforcement officer in the United States, and had been assigned to the National Police rural combat force in Vietnam. The DSO was fully mobile—it had modern vehicles and radios—and was well armed—it was the only unit in the Dominican Republic which carried the U.S.-made 7.62mm M-14 rifle. In 1971 and 1972, the DSO was considered the best-trained ground formation in the country.

ARMY CAPABILITIES AFTER BALAGUER'S REELECTION

An evaluation of the Dominican ground forces one year after President Balaguer began his second elected term in August 1970 was generally positive. Internally, the Army was capable of repelling small armed groups who opposed the government, of countering a limited-size insurgency threat, and of acting as a back-up to the National Police for any serious civil disturbances. It was capable of defending against a conventional invasion from Haiti, but did not have the ability to conduct sustained offensive operations in that country, mainly because of logistical limitations. (Both scenarios were highly unlikely.)

The three battalions of the 1st Brigade in the capital area and the 9th Battalion, 2nd Brigade, in the northern Cibao Valley, had received U.S. Military Assistance Program (MAP) support, thus providing those tactical light infantry units with the capacity to engage insurgents with a reasonable chance of success. In July 1971, planning was underway to establish a fifth MAP-supported battalion.

Seven battalions of the Dominican Army had a constabulary role only. The 5th, *General Fernando Valerio*; the 6th, *General Gregorio Luperón*; the 7th, *General Olegario Tenares*; and the 11th, *General Francisco Antonio Salcedo*, were assigned geographic areas in the north and along the Haitian border. The 8th, *General José María Cabral*; and the 10th, *General Francisco Sosa*, had the same mission in the south and southwest including the frontier with Haiti. And the 4th, *General Juan Sánchez Ramírez*, was geographically responsible for the entire area east of the capital. Throughout the country, there were 26 companies, 46 detachments, and 131 posts of constabulary-type Army units. A company was led by a captain, a detachment by a lieutenant, and a post by a sergeant. The last two units normally numbered no more than 20 and 6 men, respectively. This vast rural network meshed well with the peasantry which had a tradition of supporting the Army.

Major unit locations were as follows:

Unit	Authorized Strength	Location	Commander
1st Brigade	2,198	*16 de Agosto* Military Camp	B. Gen. Neit Nivar Seijas
1st Battalion		*16 de Agosto* Military Camp	
2nd Battalion		*16 de Agosto* Military Camp	
3rd Battalion		San Cristóbal	
2nd Brigade	2,482	Santiago	B. Gen. Guarionex Estrella Sahdalá
5th Battalion		Santiago	
6th Battalion		La Vega	
7th Battalion		San Francisco de Macorís	
9th Battalion		Mao	
11th Battalion		Dajabón	
3rd Brigade	1,285	San Juan de la Maguana	Col. Francisco Medina Sánchez
8th Battalion		San Juan de la Maguana	
10th Battalion		Barahona[59]	

The 1st Brigade's principal weapon was the Belgian 7.62mm FAL rifle. In addition, it was equipped with U.S.-made 7.62mm M-60 machine guns, 81mm mortars, and 3.5 inch rocket launchers. The headquarters company of the Brigade had four U.S.-made 4.2 inch mortars, four Swedish-made 105mm Bofors recoilless rifles, and two 20mm Hispano Suiza antiaircraft guns. There existed sufficient transportation to move nine rifle companies of the Brigade into Santo Domingo at one time.[60]

The constabulary units were armed with a variety of individual weapons such as 7mm 1908 bolt action Mausers, Dominican-produced .30 caliber Cristóbal carbines, and American World War II Garand M-1 rifles, M-1 and M-2 carbines, and Thompson submachine guns. These battalions had limited communications and transportation equipment.

In the Combat Support Command, the Armored Battalion and the Artillery Battalion relied on Trujillo-era armored vehicles and guns. The Engineer Battalion was a construction unit with no combat support mission. Colonel Manuel Antonio Cuervo Gómez was the overall commander. He was authorized 1,073 personnel. The Armored Battalion consisted of a headquarters company and four line units: the Tank Company(AMX), the Tank Company(L-60), the Armored Infantry Company, and the Armored Cavalry Company. These units did not have authority over all the armored vehicles, however. All but 13 were satellited on larger non-armored organizations which had operational control of the tanks, scout cars, and personnel carriers. Consequently, there was no commander in the Dominican Republic who had total armor dominance. The distribution of the 68 armored vehicles in July 1971 was as follows:

Location	Tank, AMX -13	Tank, L-60	Tank, M3A1	A/car, Lynx	APC, M-16
Combat Spt Cmd	5	2	1	2	3
National Palace	2	2		2	1
1st Brigade *16 de Agosto*		4			
3rd Battalion San Cristóbal	2	2			
Transportation Battalion		2			
Army Headquarters					2
San Isidro Air Base					2
2nd Brigade Santiago		2			2
Santiago Air Base	1	2			2
9th Battalion Mao	1	2	1	5	4
6th Battalion La Vega	2	1		1	
10th Battalion Barahona		2			2
3rd Brigade San Juan de la Maguana		2			2[61]

The Artillery Battalion was collocated with the headquarters of the Combat Support Command at the Artillery Military Camp seven kilometers outside Santo Domingo. It consisted of a headquarters battery and six numbered batteries. The 1st Battery was attached to the 3rd Brigade in San Juan de la Maguana and the 2nd Battery was with the 2nd Brigade in Santiago. The remainder of the guns were at the Artillery Military Camp. The battery in San Juan de la Maguana consisted of four German-made 75mm Krupp pieces of questionable military value and, in Santiago, the 2nd Brigade had attached a battery of four U.S.-made 105mm M-3 howitzers (used by American airborne units in World War II). They had no sights. At the Artillery Battalion there were 12 Spanish-made 105/26 Reinosa howitzers in good condition; 36 Krupp, Schneider, and St. Chamond 75mm guns—none could be fired except for ceremonial salutes; and 14 Hispano Suiza and Bofors 20mm antiaircraft weapons. In addition, at the battalion there could be found U.S.-made 37mm anti-tank guns, Swedish-made 105mm Bofors recoilless rifles, and Spanish-made 120mm ECIA mortars.[62]

The Combat Service Support Command, the Army's logistics organization, was headquartered at *Fortaleza Ozama*. It was commanded by Brigadier General Marcos Antonio Jorge Moreno and was authorized 2,371 officers and men. Its main sub-elements were the following:

Unit	Location
Military Police Battalion	*Fortaleza Ozama*, Santo Domingo
Ordnance Battalion	Artillery Military Camp, near the capital
Transportation Battalion	Transportation Barracks, Santo Domingo
Communications Battalion	Army Headquarters, Santo Domingo
Quartermaster Company	*Intendencia*, Santo Domingo
4th Battalion	San Pedro de Macorís[63]

The 4th Battalion was a quasi-independent formation that controlled the eastern zone of the country. It had been subordinated to the 4th Brigade in San Isidro; after that brigade was replaced by the Schools Command, the 4th Battalion was nominally assigned to the Combat Service Support Command. As a constabulary unit, the 4th Battalion had nothing in common with a logistics command.

The last major organization in the Army was the Schools Command, which was authorized 399 permanent party. Its director was Colonel Salvador Escarramán Mejía. In addition, the Dominican Army contained the Presidential Guard Battalion (it was authorized 237 positions), and the Medical Company and Military Hospital, *Dr. Enrique Lithgow Ceara* (they were authorized a total of 418 billets).[64]

On June 30, 1971, the actual strength of the Dominican Army was 10,463[65]; it was led by Brigadier General Rafael Valdez Hilario, the chief of staff. The sub-chief was Colonel Rafael de Jesús Checo. Neither officer had successfully completed any advanced military studies nor did either have a reputation for military professionalism. The Army General Staff was organized in accordance with U.S. doctrine. Each of the principal staff officers was designated an *Auxiliar de Estado Mayor* followed either by "G-1," "G-2," "G-3," "G-4," or "G-5." The G-1 (personnel) was Lieutenant Colonel Luis García Recio, the G-2 (intelligence) was Lieutenant Colonel Narciso Elio Bautista de Oleo, the G-3 (plans and training) was Colonel Miguel Alvarez Belén, the G-4 (logistics) was Lieutenant Colonel Héctor Valenzuela Alcantara, and the G-5 (civil affairs) was Lieutenant Colonel Cayetano Vidal Reyes. These men were considered competent members of the officer corps at the time. Lieutenant Colonels García Recio, Valenzuela Alcantara, and Vidal Reyes were all graduates of the Command and Staff Course at the U.S. Army School of the Americas.[66] They represented the vanguard of the new professionalism in the Dominican Armed Forces. Colonel Alvarez Belén had taken a staff orientation course in 1963[67] and was known for being a serious-minded career officer. Although not staff college trained, Lieutenant Colonel Bautista had received a doctorate of laws in 1961[68] and was considered well informed and an efficient manager of the Army's intelligence system.

The 15 member Special Staff was organized in the same manner as the headquarters of an U.S. infantry division. The officers who made up the Special Staff fell into two categories: staff specialists in technical fields, such as the legal or medical profession; and commanders of units who also performed as staff advisers, such as the commanders of the Engineer and Communications Battalions who were simultaneously the engineer officer and the communications officer on the Special Staff. Examples of the former grouping were recently promoted Brigadier General Clarence Charles Dunlop, the medical officer, and Colonel Juan Rodríguez Pérez, the equivalent of the staff judge advocate. (General Charles had been a physician since 1946[69] and Colonel Rodríguez entered the Armed Forces as a lawyer in 1956.[70]) The commander/staff officer category was best represented by the highly qualified Colonel Manuel Antonio Cuervo Gómez, who, as commander of the Combat Support Command, filled the two Special Staff positions of armor officer and artillery officer. Lieutenant Colonel Eddy Anibal Bobea Pérez, the engineer officer and engineer battalion commander, was a long-time licensed engineer. The commander of the Communications Battalion was Lieutenant Colonel Antonio Rosario Japa. The Special Staff signal officer had begun his communications career as a non-commissioned officer in the Communications Company in the early 1950s[71] and had risen through the commissioned ranks as a technical officer in communications.

There were strengths and weaknesses in the Dominican Army's General and Special Staffs. The structure was adequate, but it should have been expanded beyond the infantry division model. For example, there was no officer who performed as a comptroller or program budget director at the general staff level. The General Staff had a coordinating staff mission, but there was no one with the responsibility to internally coordinate the G-1 through G-5 sections. Colonel Checo, as the sub-chief, should have accomplished this essential requirement for the General Staff, but he had no training, experience, or inclination to undertake general staff work. Consequently, another officer became the dominant force on the General Staff. In most armies one would expect the operations officer to fill that void, but in the Dominican Army, G-3s were not traditionally predominant. In 1971, it was Lieutenant Colonel García Recio, the G-1, who rose to the position of being General Valdez Hilario's most influential General Staff officer. (Despite Colonel Checo's flaccid performance as sub-chief, he was promoted to brigadier general on July 12th, and became the new chief of staff on August 4th.[72])

An obvious strength of the Special Staff was that qualified personnel had been selected to fill many of the special staff officer positions. For example, there were no officers in the Dominican Army who had more expertise or more dedication than Colonel Cuervo Gómez as a tanker, or Lieutenant Colonel Rosario Japa as a signal specialist. But, in some cases, the Special Staff did have deficiencies caused by a poor selection process. The most notorious example was the *intendente general* or quartermaster general (Colonel Juan Bautista Tejeda); he was not a logistician but an officer appointed, as a reward, to that post for not more than six months so that he could augment his income by pocketing 10% of quartermaster funds. The inspector general of the Army (Colonel Jacobo Fernández Mota) did not formally review the state of discipline, performance, or economy of the institution for the chief of staff, nor did he have a program to investigate complaints. That position was usually held by a senior officer whom the leadership wanted to keep in politico-military limbo.

Despite the defects noted, the Dominican Army at the beginning of President Balaguer's second elected term was probably in the best overall condition in its history. Aging armor and artillery and a large number of untrained officers and units did not eclipse two facts: First, the U.S. MAP-supported infantry battalions were superior to anything the government's opponents could field in Santo Domingo, which was significant because the highest national priority was to control the capital. And, second, the constabulary battalions were the masters of the countryside principally through their contact with the peasantry at the grass roots of the Dominican Republic.

THE STATUS OF THE AIR
FORCE AND THE NAVY

In the 1970s, the Dominican Air Force should have been capable of providing the tactical light infantry battalions with close air support and air mobility. In turn, the Navy should have been able to prevent, through surveillance, a hostile incursion into the Dominican Republic from the sea.

The inventory of functioning FAD aircraft in 1971 was as follows:

P-51 (rehabilitated by Cavalier)	10
Vampire De Havilland	6
T-28 North American	6
T-41 Cessna	4
C-47 Douglas	7
OH-6A Hughes	7
H-19 Sikorsky	1
Alouette II helicopters	2
Alouette III helicopter	1[73]

In theory, the P-51s could have been utilized in a close air support role; however, guerrillas on the ground made difficult targets, and the Air Force did not have an effective forward air controller system. Air mobility for the Army was also restricted because the OH-6A and Alouette helicopters had limited passenger space; they were more appropriately utilized for command and control and for reconnaissance purposes. Thus, there remained only one helicopter, the aging H-19, for airmobile operations.

The Air Force had 3,794 personnel in the beginning of President Balaguer's second elected term. The Base Defense Command, made up of two security squadrons and two air police squadrons, was not prepared for offensive operations against guerrillas. The 330 man airborne Special Forces Group, however, was capable of such a mission.[74]

The U.S. Embassy reported that the Navy, in 1969, was capable of deploying "14 combatant-type" vessels, with at least one ship stationed "in ready duty status in Santo Domingo, Manzanillo, Puerto Plata, Samaná, La Romana, San Pedro de Macorís and Barahona."[75] In the 1970s, however, this deployment was no longer possible. The inventory of principal Navy vessels which were functional at mid-point in President Balaguer's 1970–1974 term was as follows:

Frigate 1	*Mella*
Corvette 1	*Juan Alejandro Acosta*
Patrulleros (ClassB cutters) 2	*Libertad, Restauración*
Guardacostas (Sewart boats and PGM) 5	*Bellatrix, Proción, Capella, Aldebarán, Betelgeuse*
Tugs 2	*Caonabo, Macorix*[76]

The Navy numbered a total of 3,438 officers and men at the time the 1970–1974 Balaguer term began.[77] Only a small percentage of those personnel would be dedicated to manning and maintaining the five *guardacostas* and the two tugs; these vessels were in the best condition, compared with the rest of the Navy, for reconnaissance work. The corvette and the two cutters could be utilized in an emergency, while the frigate *Mella*, in 1971, was mainly useful as a site for conferences and social events even though it was capable of leaving the dock.

V

Officer Corps Attitudes During Balaguer's Second Term

By Balaguer's second elected term, a measure of stability had returned to the officer corps; however, the long Trujillo dictatorship, the turmoil of the early 1960s, and the 1965 civil war continued to influence the thinking of Dominican officers. Added to those factors was the impact of the new American military advisory effort on the attitudes of Balaguer's officers.

POLITICS

There were few surprises in the early 1970s on how officers aligned themselves with the politicians of the Dominican Republic. They were decidedly anti-left. The vast majority was convinced that Juan Bosch and his non-radical, left-of-center, legal party, the *Partido Revolucionario Dominicano* (PRD), were Communists. The miniscule number of officer corps members who were well-educated knew that Bosch was too ideologically complicated—or too erratic—to be a well-defined Communist, but they also knew that they had to oppose the former president because Bosch's policies were inimical to the interests of the officer corps. It followed, consequently, that any politicians or groups which were to the left of the PRD were automatically beyond the pale.

On the right of Balaguer's center-rightist governing party (the *Partido Reformista*), stood Wessin y Wessin's new *Partido Quisqueyano Demócrata* (PQD). Even most ex-CEFA officers rejected the PQD as a poor substitute for what Balaguer's administration could do for them. This self-serving view on the part of Wessin's former officers was also shared by the defunct San Isidro Group, the Navy's officers, and, of course, the old San Cristóbal clan.

RELIGION

Reportedly, Trujillo wanted only Roman Catholics in the officer corps.[1] Although he openly favored the Church as an institution, and he personally enjoyed its ceremonial pomp, very few of his officers followed their religion beyond attendance at the obligatory masses and other religious state functions. This attitude continued in the 1960s and 1970s. There were exceptions among the officers (e.g., Wessin y Wessin and Cuervo Gómez), but to the majority, religion played no substantive role in their lives.

The Church in the early 1970s was not a strong political force in the Dominican Republic. Although there was some grumbling against the archbishop/primate and the papal nuncio for their occasional interference in government affairs when humanitarian circumstances demanded it, by and large Balaguer was able to deal effectively with the Church hierarchy without the Armed Forces' heavy hand being present. In short, Church-military relations under Balaguer never reached the turbulent nature of El Salvador in the 1970s nor of Nicaragua in the 1980s.

CLASS

The officer corps, as a group, was held in disdain by the wealthy upper class of the Dominican Republic. This attitude was evident during the U.S. Marine occupation and it continued into the 1970s. Pejorative descriptions of the military such as *gorila* and *bruto* were common. Some naval officers and a very small number of well-educated, European-looking Army and Air Force members escaped this treatment, but normally the oligarchy lumped all men in uniform into an inferior category. One policy begun by Trujillo was his own version of the proverbial Napoleonic private carrying a marshal's baton in his knapsack— Dominican enlisted men were encouraged, if they demonstrated sufficient loyalty, to enter the commissioned officer corps. In 1948, a second lieutenant who had recently been promoted from the non-commissioned ranks wrote an article lauding *El Jefe* and the Dominican Army because there was no obstacle in the institution for enlisted men to become officers.[2] The author was living proof of the accuracy of his 1948 writings—in 1979, Diógenes Noboa Leyba retired as a brigadier general.

This egalitarian policy had a strange aspect to it, however. Dominican officers in the early 1970s normally treated their soldiers contemptuously. The source of the officers' commission—the academy, cadet school, or direct from the ranks—was irrelevant. The social and physical abuse toward enlisted men was so pervasive that a few far thinking officers seriously were concerned that the maltreatment of the troops was the potential breeding ground for insurgency.[3]

RACE

Generally speaking, there were few prejudices in the Armed Forces which were based on race. The officer corps, like Dominican society as a whole, was almost totally mixed racially. Among the officers, there was a wide range of skin tones from African black to European white. Despite this broad acceptance of all hues of complexion, isolated examples of bias would surface. *El Jefe* supposedly opposed the assignment of black officers to elite units.[4] Although this bigotry never became policy after the Trujillo regime, in the early 1970s Air Force pilots and naval officers tended to be more European in appearance. In Balaguer's Army, a level playing field was the rule, but racial slurs, nevertheless, were not uncommon. The much respected General Pérez y Pérez was a good example of race being no barrier to advancement, yet he was the subject of disparaging racial remarks by his enemy General Nivar Seijas. But was Nivar a racist? In his inner circle was General Checo, who was as African in appearance as Nivar's and Checo's foe, General Pérez y Pérez.

The overall liberal attitude that the Dominican Armed Forces held concerning race did not extend across their western border, however. To the officer corps (as well as to most of their countrymen), Haitian blacks were not the equals of Afro-Dominicans, but were considered almost subhuman.

HAITI

The citizens of the Dominican Republic viewed Haiti as their natural enemy. Santo Domingo spent a good part of the first half of the nineteenth century attempting to free itself from a brutal Haitian occupation, and the remainder of the period seeking a means to protect itself from further encroachments by its neighbor. Dominicans of all classes were taught at an early age to fear and despise Haitians and to look to the Armed Forces to defend them from Haiti. In the twentieth century, Trujillo kept alive the anti-Haiti issue. During October 1937, he ordered the Army to slaughter at least 12,000 Haitian men, women, and children living in the Dominican Republic along the northern border.[5] There was little adverse reaction on the part of Dominicans to the massacre. The Generalissimo never attempted to reduce the antagonism in the Armed

Forces toward Haiti, and, in fact, Trujillo reportedly boasted that his Army could invade and defeat Haiti in less than a day.[6]

With the end of the Trujillo era, there was no reduction in anti–Haitian rhetoric within the Armed Forces. One daily reminder to the Army was the new names of many of its installations and battalions. The departure of the Trujillo family required different heroes—among those chosen were the host of Dominican generals who had fought the Haitians in the previous century. President Juan Bosch, on April 27, 1963, also took advantage of Dominican irrational hostility toward Haiti by unwisely proposing a military invasion of Haiti in response to a perceived violation of the Dominican embassy's diplomatic status in Port-au-Prince. At first the military was delighted to rattle sabers, but, by May 5, they lost their enthusiasm when faced with the many logistical problems that the Dominican Armed Forces would encounter in a campaign against Haiti. (The only land route to Port-au-Prince was an almost impassable southern road. The CEFA had been able to concentrate two tank companies, two artillery batteries, and two rifle companies at Jimaní, the Dominican terminus of the road, but Colonel Wessin y Wessin had little possibility of going further.) Thus, the leaders of the Army, Navy, and Air Force were easily able to convince themselves that Bosch was attempting to distract the Dominican people for political reasons by engaging in a popular war. Speaking for all the service chiefs, Colonel Wessin informed the President that the military did not have the capability to invade Haiti at that time.[7]

The military setbacks of 1963 did not dampen jingoistic talk about invading Haiti, however. When President Francois Duvalier's death was announced on April 22, 1971, in Port-au-Prince, General Nivar Seijas and his officers in the 1st Brigade blustered that they would seize Haiti's capital before Haitian enemies of the Dominican Republic took over. Chauvinistic Nivar men bragged to their friends that they wanted the names of the best hotels in Port-au-Prince.[8] At the time there was also much commentary by Dominican officers that the "pacific invasion" or illegal border crossing of Haitians into the country looking for work must be stopped by military force. In a less strident vein, for almost all of the first six months of 1971, Colonel Ramiro Matos González had worked on an historical and cartographic study which took the position that a sizeable slice of central Haiti, along the border with the Dominican Republic, was rightfully Dominican territory.[9] And, on May 6, 1971, General Valdez Hilario, chief of staff of the Army, officially made the recommendation to the government that 46 localities in the southwest of the Dominican Republic with Haitian designations should be converted to Dominican names.[10] It can be seen that detesting Haiti in the Armed Forces came just as easily in the early 1970s as in the previous 150 years.

Despite the alarmist talk associated with Haiti, thoughtful military planners had concerns about the only country that shared a border with the Dominican Republic. On April 19, 1971, the U.S. Embassy dispatched a message to Washington identifying the following Dominican fears:

> At some future point widespread disorder in Haiti could cause large numbers of Haitians to flee over the border.
> A weak and distracted Haiti could be used as a base or a staging area for external forces, possibly led by Caamaño, to invade or otherwise launch guerrilla-type incursions into the Dominican Republic.[11]

Any general staff that ignored those contingencies would be delinquent. The fundamental attitude of the Dominican officer corps toward Haiti, however, was not derived from an official estimate, but was based on a visceral fear and loathing of the Haitians.

HISPANIC CARIBBEAN COUNTRIES

Trujillo had excellent relations with those Spanish-speaking countries of the Caribbean Basin which were governed by military strongmen. Specifically, he felt politically comfortable with Cuba under Fulgencio Batista, Venezuela under Marcos Pérez Jiménez, and Nicaragua under Anastasio Somoza. For the officer corps, this closeness was translated into military exchange programs that involved some substantive matters and many symbolic gestures. Among the three countries, Venezuela provided the most useful, albeit modest, contribution through limited officer training. For example, in Venezuela, Matos González had received infantry instruction,[12] Cuervo Gómez had graduated from the armor school,[13] and two Dominican cadets had completed the naval academy's four-year course at Maiquetía.[14] A typical display of solidarity, which *El Jefe* enjoyed more than the professional exchanges, was Batista's and Somoza's sending the *Brigada de Infantería, Presidente Batista*, and the *Primera Brigada, Presidente Somoza*, respectively, to march in a Santo Domingo parade with the Dominican Armed Forces on August 16, 1952.[15]

By the beginning of the 1960s, the political situation in the Caribbean Basin had changed dramatically. Although the Somoza family still controlled Nicaragua, it was not likely to support Trujillo, and Venezuela and Cuba were ruled by governments that wanted to end the Trujillo regime. The collapse of the Trujillos in 1961 reopened the opportunity for an interchange with foreign officers. The Spanish-speaking country that most took advantage of the new political climate was once again Venezuela. Representative of Caracas' policy was the enrollment, in August 1963, of two first-year students from the Military Academy, *Batalla de las Carreras*, in Venezuela's *Escuela Militar de Venezuela* for the four-year infantry cadet course.[16] The Venezuelan effort continued into the Balaguer years—for example, in 1968, the Dominican Army and National Police received instruction on setting up a literacy program[17] and, in 1972, six Dominican enlisted tankers received training for seven weeks on the AMX-13 at the *Centro de Instrucción de Tropas* in Maracay[18] (The Venezuelan Army also had French AMX tanks in its inventory.)

The U.S. Embassy looked favorably on the Dominican military's being exposed to democratic, civilian-governed Venezuela, but there was a lack of enthusiasm on the part of the Dominican officer corps toward the new Venezuela's programs. It was difficult to determine if Dominican officer attitudes stemmed from irritation with oil-rich Venezuelan officiousness, or with the small amount of military aid being provided by Caracas. In contrast, there was no doubt how the officers felt when President Anastasio Somoza (the son of Trujillo's Nicaraguan counterpart), visited the Dominican Republic. From the 8th through the 10th of March, 1972, General Somoza received the adulation of the officer corps. Even arrogant generals such as Neit Nivar Seijas appeared overwhelmed in Somoza's presence. The Nicaraguan visitor observed all three Dominican services: tank-infantry demonstrations at the 1st Brigade, Vampire jets in a simulated attack of targets on the ground, and the naval base at the mouth of the Ozama River. In addition to formal speeches, Somoza, on March 9th, also spoke to an assembled group in a closed, informal setting. The audience, made up of young as well as senior officers, was captivated by him. It was a reaction similar to the one observed when retired General Fausto "the Butcher" Caamaño visited the 1st Brigade. Dominican officers would have been crushed if they knew that when "Tacho" Somoza returned to Nicaragua he commented on the low professional caliber of the Dominican Armed Forces.[19]

UNITED STATES

President Balaguer was quite content to allow the Americans to conduct an active military assistance program in the Dominican Republic as long as there was no major financial cost to the government. Neither he nor the leadership of the Armed Forces allowed sentiments such as nationalism to prevent or obstruct the receipt of extensive U.S.-funded equipment and training. And the officer corps at every level made no attempt to disguise the presence of American advisers attached to all branches of the Dominican military. This is not to say, however, that there was no resentment when the MAAG pressured the officer corps to adhere to an American concept of professionalism. As has been seen during the creation of the military educational system, older officers could not appreciate the value of returning to the classroom at different phases of an officer's career and, from the President down, there was dissatisfaction with any effort to remove pro-government political activity from an officer's mission. But, by and large, Dominican officers accepted United States advice, and, in some cases, interference, without any significant disapproval.

There were isolated examples of anti-American attitudes in the officer corps, but they involved a specific complaint rather than an overall disposition. Two cases of interest were those of an Army lieutenant colonel and a Navy *capitán de navío* (captain). The Army officer reportedly was unhappy with the MAAG and the U.S. Embassy because he had been relieved, at the insistence of the advisers, of command of a MAP-supported battalion for continuous public drunkenness. And the naval officer was hostile to the United States in general because a member of his family had been abused by American Marines during the occupation. In a large officer corps, it is remarkable that these were the only instances noted of anti-U.S. attitudes.

In contrast, the examples among officers of pro-U.S. sentiment and acquiescence to American wishes were legion. General Nivar Seijas, not an open or overly friendly individual, was genuinely fond of two of his 1st Brigade advisers—U.S. Army Majors Mario A. Burdick and Orlando P. Rodriguez—and almost always accepted their advice on purely military affairs. This type of influence was evidenced throughout the institution even though it was not as personal as it was between Nivar and the two majors. When the last of the MAP-supported tactical infantry battalions was being established during 1971–1972 in Constanza, it was designated the *Batallón de Cazadores* ("hunter" or light infantry battalion) at the strong suggestion of the chief of the Army Section of the MAAG, Lieutenant Colonel Edward J. Kelly. There was no tradition of *cazador* units in the Dominican Republic, but Lieutenant Colonel Kelly had been exposed to them in Venezuela where they had been set up by Americans, and the Dominicans did not want to oppose the MAAG. The American Army captain who was the adviser to the new battalion in Constanza designed its shoulder patch and headgear. It was no accident that the former looked like the 101st Airborne Division patch and that the latter were green berets—the adviser had been in those two U.S. Army units earlier in his career.

Influence, on occasion, became more like dependence, however. It was not uncommon for a senior Dominican officer, when pressed by his adviser to prepare a major study or plan, to simply tell the American officer to write the required document and the Dominican would sign it as his own work. U.S. officers also became useful for the acquisition of assignments and other favors. This arrangement went beyond close friends or counterparts. Dominican officers would approach any American military man, acquaintance or stranger, and ask for help in being transferred or in acquiring a visa for a family member. Sometimes an officer would attempt to impress the Americans with how receptive he was to modern U.S. training, but would inadvertently reveal that he still clung to the old *Trujillista* style of operating. The Army commander in the province of San Francisco de Macorís demonstrated this attitude when he proudly explained that he was a graduate of the U.S. Army's civic action course and that he knew how to apply his new American skills. First, he gave the people in his jurisdiction a little civic action—if they did not respond, he gave them *"palo"* (a blow with a club)—he would repeat the cycle again and again until he received the response he desired. Of course there were some Dominican officers that refused to defer to the Americans. When Brigadier General Guarionex Estrella Sahdalá was returned to active duty after an absence of 10 years, President Balaguer gave him the important regional command of the 2nd Brigade in Santiago. With the post came an U.S. Army adviser. During their first meeting, the American major recommended that the elderly general request a helicopter when he planned to visit his subordinate units in the Cibao Valley and along the north coast. The Dominican seemed surprised at the advice. Why would he need a helicopter, he asked—air travel would prevent him from being close to the people so he could determine the mood of the population.

Ironically, in the early 1970s, the main brake on U.S. military personnel's exhibiting too high a profile in the internal affairs of the Dominican Republic was not the President or his officers, but the American ambassador, Francis Meloy. The U.S. Chief of Mission established a firm policy that advisers would work discreetly rather than provide the impression that the U.S. military was running the government or the Armed Forces. In 1966, the MAAG had had advisers assigned down to each rifle company in the 1st Brigade. Five years later, during Ambassador Meloy's tour in Santo Domingo, the advisory effort went no lower than battalion. By 1971, there were a total of 16 officers from all services in the MAAG. The following year he was able to reduce further the size of the MAAG to ten officers.

In conclusion, Dominican officers generally did not object to an American military presence in their country and were quite willing to accept direction from their advisers. When it came to subjects such as corruption and political activity, the officer corps quietly rejected American reforms, but there were very few examples of rifts developing between the officers of the two nations concerning those issues, or, for that matter, any other issue. This easy relationship between Dominican and American personnel should not be a surprise since it must not be

forgotten that even though Santo Domingo was the oldest European set-
tlement in the New World, the customs and traditions of its military institution extended no further back in history than the U.S. occupation of
1916–1924.

MILITARY CAREER

Even though Balaguer's second elected term was a period of relative stability for the officer corps, its members did not feel totally secure.
There were many factors outside the control of an officer which endangered his job security within the institution. Abrupt dismissal could come
from a "*denuncia*" or accusation from any quarter. The most serious
charge was political disloyalty. The defendant had little protection against
such an accusation if he did not have a strong patron. The accused did
not have the right to confront the accuser and the aggrieved could not
rely on the law to guarantee him a fair hearing. Consequently, he could
be summarily expelled from the Armed Forces by having his commission annulled (*cancelado*) without the benefit of judicial or administrative due process.[20]

As with job security, advancement (and financial success) did not
depend on regulations concerning career development. Individuals were
not promoted based on fitness reports, on the screening of a selection
board, on standing in the *escalafón* or officers register, or on military
schools attended. Promotion and appointment to key positions were normally acquired as a result of having the sponsorship of a strong leader
and his clique within the Armed Forces. And in the early 1970s, the factions with the most influence were the group or groups which Balaguer
supported at any given time. Thus, any wavering in loyalty toward the
President meant a threat to one's future.

For those officers whose careers resembled the professionalism practiced in the United States, in Western Europe, or in more developed
Latin American countries, there existed the fear that resentment held
by their less-prepared superiors would cause retaliation. A common
response to an American officer's compliment that a Dominican officer
had performed professionally was a plea for the American not to tell the
Dominican's chief.

Dominican officers who reacted in that cautious manner were quick
in private to denigrate their countrymen for their backwardness and lack
of sophistication. Curiously, that small group of military professionals
spoke very much like many of their civilian counterparts who were
trained as engineers, physicians, or attorneys. U.S. Ambassador Martin
wrote of this phenomenon among the educated as the "Dominican con-

tempt for Dominicans,"[21] and Professor Howard J. Wiarda, a recognized authority on the Dominican Republic, described this trait as the "national inferiority complex."[22]

In almost all the countries of South America and in El Salvador and Guatemala of Central America, this lack of pride on the part of the officer corps did not exist. General staff colleges in those nations emphasized the elite politico-military status of their students, thus reinforcing the officers' view of themselves as the leaders and guardians of their countries' future. For them to be designated a *"Diplomado de Estado Mayor"* or "DEM," was to receive the credentials confirming their exclusive standing. Since most of the mid-career professionals of the Dominican Armed Forces were graduates of the Command and Staff Course in the Canal Zone, they were not indoctrinated in the same way as the DEM officers of Latin American staff colleges. The U.S. Army's general staff course in Panama was purely technical; it steered clear of the political and socio-economic themes found elsewhere in the Hemisphere. Although Dominican graduates received their staff college training under the auspices of a foreign army, they still felt this accomplishment was important. Even though they did not obtain the recognition in the Dominican Republic that was given to general staff officers of other Latin American republics, they believed they had a role in the improvement of the Dominican military. They brought back from the Canal Zone the capacity to plan operations, to manage resources, and to direct an efficient institution. But they had to step lightly.

It was unusual for a Dominican officer to follow the custom seen in other parts of Latin America in which graduates of a staff college advertised their successful completion of the advanced study program by including the equivalent of a DEM in their title or by some other visible means. When Colonel Cuervo Gómez returned from Spain where he graduated from the Spanish Army staff college, he used the title *"Coronel de Estado Mayor,"*[23] but after 1968, he discontinued this practice. Colonel Medrano Ubiera (a Canal Zone graduate) utilized the DEM after his name in 1969,[24] but he too stopped using the designation in the Dominican Republic. During the early 1970s, only one officer consistently brought attention to the fact that he was a *"Diplomado de Estado Mayor"* by adding DEM to his rank—he was Lieutenant Colonel Romero Pumarol, an officer who personified the dilemma of the mid-career professional in the Dominican Republic.

As stated earlier, Second Lieutenant Romero Pumarol was a member of the Military Academy faculty when the most promising officers in the Armed Forces were concentrated there in the late 1950s. He remained in the CEFA after the fall of the Trujillos and attached himself to Wessin y Wessin when that officer dominated Dominican politics

as the director of the CEFA. With the title of sub-director, Romero
Pumarol became the slow-witted Wessin's key staff operative.[25] After the
civil war, Romero Pumarol avoided public attention by attending the
1966 Command and Staff Course in the Canal Zone,[26] and, following a
short stint at the San Isidro Officers School, by returning for a second
tour at the School of the Americas as the first invited instructor from
the Dominican Republic—he taught general staff subjects. Like so many
of his ex-CEFA staff college graduate colleagues, he was distrusted by the
Balaguer government. They had resigned themselves to receiving assignments away from troops—usually they congregated at the Schools Command or the Army General Staff. But Romero Pumarol skillfully returned
to prominence by allying himself this time with Wessin's archenemy, General Nivar Seijas. In 1970 and 1971, he became the equivalent of Nivar's
chief of staff for military affairs—he was the operations and training executive of Nivar's command. Romero Pumarol was the only mid-career professional who was agile enough to have made the transition from
Wessinista to *Nivarista* even though he spent approximately three years
in the political wilderness in the interim between the two generals. Of
course, in the Armed Forces of Joaquín Balaguer, ascendancy was never
permanent. When the President undercut General Nivar's power base
in October 1971, Romero Pumarol lost his patron. He joined the ranks
of most of the other staff college graduates—he was assigned to a position without authority and with little potential to augment one's salary.
(His new job was Army liaison officer to the National Police.) Consequently, he was reduced to devoting the majority of his time to writing
articles.[27] Even Romero Pumarol, the most adroit survivor of the military professionals, was unable to find a guarantee for career stability in
the Dominican Republic.

LAW

It is difficult to generalize on the attitudes of Dominican officers concerning the law other than that the vast majority of them simply believed
that the nation's laws did not apply to them. This view did not appear
to be based on a statute such as the traditional *fuero militar*, which was a
privilege granted to the military by the king of Spain allowing officers
to be excluded from the authority of civil and criminal courts. The *fuero
militar* created a separate legal jurisdiction for the Army in the Spanish
colonies and was continued in most countries after independence.[28] In
the Dominican Republic of the early 1970s, however, the sentiment of
immunity seemed to stem more from Trujillo's policy that only he, not
judges or legislators, had the right to rule on issues involving the officer

corps. Illustrative of this disposition were comments expressed in 1971 by a lieutenant colonel assigned to Army Headquarters. He said, half jokingly, that being an officer prevented him from ever being in need of the basics such as food. If he were hungry, all he had to do was point his pistol at someone and give the order: "I am hungry!"

More significant was the remark made by an educated flag officer in March 1973 that it would be more beneficial to society if a convicted bank robber, who had escaped from prison and had been recaptured, be summarily executed rather than returned to jail. Also telling was the statement made in July 1971 by an uncharacteristically erudite and urbane Army colonel that even though he had a law degree he would not practice in the Dominican Republic because its weak and corrupt civil courts usually released the guilty. A bizarre twist in ethics occurred when Dominican officers spoke admiringly in 1972 of an Army colonel and a National Police lieutenant colonel because they had had the fortitude, despite international conventions, to execute personally prisoners during the 1965 civil war.

Much of the above was kept within the institution; however, there were many examples of the Dominican officers' contempt for the law that were exposed to the public. Two notorious cases were widely discussed. The first involved police Captain Félix "Polanquito" Polanco González of the President's Corps of Military Aides. On May 3, 1970, according to one version, Polanco's car was hit from the rear by a second vehicle on a major Santo Domingo avenue. The infuriated captain got out of his automobile and shot to death the other driver. Even though the incident, in the U.S. Embassy's words, "provoked public indignation and sharp protests,"[29] Polanco's career was not seriously affected. Initially, Polanco was dropped from the National Police and turned over to the civil courts[30] (acts which ex-President Bosch praised on May 5th[31]). But, after a decent interval, Polanco resumed his duties as a presidential aide-de-camp and was promoted to major in the Army, his original service. He retired in November 1978 with the rank of colonel.[32]

The second incident was also a homicide in a public place. On April 11, 1971, Air Force Colonel Guarién Cabrera Ariza (who was mainly known for playing polo with Ramfis and for subsequent run-ins with the law) was sitting in the La Posada restaurant on the waterfront of the capital when a man at a table near Cabrera, who had drunk too much, began to criticize the Colonel for being a *Trujillista*. Cabrera responded by shooting the inebriated diner dead with his pistol and his bodyguard's shoulder weapon. A second man also was killed by the gunfire. The Colonel then telephoned General Pérez y Pérez and informed him of what had occurred. The General instructed Cabrera to report immediately to San Isidro Air Base. (When the story circulated in Santo Domingo, peo-

ple quipped: "Did the Colonel ask for directions to get to San Isidro?"—
a reference to the fact that he had been an Air Force officer in name
only since Ramfis departed the country in 1961.) Cabrera was required
to face a judge—his initial defense was that he had killed the individuals in the restaurant because he had been "provoked." The judge, on
September 2nd, sentenced Cabrera to one month in jail and the equivalent of a 100-dollar fine. Two weeks later Cabrera departed legally for
Miami on a commercial flight. Well-informed Dominican civilians were
incredulous, but there was more to come. It was expected that any further publicity for the Colonel would be avoided, thus bringing the outrageous incident to closure; however, on April 26, 1973, President
Balaguer promoted Cabrera to brigadier general and appointed him the
sub-secretary of state of the armed forces for air with an office in the
National Palace.[33]

VI

Nivar versus Pérez y Pérez: A Politico-Military Rivalry

Before the 1965 civil war, one of the most virulent factional struggles within the officer corps had been the dispute between the San Cristóbal Group and the CEFA officers of San Isidro. From the July 1966 inauguration of President Balaguer through his second elected term, this internecine conflict evolved into a personal rivalry which pitted General Neit Nivar Seijas against General Enrique Pérez y Pérez. Nivar had not been the senior member of the San Cristóbal Group and Pérez y Pérez had never belonged to the CEFA, but, by the end of 1971, they led the two dominant cliques in the Dominican Armed Forces, which were the outgrowths of *Clan San Cristóbal* and *Clan San Isidro*.

There have been many accounts as to the origin of the feud between the two generals—those stories were similar to the numerous colorful anecdotes passed on by word of mouth about *El Jefe* and his entourage of officers. Beyond these Trujillo-era rumors, there does exist one indisputable reason that Nivar resented Pérez y Pérez, and it did not stem from the days of the Generalissimo. Nivar had devoted a great deal of energy and sacrifice to returning Balaguer to the presidency, which included the time they shared in U.S. exile. Nivar believed no military man had given as much of himself as he had to Balaguer's cause; therefore, he assumed that the incoming president would appoint him to the new cabinet as the head of the Armed Forces. Nivar and the officer corps were surprised (as they would be many times in the future with presidential appointments) when Balaguer retained his predecessor's minister, Pérez y Pérez, rather than select a *Balaguerista* to the post. (The General was the only member of the García Godoy cabinet who remained in office under Balaguer.) The insult to Nivar was heightened when the President also refused to appoint him to a position which carried the automatic promotion to brigadier general such as chief of staff of the Army. Instead, Balaguer re-integrated Nivar on the active list in his old rank of colonel and placed him in charge of the Corps of Military Aides—an assignment which, in 1966, offered no leverage in the military and police establishments. Nivar sulked, but, as would be seen later in his career, he put aside his disappointment quickly and began to convert his weak post into an independent power base. Therefore, the beginning of the personal struggle between Nivar and Pérez y Pérez can effectively be traced to July 1966 when the two faced off—the former as Balaguer's chief aide-de-camp against the latter who was the President's defense minister.[1]

THE TRUJILLO ERA

If the two officers' experiences before 1966 are reviewed, the differences are quite significant even though both individuals were the products of Trujillo's Armed Forces. Pérez y Pérez, a black man, was born on July 9, 1923, in Duvergé near the border with Haiti, thus making him susceptible to attacks from his opponents that his family could have been of Haitian origin, a common slur in Dominican cutthroat politics. In contrast, Nivar, who was of Hispano-European appearance, was born approximately one year later (August 14, 1924) in Trujillo's birthplace of San Cristóbal.[2] It was rumored that Nivar's family tree—as a result of an illegitimate liaison—included *El Jefe*, a charge some Dominican wags would claim was never denied by Nivar.

Nivar entered the Army as a cadet on March 1, 1945, while Pérez y Pérez joined the same service as an enlisted man on January 26th of the same year. It was not until February 1, 1949, that he was appointed a cadet. Both young men attended secondary school and received their pre-commissioning training in the Army's *Escuela de Cadetes* before they were designated second lieutenants of infantry. Nivar was appointed in November 1947—at that juncture, his formal education came to an end. Pérez y Pérez was commissioned in February 1951; during the next year, while he was assigned as an instructor of recruits, he became a student at the University of Santo Domingo.[3]

Subalterns in Trujillo's Army of the 1940s and 1950s normally were assigned to constabulary-style companies and detachments throughout the countryside. Initially, Nivar was no exception. Just as his peers (such as the future Generals Braulio Alvarez Sánchez, Rafael de Jesús Checo, Rafael Valdez Hilario, and Marcos Antonio Jorge Moreno), Nivar spent his first years as a company grade officer in the interior. He was posted to Elias Piña, Hato Nuevo, Restauración, and San Cristóbal. Nivar's assignment pattern from the mid–1950s, however, was different—he had had almost continuous duty in the Presidential Guard. In 1954, as a first lieutenant, he served as an adjutant in the Guard. In the same year, he was promoted to captain. On March 15, 1956, he was appointed president of the Guard's military court, and, on April 11, 1958, he was promoted to major in that elite unit. Ten days after that promotion, he was designated the *auxiliar* or staff assistant to the commander of the Presidential Guard, who was a member of the Trujillo family.[4]

Because of his race, Pérez y Pérez would not have been accepted in the Presidential Guard; however, he does appear to have escaped some of the tedium of the constabulary Army by serving as commander of tactically-oriented units that occasionally were sent to the field. In 1955, as a first lieutenant, Pérez y Pérez led an 81mm mortar platoon, and, after his September 6, 1956, promotion to captain, he commanded a heavy weapons company, a post he retained into 1958. During that period, Pérez y Pérez was assigned to the capital-based 1st Battalion, *Generalísimo Trujillo* Regiment, which was the precursor in regimental lineage to the 1st Battalion, *Juan Pablo Duarte*, of the 1960s and 1970s. Concurrent with his military duties was his pursuit of a university education. In 1954, he received the equivalent of a bachelor's degree and he began law school classes at night. By 1961, he had advanced to being a fourth-year law student, but was forced to withdraw due to the October closing of the university for political reasons.[5]

In the last years of the Trujillo regime, Nivar was in far better circumstances than Pérez y Pérez. On March 3, 1959, Nivar was promoted to lieutenant colonel and was given command of the 3rd Regiment in San Pedro de Macorís. In the following two years, Nivar gained the reputation of being the dictator's facilitator and brutal enforcer in the eastern sector of the country. Whenever Trujillo traveled in that region, Nivar became part of his coterie.[6]

The much less visible Captain Pérez y Pérez had an opportunity to expand his professional experience when, in the beginning of 1959 after the collapse of the Batista regime in Cuba, he was assigned to the military group that was training an anti-Castro expedition in the Dominican Republic.[7] The invasion force consisted of Cuban exiles, under the command of a Batista officer, General José Eleuterio Pedraza, and the newly established Foreign Legion, made up primarily of Europeans. Initially, the volunteers were assembled in the *Las Calderas* Naval Base, and then they were transferred to Constanza for training, but, by mid–August, the project had miscarried.[8] Pérez y Pérez was promoted to major (July 16, 1959)[9] before the scheme failed, and he was advanced to lieutenant colonel (June 8, 1961) less than one month after Trujillo was assassinated.[10]

THE TURBULENT YEARS

From the November 1961 fall of the Trujillo family to the end of the civil war in 1965, the Dominican Republic passed through a period of continuous turmoil, allowing Nivar to be thrust prematurely into national prominence. Members of the officer corps sought out new loyalties during this highly fluid political experience; Nivar felt that associating oneself with Balaguer was most in his interest.

After San Pedro de Macorís, Nivar commanded regiments in Mao and Puerto Plata. At the latter station, on the 1st of December, 1961, he was promoted to colonel. He was then sent to the 3rd Brigade in San Juan de la Maguana. In all three posts, he furthered his reputation as a repressive provincial commander. On the night of January 3, 1962, a political opponent of Nivar was shot by a soldier assigned to Nivar's garrison. The murder of José Alfredo Achecar, an owner of a radio station, was blamed on Nivar; however, the Colonel insisted that he was innocent, maintaining that he had left San Juan de la Maguana at 3:30 P.M. on January 3rd to take command of his new unit in Mao. Army headquarters announced on January 5th that a full investigation would be launched, but no action was ever taken against Nivar. On the same day as the assassination, Colonel Nivar took over the command in Mao, which at the time was designated the 5th Brigade. Six days later he dispatched an open letter with the signatures of his officers to the first Council of State taking a political position favorable to Balaguer. On January 16th, Nivar participated in the coup d'état against the Council of State with the objective of permitting Balaguer to remain in power. For two days, Colonel Nivar was a principal member of the Civilian-Military Junta before Colonel Wessin y Wessin and the CEFA unseated the new government and established the second Council of State. Balaguer went into exile in New York and Nivar remained unassigned while it was being determined whether he should be punished by military authorities. During the period following Nivar's expulsion from the Junta, civilian professional and commercial groups such as the physicians' and attorneys' guilds and the sugar growers' and cattlemen's associations demanded that he be tried for "crimes and abuses" that he had reportedly committed while he commanded in San Pedro de Macorís, Mao, Puerto Plata, and San Juan de la Maguana. Even though the new government, in April 1962, had him on a list of 18 officers to be purged, Nivar evaded both military and civilian justice—in June, he was exiled to Colombia as a military attaché. Nivar would not return to the Dominican Republic until the following year.[11]

Compared with Nivar's political machinations, Pérez y Pérez's activities after the fall of the Trujillo regime appeared bland. With the collapse of the dictatorship, U.S. security assistance was resumed for the Dominican Republic. This change in Washington policy provided Pérez y Pérez with the opportunity to receive U.S. Army training in the Panama Canal Zone. During the second half of 1962, he was a student in the five-month *comando y plana mayor* course followed by a two-week orientation on counterinsurgency. The *plana mayor* block of instruction primarily encompassed battalion and brigade level subjects, to include the basic S-1 through S-4 staff functions for those tactical units. While in Panama, Pérez y Pérez had requested a transfer to the Air Force. This personnel action was approved effective November 30, 1962—the day that he completed his training in the Canal Zone. Pérez y Pérez had not acquired general staff officer credentials; however, in the years to come, he would be one of the first Dominicans in a position of authority to advocate a military educational system capped off by a nine-month command and general staff college course.[12] In contrast, Nivar had no military schooling after his pre-commissioning instruction, and devoted little of his energy to professional military issues.

Pérez y Pérez had taken a new direction in his career when he was transferred out of the Army. He was assigned to the staff of the post-Ramfis air service as a ground officer. He had not been close to the National Palace, he had not been part of the CEFA clique, and he was a non-pilot in the Air Force.

In less than a month following Pérez y Pérez's transfer, he participated in an Air Force-CEFA joint exercise, which included elements of the Armored Battalion and the Artillery Group, and paratroopers and FAD infantry. They were supported by P-51 fighters, Vampire jets, and C-47 transport aircraft. (The purpose of the maneuvers was to provide a show of force to the public prior to the December 1962 elections.) That experience gave Pérez y Pérez an opportunity to assess military officers to whom he had not had extensive exposure in the past. The task force commander was the less than impressive Colonel Wessin y Wessin; however, the battle staff (of which Pérez y Pérez was one of four principals) was far different. During the operation, Pérez y Pérez worked with two of the keenest minds in the Armed Forces. They were Lieutenant Colonels Pedro Medrano and Ramiro Matos González. At the time, the former led CEFA's artillery and the latter was head of the Air Force's base security infantry.[13]

With the termination of the field exercise, Pérez y Pérez was able to settle into his new job on the air staff as director of intelligence, A-2. In that position, he interfaced with the Air Force's *Grupo de Anti-guerrillas* that later was amalgamated with the airborne company to form the Special Forces Group. It was through work with these units that Pérez y Pérez came into contact with the young, charismatic Major Lluberes Montás. As the A-2, Pérez y Pérez also was responsible for counterintelligence and the prevention of arms smuggling by air—in these functions he was aided by his earlier legal training as well as his knowledge of management procedures.[14]

On February 27, 1963, Juan Bosch became the country's first freely elected president in 38 years. During the new constitutional government, Colonel Nivar was allowed to resume his career in Santo Domingo as the director of Army training. Pérez y Pérez was also designated the training director for his service. (He was promoted to colonel in the Air Force on April 4th, more than 16 months after Nivar.) The difference between the two officers was that Nivar devoted his energy to returning Balaguer to the presidency, while Pérez y Pérez concentrated on subjects such as guerrilla warfare. Nivar joined the temporary military coalition led by Colonel Wessin y Wessin to overthrow Bosch and, when the coup d'état took place on September 25, 1963, Nivar was one of the 25 flag and field grade officers who signed the manifesto removing the President from office.[15] Pérez y Pérez played no individual role in the affair.

It was after the ouster of Juan Bosch that Nivar would reach his highest point as political conspirator and military coup plotter. As the most active and talented member of the San Cristóbal Group, Nivar became the principal operative in the plan to overthrow the Triumvirate government which had succeeded the Bosch administration. For Nivar to eliminate the Triumvirate, it would be essential to neutralize its main source of authority—the military power of the new Brigadier General Wessin y Wessin and the CEFA. Nivar would devote the remainder of 1963, and all of 1964, to seeking a formula to compensate for the massed force at San Isidro.

The San Cristóbal Group pursued the traditional preparations for staging a military *golpe*—potential supporters in key units were approached and, if possible, won over. Nivar, however, provided an additional dimension; he made contact with PRD civilian officials who were also contemplating the downfall of the Triumvirate, although they were seeking a different end game than Nivar. For the left-of-center politicians, such as José Francisco Peña Gómez and Pablo Rafael Casimiro Castro, the goal was the reinstatement of Juan Bosch, not Balaguer, as president. Meetings between Nivar and Peña Gómez began in the summer of 1964 although, reportedly, the relationship between PRD leaders and Nivar had started as early as 1961 when the Army officer was saved by the PRD from a mob in Puerto Plata. Nivar claimed that his contacts with the PRD were solely tactical—his objective in 1964, according to Nivar, was to overthrow the Triumvirate government, to form a military junta, and to open the door for a Balaguer presidency. Juan Bosch would be excluded from power because Nivar was convinced that the former president was a Communist.[16] Nivar, however, never terminated his contacts with the PRD—a factor that the inflexible Pérez y Pérez would consider over the years to be tantamount to treason.[17]

Despite Nivar's efforts in 1964, the San Cristóbal Group failed to become strong enough to launch a successful coup. Politically, he and his colleagues were continuously denounced by the non-radical civilian parties, as well as receiving the expected attacks from the extreme left. Nivar countered by agitating against members of the Triumvirate. He was able to force the resignation of one triumvir—Dr. Ramón Tapia Espinal— but Nivar's position remained weak. After the removal of Tapia, Nivar in April 1964 personally was the subject of new petitions from civilian professionals in San Pedro de Macorís and Santiago demanding his dismissal, and of attempts by President Reid Cabral to rid himself of the Colonel by proposing he study abroad.[18] On April 14th, the U.S. Embassy reported to Washington that "Nivar is generally regarded among Dominican politicians as one of the worst of the remaining *Trujillistas* in the Armed Forces."[19] The American Embassy further informed the State Department on June 6th of the Dominican reaction to an official Nivar visit to the town of Moca in the rich Cibao region. The memorandum stated: "... the memories of the excesses of the Trujillo regime permeate almost every home in that area, and Nivar Seijas is known as one of the worst of Trujillo's henchmen."[20]

The inadequacy of the San Cristóbal Group was not only its lack of popular support, but also its military weakness. In mid–1964, Nivar held the joint positions of director of military training and commander of the old *16 de Agosto* Military Camp, located, at that time, on the east bank of the Ozama River, not too distant from the CEFA at San Isidro. Nivar had had many opportunities to compare the capabilities of his Army training center at the *16 de Agosto* facility with its main rival, the CEFA. It had to be evident to Nivar that his troops, and those of his collaborators in the interior, would have difficulty opposing Wessin's armored phalanx and modern artillery. Despite this lack of strength, however, the San Cristóbal Group decided in the fall of 1964 to move against the Triumvirate. Nivar alerted the PRD,[21] but he never had the opportunity to follow through.

On September 28th, the government took its first step against the San Cristóbal Group by relieving Nivar of his command, which included a battalion of troops, and appointing him the *intendente general* of the Army. Even though the quartermaster general's post was financially lucrative, Nivar refused the assignment because he knew that if he gave up the *16 de Agosto* Military Camp, he would be militarily and politically impotent. For two days, rumors circulated in the capital that a revolt was imminent within the Armed Forces. President Reid Cabral, on October 1st, confronted the Colonel and demanded that he surrender his command. Nivar protested emotionally to no avail, because the CEFA had already gone on full alert. Nivar backed down. He passively assumed the staff position of *intendente general*, thus allowing Armed

Forces headquarters, on October 3rd, to issue a communiqué to an anxious Santo Domingo stating that the Triumvirate's orders had been obeyed.[22]

In the months that followed, the government and the CEFA continued to move against San Cristóbal Group members. The most significant event in this purge occurred on the morning of January 27, 1965. At 11:00 A.M., the President arrived at the National Palace accompanied by a detail of CEFA officers in battle dress. Reid Cabral then took the following actions: He fired Nivar as quartermaster general, and, in the words of the Triumvirate's decree, placed him in "immediate retirement."[23] Nivar and approximately 15 relatively junior officers, however, continued to plot the overthrow of the government. An exasperated president deported the retired Colonel to Puerto Rico on April 12th.[24] From there, Nivar joined Balaguer in New York.

Twelve days after Nivar's flight departed the Dominican Republic, the civil war began. The rebellion would alter the course of Colonel Pérez y Pérez's career. When the insurrection started, he was a member of the Air Force chief's headquarters staff. In that capacity, on the second day of the crisis, he was sent as an envoy to negotiate with the rebels. Pérez y Pérez, rather than a pilot, was chosen because he had friends among the insurgent Army officers. His mission failed,[25] but the civil war would open opportunities of a different type for him.

After the CEFA performed poorly at the Duarte Bridge, other combat leaders would surface. Beginning on May 15th, the government launched its first serious offensive in Santo Domingo since the CEFA setback at the river. The purpose of the unilaterally planned operation, entitled *Operación Limpieza*, was to clear the rebels out of the northern sector of the capital and to gain control of Radio Santo Domingo, the so-called "voice of the revolution." To accomplish these objectives, over 2,000 loyalist troops would have to deploy behind the insurgents, and sweep from west to east until they reached the Ozama River.[26] Pérez y Pérez was selected to be one of the principal ground commanders. He led a mixed battalion-sized unit made up of Air Force infantrymen and Army and National Police personnel. First Lieutenant Juan A. Montes, an American Army paratrooper, observed the Dominican colonel throughout most of the operation. (Lieutenant Montes was attached to Pérez y Pérez's task force as a liaison officer from the U.S. XVIII Airborne Corps. They would meet again in 1972 when Major Montes was assigned as the 1st Brigade adviser.) The American lieutenant described Pérez y Pérez as having the natural ability to command. He coolly led his troops in bloody house-to-house fighting, from phase line to phase line, without any display of emotion or irresoluteness. Although Pérez y Pérez spoke few words, he was popular with and respected by his men.[27] Operation *Limpieza* was a success and Pérez y Pérez had established himself with American representatives in country, as well as with Dominicans, as a military leader.[28]*

By September 1965, Colonel Pérez y Pérez was, as head of the FAD Base Defense Command, in charge of all the Air Force infantry at the San Isidro installation. In the following month, the focal point for the entire Dominican conflict had shifted to the *Fortaleza Ozama* and its environs. On October 18th, FAD troops successfully occupied the colonial fortress, but sporadic combat action continued outside its walls for the remainder of October. During that period, Pérez y Pérez was given the added responsibility of collecting arms from the rebels and the civilian population in that sector of Santo Domingo. On the last day of October, Pérez y Pérez was transferred from the Air Force back to the Army—this action was promulgated on November 3rd. He continued his mission of pacifying the city throughout the month. In that effort, a major government step was taken when the Army's reconstituted 1st Battalion, *Juan Pablo Duarte*, moved into the old fort. Pérez y Pérez's role in the process was formalized on December 10th when he assumed command of *Fortaleza Ozama* as an Army colonel.[29] *Fortaleza Ozama* was the traditional headquarters for the leader of ground units in Santo Domingo—and, during the closing phase of the civil war, it would be something more. *Fortaleza Ozama* was to become the garrison of the first units of the Dominican 1st Brigade to receive U.S. MAP support. Pérez y Pérez energetically took up his new responsibilities as the capital's premier troop commander, but his good fortune had just begun. In less than two months, he was under serious consideration to head the entire Army of the Dominican Republic.

Colonel Pérez y Pérez's leap from field command to national-level office can be attributed to many elements, but the deciding factor was his seemingly neutral background within the institution. He appealed to the military professionals in the U.S. occupation forces as well as to the small segment of like-minded Dominican officers, but to provisional President García Godoy his main attribute was that he was not tainted with membership in one of the feuding factions. Pérez y Pérez had not been in the San Cristóbal Group, the CEFA, or the Constitutionalist movement. Although he had served on the Air Force staff at San Isidro Air Base, he had been an outsider there because of his previous lengthy career in the Army. And when he had been in the Army, he had steered clear of becoming a provincial political chieftain.

*Accusations have been made that loyalist troops committed human rights violations during the May 1965 military operation in the northern sector of the capital. Pérez y Pérez was never linked to those alleged incidents, but at least two officers who were members of the Pérez y Pérez faction after the civil war were singled out as having executed prisoners. This connection was unfair to Pérez y Pérez; however, the association became one more factor in fortifying his image of ruthlessness.

The general public first became aware of Colonel Pérez y Pérez when the President, on January 6, 1966, announced that he had selected a new high command, that he had assigned the outgoing minister of the armed forces and two chiefs of staff to military attaché posts, and that he had submitted a list of 34 officers to study abroad. Commodore Jiménez was designated the incoming minister; *Capitán de Navío* Amiama Castillo would lead the Navy; the pilot Colonel Luis Beauchamps Javier would replace Brigadier General de los Santos as head of the Air Force; and Pérez y Pérez would become the chief of staff of the Army.[30] These appointments were rejected by the designees on January 7th because of the adverse reaction to the order within the Armed Forces. The members of the high command who were relieved by the President, as well as the loyalist officers who were on García Godoy's list, refused to go abroad. Thus, the new appointees demonstrated their solidarity with the institution by declining to accept the January 6th leadership posts.[31]

An irate President informed the U.S. government that he was considering going alone to *Fortaleza Ozama* and ordering the head of the Dominican Army "to produce Colonel Pérez y Pérez for [the] purpose of taking [the] oath as Army chief of staff then and there." García Godoy asked if he could count on the support of allied troops. A less than enthusiastic reply from American officials caused the President to drop that approach.[32]

The ensuing crisis dragged on for a month until a partial solution was reached: Commodore Rivera Caminero was prepared to vacate his cabinet post as head of the Armed Forces and to become the naval attaché in Washington. Although it was patently obvious that the U.S. Embassy had favored Commodore Jiménez for minister of the armed forces in place of Rivera Caminero since at least October 23, 1965[33] (and the President shared this view[34]), American backing for Jiménez appeared to have shifted by the end of January 1966. On January 29th, Rivera Caminero told the new commander of U.S. forces in country, Brigadier General Robert Linvill, that Colonel Pérez y Pérez had the strong character necessary to fill the top military leadership position in the Dominican Republic. The Commodore added that his protégé, Commodore Jiménez, and the 4th Brigade commander, Colonel Perdomo Rosario, fell short of having the necessary qualities for the job. On the following day, Rivera Caminero and the U.S. Ambassador met to discuss the same subject.[35] Undoubtedly, Rivera Caminero repeated his recommendation to the ambassador.

By February 2nd, Rivera Caminero had totally abandoned Jiménez's candidature and decided to submit a list of three Army nominees for minister to the President. One of the triad would be Pérez y Pérez.[36] After consultation with different sectors of the military establishment, the three officers selected by the Commodore were Colonels Perdomo Rosario, Valdez Hilario, and Pérez y Pérez. The list was delivered to the President on February 4th.[37] One day later, the public became aware of what had occurred; however, Colonel Juan Pérez Guillén's name was cited in lieu of Pérez y Pérez.[38] That lineup suggested that they were selected because they were the brigade leaders who commanded the three geographic military zones in the interior. (Valdez Hilario was the commander of the 2nd Brigade in the north, Pérez Guillén was the commander of the 3rd Brigade in the south, and Perdomo Rosario was the commander of the 4th Brigade which had the responsibility for the east.) On February 7th, Dominicans became aware that Pérez y Pérez, not Pérez Guillén, was one of the candidates.[39] The next day the President personally selected Pérez y Pérez.[40] Temporary Brigadier General Pérez y Pérez was sworn in as minister of the armed forces on February 11th.[41]

President García Godoy's decision to select Pérez y Pérez could not have been a difficult one. Colonel Perdomo Rosario was the CEFA tank commander who replaced Wessin y Wessin in September 1965 when the CEFA leader was forced into exile, and Colonel Valdez Hilario was a long time Army commander in the interior with strong links to the previous government. Not only did Pérez y Pérez carry no similar complicating baggage, he also was considered "moderate"[42] and "one of the Army's most qualified officers"[43] by the U.S. government's representatives in Santo Domingo. (Curiously, from exile in London, Caamaño also expressed his approval of the Pérez y Pérez appointment.[44])

The new minister has been credited with skillfully managing the Armed Forces during the tense final months of President García Godoy's provisional administration.[45] Notably, Pérez y Pérez was instrumental in bringing to a close on February 26th the general officer assignment crisis that began on January 6th. (The dissatisfied generals were accommodated by creating domestic billets for them to fill without loss of rank. Shortly after, García Godoy rewarded Pérez y Pérez by designating him a permanent brigadier general and a temporary major general.)[46] Pérez y Pérez also was able to prevent the antagonism felt toward the transitional government on the part of the *Wessinistas*, on the right, and the Constitutionalists, on the left, from spiraling out of control. And, finally, he was successful in orchestrating (with substantial U.S. assistance) the build-up of the security apparatus in preparation for the June 1st presidential elections.

From the outset, the new minister had captivated the American Embassy. On March 16th, Ambassador Bennett dispatched to Washington an extraordinary description of Pérez y Pérez:

> [He] has made dramatic rise from private in 1945 to highest Dominican rank, having received second star since nomination as minister of defense.

He studied law at University of Santo Domingo.... He is man of quiet dignity and considerable poise and impresses one with his restraint and a breadth of viewpoint unusual in Dominican officer ... at my residence ... [the] minister of defense was easily lion of evening. He handled himself well and ... critical group of [foreign] ambassadors uniformly expressed themselves as much impressed by him.[47]

It was during the beginning of the general's tenure as minister of the armed forces that Pérez y Pérez began emphasizing the policy that the military establishment would be apolitical. Although there exists significant evidence that Pérez y Pérez's real sentiments on the subject did not match his public statements to Dominicans and his private remarks to the U.S. Embassy, he consistently made the policy a matter of record. During March 2nd, *Radio Continental* reported that the minister had dispatched a circular to the chiefs of staff of the three services on the first day of the electoral campaign (March 1st), directing them to inform their personnel that the military was apolitical and that any violation of that position would result in dismissal.[48] These words were repeated to the American Ambassador on March 15th.[49] On the 4th of April, the magazine *Ahora* published an interview with Pérez y Pérez; in that conversation, he claimed that the Armed Forces were and would be "eminently obedient to civil authority."[50] *Radio Comercial* reported on May 19th that the minister had stated the day before that, while he was in office, the military establishment would be apolitical. He added that if anyone in the military, regardless of rank, participated in politics, he would be punished.[51] Pérez y Pérez would repeat those words for the remainder of his public life.

While the new minister of the armed forces articulated one policy concerning the prohibition of politics in the military institution, he was quite willing, on occasion, to look the other way when it came to the implementation of that policy. This was not the case with Colonel Nivar; he had never made a secret of his partisan political activity before going into exile, and, in the latter part of 1965, while in retirement, he was even more obvious. Former President Balaguer returned to the Dominican Republic in the end of June 1965 to prepare his campaign for the following year. On September 3, 1965, Nivar, who had already devoted almost all of his financial resources to Balaguer, also arrived in the Dominican Republic, where he tirelessly worked to build support for Balaguer within the active duty Armed Forces. In addition, Nivar was responsible for Balaguer's personal security and he raised campaign funds both in the Dominican Republic and in Puerto Rico.[52] On June 1, 1966, Joaquín Balaguer was victorious at the polls, and, one month later, he was sworn in as constitutional president of the nation. On that day, when the inaugural parade passed in review before the diminutive new commander in chief of the armed forces, Colonel Nivar and Major General Pérez y Pérez were at his side.[53]

Before the end of July, the U.S. Embassy prepared an evaluation of the new Balaguer government. In the cable transmitting the assessment to Washington, the American diplomats inadvertently provided the first indication of the divisiveness that would develop within the leadership of the officer corps: They wrote that there was satisfaction with General Pérez y Pérez's management of the Armed Forces, but, in contrast, senior Dominican military officers who were working with Nivar were "uneasy" with the Colonel's reputation and style. Significantly, it was reported that the American Embassy's military and civilian officials had the same reaction to the new President's chief military aide-de-camp.[54]

THE BALAGUER PRESIDENCY, 1966–1970

It quickly became apparent that Balaguer's retention of General Pérez y Pérez as head of the Armed Forces was not an isolated appointment, but part of a larger policy to dominate the officer corps. Colonel Nivar attempted to influence personnel assignments by having his collaborators placed in key posts, but the new president periodically disregarded his chief aide-de-camp's advice. Balaguer was willing to give field commands to old San Cristóbal Group loyalists such as Colonel Braulio Alvarez Sánchez and Lieutenant Colonel José Manuel Pérez Aponte; however, he also opened the door to certain former CEFA officers who did not object to turning their backs on Wessin y Wessin. Consequently, Perdomo Rosario, the CEFA tanker; Beauchamps Javier, the Wessin infantryman; and Lluberes Montás, the San Isidro parachutist, all found a place in Balaguer's elaborate balance-of-power scheme. But the President—who had observed Trujillo govern for almost three decades—did not set this mechanism of checks in motion and then focus his attention elsewhere. He maintained an active internal informant system with the objective of monitoring the ex-*Wessinistas* as well as other potential opponents of the regime. The control of this process was not restricted to a single agency or bureau; however, there was one individual who devoted more energy than any other to the project—he was the new Chief of the Corps of Military Aides.[55]

Normally, Colonel Nivar's responsibilities would have been limited to the physical protection of the president. In addition, however, Nivar developed an autonomous intelligence service which emphasized the collection of political information. The new organization soon began to encroach on the turf of the official presidential *Departamento Nacional de*

Investigaciones (DNI) and the security services of the Armed Forces and National Police. Then Nivar broadened his operations from reporting on disloyalty to engaging in political manipulation and deception; this quickly became an irritant to many loyal Balaguer followers within the National Palace and the Armed Forces.[56] As early as one month and ten days after the inauguration, Santo Domingo was awash with rumors that Pérez y Pérez was to be sacked and Nivar appointed minister of the armed forces. Although Nivar denied that he had anything to do with these

reports,[57] there were indications that he was responsible. The tension in the government was so well known that, on September 11, 1966, the Cuban news agency *Prensa Latina* broadcast from Havana that there was a "deep split" in the Dominican Armed Forces between the officers stationed at San Isidro and the "chief of the [presidential] guard, Nivar Seijas."[58] By the end of the year, Nivar was clearly a liability for Balaguer as long as the Colonel remained in the National Palace. On December 9th, the U.S. Embassy sent a cable to Washington stating "… Balaguer now aware that despite personal loyalty to him [,] Nivar's 'machinations' had reached point of seriously disturbing intra-regime relationships."[59]

Brig. Gen. Neit Nivar Seijas in his office in April 1972. He was the chief of National Police. (*Listín Diario*)

The general public (and the American Embassy) thought Nivar had been removed from his post on February 15, 1967, as part of routine reassignments in the Armed Forces. (In that presidential decree, Colonel Juan Pérez Guillén was appointed the head of the Army and a handful of old *Balagueristas* received important positions.)[60] Nivar, however, lingered on as the President's chief aide-de-camp.

In the beginning of March 1967, U.S. officials in Santo Domingo were perplexed as to why the President was still tolerating Nivar's presence in the National Palace. It was known that Nivar was not liked nor

Maj. Gen. Enrique Pérez y Pérez with other general officers, December 1973. From left to right (seated) Medical Brig. Gen. Clarence Charles Dunlop, Army Brig. Gen. Joaquin Méndez Lara, Air Force Brig. Gen. Juan Folch Pérez, Army Brig. Gen. Juan Beauchamps Javier, Army Maj. Gen Pérez y Pérez, Army Brig. Gen. Elio Perdomo Rosario, and Air Force Brig. Gen. Ramiro Matos González. They are attending a field exercise involving AMX-13 tanks, artillery, and an infantry battalion. Brig. Gen. Manuel Cuervo Gómez (not shown) is providing the briefing.

trusted by most high-ranking officers, and he had minimal military clout; therefore, the American Embassy did not understand why he was not transferred. Observers did not yet appreciate the full extent of Balaguer's balance-of-power policy for the Armed Forces, but they did, at least, recognize that Nivar had some value for the President as a club over the heads of other officers. Nivar was a potential replacement for the Armed Forces secretary, for the chief of the Army, or for any field commander who failed to subordinate himself to the President.[61]

To Balaguer's satisfaction, in this early period of his government, Nivar's opponents were equally lacking in politico-military strength. General Pérez y Pérez was exhibiting an administrative style that, although efficient, was highly unpopular. His policy was to centralize the management of the Armed Forces at his level at the expense of the service chiefs. This effort included the control of logistics, which, because it involved money, especially irritated the heads of the three branches of the military. The President described Pérez y Pérez's approach as professional but "severe."[62] Consequently, since the Armed Forces secretary had few close friends and General Pérez Guillén, the new chief of staff of the Army, was a weak leader, there existed little threat to the President's authority among the anti-*Nivaristas*. The result was that there was a modicum of balance between Nivar and his enemies.

On March 21, 1967, the Dominican Republic was immersed in gossip after hearing that Antonio Imbert Barrera, one of the two survivors of the Trujillo assassination plot and subsequently the president of the Government of National Reconstruction during the 1965 civil war, had been gunned down by unidentified assailants in an affluent section of the capital. Imbert survived the murder attempt and Balaguer ordered an extensive investigation. Two days after the incident, a bandaged Imbert, at a press conference in the hospital, stated that he had been attacked by a *Trujillista* cabal.[63] In some circles, it was believed that Colonels Nivar and Marmolejos were behind the assassination conspiracy. Arrests were made to include Nivar's close civilian associate Salomón Sanz, a prominent businessman, but no charges were filed.[64] Nivar, still in the National Palace, blamed "foreign elements" for the crime,[65] but the investigation was inconclusive. Years later Balaguer would write that the assault was most probably conducted by a group within the Dominican Armed Forces, but he had been unable to identify the guilty due to the unwillingness on the part of the military institution to cooperate.[66]

The Imbert affair gave Balaguer's allies who opposed Nivar the rationale they needed for pressing for his removal from the executive offices of the President. Even though Balaguer felt obligated to Nivar for the Colonel's past services and he valued Nivar as a counterweight to other military leaders, the President recognized that Nivar had to be removed from the National Palace.[67] Nivar was informed officially on April 4th of what had been in the works for some time. He was to be transferred out of the presidential household and given command of a military unit—the 1st Brigade. The decree was promulgated three days later and obeyed.[68]

At first glance, it appeared that Nivar's politico-military power had been severely reduced. He no longer had official access to the President; instead, according to the chain of command, he was subordinated to the chief of staff of the Army, who, in turn, reported to General Pérez y Pérez. Nivar was co-equal with the commanders of the 2nd Brigade in Santiago, the 3rd Brigade in San Juan de la Maguana, and the 4th Brigade in San Isidro. More important, the 1st Brigade did not have unit cohesion. The three 1st Brigade commanders who had preceded Nivar since the July 1st inauguration—Colonels Maximiliano Ruiz Batista, Angel Urbano Matos, and Braulio Alvarez Sánchez—had not welded the Brigade's scattered battalions into a solid force (which, of course, was precisely the weakness that President Balaguer desired). Nivar had not chosen his battalion commanders and, in fact, the 1st Battalion at *Fortaleza Ozama* was led by an officer known to support Pérez y Pérez. Nivar had further problems. He now was isolated from the levers of political power that he had utilized in the National Palace. His intelligence service was no longer easily responsive to him, and he had lost the daily contact he had maintained with members of the government. But Nivar, characteristically, refused to suffer defeat for long. Even though he had been placed in a disadvantageous position, he soon took the initiative. Nivar began to build a new base, forcing his enemies to react to his actions again rather than having them continue on the offensive. The instrument that Nivar would utilize to regain power was to be the Dominican Republic's "new CEFA"—the 1st Brigade.

It is not known precisely when Nivar was inspired to build an independent unit around Santo Domingo and link this source of politico-military strength with the wide net of military contacts he already had in the interior, but, undoubtedly, the humiliations that he had been subjected to at the hands of Wessin y Wessin prior to 1965 must have influenced him. In 1967, the 1st Brigade did not have the armor and artillery that had made the CEFA a threat to Wessin's enemies, but it would be misleading to suggest that before Nivar took command the unit was without any military clout. When he became the commander of the 1st Brigade, it had already had training and materiel support from the U.S. Army for over one year as part of Washington's military assistance policy to provide security for the June 1966 elections and July 1966 installation of the new president. In October 1966, the public had been informed that the 1st Brigade "will become the country's elite unit."[69] But the Colonel desired more. His organization would have to have the capabilities of the old CEFA—it must be the final arbiter on any political issue in the Dominican Republic. To accomplish his goal, Nivar had to reach the following objectives with the 1st Brigade:

The actual chain of command must be directly from Balaguer to Nivar.
The Brigade's commanders must be loyal to Nivar and opposed to his enemies.
The Brigade staff would require at least one professionally-oriented member to handle military matters.
The junior officers and enlisted men must be dependent on Nivar personally.
The armament must be increased.
The advisers from the U.S. MAAG must be won over.

From the outset, Nivar dealt directly with the President. It was apparent that when Balaguer departed for the April 11–14, 1967, Punta del

Este conference in Uruguay, Nivar had the impression that the security of Santo Domingo, thus the nation, was his responsibility.[70] For as long as General Pérez Guillén was chief of staff of the Army, the 1st Brigade commander ignored him. Nivar either refused to obey, or arbitrarily changed, orders that came down from Army headquarters.[71] General Pérez y Pérez had no intention of allowing Nivar to treat him in the same manner; however, he did not take a stand on the issue immediately. Initially, the secretary of state of the armed forces attempted to consolidate his authority in other sectors of the Army and with the leaders of the Air Force and Navy (as well as to gain the support of the U.S. Embassy).[72]

Acquiring loyal battalion and company commanders who had the same outlook on the Brigade's political role as did Nivar was not a rapid process, but, ultimately, the Colonel was successful. His first pro-Nivar battalion commander was Lieutenant Colonel Pérez Aponte, who was assigned to the 3rd Battalion in San Cristóbal on September 6, 1967. This appointment was important because Nivar considered San Cristóbal his personal fiefdom. The 3rd Battalion had an additional company with constabulary responsibilities; the installations in Baní and in Haina, as well as Fort *General Antonio Duvergé* (formerly Fort *Generalísimo Trujillo*) in the city of San Cristóbal, were manned by 3rd Battalion troops. Pérez Aponte had been an old San Cristóbal Group member and had commanded the unit at the outbreak of the 1965 civil war. After leading the 3rd Battalion a second time through 1968, he was appointed to the coveted post of *intendente general* of the Army on March 11, 1969. Pérez Aponte was replaced by Lieutenant Colonel José Napoleón "Papito" Pimentel Boves, an officer whose family had been part of local San Cristóbal politics during the Trujillo years. (As early as 1930–1934, Pimentel Boves' father, Don José, an Army colonel, had been *El Jefe*'s man in San Cristóbal, and Pimentel Boves' sister, Josefina, had been the province's governor in the 1950s.)[73] Nivar's brigade headquarters and his 1st Battalion were in Santo Domingo—after the officer commanding that battalion was relieved, Nivar had his own man, Lieutenant Colonel Luis Reyes Pérez, take over the 1st Battalion. Reyes Pérez was an uncomplicated officer who had spent the majority of his career in the provinces. The 2nd Battalion, located in the new *16 de Agosto* Military Camp, 25 kilometers northwest of the capital, was eventually commanded by Lieutenant Colonel Manuel Antonio Lachapelle Suero, a *Balaguerista* officer who had served under Nivar in the Corps of Military Aides.[74] Pimentel Boves, Reyes Pérez, and Lachapelle Suero were the backbone of Nivar's brigade. What was needed, in addition, was an accomplished staff officer who could interface with the American mission but would not be involved in the all-important, national political role of the Brigade.

One of Nivar's strongest attributes was his ability to select the appropriate subordinate for each task. To be his operations officer (S-3), he acquired Lieutenant Colonel Romero Pumarol, a U.S. Army Command and Staff Course graduate and former general staff instructor at the School of the Americas in the Panama Canal Zone. Romero Pumarol would be the perfect officer to handle purely military matters and to dialog directly with the MAAG on training issues. The fact that Romero Pumarol had been a key CEFA figure under Wessin did not deter Nivar because Nivar knew that his S-3 was desperate to attach himself to a new patron. The last important assignment to fill was the position of brigade intelligence chief (S-2). This sensitive post went to Captain Manuel Emilio "Nivarito" Nivar Pellerano, the Colonel's nephew.

To secure the loyalty of his junior officers and enlisted men, Nivar took a page out of Wessin y Wessin's book—he bought their allegiance. Nivar combined the traits of a good commander with that of a mafia godfather. First, he provided his men and their families with the best housing, medical care, and rations in the Armed Forces.[75] For example, during one Christmas at the *16 de Agosto* Military Camp, he turned over 50 newly built houses to his enlisted men. Each set of quarters had a living room, a dining room, a kitchen, three bedrooms, indoor plumbing, and a terrace. For corporals and sergeants who had been peasants before enlistment, this was a major event in their lives. During the same Christmas celebration, it was announced that the construction of a school and a medical dispensary was completed and houses for officers would be built.[76] Beyond these acts befitting a wise commanding officer was Nivar's use of special funds to distribute gifts in the form of money and to grant small loans, and, especially for the officers, to facilitate easy access to graft.[77]

Nivar recognized that if he were to reach the same level of politico-military power that Wessin y Wessin in the CEFA had attained, it would be necessary to acquire more weapons than what the Americans had provided as part of their security assistance program. The U.S. MAP-supported light infantry battalion did not include rifles; therefore, Nivar personally persuaded the President to approve the purchase of Belgian 7.62mm FALs manufactured in Argentina.[78] His requests for tanks and artillery; however, were less willingly received. Nivar's means of making his case would be through the Americans in the MAAG.

Colonel Nivar had been exposed to American advisers from the MAAG since 1963 when he was the Army's director of military training; however, according to U.S. standards, he had never developed into a proficient military officer. As a professional, he was deficient in both training and experience. Nivar not only lacked an adequate formal military education, he also had failed to participate in any of the Dominican armed conflicts that had occurred during his career. Nivar had not taken part in the military operations conducted against the anti-Trujillo 1949 coastal incursion at Luperón nor at the 1959 air and sea expedition at Constanza, Maimón, and Estero Hondo; he had not been utilized in the counterguerrilla campaign of 1963; and he was in exile during the1965 civil war. Impartial observers in his headquarters believed he could not even perform the basics associated with military planning and operations.[79]

Nivar was skilled, however, in selecting others with the appropriate credentials to represent his interests. It would be the MAAG that would become Nivar's facilitator in his drive to create the "new CEFA." The Colonel and his staff were tutored by his U.S. advisers on the value of the 1st Brigade's becoming a self-sufficient, combined arms unit. For example, a brigade needed to have artillery, anti-tank, air defense, and tank-infantry capabilities to be combat ready. Using the MAAG's information as justification, Nivar pressed for as much armament as he could acquire. He was able to add 4.2 inch mortars, 105mm recoilless rifles, and 20mm antiaircraft guns to the Brigade's inventory. In the case of field artillery and tanks, however, he was promised their support only when needed. Nivar then requested tanks to participate with his infantry in a training exercise and live fire demonstration. A platoon of armor was attached to the 1st Brigade for the project; and, after the field work was completed, Nivar refused to return the vehicles.

By December 1967, General Pérez y Pérez's patience with Nivar had been exhausted. On the 19th, he requested the President to relieve the Colonel of command of the 1st Brigade. The Armed Forces secretary told Balaguer that Nivar was attempting to make his unit an "autonomous command" like the former CEFA, and that Nivar refused to recognize the chain of command. General Pérez y Pérez informed the President that not only he, but also Pérez Guillén, the chief of staff of the Army, and other officers were "alarmed" by Nivar's actions. Allegedly, Pérez y Pérez informed Balaguer that if Nivar were not removed from the 1st Brigade, the secretary would resign.[80] The President's exact reply is not known, but it can be assumed that Balaguer mollified the General by promising him that the President would make the Colonel change his ways in the 1st Brigade.

If Colonel Nivar became more cooperative, it did not last for long. In mid–1968, Nivar was described by the U.S. Embassy as being "scornfully insubordinate to the Chief of Staff of the Army, and a bitter enemy of Secretary of State for the Armed Forces Major General Enrique Pérez y Pérez."[81]

Nivar's hatred of Pérez y Pérez was revealed once again when, in early August, the Colonel dispatched a letter directly to the President insisting that his superior, Pérez y Pérez, be removed. Members of Nivar's clique, such as General Alvarez Sánchez and Colonel Checo, also signed the document. In addition to the letter, Nivar's friends circulated rumors in the capital that Pérez y Pérez was to be sacked.[82]

The Armed Forces secretary did not take strong measures against the Nivar faction because he was convinced that the President was ignoring the Nivar demands. In a calm manner, Pérez y Pérez explained to U.S. military officers that Balaguer approved his policies, which were the following:

> Loyalty to the constitutionally elected president
> Promotion of an apolitical military
> Centralization of command[,]control and logistics support ...
> Support for Balaguer[83]

(The second item calling for an apolitical military was probably cited for American Embassy consumption. Pérez y Pérez most likely really meant: "refusal to support any political party except the President's political party")

General Pérez y Pérez's low-key methods did not mean he was not actively attempting to reduce the Colonel's influence. For example, on May 24th, the MAAG presented to the Dominican government a reorganization plan for the Army. A small part of this proposal was the U.S. recommendation that when the 4th Brigade at San Isidro was disbanded, its 4th Battalion in San Pedro de Macorís be assigned to Nivar's 1st Brigade. (Nivar had commanded in San Pedro de Macorís during the Trujillo regime.) General Pérez y Pérez objected to only one segment of the MAAG plan—the transfer of the 4th Battalion to Nivar. Accordingly, the proposal was altered to reflect that the 4th Battalion (which controlled the eastern sector of the Dominican Republic) would be subordinated to the Combat Service Support Command in the capital.[84] Small victories for Pérez y Pérez did not alter the overall situation, however. During that period, the American Embassy informed Washington that "Col. Nivar Seijas' command of the well-equipped and trained First Brigade and the apparent extension of his influence over other military officers and their units have generated considerable speculation as to the true nature and limits of his personal ambitions."[85]

The year 1969 began with the conjecture that Nivar was to be promoted to brigadier general and moved out of the 1st Brigade. Nivar had stated in response to questions concerning the promotion that he had been offered the temporary rank of brigadier general, but had declined it because he preferred to wait for a permanent promotion.[86] The truth of Nivar's answer is highly doubtful, unless the offer of promotion came with the proviso that Nivar would only be promoted if he relinquished control of the 1st Brigade. In any event, Nivar remained in command of the "new CEFA" and was not promoted until one year later.

During 1969–1970, the MAAG would inadvertently again provide assistance to Nivar at Pérez y Pérez's expense. Left to his own devices, Nivar would probably have been content to keep the 1st Battalion at *Fortaleza Ozama* and move his brigade headquarters to his political stronghold in San Cristóbal. Nivar favored this arrangement before the MAAG provided him with new military advice. The American recommendations were sound from a tactical and technical point of view: The 1st Battalion should be transferred from *Fortaleza Ozama* to the *16 de Agosto* Military Camp because, if it remained in the colonial, urban fortress, it could be rendered ineffective by a force much smaller than the 1st Battalion. It was militarily inappropriate, the MAAG explained, for a maneuver element of the 1st Brigade to be bottled up in a corner of Santo Domingo as had been the case with the *Cascos Blancos* during the 1965 civil war. In addition, it was pointed out that training would be far more efficient if it were undertaken at the *16 de Agosto* Military Camp where more space and equipment existed.[87] It followed that the best location for brigade headquarters would be with the 1st and 2nd Battalions rather than at *Fortaleza Ozama* or San Cristóbal. Nivar enthusiastically embraced these proposals. Whereas the Americans were thinking of the most sensible means to train and deploy a tactical light infantry battalion, Nivar saw himself at the head of a concentrated two-battalion force, with a third battalion in San Cristóbal, only an hour's motor march away. Wessin y Wessin had never had more than one infantry battalion under his immediate control.

General Pérez y Pérez strongly opposed the concept for obvious political reasons. The chief of staff of the Army, General Pérez Guillén, went along with the secretary (although he was primarily motivated by the simplistic conviction that it was traditional for the Army to man *Fortaleza Ozama*). For approximately one year, Nivar's opponents argued against the proposal citing the fundamental policy that it was essential to have one battalion stationed in the capital as a show of force.[88] A politically unsatisfactory compromise for Pérez y Pérez was reached by creating a mixed-service military police battalion to replace the Army's 1st Battalion at *Fortaleza Ozama*, thus providing the visual deterrence claimed to be essential within the city limits of Santo Domingo. The movement of 1st Battalion troops began in stages in 1970. General Nivar built new quarters for the arriving units and a headquarters for himself at the *16 de Agosto* Military Camp. (Nivar set up a desk in his personal office for his U.S. Army adviser.) The 15th Company, 1st Battalion, was the last 1st Brigade unit to depart *Fortaleza Ozama*.[89] General Nivar had won a significant victory in his endeavor to create the "new CEFA."

By the end of Balaguer's first elected term, General Pérez y Pérez had not been able to prevent Nivar from establishing a formidable politico-military base with the 1st Brigade at its core, but Pérez y Pérez (with Balaguer's decided approval) had formed a partial counterweight to Nivar through alliances with other officers. The most advantageous appointment for Pérez y Pérez came on September 6, 1967, when the President designated Lieutenant Colonel Lluberes Montás head of the Air Force.[90] The new parachutist brigadier general brought the airborne Special Forces Group, which was loyal personally to him, and the Air Force infantry, into the equation. This step was followed by Balaguer's appointing an opponent of Nivar, Colonel Cuervo Gómez, to be the commander of the Artillery Battalion, the unit in the vicinity of the capital which contained the Dominican Army's modern howitzers.

Nivar, however, had no cause for serious concern with the Lluberes Montás and Cuervo Gómez appointments. His own collaborators continued to be represented in the Armed Forces and National Police. On the same day that General Lluberes Montás was named chief of staff of the Air Force, President Balaguer designated the San Cristóbal Group activist Alvarez Sánchez chief of the National Police.[91] And woven into the fabric of the military institution were Nivar men to keep the 1st Brigade commander informed. The sub-chief of the Army would be Colonel Checo, the commander of the San Isidro Air Base already was Colonel Marmolejos, and the new Military Police Battalion at the *Fortaleza Ozama* was to be under the control of Colonel Jorge Moreno.

The shifting of the chess pieces to improve the balance of power did not usher in a period of relaxed tensions within the officer corps. Rather than a modus vivendi, agitation between Nivar and Pérez y Pérez continued. For example, in June 1968, the President appointed General Pérez y Pérez to lead a commission to investigate allegations of crimes committed by General Alvarez Sánchez's National Police,[92] and, in September 1969, the President, reportedly, directed Colonel Marmolejos to take actions in the Air Force without the prior knowledge of General Lluberes Montás, thus causing further divisiveness between the two factions.[93]

In the beginning of 1970, the scales were tipped in Nivar's favor when the post of Army chief of staff suddenly became vacant. The tragic General Pérez Guillén had tried to be supportive of General Pérez y Pérez, but he had been powerless against Nivar. On March 13th, at 4:00 A.M., Pérez Guillén shot himself in the chest in his office at Army headquarters. The suicide attempt failed, but he was unable to continue as head of the Army.[94] One month later, the President appointed Brigadier General Valdez Hilario to replace Pérez Guillén. Pérez y Pérez had not been in favor of the Valdez Hilario selection, but Nivar was delighted.[95] For the first time since Balaguer became president in 1966, Nivar had an ally who was a service chief.[96] (The Air Force had consistently opposed

Nivar[97] and Commodore Jiménez had remained neutral—the Navy was not capable of any other position. Nivar had contemptuously told his officers that Jiménez's strength consisted only of "children's toy boats."[98]) The new chief of staff and Nivar had similar roots—Valdez Hilario had belonged to the conventional Trujillo Army, he had been a senior provincial commander, and he had not been associated with the CEFA. The fact that Valdez Hilario had failed to graduate from the U.S. Army's Command and Staff Course in 1967 was not a detractor for either Balaguer or Nivar. Thus, as the presidential elections of May 16, 1970, approached, the Nivar-Pérez y Pérez feud was very much alive.

Traditionally, President Balaguer celebrated the arrival of a new year by making high-level governmental appointments and by promoting a select group of officers. The agenda for the beginning of 1970 featured the promotion of Nivar to permanent brigadier general. Nivar's opportunity to have national attention focused on him was diminished, however, because Balaguer had included an inordinate number of Nivar's enemies and rivals on the promotion list. Also advanced to permanent brigadier general were three ex-*Wessinistas*—Perdomo Rosario, Beauchamps Javier, and Lluberes Montás. In addition, a fifth officer received a general's star; Anselmo Pilarte was not a former CEFA officer, but for other, personal reasons, he too was a foe of Nivar. The commander of the 1st Brigade could take some small comfort, however, by the presence on the list of his ally from Valverde Province, Carlos Jáquez Olivero, who was promoted to permanent colonel.[99] Looking beyond the Armed Forces intramural aspects of the affair, Balaguer's opponents maintained that the President had sent a message to the nation. Legal opposition political parties and the extreme left interpreted the promotion list to signify that the President was preparing his military-civilian team for the reelection campaign of 1970.[100]

Other than General Pérez y Pérez's stock speeches that the Armed Forces were apolitical, there was little evidence that the military had been restrained from participating in partisan activities during the weeks leading up to the 16th of May elections. General Nivar and the 1st Brigade were especially visible during the campaign. Whenever the President traveled outside the capital, 1st Brigade motorized troops provided a cordon of security for Balaguer. The procedure was for Nivar's men to establish a perimeter defense around the town or village that the President visited. Planning and coordination were the responsibility of Nivar's intelligence officer, Captain "Nivarito" Nivar Pellerano.[101] These presidential caravans had the dual effect of intimidating the opposition and impressing the peasantry.

In addition to staging these swings through the countryside, General Nivar was an active campaigner himself. In this respect, he was in the company of many provincial commanders who came out strongly for Balaguer's continuation in office. This overt political support at times turned into strong-arm tactics used against members of the opposing parties. Protests were repeatedly filed against Nivar, Checo, and Jáquez Olivero, as well as three other Nivar supporters—Colonel Eligio Bisonó Jackson, the National Police chief in Santiago, Lieutenant Colonel José Almonte Mayer, the Army commander in Dajabón, and Lieutenant Colonel Darío Morel Ramos, the Army commander in Barahona.[102] General Pérez y Pérez did not escape the accusations of Balaguer's opponents. Ultra-rightists in opposition to the President denounced Pérez y Pérez for allegedly telling Air Force pilots at San Isidro that it was their duty to assist in the reelection campaign.[103] On April 7th, five opposition parties met and agreed on a communiqué that called for Balaguer to resign before participating in the May 16th elections. Included in the resolution was the demand that Pérez y Pérez, Nivar, and Checo should also resign; they were identified as "principal reelectionist elements within the Armed Forces."[104] (The officers ignored the charge.) Although there is no confirmed information that General Pérez y Pérez played a major pivotal role in the military establishment's push to reelect Balaguer, it is clear that he did not oppose the political activities of Nivar and his collaborators.

On the 16th of May, Balaguer was elected with 56.54% of the total votes cast. The U.S. Embassy stated that there were "undoubtedly isolated instances of electoral fraud and some pressure imposed…," but it concluded that "… the people had the opportunity to vote for the candidate of their choice."[105] There is no doubt that the Armed Forces and National Police contributed to shaping the outcome of the elections and that the most prominent Balaguer activist in uniform had been General Nivar. Although there had been a loose alliance between Generals Nivar and Pérez y Pérez during the campaign in that they both supported Balaguer's retention of the presidency, their rivalry had not abated, and it appeared that the commander of the 1st Brigade was continuing to gain strength.

VII

The Rivalry Continues

The beginning of Balaguer's second elected term saw General Nivar in the ascendancy while General Pérez y Pérez appeared to have been relegated to the side lines. On October 25, 1970, John J. Crowley, the U.S. Chargé, reported to Washington that Nivar "… is undoubtedly the most important military figure in the Dominican Republic today, " while, the Embassy continued, Pérez y Pérez has been "shunted aside" in a position that was weak both militarily and politically.[1] In forming his new cabinet, the President shifted Pérez y Pérez from secretary of state of the armed forces to secretary of state of interior and police. The latter post did not control the National Police or any other organization that exerted any leverage. Both Pérez y Pérez and Nivar had attempted to influence Balaguer in the selection of a new Armed Forces chief, but the President appointed Joaquín Méndez Lara, a member of neither faction and professionally inept. (Nivar spread the unlikely story that he had been offered the Armed Forces post, but declined it preferring to remain in the 1st Brigade.[2]) For the remainder of 1970, Pérez y Pérez, although still holding the highest active duty rank in the Armed Forces, ceased to be a visible player in the politico-military competition for power in the Dominican Republic. In contrast, evidence of Nivar's military and political clout in the second half of 1970 and the beginning of 1971 could be seen throughout the country.

MILITARY STRENGTH

In the capital area, Nivar commanded the 1st and 2nd Battalions at the *16 de Agosto* Military Camp and the 3rd Battalion in San Cristóbal, and his ally, Colonel Jorge Moreno, controlled the new Military Police Battalion at *Fortaleza Ozama*. The Presidential Guard Battalion and the National Police's infantry-type battalion, the Duarte Department, were nonaligned, while Nivar opponents commanded the Artillery Battalion and the Air Force's ground units at San Isidro. This distribution of force gave Nivar a slight edge, but what altered the balance decidedly was the new deployment of armored vehicles in the vicinity of Santo Domingo. The October 1969 transfer of armor to the Haitian border zone had left the capital with few tanks under any one commander. This picture was changed in September 1970, however, when Nivar refused to return the platoon of tanks that he had used in a training exercise and live fire demonstration during the first week of the month. Thus, the General had a total of two French-made AMX-13 tanks and six Swedish-made L-60D tanks in the 1st Brigade. To oppose him in Santo Domingo were four tanks in the National Palace and two in the Transportation Battalion—they were under the control of neutral officers. For the first time since Balaguer had begun his redistribution of armored vehicles there was one officer who had the monopoly of tanks at the center of gravity—the capital—and that officer was Nivar.[3]

Added to Nivar's strength in Santo Domingo was the fact that he had built alliances in the interior, a situation that Wessin had never enjoyed in the early 1960s. Even though this support in the country-side would mean little in a physical showdown for control of the country—that could only be accomplished in Santo Domingo—it provided Nivar with a psychological advantage which could not be ignored. The Army commanders in San Juan de la Maguana, Mao, San Francisco de Macorís, San Pedro de Macorís, Barahona, and Dajabón were all con-sidered Nivar's allies. They were Colonels Francisco Medina Sánchez and Carlos Jáquez Olivero and Lieutenant Colonels Rafael Grullón Hierro, Daniel Rosario González, Darío Morel Ramos, and José Almonte Mayer, respectively.[4] Brigadier General Juan René Beauchamps Javier, who, in the beginning of 1968, had taken com-mand of the 2nd Brigade in Santiago, was not firmly in Nivar's camp; however, in 1970, it was understood that they had come to terms and the former *Wessinista* was leaning in favor of Nivar. (The only major provincial Army commander not clearly linked with Nivar was Lieuten-ant Colonel José Antonio Rodríguez Fernández who led the 6th Bat-talion in La Vega. A review of his career, however, suggests that in a crisis he would have been inclined to support Nivar rather than Pérez y Pérez.)

ECONOMIC AND POLITICAL POWER

In the U.S. Chargé's report to Washington of October 25th, 1970, it was emphasized that General Nivar's strength went further than his control of Armed Forces units and personnel: The American Embassy communication stated that "Nivar had acquired wealth, position and political influence well beyond that enjoyed by any other military leader in the Dominican Republic."[5]

During Balaguer's first elected term, Nivar had utilized civilian advisers to assist him in amassing a personal fortune. Chief among them was the prominent businessman Salomón Sanz. He had aided Nivar in obtaining ownership of *Radio Clarín*, which had begun broadcasting in November 1969.[6] Another acquisition engineered by Sanz was an interest in the Perla Antillana racetrack. But by far the most impressive business venture was being negotiated for Nivar in the beginning of 1971. It was the opening of the Alas del Caribe airline which would connect Santo Domingo with eleven localities in the Dominican Republic. Four "Islander" two-motor aircraft were to be based at the new Herrera airport west of the capital, which was being built by 1st Brigade troop labor. The General had arranged for off-duty FAD pilots to fly the airplanes. When it became known that Nivar had holdings in Alas del Caribe, Dominican gossips immediately started saying that the General had bought himself a private air force. These projects, plus extensive involvement in government contracts, had made Nivar immensely rich. Part of this newly acquired wealth was sent abroad, in increments of $100,000, to be deposited in Nivar's foreign bank accounts.[7]

Although Nivar reveled in the role of a man of affluence, he above all desired to be recognized as a national political *caudillo*. By 1970, the General had inserted himself into the civilian political affairs of the country at the highest levels. As a *Balaguerista* party operative, Nivar had acted for the President in numerous instances. After the May 1970 elections, the General had facilitated a split in the opposition PQD by offering jobs in the new government to a dissident faction of Wessin's party. In September 1970, Nivar mediated between the administration and the *Movimiento Nacional de la Juventud* (MNJ), which had supported the President in the 1970 elections, in a dispute over patronage. During the second half of 1970, the General maintained important links with the opposition *Partido Revolucionario Social Cristiano* (PRSC) and the *Movimiento de Conciliación Nacional* (MCN).[8] There also existed evidence that Nivar was involved in certain political activities strictly on his own behalf. As had been revealed earlier, Nivar and Juan Bosch's PRD had been in contact since the early 1960s. It was suggested by the Political Section of the U.S. Embassy in October 1970 that the General respected the PRD's superior mass organization and saw it as a possible tool for his own political aspirations. The PRD, in turn, relied on Nivar to intercede with the government to prevent the persecution of its members.[9] On December 18, 1970, the American ambassador informed the State Department that the "opportunistic, power-hungry and ruthless" Nivar was engaged with the opposition "more than Balaguer has asked him to ... and more than Balaguer knows."[10]

Although Nivar's horizons were widening, in the end of 1970 and the beginning of 1971 he still did not appear to be a political entity in his own right. At that time, he was very much in Balaguer's shadow. His political views were ill defined and simplistic—for example, he considered all leftists to be Communists. (Dr. Santiago Rey Perna, a former Cuban minister of government and friend of Balaguer, and a close observer of Nivar, summed up the General at that time as having the "political intellect of a sergeant."[11])

Despite Nivar's lack of formal education and his hazy understanding of political philosophy, he excelled at being cunning and manipulative. Nivar felt very much at home in the intrigue and maneuvering of Dominican politics. Although adroit in furthering Balaguer's interests—especially within the military and police establishments—he had characteristics which would not help him as a popular figure among the civilian body politic. Nivar was a poor public speaker (as he demonstrated when his December 22, 1970, Christmas speech was broadcast live to the nation)[12] and he was ill at ease whenever he was with groups other than his own entourage. When surrounded by members of his clique, he most enjoyed being compared to Trujillo. (One incredible example of this occurred when he hosted an outdoor *asado* or barbecue for his officers—behind him at the head of the table were three musicians who followed the slightly intoxicated Nivar everywhere, to include the bathroom, playing the *Jefe's* favorite merengue *San Cristóbal*. The first line of the banned song stated that San Cristóbal was the *cuna* or cradle of Trujillo which, of course, was also the birthplace of Nivar.) His lack of skills necessary to succeed in elective politics did not prevent him from gaining some influence with the left-of-center PRD, however. The leaders of that party saw the advantage in maintaining contact with Nivar, and they made no secret of the fact that the PRD and Nivar had conspired together in 1964 to overthrow the government.[13] However, even though the PRD chiefs spoke well of him in public, they did not see him as a military reformer. When the leftist Uruguayan author Carlos María Gutiérrez visited the Dominican Republic in April and May 1971 and asked various left-wing politicians if Nivar could lead a progressive movement similar to that of Peruvian officers in 1968, the Dominicans were quick to disabuse Gutiérrez of that idea.[14]

There was little doubt that the General did not have the necessary attributes to be a successful figure in national public affairs, but he was an important player in the Dominican political ferment for one overriding reason: Nivar openly told many people that if Balaguer was unable to continue as president, the vice president would not succeed Balaguer because he (Nivar) would seize the government immediately.[15] He drove that point home in December 1970 when he boasted to the U.S. Army attaché that "The President is the President and I am the power."[16] Those *pronunciamientos* were significant in the beginning of 1971 because Nivar was totally capable militarily of following through.

BALANCE OF POWER RESTORED

In early 1971, Nivar's political and economic status would continue to grow, but the President would check the commander of the 1st Brigade militarily. The return to a more evenly balanced distribution of military power in the Dominican Republic would be accomplished by Balaguer's utilization of General Pérez y Pérez and his supporters.

The first step in countering Nivar's strength was to alter the deployment of armor in the capital area. As we have seen, in October 1969 the armored vehicles remaining at San Isidro were sent to Neiba and Dajabón in the vicinity of the Haitian frontier. In the end of 1970, the President appointed Colonel Cuervo Gómez the new commander of the Combat Support Command, thus giving Cuervo Gómez the Armored Battalion in addition to the Artillery Battalion which he already commanded. Colonel Cuervo Gómez was a serious military career officer who supported General Pérez y Pérez and disliked General Nivar. Cuervo Gómez's opposition to Nivar was based on the Colonel's distaste for Nivar's lack of integrity and professional qualifications. (Nivar, in turn, held the new commander of the Combat Support Command in contempt because Cuervo Gómez was an ex-CEFA official and made no secret of his Spanish Army staff college credentials and his intellectual accomplishments in the study of history, revolutionary war, and the law.) After taking over the Armored Battalion, Colonel Cuervo Gómez submitted a staff study recommending that his new unit's assets be concentrated in accordance with traditional tank doctrine. The President approved elements of the recommendation that would have an impact on the immediate Nivar problem. Accordingly, during the months of December 1970 and January and February 1971, a realignment of armor strength occurred in the Dominican Republic. From Neiba, thirteen armored vehicles, which included eight tanks (five AMX-13s, two L-60Ds, and one M3A1), were sent to Cuervo Gómez's Artillery Military Camp outside the capital. To complete the overall elimination of armor on the border, thirteen armored vehicles in Dajabón were transferred east to the 9th Battalion in Mao.[17] From a purely military point of view (which appealed to the American advisers in the MAAG), the Dominican Army had redeployed its armor so it could operate more efficiently with U.S.-trained infantry; however, the real objective was to terminate General Nivar's hegemony of tanks around the capital.

In December 1969, the President needed a tough-minded, resolute officer to take over the difficult (and thankless) post of National Police chief. The selection of Pérez y Pérez would fill this requirement, and it would provide Balaguer with the second step in restoring politico-military equilibrium in the capital. General Pérez y Pérez's control of the police *Cascos Negros* (the Duarte Department "infantry battalion"), plus General Lluberes Montás' Special Forces and infantry at San Isidro Air Base, and Colonel Cuervo Gómez's reinforced Combat Support Command, would be a significant counterweight to General Nivar's 1st Brigade and Colonel Jorge Moreno's Military Police Battalion. On January 1, 1971, Army Major General Pérez y Pérez took command of the National Police[18] and began the deliberate process of shuffling its officers so that the security force would be responsive to him.

The dynamics of the military balance remained essentially the same for the next ten months. During that period, the President made changes among the high-ranking officers of the Armed Forces, but the distribution of power was not appreciably affected. On the 12th of July, the President replaced General Méndez Lara with Commodore Ramón Emilio Jiménez, Jr., as secretary of state of the armed forces. Other than the fact that the naval officer commanded more respect than Méndez Lara, there was little of significance in the July appointment. The new temporary rear admiral did not bring anything additional to the high stakes game of politico-military power in the Dominican Republic. The transfer of General Lluberes Montás from Air Force chief to secretary of state of interior and police at first glance seemed important because he was giving up direct command of the ground forces at San Isidro, but Lluberes Montás still maintained a hold on that element of the equation through Lieutenant Colonel José Isidoro Martínez González, the commander of the Special Forces Group of the Air Force. They were close friends and fellow paratroopers since they had been together in the Spanish airborne school during 1959. (In March 1970, the two officers returned to the *Escuela Militar de Paracaidistas* as guests of the Franco government.) General Lluberes Montás was relieved by Brigadier General Juan Folch Pérez, a pilot since 1948 and chief of staff of the Air Force in 1966. Folch Pérez focused on airplanes and improving his own financial portfolio, not on the Air Force infantry. On the same day, Brigadier General Guarionex Estrella Sahdalá was returned to active duty after being cashiered ten years earlier because his brother had been one of the Trujillo assassination conspirators. Two weeks later, Estrella assumed command of the 2nd Brigade in Santiago. The old general soon made it clear that he wanted no part of the Nivar-Pérez y Pérez feud nor any involvement in the intrigues of the capital. Finally, on July 12th, the President promoted two Nivar supporters to brigadier general—Rafael de Jesús Checo and Marcos Antonio Jorge Moreno.[19]

The Nivar faction appeared solid if not predominant in the summer of 1971; however, internal friction had developed between Nivar and his crony, Army chief of staff Valdez Hilario. Under Valdez Hilario, the 1st Brigade was allowed to continue acting as an autonomous organization, but Nivar went further by presenting new demands to Army headquarters: Nivar wanted his unit's personnel strength to be brought up to authorized levels at the expense of other elements of the Army. The chief of staff was caught between Nivar and Valdez Hilario's G-1, Lieutenant Colonel Luis García Recio. García Recio was a bright, but arrogant, young former CEFA officer and a graduate of the U.S. Army's staff college course in the Canal Zone. He advocated an equitable distribution of resources throughout the Army. Consequently, García Recio pressured Valdez Hilario to exert his mandate as head of the Army by standing up to Nivar who, in theory, represented only a segment of the institution.[20] Although not an exceptional officer, the U. S. Embassy in April 1970 considered Valdez Hilario to be "dedicated and hard working and receptive to suggestions."[21] He lived up to this description. Valdez Hilario accepted García Recio's recommendations over Nivar's demands, and, on August 4th, 1971, this cost him his position. The 1st Brigade commander engineered the transfer of Valdez Hilario and the appointment of Checo to be Valdez Hilario's relief. Valdez Hilario spent the remainder of Balaguer's second elected term working on civilian frontier problems for the President with the rank of secretary of state.[22] The champion of the General Staff's authority to manage the Army's resources was less fortunate. García Recio was sacked along with his chief and, after eighteen months of meaningless jobs, was sent to Ecuador as military attaché.[23] With Checo as chief of staff, Nivar dominated the headquarters of the Army, although Balaguer prevented Nivar from extending his influence over the entire Army.

HIGHER STUDIES AND FACTIONALISM

It would not have surprised an observer in the Dominican Republic that leftist intellectuals, in the spring of 1971, categorically rejected the possibility that General Nivar would be willing to lead a progressive movement similar to the type advocated by officers in Peru. This disinterest in the Peruvian experiment on the part of Nivar was evident also among the members of his faction. Moreover, the same view was shared by Nivar's enemies in the Pérez y Pérez group. Opposition to the new leftist doctrine in Peru did not signify that Nivar's and Pérez y Pérez's cliques were inclined toward the contrasting, more rightist, concepts being developed in the Brazilian military. In realty, the vast majority of

Dominican officers in the early 1970s were oblivious to the politico-military innovations underway in both Peru and Brazil.

In 1950, Peruvian officers, inspired by their pre-World War II French Army advisers, established a center of higher studies named the *Centro de Altos Estudios Militares* or the CAEM.[24] This war college officially stated that one of its key objectives was "... to develop planning standards oriented to achieve the general well-being for all the nation's inhabitants in an environment of complete security."[25] To accomplish this goal, the students (who were colonels and civilians) were exposed to geopolitics, economics, agrarian reform, social planning, and development of the national infrastructure.[26] Critics of the CAEM, however, described the war college's impact as causing a "'leftward drift' of the officer class toward a neo-Marxist corporatist position on socioeconomic development..."[27]

Although the Brazilian Army had also been advised by the French military before World War II, its Armed Forces established the *Escola Superior de Guerra*, or ESG, in 1949, along the lines of the U.S. National War College with some important exceptions. Whereas the American institution focused on defense and foreign policy for an industrialized nation, the Brazilian war college emphasized internal development and security for a developing country. Another difference from the National War College was that civilians in the Brazilian student body would be drawn from sectors such as education, banking, and industry, as well as from government service. (Civilians who would not mesh well with the members of the class, such as leftist-oriented trade union leaders, were not accepted.)[28] The official charter of the ESG stated that its mission was to prepare "civilians and military to perform executive and advisory functions especially in those organs responsible for the formulation, development, planning, and execution of the politics of national security."[29] Like the CAEM, its counterpart in Brazil studied subjects such as economics, agrarian reform, sociology, and modernization of the infrastructure, but, unlike the CAEM, the ESG placed great emphasis on the vulnerability of developing nations to the Communist threat. The Brazilian officers were taught that their country was an integral part of the global cold war.[30]

When a coup d'état established military governments in Brazil in 1964 and in Peru in 1968, the two war colleges assumed special importance. Prior to the ousting of the two civilian administrations, the ESG and the CAEM had principally influenced only the officer corps of the two countries, but with the installation of military governments in Brazil and Peru, the two war colleges became an ideological force that permeated all sectors of society. By the beginning of the 1970s, many officers throughout Latin America were considering how the ESG and the CAEM could be relevant to their own nations. In the Dominican Republic, however, this attitude was highly unusual. Three colonels—Cuervo Gómez, Matos González, and José Ernesto Cruz Brea—were curious as to what had occurred in the Brazilian and Peruvian war colleges, but this focus was purely for intellectual reasons. (Colonel Cruz Brea, the Armed Forces intelligence chief, was a possible exception; the CAEM also interested him for counterintelligence purposes.)

The officer corps of the Dominican Republic was not totally unfamiliar with higher studies institutions. From 1963 to 1968, fifteen of its members had graduated from the Inter-American Defense College.[31] That senior service school was located in Washington, D.C. at Fort Leslie J. McNair, directly across the quadrangle from the National War College and the Industrial College of the Armed Forces. The Inter-American Defense College was founded in 1962 with the intention of providing Latin American colonels and lieutenant colonels, and their naval and aviation equivalents, a war college course of study similar to that of the U.S. National War College and the NATO Defense College. A prerequisite for military students was graduation from a staff college. (This requirement was waived for most Dominicans.)

The Inter-American Defense College differed from the CAEM and the ESG in that it did not concentrate on socioeconomic planning as did the Peruvian center nor on internal defense as did the Brazilian school. The official mission of the Inter-American Defense College was "to function as a military institution for advanced studies, with the purpose of preparing military personnel and civilian officials of the American States through the study of the Inter-American System and the political, social, economic and military factors that constitute essential elements for the defense of the Hemisphere."[32] More simply put, the purpose of the College was to foster the spirit of "Hemispheric cooperation." In the early 1970s, it was considered that optimum results had been achieved during the nine-month course if the graduates had had the experience of working together on serious international issues. It was understood that it was unlikely that Inter-American Defense College plans would ever be implemented, but the collaboration on formulating those plans by South, Central, Caribbean, and North American students would have a beneficial effect that would last years after graduation.

The Dominican Republic would discover another utility for the Inter-American Defense College: The various Santo Domingo governments of the 1960s found a place to exile politically undesirable officers. Among the fifteen graduates, one can identify key individuals belonging to four officer corps factions. For example, a leader of the pilots' clique at San Isidro Air Base, the troublesome Colonel Luis Beauchamps Javier, finished the Inter-American Defense College in 1964. He had been sent to Washington after the fall of the Bosch government. The politically active Colonel Alvarez Sánchez graduated with the class of 1965. He had been assigned to the College by President Reid Cabral because he was a San Cristóbal Group conspirator. (No Constitutionalists attended at the end of the 1965 civil war; they were considered too far beyond the pale to send to a course of study that lasted less than one year.) Alvarez Sánchez was followed by the most well known graduate in Dominican history. The former secretary of state of the armed forces in the Government of National Reconstruction, ex-Commodore Francisco Rivera Caminero, was exiled by President García Godoy in February 1966 and enrolled in the 1966–1967 class at the College as a *capitán de navío.* As that academic year was about to begin, the new president, Joaquín Balaguer, added the *Wessinista* Lieutenant Colonel Rafael Luna Peguero to the class. Luna was the last commander of the Artillery Group, *General Gregorio Luperón,* before it was disbanded as a part of Balaguer's purge of the 4th Brigade, the renamed CEFA.[33]

Balaguer would never have tolerated a CAEM or an ESG, but, fortunately for the President, the various factions within the Dominican officer corps were not drawn toward either war college's experiment in advanced studies. Thus, Balaguer never had to face a Peruvian- or Brazilian-type problem. The case of the Inter-American Defense College, however, was more complex for the President. He was never enthusiastic about the Washington-based institution, but he always wanted to cast the image of being an advocate of the "Hemispheric system" and of U.S.-supported projects. Therefore, Balaguer was willing to provide students to Fort Leslie J. McNair, but in limited numbers only. For the 1968 class, he sent merely one officer (who, the following year, was dropped from the Armed Forces). Three new annual *promociones* would graduate before a second Dominican attended the College.[34] When the President was queried by the secretariat of the Armed Forces as to whether he would have nominees in 1972, Balaguer responded that funds were not available, although the money had already been allocated. It was believed by observers in the National Palace that the President's reluctance to allow members of the officer corps to study at the Inter-American Defense College was rooted in his basic distrust of an educated, foreign-trained officer caste.[35] It was only after any danger from Wessin y Wessin's followers was extinguished that Balaguer allowed another Dominican to attend the College.

VIII

The Wessin y Wessin Question

Running parallel to the Nivar-Pérez y Pérez struggle was the adversarial relationship between the Balaguer government and retired General Wessin y Wessin. As during the 1970 electoral campaign, Generals Nivar and Pérez y Pérez found themselves working in tandem as part of the President's endeavor to render Wessin an impotent figure in Dominican politico-military matters.

Nivar's and Pérez y Pérez's past connection with Wessin had been decidedly different. In the case of Nivar, it was a virulent and acrimonious association. The former CEFA commander in 1961 had overthrown the Civilian-Military Junta, of which Nivar was a member, thus driving Nivar into exile. In 1964 Wessin had opposed the San Cristóbal Group and its most notorious operative, Nivar, which culminated in the 1965 forced retirement and deportation of Nivar. In the Balaguer presidency of 1966–1970, Nivar and the pensioned Wessin were not merely political opponents—Nivar was denounced for planning the assassination of Wessin.[1] In contrast, Pérez y Pérez had had little involvement with Wessin during the chaotic period between the 1961 end of the Trujillo family regime and the opening of the 1965 civil war. It was only after Wessin had discredited himself militarily, and Pérez y Pérez's Armed Forces leadership had become public knowledge, that their differences surfaced. And the contention between them was not personal, but rooted in the fact that Wessin represented the CEFA era in the Dominican Republic while Pérez y Pérez was part of two governments (García Godoy and Balaguer) which were anti-CEFA. There was no talk of Pérez y Pérez's wanting to murder or jail Wessin, only of Pérez y Pérez's policy to dismiss the most troublesome *Wessinistas* from the Armed Forces and to aid Balaguer in defeating Wessin at the polls.

THE WESSIN Y WESSIN LEGACY

Although General Wessin y Wessin devoted twenty-one years to an Armed Forces career, his impact on Dominican history was exclusively political. He left no positive imprint as a military professional during the counterguerrilla operations of 1959 and 1963, nor in the course of the civil war of 1965. If anything, during the last conflict, he gained a reputation for incompetence. It was from the fall of the Trujillo family in November 1961 to the beginning of the Constitutionalist rebellion on April 24, 1965, that Wessin y Wessin's influence on the political affairs of his nation was most evident. At that time, he was the single most powerful individual in the country solely because he was the commander of the nation's strongest military organization. In that position, his decisions and views shaped political events in the Dominican Republic to such an extent that no civilian government could survive for long without his support.

For seventeen years, Wessin y Wessin was an obscure member of the Generalissimo's military establishment before he was thrust into public view during the last days of 1961. On November 19th, while commanding the air arm's 3rd Battalion of infantry in Santiago, recently promoted Lieutenant Colonel Wessin y Wessin collaborated with General Pedro Rafael Rodríguez Echavarría in the expulsion of the Trujillo family from the Dominican Republic. The General made himself head of the Armed Forces and he rewarded Wessin on November 24th by giving him command of the CEFA. With the new post came the simultaneous promotion to permanent colonel.[2] The first Council of State was set up, but, on January 16, 1962, General Rodríguez Echavarría dissolved it and installed the Civilian-Military Junta. Two days later, Wessin turned against his benefactor by participating in the arrest and exile of Rodríguez Echavarría.[3] The Junta's successor organization, the second Council of State, was established in the shadow of the CEFA—thus began Wessin's quasi-political career.

Wessin y Wessin brought to his new command traits not normally associated with an officer in the Dominican Republic. (In fact, Wessin would have been more at home in Franco's Spanish Army than in his own.) Wessin rarely drank, he lived in a simple house, he did not womanize, and above all, he was deeply religious. Wessin's contemporaries, like most Latin American males, only paid lip service to the Roman Catholic Church. In contrast, Wessin y Wessin was a devout Catholic who practiced his faith out of conviction and expected his subordinates to follow his example. In the CEFA, he instituted mandatory Christian training for the troops, compulsory Sunday Mass, and three-day officers' seminars supervised by the clergy. Wessin surrounded himself with vestiges of his faith. His plain office at San Isidro had more than the expected number of religious symbols on display and, reportedly, his closest adviser was a Spanish Jesuit military chaplain.[4]

Wessin y Wessin also stood out in the officer corps as a rabid opponent of Communism. Wessin's views on this subject were far more intense than the simplistic anti-left/anti-reform position common with Dominican officers. For Wessin, his hatred of Communism bordered on fanaticism. American Ambassador Martin described Wessin's attitude thusly:

> ... anti-Communism was his whole politics—he knew nothing else whatever about politics and did not want to know. Indeed, he did not even regard Communism as a political matter, but, rather, as a moral or religious question.[5]

As with religion, Wessin's private ideological beliefs were translated into bureaucratic policy for the CEFA. Classes on the Communist threat were established for all personnel. These scheduled lectures were augmented by special presentations to officers in which Wessin personally instructed his audiences on the means to protect their troops from Marxist subversion.[6] Wessin also wrote numerous articles on the dangers of Communist exploitation. In one piece, addressed "To All my Brothers in Arms," in the *Revista de las Fuerzas Armadas*, he cautioned that a principal objective of Communism was to infiltrate the Armed Forces. His historical example was the pre-Castro Cuban Army which, he stated, no longer existed because of Communist subversion.[7]

Wessin y Wessin's unrelenting indoctrination on the virtues of Catholicism and the perils of Communism would not have left a lasting impression if they were all that he provided individuals in the CEFA. What made the difference between him and other commanders for Wessin's men was the tangible proof that he cared for the welfare of his troops. Although he was not an exceptional military leader, he did understand how to gain the loyalty of his subordinates. He increased the benefits that the already-privileged members of the CEFA received. Officers were granted homes, automobiles, and special perks, while enlisted men were the best paid, fed, clothed, and housed in the Armed Forces.[8] Wessin's solicitous behavior toward his soldiers was reciprocated—they provided him with a powerful massed force during the turbulent years from 1962 to 1965.

The second Council of State was the first Dominican government to receive protection from the CEFA. On April 17, 1962, Wessin was approached by a group of officers, headed by General Andres Rodríguez Méndez, who were plotting a coup d'état. Wessin was asked to join the conspiracy; instead, he reported the incident to the president of the Council, Rafael Bonnelly. With the CEFA behind the government, the rebellion was crushed before it had an opportunity to begin and the plotters were jailed. The CEFA had not been required to fire a shot.[9]

Other intrigues followed throughout 1962, but none caused as much

The French-made AMX-13 (May 1969). It was the most powerful tank in the Armored Battalion. From 1962 to 1973, control of the Armored Battalion was a key factor in the balance of power within the Dominican Armed Forces.

tension within the Armed Forces as the quest for a generalship by Trujillo's civilian assassin, Antonio Imbert Barrera, a Council member. From October to December, meetings in the military establishment took place to debate whether the commission should be granted and what would Imbert's responsibilities be in the Army and/or the National Police. The threat of a coup hung over these deliberations. For Wessin y Wessin, the significance of this episode was that the CEFA commander was treated during the conferences as an equal with the Army, Air Force, and Navy chiefs of staff, and that the U.S. Ambassador believed Wessin's final decision would determine the outcome of the controversy because Wessin "owned the tanks."[10]

The Council of State had selected December 20, 1962, as the date for the first free election in 38 years. Juan Bosch, the PRD candidate, encountered strong opposition from Jesuits and other priests, who, in the press, denounced him as a Communist.[11] Wessin y Wessin followed government policy and avoided taking an overt position during the campaign even though he was accused by two Council members of being involved in politics.[12] Bosch won and the obviously dissatisfied CEFA commander explained his silence the day after the election by claiming to his wife that he had performed his duty to the best of his ability.[13] As the Bosch presidency progressed, Wessin y Wessin's interpretation of fulfilling his duty would go through many transformations.

Charges that Bosch was implicated with Communists increased after his February 27th inauguration. This issue caused rumors to spread that military plotting to overthrow the President was underway. Wessin y Wessin put those thoughts aside in late April 1963 when Bosch proposed a military invasion of Haiti. As stated before, initially the Armed Forces chiefs were enthusiastic; however, they soon realized that they did not have the technical capability to mount the operation. Colonel Wessin y Wessin commanded only one-third of the forces prepared to invade, but it was he—not the generals and commodore who headed the Army, Air Force, and Navy—who confronted the President with the cold fact that the invasion could not take place.[14] Even though the Armed Forces leadership lost heart for logistical reasons, Wessin later took the personal position that the enterprise was opposed because Bosch allegedly planned to make public his new, controversial constitution while the Dominican citizenry was distracted by military operations in Haiti.[15]

With the Haitian affair behind him, Wessin y Wessin again turned to the threat of Communist subversion. Extreme leftists had become more visible in the Dominican Republic and Wessin had begun to focus his attention on their activities. He had established an intelligence service in the CEFA to infiltrate various groups which Wessin considered dangerous.[16] By July, the CEFA commander had lost all patience with the Bosch government's appearance of disinterest in controlling the Communists. On the twelfth day of the month, Wessin summoned the President and the military and police chiefs to a meeting at his headquarters at San Isidro. Astonishingly, Wessin's superiors, to include Juan Bosch, complied; the conference was held early the following day. Although a colonel among generals, an arrogant Wessin took the lead during the meeting. He presented Bosch with a list of demands for action against the Communists in the Dominican Republic. The President responded by stating that the officers present had ceased being apolitical servants of the nation, but were acting as politicians. Under those circumstances, reasoned Bosch, he could not continue in the presidency and would resign. The request was made that Bosch reconsider his resignation. The President responded that he would give it some thought.[17]

After the meeting, a furious Bosch concluded that Wessin y Wessin was the leader of the military opposition to his government and that it was necessary to send the Colonel abroad. The President lost his nerve, however, and decided instead to move against a chaplain, Father Rafael

Marcial Silva, who was close to Wessin. The priest, a captain, had been instructing young CEFA officers in political as well as religious matters. Another target identified by the President was a highly vocal, anti-Bosch Air Force lawyer, Major Rolando Haché Rodríguez. Both were cashiered on July 17th. On the same day, Bosch met alone with Wessin y Wessin in the National Palace. At that time, the President gave the Colonel his personal guarantee that Communists would not be allowed to take over the country. Wessin indicated that he was satisfied.[18]

The immediate crisis had passed, but the steady stream of information Wessin received continued to alarm him. Communist training centers (such as the Dato Pagán Perdomo school) were still operating and a leftist peasant militia under a Bosch crony was alleged to be forming.[19] Wessin's anxieties were further fueled by ex-Chaplain Marcial Silva, who had not stopped exerting influence over Wessin. Beginning on August 4th, the priest and other members of the clergy broadcast attacks against the President, which included accusations that he was a "Marxist-Leninist" and "Godless."[20] Rumors again began to circulate that the military, along with right-wing civilians, were engaged in coup plotting. The U.S. Ambassador prepared an assessment of the situation on August 23rd; he concluded that Wessin y Wessin would be the pivotal individual in any attempt to overthrow the government.[21]

During the first three weeks of September, the political environment in the Dominican Republic deteriorated rapidly. The nation's stability was further shaken on the 20th when rightist businessmen staged a strike in Santo Domingo with the goal of inducing the military to drive the President from power.[22] The Armed Forces minister and the head of the Army were reluctant to move, but, by September 24th, it was apparent that Wessin y Wessin, on his own, planned to end the Bosch government.[23] The President attempted to gain support in the Armed Forces for the sacking of Wessin by exploiting the fact that the Army resented the CEFA's dominant position within the military establishment. Although the Armed Forces minister and the Army chief of staff were tempted to go along with the transfer of Wessin to an assignment where he would not control the country's tanks, they ultimately decided to maintain a united front with Wessin. At approximately 2:30 A.M. on September 25th, Bosch was placed under arrest.[24] The next day Wessin y Wessin was promoted to permanent brigadier general.[25]

The government that Wessin and his cohorts created to replace the Bosch regime was made up of three "presidents" acceptable to the military institution. This junta, or "Triumvirate" as it was called, therefore had only one constituency—the Armed Forces. And within the Armed Forces, the power was the CEFA. Consequently, for nineteen months after the fall of Juan Bosch, Wessin y Wessin was both the protector and the enforcer of the executive branch of the Dominican government.

Although the Triumvirate was accountable only to the officer corps, some of the Triumvirs (membership in the Triumvirate changed occasionally) were committed to doing the very best for the people of the Dominican Republic. This spirit of public service was most exemplified by Dr. Donald Reid Cabral, a wealthy businessman. During the period when he was president of the Triumvirate, Reid felt it necessary to dismiss conspiratorial and/or corrupt officers. Reid relied on Wessin y Wessin to provide the muscle to his policy of cleansing the officer corps. The interests of the two men converged, although Reid's motivation was for the good of the Republic, while Wessin's was merely to eliminate his numerous enemies.

Reid began his presidency of the Triumvirate by replacing the head of the Navy, and, subsequently, by appointing a new chief of staff of the Air Force.[26] Neither case was controversial enough to necessitate a show of force by the CEFA. Beginning in September 1964, however, this situation changed. The San Cristóbal Group was actively plotting an overthrow of the government; therefore, Reid had to strike first. On October 1, 1964, he insisted that Colonel Nivar give up his command. Nivar resisted, but when the CEFA went on a war footing in support of the Triumvirate, Nivar backed down.[27] The following day, with Wessin y Wessin behind him, Reid sent San Cristóbal activist Colonel Alvarez Sánchez, the sub-chief of staff of the Army, to study abroad.[28]

Reid and Wessin y Wessin selected a new target in January 1965— they both decided to remove General Belisario Peguero Guerrero from the National Police. Reid wanted Peguero replaced because the police chief was notoriously corrupt and a political reactionary. Wessin y Wessin's motivation was that Peguero aspired to expand the National Police and provide it with armored vehicles, thus presenting a challenge to the CEFA.[29] Reid was slow to move, causing Wessin to let it be known that if the Triumvirate did not fire Peguero, he would send his tanks into the capital to get the job done. Bowing to this pressure, Reid issued the order relieving Peguero on January 18th.[30]

The San Cristóbal Group was still actively involved in anti-regime plotting; therefore, the Triumvirate president's attention returned to his original objective. Nivar was retired against his will on January 27th, and the San Cristóbal Group associate, General Félix Hermedia, Jr., was left without a position when his post as sub-secretary was abolished.[31] Also on that date, the secretary of state of the armed forces, Major General Víctor Elby Viñas Román, in a surprise move, was transferred to Washington as the Dominican delegate to the Inter-American Defense Board. Wessin's reason for getting rid of the minister, who had continually supported him since 1962, was a disagreement over who would assign CEFA personnel. Viñas Román had had the temerity to replace three lieutenant colonels in Wessin y Wessin's command without Wessin's concurrence.[32] The end of Reid's and Wessin's purge came on February 17th when the chief of staff of the Army, General Montás Guerrero, was sacked, and the ex-police chief Peguero was forcibly retired.[33] No member of the high command who had overthrown Juan Bosch on September 25, 1963, remained. Of the senior conspirators, Wessin y Wessin was the sole survivor.

From 1962 to the rebellion of April 24, 1965, Wessin y Wessin had run roughshod over the various factions of the Armed Forces. His arrogance in dealing with the Army, of which the San Cristóbal Group was only a part; with the Air Force's pilots; with naval officers; and, outside the military, with the National Police; had resulted in deep-seeded resentment of the CEFA commander. Consequently, when the Constitutionalist revolt began, there were few officers, other than those in the CEFA, who were willing to offer Wessin any cooperation.

The civil war not only revealed Wessin's inability to gather allies to his side, it also exposed Wessin y Wessin for actually what he was—a military incompetent. Since 1962, he had been free to utilize the CEFA as a cudgel to intimidate opponents, but he never had been called upon to exercise command of the CEFA while shots were being fired in anger. (The only time he had been in a dangerous situation, according to General Rodríguez Echavarría, was when a nervous Wessin almost lost control of his own pistol while attempting to arrest the General.[34]) When the opportunity finally arose for him to lead in combat at the Duarte Bridge, he remained safely in his office at San Isidro. The failure of the CEFA to hold its positions on the western approach of the bridge and to quell rapidly the insurrection in Santo Domingo marked the beginning of his steady decline as a professional officer. By the end of the civil war, he had become militarily irrelevant.

WESSIN Y WESSIN AND BALAGUER

A review of Wessin y Wessin's public life from his expulsion by U.S. troops on September 9, 1965, to his humiliation before the entire nation by President Balaguer on June 30, 1971, can only be characterized as pathetic. During his forced departure from Santo Domingo, the American and Brazilian commanders, who were attempting to ease Wessin out of the country, informed him that the Dominican government had appointed him consul general in Miami.[35] On September 10th in Florida, Wessin wrote a bitter letter to provisional President García Godoy in which he refused to accept the post of consul general and declared that the official Washington foreign policy establishment was infiltrated with Communists.[36] On October 1st, Wessin testified before a U.S. Senate subcommittee on the events that had transpired during the 1965 civil war. In his testimony, he accused a wide assortment of Dominicans, to include oligarchic President García Godoy, of being Communists. (Later he denounced Balaguer as a Communist sympathizer.)[37] The September 10th letter and the subsequent Congressional hearing set the tone of Wessin's next three years in exile.

While General Wessin suffered the inconveniences of exile, a small number of his supporters in the 4th Brigade maintained contact and agitated for his return to the Dominican Republic. Coupled with this was talk of a coup and of a new junta led by Wessin. Undoubtedly, these rumblings contributed to the new president's decision to disperse the strike force of the 4th Brigade beginning in September 1966.[38] When, on the 5th of September, Balaguer announced to the nation that his plan was the "integration of the 4th Brigade into the National Army," he also informed his listeners that Wessin was to be appointed ambassador, alternate delegate, and military adviser to the diplomatic mission at the United Nations, but that he would not be allowed to return to the Dominican Republic at that time.[39] Wessin reversed his position of one year before and accepted the governmental appointments. The reality was that Wessin desperately needed the money that came with the postings. But, even though the retired general became an ambassador to the United Nations, he refused to move from Miami to New York City, and he never fulfilled his responsibilities as a diplomat.[40] Therefore, in southern Florida at the age of 43, the under-employed former "strongman" of the CEFA became an eager spokesman for anti-Communism and an aspiring *caudillo* waiting for a recall by an adroit president who always had opposed him.

Balaguer manipulated the issue of Wessin y Wessin's return carefully from 1966 through 1968. The longer Wessin was kept out of the Dominican Republic, the less opportunity the General had to organize a political opposition to the President. This delaying tactic was weighed against the possibility that Balaguer could create resentment against his government if he appeared unreasonable in denying Wessin the opportunity to return to his home and family. The controversy was kept alive by gossip that *Wessinistas,* with the ex-CEFA chief at their head, were plotting to overthrow the government. In the beginning of July 1967, a rumor heard in Santo Domingo was that military supporters of Wessin were prepared to seize the international airport, thereby allowing Wessin forcibly to re-enter the country. Balaguer publicly stated that the story was "pure fantasy"; however, he continued to have his security services monitor

Wessinista activities. A major approach to the issue was for General Pérez y Pérez to retire or dismiss the most active military conspirators and to isolate others who could become problematic.[41]

In an obvious effort to distance themselves from *Wessinista* activists, thirty officers who had past links to the former CEFA commander dispatched a letter to Wessin in Miami on August 12, 1967, allegedly for the purpose of alerting the General that anti-regime politicians wished to exploit his name. Undoubtedly, the letter, which was made public on August 16th, was a means for the officers to go on record that they were not plotting against the Balaguer government. Two of the signatories of the letter were Colonel Perdomo Rosario, then an inspector in Army headquarters, and Lieutenant Colonel Lluberes Montás, the new head of the FAD's Combat Support Command.[42]

The nature of the Wessin question changed dramatically in January 1968 when Wessin, in the United States, declared himself a candidate for the presidency in the 1970 elections. His new party, the *Partido Quisqueyano Democrático* (PQD), was recognized by the Central Electoral Board in Santo Domingo on January 19, 1968. After Wessin's announcement, PQD members stated that under the circumstances the retired General should be permitted to return home. One month later, at an assembly of the PQD in Santo Domingo, a communiqué was released demanding that the government lift the ban on Wessin's travel to the Dominican Republic. On April 14th, at a PQD rally in New York City, Wessin again called for his return, citing that the electoral board had recognized the party, thereby making his exile a violation of democratic principles.[43] Twelve days after the PQD meeting, the secretariat of foreign affairs in Santo Domingo issued the laconic statement that Wessin's status remained unchanged, and that the $1,350 a month which the General had requested for rent, salary, and expenses, was approved.[44]

The President attempted to reduce tensions concerning Wessin's exile by stating during a May 15, 1968, speech that "Former General Wessin ... will be able to return to the country in sufficient time to take part in the general elections of 1970. He will be given complete guarantees and the same opportunities as all other candidates."[45] Wessin was not mollified, however. The day following the Balaguer address, he informed a Santo Domingo newspaper (*Listín Diario*), during a long distance telephone interview, that the President was "violating the constitution when he enforces [my] banishment from the country."[46] The PQD in the Dominican Republic reiterated forcibly that theme for the remainder of the year.[47]

While the pressure built up for Wessin to be allowed back into the country, General Pérez y Pérez stepped up his actions against Wessin's supporters. On March 18th 1968, a circular from the secretary to the service chiefs was dispatched prohibiting former officers who had political links from entering military installations. This directive was aimed at PQD operatives.[48] From the United States, Wessin had been criticizing the secretariat of the Armed Forces for purging young officers who were sympathetic to him; moreover, on April 14th, Wessin broadened the target of his accusations to include Colonels Nivar and Checo in addition to General Pérez y Pérez.[49] On September 10, 1968, during a press conference, the President denied that 23 personnel had been retired for being *Wessinitas*.[50] Three days later Pérez y Pérez stated that there had been no political motivation for recent retirements. It was obvious that these comments fell short of being accurate. Among the officers affected were Lieutenant Colonel Ramón Tatis Núñez, formerly commander of the CEFA's Infantry Battalion, *Enriquillo*; Lieutenant Colonel Grampolver Medina Mercedes, the past sub-commander of the CEFA's Armored Battalion; Major José Antonio Fernández Collado, Wessin's adjutant in the CEFA; Major José Féliz Cuevas, a former tank company commander in the CEFA; Captain Rafael Marcel Holguín, an ex-CEFA artillery officer; and Lieutenant Carlos Miguel Wagner, earlier a CEFA platoon leader. Also included in the group were *Wessinista* Lieutenant Colonel José Manuel Martínez Polanco of the Air Force and Wessin's *compadre* Lieutenant Colonel José Ramón Puente Eusebio of the Army.[51]

On September 26th, retired Lieutenant Colonel Grampolver Medina addressed an open meeting of the PQD. To the members of the party, the veteran CEFA tanker, who had been wounded in the civil war, emotionally exclaimed that it was a "crime in the country for a soldier to be Wessin y Wessin's friend" and for that reason he had been dismissed. Medina accused the Balaguer government of "being ungrateful to those who struggled on Wessin y Wessin's side." He closed with the strong statement that "notwithstanding this ingratitude, the men of San Isidro made it possible for President Balaguer to return to the Dominican Republic."[52] These inflammatory words were broadcast nationally.

The end of Wessin's exile was finally announced during a press conference at the National Palace on December 11, 1968. Balaguer informed the newsmen that "by 10 January at the latest" the ban for entry into the country would be lifted.[53] After more than three years abroad, the once powerful general arrived at the international airport at 7:00 A.M. on January 12, 1969.[54] There were no spontaneous demonstrations of support from the barracks, to include the 4th Brigade at San Isidro. Any indication that the former strongman of the CEFA would be swept into power by his comrades of 1962–1965 was absent. In fact, 1969 would be another year of virulent rhetoric only. While Wessin's friends in the PQD lodged accusations against the Balaguer government, General Pérez y Pérez continued to isolate the *Wessinistas* in the Armed Forces. The one difference in the new year would be that Colonel Nivar would become more visibly involved in the anti-Wessin effort.

Six days before Wessin's return, his party accused former San Cristóbal Group officers (without identifying them) of forcing the *Wessinistas* out of the military.[55] On the 12th and 15th of February, the PQD became more vicious and specific. The first PQD communiqué stated that Nivar presided over a meeting in which the assassination of Wessin was discussed. In the second report, Wessin's spokesman provided details: On January 26th, in the Hotel Londres in Santo Domingo, Colonel Braulio Alvarez Sánchez, Nivar, and some civilians (to include a professional assassin) met to plot the murder of Wessin.[56] In the following month, retired Lieutenant Colonel José Alejandro Rodríguez Alba, the former CEFA press officer, began a PQD-supported public information campaign denouncing so-called "uncontrollable forces" for imposing a reign of terror on Balaguer's opponents. At first, Rodríguez Alba said that he would not identify the "uncontrollable forces"; however, on April 29th, the PQD central executive committee issued a formal communiqué stating that Nivar was one of ten military leaders who made up the "uncontrollable forces" and that Nivar and his officers at the *16 de Agosto* Military Camp were planning to kill PQD officials.[57] Colonel Nivar promptly denied the charges and made the statement that "never in my life have I thought of killing anyone."[58] (Those individuals who knew Nivar would surely have been amused at that remark.) On the 4th of May, Nivar wrote a letter, which was publicized, to the President requesting that Balaguer initiate an investigation to determine if he was guilty of the PQD charges. Three days later, the President told the press that there was not sufficient evidence to remove Nivar from his command; however, he would have the reported assassination plot investigated.[59] From the government's point of view, that terminated the issue. Rodríguez Alba continued his attacks throughout 1969, adding Colonel Marmolejos to his list of alleged assassins.[60] Although these unsubstantiated accusations appear ineffectual, it must be remembered that public opinion was already attuned to linking Nivar and Marmolejos with assassination schemes. The case of the 1967 attempted murder of Government of National Reconstruction president Antonio Imbert Barrera was a good example. The truth is hard to determine as to whether a Nivar plot to eliminate Wessin actually existed, but there is no doubt that General Pérez y Pérez had every intention of denying *Wessinista* officers the opportunity to have access to troops and equipment which could be used against President Balaguer.

In late August 1969, the political opposition claimed that orders had been prepared by the secretariat assigning three prominent former CEFA officers to posts abroad. The initial report stated that Lieutenant Colonel Romero Pumarol was to be assigned to Panama as a military attaché, Lieutenant Colonel Gildardo Pichardo Gautreaux was to have the same post in Madrid, and Colonel Medrano was designated the new delegate to the Inter-American Defense Board in Washington, D.C.[61] This information was only partially true. Romero Pumarol had returned from Panama on August 25th after two tours in the Canal Zone. He would eventually be accepted into Nivar's 1st Brigade. Colonel Medrano was indeed to be the new representative to the Inter-American Defense Board, but many factors had contributed to his assignment overseas. It was Pichardo Gautreaux who was potentially the most dangerous as a *Wessinista* operative. He had been a key member of the CEFA Armored Battalion and had commanded that unit in 1966 when the CEFA was renamed the 4th Brigade. Evidence indicates that General Pérez y Pérez was justified in creating a gulf between Pichardo Gautreaux and the Dominican tank force. Coupled with the possible assignment abroad of the three ex-CEFA officers was the rumor that General Lluberes Montás was to be replaced.

Because Lluberes Montás had been a favorite of Wessin and the parachutist was highly regarded by former young CEFA tanker, infantry, and gunner officers, as well as by paratroopers, Lluberes Montás had always been vulnerable to charges that he was conspiring with Wessin. It was advantageous for Balaguer's political opponents to keep that story alive (as well as for Nivar, who considered Lluberes Montás a competitor and an ally of Pérez y Pérez). The National Palace, on August 28th, formally denied that the head of the Air Force was to be replaced[62]; however, two weeks later, further speculation arose in Santo Domingo that Lluberes Montás had defied Balaguer's authority and was to be sacked. On September 22nd, the U.S. Ambassador explained to Washington that the most recent account of Lluberes Montás' alleged disloyalty was most likely untrue and was merely one of "several stories and rumors linking him to plots against the government."[63] The American Embassy went on to inform the State Department that the General had issued an open letter on September 13th reaffirming his allegiance to the President. (The letter had been approved in advance by Balaguer.)[64] Talk of the Wessin-Lluberes "connection" did not disappear, however. On October 3rd, the transfer of the armored vehicles that remained in San Isidro to the Haitian border area was interpreted by some to be a result of the government's fear that Wessin and Lluberes Montás were in collusion. General Pérez y Pérez informed the U.S. Embassy privately that Lluberes Montás was not the cause for the tank redeployment. Wessin's culpability was not denied, however.[65]

In the beginning of 1970, the secretary of state of the armed forces had to direct his attention to those Wessin officers who were already in retirement. Some of the newly pensioned *Wessinistas* such as José Rodríguez Alba and Grampolver Medina were easily monitored because they were very vocal in their support of Wessin's candidacy.[66] It was the covert political activity on the part of some retirees that required General Pérez y Pérez to take special action. Such was the case with retired Lieutenant Colonel Puente Eusebio, a member of Wessin's new "personal escort" or group of bodyguards. Intelligence reports had revealed that Puente Eusebio was involved in clandestinely purchasing large quantities of weapons from active duty military personnel. The matter was not handled through legal proceedings—Pérez y Pérez simply ordered Puente Eusebio's retirement pay to be discontinued. The PQD charged that the secretary had cancelled Puente Eusebio's pension because the retired lieutenant colonel was a part of Wessin's entourage, but Pérez y Pérez responded that the justification for his order was that Puente Eusebio had been involved in "subversive activities."[67]

Thus, when Election Day, May 16, 1970, arrived, the two enemies, Generals Pérez y Pérez and Nivar, had each contributed in his own way to debilitating General Wessin y Wessin. Although Wessin had campaigned extensively, he only received 13.24 % of the total national vote. Wessin had appealed mainly to ultraconservatives including *Trujillistas* and anti-Balaguer military men.[68] For one year after his failure at the polls, relations between Wessin and the government's senior officers remained bitter, but not violent. Before the August 16, 1970, inauguration, General Pérez y Pérez had to contend with the possibility that Wessin and his supporters would engineer incidents to mar the inauguration. As a precautionary measure, troops were posted visibly near the PQD candidate's home during the week of the ceremony.[69] And General Nivar, on July 30th, had to answer charges from Wessin that Nivar had removed Wessin's nine man Army security detail provided during the electoral campaign because Nivar supposedly intended to kill him. General Nivar countered that the armed soldiers were withdrawn because Wessin was conspiring to prevent Balaguer's taking the oath of office on August 16th.[70] After the inauguration passed without incident, Pérez y Pérez and Nivar became absorbed in other controversies. In the first months of 1971, both officers were focused on politico-military issues which did not relate to Wessin or his small group of followers. It was at that time that the former commander of the CEFA turned his attention to seizing the Dominican government by force.

In 1965 Wessin y Wessin failed as a military commander, in 1970 he failed as a legitimate politician, and in 1971 he would fail as a *golpista*. He and his supporters planned to launch their coup d'état on July 2, 1971,[71] yet when they were exposed on June 29, 1971, it was evident that their preparations were nothing short of absurd. The plan that Wessin had formulated for seizing power was weak and incomplete. He had not won over any military or police units at the center of gravity—the capital—nor had he gained the collaboration of any key individuals who could provide him with armed force or sway public opinion.

Wessin's plan was for a small group of *Wessinistas* to take possession of the National Palace with commandeered tanks, to apprehend General Pérez y Pérez, General Nivar, and Commodore Jiménez, and to broadcast a tape proclaiming to the nation that Wessin had assumed control of the government, the Armed Forces, and the National Police.[72] These paltry efforts could never have succeeded. Wessin would have faced the three battalions, with armor support, of Nivar's 1st Brigade. The battalion commanders were Colonel Pimentel Boves and Lieutenant Colonels Lachapelle Suero and Reyes Pérez; all were loyal to Nivar and had no past connection with Wessin. The ex-CEFA commander believed he had a better chance of success within the Armored and Artillery Battalions; however, their overall commander, Colonel Cuervo Gómez, though a former CEFA officer, admired President Balaguer, and was opposed, in principle, to the coup d'état as a means of acquiring the presidency. The potentially most fertile area for exploitation by Wessin was the ground force at the San Isidro Air Base, but the paratroopers would only obey General Lluberes Montás and, in Lluberes' Air Force, the remainder of the infantry would follow the airborne. In the National Police, the commander of the Duarte Department or *Cascos Negros*, Lieutenant Colonel Virgilio Payano Rojas, was considered to be in General Pérez y Pérez's camp. The Military Police Battalion at *Fortaleza Ozama* was under the control of an old San Cristóbal Group member, Colonel Jorge Moreno, and the Presidential Guard Battalion commander, Lieutenant Colonel Luciano Díaz, had been appointed by Balaguer in 1966, and was still the President's man. The conspiracy made almost no headway within those organizations. There were a few enlisted men in the Armored Battalion who were drawn into the plot, but none were in a position to do harm to the government. Also, Wessin was led to believe that he had support from some combat policemen in the Department of Special Operations, stationed in Manoguayabo, nine kilometers west of Santo Domingo; however, its commander, who had been in that position for five years, lived up to his reputation of always adhering to the legal chain of command. Major Pascual Féliz Fernández ensured that the DSO remained loyal in June 1971.

The one organization where the conspiracy took root was the *Centro de Operaciones de las Fuerzas Armadas* (COFA); however, the importance of the COFA to Wessin was highly overrated. The Center's charter was to be the Armed Forces' operations organization where information could be received and orders issued in an efficient manner to the three services and police throughout the country during a period of military or civil crisis. The establishment of the COFA had been a project of the MAAG—the U.S. security assistance program provided the communications equipment and advice necessary to set up the operation. The COFA had functioned effectively during the 1968 municipal elections, the July 1969 visit of Nelson Rockefeller to the Dominican Republic, and the 1970 presidential elections. During the 1970 electoral period, the chief of staff of the Army was designated the COFA director and the Center was augmented with trained staff officers. The capital was divided into 12 zones which all reported to the COFA.[73] This image of military efficiency did not accurately portray the Center during normal duty conditions, however.

The COFA was made up of a representative from each service (to include the police), communications specialists, and clerks. Since 1968, the practice had been to appoint to the Center a senior field grade officer who was either being punished or being kept from public view. Two delegates who had been assigned to the COFA since the 1968 municipal elections were Army Colonel Julio Calderón Fernández and Navy *Capitán de Navío* Moisés Cordero Puente. The high point of Colonel Calderón's career was his selection by Juan Bosch to be the chief of the President's Corps of Military Aides. In Balaguer's presidency, however, the kindly old gentleman had been relegated to the equivalent of internal exile—he was sent to the COFA.[74] Navy Captain Cordero also had complications in his past. In 1954, he was convicted and demoted by a court-martial for negligence and mismanagement.[75] Although he was able to rehabilitate himself in the first half of the 1960s, he was not acceptable in the mainstream Navy to Commodore Jiménez.

The Air Force representative at the time of the Wessin y Wessin affair was a different type of officer. Colonel Ramiro Matos González was one of the most outstanding professionals in the Armed Forces. He had been sub-chief of staff of his service, he had a reputation as a counterguerrilla operations leader, and he had a first class mind. On January 23, 1970, however, he would suffer a career setback while making a routine visit to a hospital in Santiago in his capacity as chief of the Air Force's North Command. There, he intervened in an enlisted men's brawl. In the scuffle, Colonel Matos accidentally shot a policeman.[76] For public relations purposes, he was relieved of his command and exiled to the COFA. While the other personnel in the Center appeared to have succumbed to the boredom of shift work in an organization where nothing of interest took place, Colonel Matos submerged himself in numerous intellectual projects. Among these tasks, he undertook an historical study of the Haitian-Dominican frontier, which included the preparation of maps going back to the seventeenth century, and he wrote a course on map reading. (The first article in this series was published in the Armed Forces *Revista,* or journal, in its August-September-October 1970 issue.) In short, the COFA of June 1971 was not the command center of the Dominican Armed Forces, but a sleepy backwater that was not scheduled to come to life again until 1974 when it would be given the authority and personnel to operate during the presidential elections. Wessin, apparently, was not aware of how impotent the COFA was when he attempted to recruit its members to his cause. Colonel Calderón and Captain Cordero joined Wessin's enterprise; however, Colonel Matos refused. The irony was that only Colonel Matos had been in Wessin's CEFA.

The other officer corps participants in the scheme to overthrow the government were not on active duty; consequently, they did not control troops, much less command units, in the Armed Forces. The most engaged in the plot were Grampolver Medina Mercedes, Ramón Tatis Núñez, and José Ramón Puente Eusebio. Others who were involved were José Alejandro Rodríguez Alba, Gildardo Pichardo Gautreaux, José Manuel Martínez Polanco, Miguel Veras Toribio, José Fernández Collado, José Féliz Cuevas, and Leopoldo Puente Rodríguez. And from the National Police, retired Major Julián Tirso Chestaro Mejía and Captain Joaquín Fung had also joined.[77] It was a pathetic roster of conspirators. There were no high-ranking individuals included, and General Pérez y Pérez had effectively neutralized the field grade officers by retiring them in 1968–1969.

From the outset, General Pérez y Pérez took the lead within the military and police establishments in rolling up the Wessin y Wessin conspiracy. In contrast, General Nivar was barely visible during the entire affair. Wessin's residence had already been under surveillance by Pérez y Pérez's men when police Sergeant Antonio Espaillat Núñez of the Department of Special Operations provided his superiors, on June 28th, with the most conclusive proof of the existence of a Wessin plot—the tape with Wessin's proclamation. The noncommissioned officer had been entrusted with the recording by Wessin with the instructions that the sergeant was to have it broadcast as soon as the coup began.[78] (How the enlisted man was to accomplish this task has never been made clear.) Arrests of *Wessinistas* were immediately ordered, causing the former CEFA commander to call a quick press conference in his home for the afternoon of June 29th. In front of a small group of newsmen, Wessin charged that he was targeted for assassination or deportation. He insisted that he was not part of any plan to overthrow the regime.[79] On the following day, at 11:30 A.M., Wessin was apprehended by senior officers of the National Police and taken to police headquarters in Santo Domingo. He was interrogated until 7:00 P.M. by officers from the upper echelon of the institution—one was Lieutenant Colonel Usino Osvaldo Guzmán

Liriano, an *hombre de confianza* (or "man of trust") of General Pérez y Pérez. During the interrogation session, Wessin admitted that he had planned and directed the conspiracy. He was then taken to the National Police chief's office for further questioning and, subsequently, General Pérez y Pérez, in person, escorted Wessin to the National Palace shortly before President Balaguer was scheduled to speak to the nation.[80] Even though General Pérez y Pérez had orchestrated the details of countering the coup, history would forever link Balaguer personally with the crushing of the Wessin y Wessin plot because of the President's televised perform-ance during the evening of June 30th.

Dominicans who watched Balaguer's speech on television that night would never forget the live drama played out before them. The physical setting in itself was riveting for viewers. At the head of a large confer-ence table stood the diminutive president in a dark suit. Seated to his immediate right, at the head of the table, was General Pérez y Pérez, the Chief of National Police, in Army uniform. To the President's left, also at the head of the table, was Wessin wearing a white shirt without a jacket or tie. Along the two sides of the table were seated the majority of the flag officers of the Dominican Armed Forces in uniform. The seating arrangement placed Generals Méndez Lara and Beauchamps Javier (sec-retaries of state of the armed forces and interior and police, respectively) in the first chairs, across from each other, on the left and right sides of the table. Then, according to protocol, were seated the sub-secretaries and chiefs of the services. General Nivar, further down the table, was almost unrecognizable.

The President remained standing as he denounced Wessin in the strongest terms. Balaguer described how Wessin had planned to over-throw the government and personally take power. It was explained by the President that "the right climate does not exist for such an adven-ture to be successful. We are not back in 1961, 1963, or 1965. Present cir-cumstances are completely different and [Wessin] has failed to see this."[81] While Balaguer continued to illustrate how Wessin was guilty of treach-ery, he would occasionally point to the seated Wessin who made no com-ment nor changed the blank expression on his face. Then the President played the captured tape provided by the police sergeant.

After the recording was finished, Balaguer went on to state that the government had other evidence proving that Wessin was guilty of trea-son. At that juncture, an unexpected twist took place in the drama, prov-ing that indeed the entire performance was live. The President called on Colonel Mario Imbert McGregor, the sub-chief of staff of the Air Force, to come forward and tell the nation what he had heard at the home of his cousin, Antonio Imbert Barrera, when Wessin had tried, unsuccessfully, to obtain support for the coup. The Colonel was unprepared for this remark and was embarrassed that he was being identified as an informant. He mumbled words to the effect that he knew nothing. Balaguer quickly stated that that was not what General Lluberes Montás had reported Colonel Imbert McGregor to have said concerning Wessin. The President then resumed his speech as if nothing had transpired. He explained how a military coup would be damaging to the country at a time when it was seeking political and financial stability. Balaguer concluded dramatically by reminding his listeners that in other times a conspirator would be placed against a wall and shot; however, he wanted to be humane. He then turned Wessin over to "his comrades in arms," with the instructions that they decide his fate before 10:00 A.M. on July 1st. Balaguer's final words were "General, I want you and the nation to know that I, as President of the Republic, guarantee your life and your safety."[82] Through the entire episode, Wessin had not said a word and when he was led away by police officers, reporters asked him if he had something to say; his reply was "no, nothing."[83] The humiliation of the former strongman of the CEFA had been complete.

The military leaders met immediately after the speech in General Méndez Lara's office one floor below the conference room. They quickly agreed that Wessin should be sent into exile again. A letter was prepared and delivered by them to the President the following morning with that recommendation and a strong statement of unconditional loyalty to Balaguer.[84] Twenty-one officers signed the document—the first name was that of General Pérez y Pérez, the thirteenth was General Nivar.[85]

For the President, the Wessin y Wessin affair brought many political gains. Wessin's involvement in the electoral campaign provided Balaguer with an opponent to his right, which tended to make the President appear more centrist. And the defeat of Wessin as a coup plotter gave Balaguer the image of resoluteness and courage. For the officer corps, the aftermath of the Wessin conspiracy resulted in a variety of reactions.

The Armored Battalion was once again the center of attention in Dominican politico-military matters. Some enlisted men were apprehended and others fled. (One of them, a tank corporal, sought asylum in the U.S. Embassy; however, he was politely turned away.) When the arrests first began, General Nivar drove into Colonel Cuervo Gómez's armor and artillery camp and took over the Colonel's office. Nivar sat down at Cuervo Gómez's desk and hurled insults at the ex-CEFA officer who remained standing in front of his own desk. The President, however, found no fault in any actions of Colonel Cuervo Gómez during the Wessin case. As a precaution, the Colonel took the firing pins out of his tanks' main guns and locked them in his safe.

Arrests in the COFA left only one colonel in the Center—Ramiro Matos González. On the first day after the roundup, he walked into the

COFA wearing the uniform of an Air Force brigadier general. One month later the new flag officer was appointed sub-chief of staff of his service.

The old sub-chief of staff, Colonel Mario Imbert McGregor, as well as others, would be punished for his inadvertent lack of support for Balaguer during the presidential speech of June 30th. While Balaguer was speaking before the TV cameras on that night, the majority of the Air Force's senior pilots were attending a reception at the retired officers club in honor of the new U.S. air attaché, Lieutenant Colonel Stanley A. Castleman. The television sets were on at the club when Colonel Mario Imbert McGregor gave the politically wrong response. A groan was heard throughout the dining area, and the sub-chief's brother, Colonel Alfredo Imbert McGregor, placed his hand across his face as if he were in pain. Although the sub-chiefs of the Army, Navy, and National Police signed the July 1st letter to the President, the sub-chief of the Air Force's name was absent. On the 6th of July, Colonel Mario Imbert claimed he was on a fifteen day leave[86]; however, on the 9th, the Air Force confirmed that he, his brother, another family member, and his *compadre* had been retired. All were colonels and pilots in the FAD.[87] During the President's weekly press conference on July 14th, Balaguer was questioned as to why Mario Imbert McGregor had been separated from the Air Force even though he was not involved in the conspiracy. Balaguer's answer was: "The uncomfortable situation which resulted from his appearance on a television program."[88]

At the same interview, the President was asked if the threat of a *golpe* still existed. Balaguer replied: "The possibility of a conspiracy always exists in the Dominican Republic. Conspiracy never stops here; danger never ceases, not for a day or even for an hour. One has to remain on the alert 24 hours a day and sleep with one eye open."[89] Dominicans were amused with the thought that the little president slept with one eye open; however, his attitude was reflected in many unseen ways. For example, Balaguer's need for assurances of loyalty after the Wessin y Wessin episode prompted him to consider closing the Schools Command at San Isidro because a large number of former CEFA officers were on the staff and faculty in that unit. He was eventually convinced, probably by General Pérez y Pérez, not to take that action, however.[90]

The Pérez y Pérez-Nivar rivalry was as intense as ever in mid–1971, but clearly the former had gained influence and public attention at the expense of the latter. The chief of the National Police had been the government's dominant official during the entire Wessin affair and his organization had been the major player. When the crisis was over, the police sergeant who had delivered the incriminating tape was commissioned a second lieutenant with duty station at the police academy, and there was extensive press coverage of the two National Police colonels who escorted Wessin on his flight to Spain and exile on July 4th.[91] On the other hand, Nivar's activities during the roll up of the Wessin conspiracy were limited. He tried to tie in a Navy incident, in which *Capitán de Navío* Luis Alberto Pimentel was placed under arrest in early June, with the Wessin plot. All that this accomplished was to embarrass Commodore Jiménez, who had taken disciplinary action against Captain Pimentel for apparently different reasons.[92] Nivar's verbal abuse of Colonel Cuervo Gómez also was meaningless. Cuervo Gómez actively supported the President throughout the tense proceedings and was one of three colonels commanding units who signed the July 1st loyalty letter that was sent to the President by the leaders of the Armed Forces and National Police.

IX

La Banda *and Showdown*

On October 14, 1971, the rivalry between the two generals had reached a flash point. The President, on that day, brought Nivar and Pérez y Pérez dangerously close to an armed confrontation. The events leading up to the near collision on the 14th of October were played out against the backdrop of the government's effort to eradicate left-wing violence by the use of the counterterror group popularly known as *La Banda*.

An explanation of the origins of *La Banda* should begin when General Pérez y Pérez was the secretary of state of the armed forces during Balaguer's first elected term. At that time, the Dominican Republic had been tormented by terrorist assaults led by members of the *Movimiento Popular Dominicano* (MPD), a Marxist-Leninist party that received some Cuban support. To blunt the escalating violence, a determined Pérez y Pérez, with the approval of the President, created in 1968 a rapid deployment unit with the mission of specifically going after individual terrorist leaders rather than entire organizations.[1] The number of personnel in the flying squad fluctuated, but it was usually made up of 12 officers and enlisted men. They were Air Force parachutists and infantry with commando-style training. Their chief was Second Lieutenant Joaquín Pou Castro. Although Lieutenant Pou was part of an established military family (his older brother Major Juan Pou, Jr., and nephews were all officers in the Army), he had had an unorthodox career beginning. In the early 1960s, Joaquín Pou had been an automobile mechanic in a government intelligence service. During the chaos of the 1965 civil war, he had been drawn into irregular warfare activities on the side of the loyalists. He eventually was appointed a second lieutenant in the Air Force infantry and received some basic special operations training. Pou gained a reputation for boldness and élan in the officer corps. By the time General Pérez y Pérez was transferred from secretary of state of the armed forces to secretary of state of interior and police, Pou's unit had had numerous successful, albeit legally questionable, operations. Most of the extremist leaders were either in jail, in exile, or dead.[2] (The most famous incident in the latter category occurred when, on July 16, 1970, Pou—by then a first lieutenant—and his men engaged Otto Morales, the head of MPD operations, in a daylight running gun battle on the streets of upper-class, residential Santo Domingo.)[3]

Although the MPD leaders were no longer operating with impunity in the Dominican Republic, they had been replaced by gangs of leftist-oriented thugs who roamed the capital at night committing atrocities against policemen and merchants. These hoodlums were not led by Marxist cadres, as had been the case earlier, but were unstructured and undisciplined.[4]

President Balaguer first chose Brigadier General Perdomo Rosario to restore order. On July 1, 1970, the Army officer was appointed chief of National Police in place of acting Brigadier General Rafael Guzmán Acosta, a career police colonel. The U.S. Ambassador reported to Washington on the following day that the selection of Perdomo was "part of most recent [government] effort to intensify campaign against leftist inspired terror and violence."[5] The inept former CEFA tank commander was unable, however, to curtail the violence that wracked urban neighborhoods. In late 1970, while Perdomo was National Police chief, there was a period when one policeman was being killed every day and the government appeared powerless to bring it to a halt.[6] On November 18th, Balaguer took the unusual step of openly criticizing his police force. He stated that National Police services were "completely inadequate," that ineffective personnel in the organization had not yet been dismissed, and that the National Police "must be made efficient to end the crime wave which is covering the country with blood."[7] On the last day of 1970, Balaguer turned to Pérez y Pérez—in a surprise move, the General was appointed chief of National Police. The presidential decree took the unprecedented measure of allowing Pérez y Pérez to retain his status of a major general in the Army while serving in the police brigadier general billet.[8]

The public only superficially understood General Pérez y Pérez's character when he became the head of the country's security forces. His commitment to duty, his self-discipline, and his control of his emotions (Dominicans called the latter having "English blood") had been commented on by the better informed, but what was not widely known was his utter ruthlessness. The General ignored the conventional wisdom that counterterror encouraged more terror, thus causing an unbroken cycle of violence. Moreover, he believed that counterterror could be organized efficiently. The usefulness of Pérez y Pérez's earlier creation—the Lieutenant Pou flying squad—tended to support this favorable view of counterterror in certain Dominican law enforcement and internal security circles. What was required in 1971, however, was a different type of instrument from what the General had utilized when he was secretary of state of the armed forces. Pérez y Pérez needed an organization that could sweep the gangs of toughs off the streets. Thus was born what came to be known as *La Banda*.

LA BANDA

Dominicans did not become aware of *La Banda* until April 1971. Before General Pérez y Pérez set his new counterterror program in motion, he began the purge of the National Police that the President, on November 18, 1970, had stated was essential. Through most of January and February 1971, police officers who did not meet Pérez y Pérez's standards were dropped from the institution or transferred to unimportant positions. The General filled the vacated billets with respected police professionals such as Colonel José Morillo López, a former chief of police, and Colonel Antonio de los Santos Almarante, an attorney. (These two officers were utilized as senior advisers to Pérez y Pérez.) The new chief did not attempt to resolve his problems solely with dismissals, however. As a top priority, he wanted to improve the Secret Department, the National Police's intelligence service (commonly called the *Servicio Secreto*), but he did not replace its chief, Lieutenant Colonel Luis Arzeno Regalado. Colonel Regalado was recognized as the best intelligence officer in the police, so Pérez y Pérez kept him on and gave him more resources—the Secret Department's manpower and budget were expanded.[9]

The large number of changes in the National Police provided Nivar with an opportunity to attack his rival. On the 19th of January, the General's radio station, *Radio Clarín*, broadcast an editorial criticizing Pérez y Pérez's new personnel policies.[10] On the same day, General Nivar claimed that he had accepted police Lieutenant Colonel Juan Bautista Germán del Villar as an officer in the Army's 1st Brigade. Germán del Villar had been removed by Pérez y Pérez from his post as chief of the Criminal Investigations Department and expelled (*cancelado*) from the National Police.[11] The President was forced to step in. On the 20th, Balaguer stated that the dismissal of "high-ranking police officers" was the National Police chief's responsibility and that the President "has given General Pérez y Pérez all the authority necessary to modernize the police."[12] Subsequently, Balaguer emphasized that point by remarking to the press that only the President could transfer Germán del Villar from the police to the Army and that he had not taken that action.[13]

While the top management of the National Police was being reshuffled, Pérez y Pérez also was making preparations to mount his counter-terror project. During the first week in January, Lieutenant Colonel Usino Osvaldo Guzmán Liriano was moved from the obscurity of the police detachment at the international airport to the center of police power—the General's personal office.[14] Guzmán Liriano had a reputation for courage during the 1965 civil war and was considered one of the most aggressive-minded mid-level officers in the National Police.[15] On January 26th, Guzmán Liriano was appointed commander of the Radio Patrol Department.[16] In addition to this important post, he, as an *hombre de confianza* of Pérez y Pérez, was given broad responsibilities within the entire police establishment. One of his new tasks was to provide the fledgling counterterror organization with operational support when it began its urban activities.

Because Lieutenant Colonel Guzmán Liriano and the Radio Patrol were to remain in the background of the counterterror effort, a liaison officer had to be appointed who would maintain full-time contact with the counterterror operatives. This job was given to police First Lieutenant Oscar Núñez Peña. The 40-year-old Núñez joined the Army at an early age and, according to one source, had been a member of the *Paleros*, a Trujillo strong-arm squad.[17] On October 21, 1970, he left an undistinguished career in the Army and transferred to the National Police. Reportedly, he was a bodyguard of General Pérez y Pérez before he was assigned to the counterterror program.[18]

The National Police's new "shock force" was made up of a motley assortment of civilian street brawlers, who were armed with nothing heavier than pistols. Mainly, they had past, low-level involvement with leftist groups (some were recruited while in jail), they were in their early twenties or younger, and they were unemployed. Thus, the $150 a month pay was a significant inducement. Approximately 400 youths joined. The formal name given to the organization was the "Anti-Communist and Anti-Terrorist Democratic Youth Front;" however, almost from the beginning Dominicans called it *La Banda*.[19] (In the Dominican Republic, the word *banda* was commonly used to mean a criminal gang as well as a musical band.) *La Banda*'s nominal leader was the former Communist Ramón Pérez Martínez.[20] He used the self-styled title of "director general" of the Front, but he was primarily known as "Macorís." (Other *La Banda* members also took colorful aliases such as "Frank el Loco," "Tony el Pelú," and "Carabina.")[21]

The initial purpose of *La Banda*, according to the so-called "April Plan," was to break up the leftist-oriented gangs operating in Santo Domingo.[22] One new recruit remarked that a police agent told him that "this is declared war against the Communists. The [teams] will be organized in all the *barrios* of the capital...."[23] *La Banda*, however, would expand its operations beyond Santo Domingo to most of the country's urban centers, and its targets would become highly diverse.

La Banda became operational during the third week of April 1971. Its first objective was to terrorize suspected leftists in public schools and the state-owned university. During *La Banda* raids, classrooms were trashed, teachers were intimidated, and students were beaten.[24] From the outset, it was obvious that *La Banda* thugs were connected with the National Police. Initially, they were seen talking with policemen; then, in the beginning of May, *La Banda* members started to apprehend individuals and drag them to police stations.[25] By mid–May, the assaults had spread throughout Santo Domingo, and deaths were being recorded. The political opposition, such as the PRD and the PQD, and university student groups made public complaints, but the President took the position that *La Banda* was not a monolithic organization, but numerous, independent ruffians who were guilty only of disorderly conduct.[26] On May 12th, Balaguer actually accused the opposition parties of using *La Banda* as a pretext to discredit the government.[27]

Throughout May, *La Banda*'s violence continued. On the night that Balaguer placed blame on the opposition, a university student association in the town of LaVega was ransacked and, on the following day, a union headquarters in Santo Domingo received the same treatment.[28] PRD offices in Santo Domingo were gutted on May 30th, causing ex-President Juan Bosch to make a well-publicized tour of the wreckage.[29]

Also in May, the Dominican Student Federation announced on the 26th that it had received a letter from Constantino Félix, the "secretary general" of the "Anti-Communist and Anti-Terrorist" group; in the letter, *La Banda* threatened to seize the entire Autonomous University of Santo Domingo with the help of "the glorious police and military forces."[30]

After the first full month of *La Banda*'s mayhem it was obvious that the scope of counterterror operations had gone beyond the original plan. Concern began to be heard from within the government. The secretary of state of education Víctor Gómez Bergés publicly revealed the anxiety of the country's teachers and principals; their fears could force the closure of the schools before the end of the academic year.[31] Another factor with which Balaguer would have to contend was General Nivar's interest in exploiting *La Banda* as a means to discredit General Pérez y Pérez.

Initially, Nivar used his station, *Radio Clarín*, to cast a shadow on the police chief's program. On May 14th, a story was broadcast that opposition and government personalities were joining together to ask the President to relieve Pérez y Pérez because of *La Banda*. Two weeks later, *Radio Clarín* relayed rumors that the National Police chief wanted a diplomatic post and also that he was under consideration for an assignment in Washington, D.C. at the Inter-American Defense Board.[32] During the same time frame, a tabloid newspaper in Santo Domingo published an article attempting to link MAAG officers and the U.S. security assistance program with *La Banda*, which was totally false.[33] Subsequently, General Nivar expressed an interest in talking with me, in my capacity as the U. S. Army attaché, at 1st Brigade headquarters. Presumably, Nivar's purpose was to send a message to the United States government (or, at least, to "the Pentagon" which many Dominicans insisted was autonomous). During that short meeting, the author was told essentially the following in earthy Spanish: "Listen, there have been no lies between you and me. Do not forget that I know how to kill Communists better than the negro Pérez y Pérez." Undoubtedly, in Nivar's mind, he believed he was strengthening his position at the expense of General Pérez y Pérez.

In June, the vigilantism of *La Banda* continued unabated. While the authorities refused to intervene, the "Anti-Communist and Anti-Terrorist" group kept up the same tempo of activity in the capital and began operations in San Pedro de Macorís and Moca.[34] Also in June, Lieutenant Núñez became more overtly associated with *La Banda*. He had been seen on several occasions with the police-sponsored thugs and he began to be identified as their leader, rather than just a liaison officer.[35] On June 7th, one of the toughs gave an interview to the press before entering the Mexican Embassy. Fernándo Aquino Maceo alleged that Lieutenant Núñez had ordered him to assassinate an anti-government newspaper editor and a union leader. According to the youth, instead of obeying the police officer, he intended to seek asylum in Mexico's embassy in Santo Domingo.[36]

During most of July, Dominicans were focused primarily on the Wessin y Wessin aborted coup; nonetheless *La Banda* continued to operate without a loss of momentum. For example, for three days, from the 14th through the 16th, the government's thugs terrorized the low-income neighborhood of Cristo Rey in the capital. Armed with pistols, *La Banda* beat its opponents then hauled them off to police stations. Members of Juan Bosch's party, the PRD, were subjected to the same treatment as were extreme leftists. Their homes were vandalized and their lives threatened. The former president, on July 24th, spoke out against *La Banda* and stated that the country had had enough of its crimes.[37]

When the bishops of the Dominican Republic attended their ninth annual assembly in the last week of July, they too added their voices calling for an end to government-sponsored violence. In the communiqué issued at the end of the bishops' conference, concern was expressed " ... over the constancy and institutionalization of violence" in the country, and "sorrow over ... the nonfunctioning of justice as concerns the abuse of force and disorder under [the] pretext of law and order."[38]

On July 26th, *Listín Diario*, the most responsible newspaper in the Dominican Republic, published an editorial strongly criticizing the President's support and tolerance of *La Banda's* excesses. The editorial further stated: "A government cannot have a gang of outlaws at its service.... We insist that the lives of these youths, who are instruments of one act of terrorism after another, be protected, but we also demand that they be stripped immediately of the immunity, protection, and encouragement they now have."[39] Balaguer refused to be swayed, however. During a routine press conference two days after the editorial, the President commented that there were several delinquent gangs loose in the country, but the press chose only to criticize one of them.[40]

It was routine for U.S. Ambassador Meloy to meet with President Balaguer to discuss issues of mutual interest. At one such meeting, on July 30th, the Ambassador brought up, on a "personal and informal basis," his concern over terrorism and counterterrorism "as well as over widespread instances of disregard for the law by the forces of public order" in the Dominican Republic. The envoy reported to Washington that he described the types of human rights violations that the press were attributing to the government, to include the connection between *La Banda* and the National Police. Tactfully, the Ambassador explained that "an unfortunate impression is being created which makes more difficult the work of those of us who wish to be helpful to the Dominican government." Balaguer responded by denying that any police support was being provided to *La Banda*. He stated, according to the Ambassador, that he (Balaguer) had "confidence in the honesty, integrity, ability, self-sacrifice and dedication at the risk of his life of General Pérez y Pérez, the National Police chief, who has greatly improved the security situation in the country and taken giant strides to correct the glaring deficiencies of the police force." The President then shifted the discussion to the "weakness and ineffectiveness" of the courts. Balaguer concluded his comments on an amiable note; however, he categorically refused to acknowledge that there was collusion between government forces and *La Banda*. Ambassador Meloy closed by again expressing his "deep concern of the impression being created in the minds of observers both at home and abroad of conditions in the Dominican Republic." Thus, on July 30th, the President was clearly aware that the U.S. government disapproved of *La Banda*.[41]

As in May and June, *La Banda*, in July, extended its arm beyond the capital. During that month, the "Anti-Communist and Anti-Terrorist" group launched assaults in Cotuí, Santiago, and San Cristóbal.[42] The foray into General Nivar's birthplace would alter the nature of the *La*

Banda affair permanently. After the San Cristóbal incident, *La Banda* would become solidly entwined in the Nivar-Pérez y Pérez struggle.

The controversy began on July 23rd when Colonel José Napoleón Pimentel Boves, the commander of the 3rd Battalion in San Cristóbal, received the report that 13 members of *La Banda* had entered the provincial capital and established a base of operations in a poor section of the town. He informed his immediate superior, General Nivar, who directed Colonel Pimentel to arrest the intruders. The *La Banda* thugs and their leader "Carabina," were incarcerated on July 24th in the Army jail located at 3rd Battalion headquarters.[43] Nivar's reason for giving the order was simple enough—he was furious that Pérez y Pérez had sent his people to operate in Nivar's personal fiefdom.[44]

Reaction to the incident quickly took on a life of its own. As early as July 24th, ex-President Bosch praised Colonel Pimentel for performing "an important service for the people."[45] Then, on July 27th, the Santo Domingo evening newspaper *El Nacional* claimed that Colonel Pimentel had stated that he took action against *La Banda* in San Cristóbal because the National Police was unable to maintain public order. At a press conference on July 28th, the President was asked how an Army officer could assume the authority to maintain public order. Balaguer responded emphatically that only the police had that responsibility. The following evening, Nivar made a statement for the record that it was he who instructed the 3rd Battalion commander to eradicate *La Banda* in San Cristóbal. On the 30th of July, Colonel Pimentel tried to repair the damage by telling the press that *El Nacional* had misquoted him and that the National Police was indeed competent.[46]

On July 30th, General Pérez y Pérez refused to respond to a newspaper's inquiry relating to the San Cristóbal incident, but, on August 2nd, he did answer the question put to him concerning his relations with General Nivar. He blandly remarked that there were no "personal disagreements" between him and the 1st Brigade commander.[47]

The issue was further complicated on August 2nd when the President dispatched Circular Number 1 to all members of the Armed Forces and National Police urging them to be alert to recent efforts of the extreme right and left to undermine their unity. In the circular, he cited a July 31st letter in which José Brea Peña, the respected PRD owner of *Radio Comercial*, charged that two police colonels were involved in a plot to blow up his radio station. Balaguer explained that Brea's letter went on to say that it would be wiser to seek protection from a high-ranking officer of the Army than from the chief of National Police, even though legally the police had the mission of maintaining order. Balaguer ended his official communiqué by writing that he was "profoundly disgusted" that certain Armed Forces officers have been the "instrument" in a conspiracy against the stability of the nation.[48] The U.S. Ambassador reported to Washington the following:

[The] communiqué appears to be directed at First Brigade commander Neit Nivar Seijas, whose recent statement publicly endorsing military commander Jose Napoleon Pimentel's arrest of 'La Banda' members in San Cristobal was widely regarded in press as challenge to police chief Enrique Perez y Perez and even to President Balaguer himself. Angered by Nivar's imprudent conduct and excessive free-wheeling, Balaguer may have decided to issue communiqué as means of reaffirming his authority and putting Nivar in his place.[49]

Two days after Balaguer signed the circular, the National Palace announced a series of reassignments in the Armed Forces. Colonel Pimentel was relieved of command of the 3rd Battalion and appointed the head of the *Armería* (Armory) located in San Cristóbal.[50] Although Colonel Pimentel had requested the move to the *Armería* almost two months earlier, the public view was that he was being punished by the President for arresting the *La Banda* cell in San Cristóbal. The American Ambassador sent a cable on August 5th to the State Department which stated: "... shift [of Pimentel] at this time is convenient for Balaguer given press' interpretation that President had criticized Pimentel's handling of La Banda members in San Cristobal. Nivar publicly endorsed Pimentel's arrest of La Banda members, hence latter's transfer should help President save face and avoid impression that Nivar had last word."[51]

The reason Colonel Pimentel wanted the *Armería* assignment was that it was a financially lucrative posting. General Nivar and the President had agreed earlier to the move, plus they expected Pimentel to continue his political work in San Cristóbal from the Colonel's new headquarters. What made command of the *Armería* desirable was access to the graft available from the products fabricated in the Armory.[52] Trujillo developed the *Armería* after World War II so that he would not be dependent on foreign armament suppliers. In 1948, an arms factory named the *Armería del Ejército* was established in San Cristóbal. By 1956, the industrial complex included factories to produce arms, munitions, and explosives. That year the entire establishment was renamed the *Servicios Tecnológicos de las Fuerzas Armadas*; however, Dominicans still continued to call it *La Armería*. Over 1,000 workers manufactured weapons like machine guns and the *Cristóbal* carabine, ammunition to include .50 and .30 caliber rounds, and explosives such as gunpowder and dynamite. To accomplish the latter, a modern chemical factory was built in Villa Mella, north of the capital.[53] When Colonel Pimentel took charge of the *Armería*, the capacity of the Technological Services organization was greatly reduced, however. The plant in San Cristóbal was partially closed and the grounds and buildings of the chemical factory in Villa Mella were in the process of being converted into the new home of Colonel Cuervo Gómez's Combat Support Command. Although the level of production seen during the height of the Trujillo era was gone, there still was sufficient money to be pocketed from the manufacture of items such as metal bed frames and cabinets as well as small arms parts and reloaded ammunition.

The August 4th transfer of Colonel Pimentel did not terminate the Nivar-*La Banda* episode. On August 9th, there was press speculation that Brigadier General Estrella Sahdalá was to take command of the 1st Brigade and Nivar was to be "exiled" at the Inter-American Defense Board in Washington, D.C.[54] Nivar was further embarrassed on the same day when Admiral Jiménez, as secretary of state of the armed forces, dispatched a memorandum to the chiefs of the services instructing them that they were the only military officials authorized to release statements to the press, and that could not be accomplished until approval was received from the Admiral's office. The secretary's directive indicated that the new order was to end the "disruptive" practice of officers' issuing public statements that did not contribute to the "monolithic unity" of the Armed Forces. The U.S. Ambassador explained in a cable to Washington that the Admiral's memorandum "was undoubtedly ordered by President Balaguer and represents indirect but pointed slap at Neit Nivar Seijas." The embassy message further stated "that the President was indeed angry with Nivar over his impulsive comments concerning the San Cristobal issue."[55]

Nivar, by the 9th, was unusually subdued after receiving constant criticism for over one week. He had withdrawn within himself and refused to meet with his normal political and press contacts. On the 10th, the President began to soften the sting received by Nivar. Balaguer met privately with the chastised general and assured Nivar that he still had presidential support. The American Embassy stated that Balaguer's objective during this phase of the episode was "to assert authority without alienating or humiliating Nivar."[56] In keeping with the President's change of approach, Admiral Jiménez attempted to reduce the appearance of friction by informing newsmen on August 10th that relations between the Armed Forces and the National Police were excellent and that the head of state had confidence in his field commanders.[57]

On the surface, the San Cristóbal incident did not appear to have had any impact on *La Banda* operations. From April through August 1971, over 50 leftists were reportedly assassinated by the "Anti-Communist and Anti-Terrorist" group,[58] and there were no indications that *La Banda* would be reined in. San Juan de la Maguana, Puerto Plata, and La Romana were added to the towns inflicted with the vigilanteism.[59] In Santiago, on August 5th, a radio station was taken over by *La Banda* and, two days later in that city, *La Banda* toughs attempted to break into a union office. In the latter case, police Lieutenant Núñez personally led the gang.[60] A report from Santiago claimed that Núñez also was demanding money from merchants for protection.[61] A prevalent sense that *La Banda* had almost become a permanent institution was strengthened when "director general" Pérez Martínez, alias "Marcorís," went on television on August 28th to charge that former President Juan Bosch was responsible for the country's violence,[62] and, subsequently, on September 4th, to explain that the "Anti-Communist and Anti-Terrorist" group was "a guarantee of national tranquility."[63]

September began in the Dominican Republic without a change in the President's policy concerning counterterror.[64] Despite the indignation of educators, the national press, the Church, labor leaders, legal political parties, and the U.S. Ambassador, Balaguer refused to restrain *La Banda*. This situation was abruptly altered during the second week of the month, however. Beginning in May, there had been some concern in business circles that the sugar quota allocated to the Dominican Republic in the U.S. market could be reduced by the American Congress. One month later the Agriculture Committee of the House of Representatives did recommend a reduction, but Balaguer believed that the final U.S. law would not be harmful to Santo Domingo.[65] When, on August 28th, a *New York Times* article, written by Alan Riding, described *La Banda*, U.S. Ambassador Meloy personally alerted Balaguer to the possibility that the National Police's illegal and brutal activities could affect American attitudes toward the Dominican Republic when the sugar quota was being debated in Washington. At the meeting, the President expressed his appreciation for the information, but he added one of his favorite phrases: "We do not live in Switzerland."[66] Balaguer's nonchalance apparently disappeared when the *Washington Post* and the *Wall Street Journal* published front-page stories on September 7th and 9th, respectively, about the government's use of terror.[67] These September articles (especially the one written by Kent MacDougall of the *Wall Street Journal*) had a profound impact on the President. The time had arrived to stop the counterterror program—further action against the left-wing gangs was no longer justifiable if the Dominican Republic's sugar quota was endangered. And, conveniently, the anti-government toughs no longer constituted a threat to public safety.

The President announced his new policy concerning *La Banda* during a special address to the nation on September 10th. Balaguer began his presentation by explaining why the U.S. sugar quota was essential to the Dominican Republic. When he moved to the subject of terrorism, he disingenuously described *La Banda* as an offshoot of the Marxist-Leninist MPD. According to the President, the schism in the MPD took place after the death of its leader Otto Morales. Policemen became involved with *La Banda* only because they were attempting to develop informants in *La Banda* so that those extremists guilty of crimes could be identified. The recruitment of *La Banda* members as sources of information made the National Police appear to be collaborating with the thugs. At that point in his speech, Balaguer stopped dissembling. He then clearly stated that he had instructed General Pérez y Pérez to dismiss Lieutenant Núñez Peña and to dissolve *La Banda*.[68]

On the same night as the speech, Pérez y Pérez placed a special 300-man police task force in the streets of the capital and, by the following day, approximately 250 members of *La Banda*, to include "director general Macorís," were in custody. In addition, the police chief relieved Lieutenant Núñez of his duties.[69] The National Police counterterror program was abruptly terminated.

Two weeks after Balaguer's address, an elated Dominican Republic obtained a substantial sugar quota from the United States.[70]

The President and General Pérez y Pérez proved that counterterror may have benefits if the rule of law, compassion, and the judgment of history are of no concern. In retrospect, the following is evident: The terrorist leaders of the extreme left were removed by the Pou flying squad, the leftist-oriented gangs were broken up by *La Banda*, and, at precisely the most advantageous time, the police officers and their subordinate *La Banda* thugs were closed down when ordered (thereby saving the Dominican Republic from the curse of autonomous death squads). In the end of September 1971, observers of Dominican politico-military affairs asked this question: Had the little doctor proven wrong the established U.S. view that counterterror begets more terror, thus creating a cycle of senseless violence?

THE FOURTEENTH OF OCTOBER

General Nivar's display of independence during the *La Banda* affair caused the President a degree of uneasiness. It became apparent to Balaguer that Nivar, once again, had accumulated too much military and political power. He had been the commander of the nation's strongest unit for the extraordinarily long period of four and one half years. And, as had been observed in the past, there was more to the General than just military strength.

Nivar's headquarters at the *16 de Agosto* installation had begun to resemble a renaissance prince's court rather than the command post of an infantry brigade. Routinely, numerous civilians passed through Nivar's office seeking favors or establishing contact in preparation for a later request. There were also civilian cronies in the headquarters building who provided knowledge of a specialized nature. Salomón Sanz continued to be part of the retinue as did other prominent businessmen such as the Spanish entrepreneur known to the Nivar following as "*El Español.*" Present also in the Nivar *camarilla* were personalities of questionable character with intelligence expertise such as "*El Coyote,*" a former Trujillo Military Intelligence Service (SIM) operative, and Dr. Frank Cabral, an *ayudante civil* of the President, who, independent of the National Palace, ran an intelligence service with a specialty in bugging telephones. It was not uncommon in Dominican society for a strongman to have these types of retainers in attendance; however, Nivar had added a new dimension to his circle of supporters. In addition to the General's military, financial, and intelligence advisers, Nivar began to utilize political and press counselors.[71]

Two of the most well known political consultants were the Cuban Santiago Rey, and an Argentine, Luis Ramón González Terrado. The former had been in Batista's cabinet and the latter had been an official in Perón's government. These two experienced politicians provided Nivar with shrewd advice although, in the field of international affairs and the economy, there may have been too much information for the General to absorb.[72] One example of Nivar's need for additional tutoring was seen when, at a social event in August 1971, a drunk Nivar attempted to repeat to the U.S. Ambassador what he had learned from Dr. Rey concerning the sugar quota. Nivar ended his garbled remarks by saying, in a hostile manner, that he knew the Dominican Republic would lose its sugar allocation to Cuba if Washington negotiated with Castro. When Nivar sobered up the following day, he sent three hand-carved humidors of cigars to the American Embassy with notes of apology. One box went to Ambassador Meloy and the other two were sent to the chief of the MAAG and the author. (No Dominican officer wanted to offend "the Pentagon.") It was obvious that Nivar would never be able to compete with Balaguer as a statesman or a diplomat, but the General, nevertheless, was honing his skills as a political operative with assistance from his Cuban and Argentine mentors.

More serious for Balaguer was Nivar's use of propaganda to embellish his public image. *Radio Clarín* served the General's interests overtly as did Nivar's associates in the press corps, who appreciated his openness with reporters. It was the covert use of newsmen, however, which caused concern in the National Palace. Nivar secretly paid reporters and columnists to write articles favorable to him and damaging to his enemies.[73]

Even though the President was uncomfortable with Nivar's activities as well as with the General's longevity in the 1st Brigade, for approximately one month after *La Banda* was terminated Balaguer took no action. Then, on October 9th, an act of violence in a poor section of Santo Domingo gave the President the pretext needed to curtail Nivar's growing power.

Before daylight, on Saturday the 9th, five youths were shot dead and their bodies were dumped in various sectors of the capital. They were identified as residents of the *27 de Febrero* neighborhood and members of the apolitical Héctor J. Díaz Sports and Cultural Club. Over the weekend, press sources passed on what they knew. They claimed that eight armed thugs, in two automobiles, had assaulted the five juveniles. The informants also stated that the assailants had belonged to *La Banda*.[74]

The murder of the five was not part of the government's counterterror program—as far as General Pérez y Pérez was concerned, sponsorship of *La Banda* ended on September 10th. But National Policemen were not uninvolved; in actuality, the Radio Patrol Department had continued to maintain contact with young slum dwellers in the area where the five were killed. Although a direct police connection was not obvious immediately after the atrocity, it would surface later in the month.

As expected, on October 11th through the 13th, political opposition leaders, student groups, and press commentators made strong protests against the government for bringing back *La Banda*.[75] The public outcry offered Balaguer the perfect opportunity to remove General Nivar from the 1st Brigade and, simultaneously, to score a political coup. Without any forewarning, the President, on the morning of October 14th, appointed Nivar chief of the National Police and Pérez y Pérez commander of the 1st Brigade. The transfers were promulgated in Decree Number1630 and were to be effective on October 15th.[76] General Nivar heard of his removal from the 1st Brigade in the same manner as the rest of the country—by the announcement of the decree on the radio.[77]

Although most Dominicans thought the President had punished Pérez y Pérez, the creator of *La Banda*, by replacing him as chief of National Police, Nivar had no illusions. Those better-informed citizens held their breath—would Nivar accept the reassignment or rebel? To appreciate the full significance of the transfer order to Nivar, one must be aware of what the 1st Brigade meant to its commander on October 14, 1971.

The Brigade was Nivar's source of power. Historically, Dominicans could not have imagined Wessin y Wessin's amounting to anything without the CEFA and, to Nivar, the 1st Brigade was his "new CEFA." As long as Balaguer continued as president, Nivar believed he would never lose control of the 1st Brigade. The General anticipated (and desired) to be appointed to a new position such as Army chief of staff or Armed Forces secretary, but he never expected the President to separate him from his politico-military base. Nivar always assumed that if he took up a new posting, Balaguer would allow the General to select his successor at the 1st Brigade, and that the new commander would be a member of Nivar's clique. That view was confirmed the month before when Nivar went on medical leave in New York. The President sent General Braulio Alvarez Sánchez, the sub-secretary of state of the armed forces for army, down to command the Brigade in Nivar's absence.[78] Alvarez Sánchez and Nivar had been closely allied since San Cristóbal Group days.

To Nivar, the appointment to head the National Police was not compensation for losing the Brigade. Since the President's inauguration on July 1, 1966, Balaguer had selected seven police chiefs. In the Dominican Republic, it was widely accepted that leading the National Police was a political dead end. It was often remarked that if a police chief lasted six months, he would inadvertently be burned. Consequently, Nivar interpreted the October 14th decree to mean he was stripped of his strength by turning over the Brigade to an enemy, and he was marked for political ruin by being assigned to the National Police.

After hearing the contents of Decree 1630, the General was stunned and then furious. During that morning, Nivar's military and civilian supporters began to congregate at brigade headquarters. Salomón Sanz remained close to the General while officers began to call for action. Lieutenant Colonel Lachapelle Suero, who replaced Colonel Pimentel Boves as commander of the 3rd Battalion, rapidly drove from San Cristóbal to the *16 de Agosto* Military Camp and rushed into Nivar's office. His first words were "*vamos al palacio.*" Other key officers took up the cry. The General was urged to give his approval for the rifle companies of the three battalions to mount up in trucks and race to the National Palace.[79]

Nivar at first said little. To give the order that his subordinates were calling for would be an act of open defiance against the President.[80] Nivar had to consider who would oppose him. Pérez y Pérez would lead his opponents. That General could count on Colonel Cuervo Gómez's armor and artillery. Also, the Air Force's paratroopers and infantry would be aligned against Nivar. General Lluberes Montás had the unconditional loyalty of the airborne Special Forces Group, and Lluberes Montás and General Ramiro Matos González, sub-chief of staff of the Air Force, together would be successful in leading the Air Force infantry. Nivar's collaborator in the Air Force, General Marmolejos, would be incapable of rallying any key ground unit at the San Isidro Air Base. General Jorge Moreno, another member of the Nivar faction, was in a pivotal position—he had the Military Police Battalion in his command at the *Fortaleza Ozama.* Nivar knew that Jorge Moreno would side with him against Pérez y Pérez, but Nivar was not sure what action the *Fortaleza*

Ozama commander would take against the President. In the National Police, General Pérez y Pérez could rely on Lieutenant Colonel Virgilio Payano Rojas, the commander of the *Cascos Negros* "infantry battalion." And, finally, the Presidential Guard under Colonel Luciano Díaz would obey Balaguer's orders.

Nivar could see that his chances of seizing power or of gaining any of his objectives through the use of brute force were not good. For Nivar to oppose both the President and Nivar's military enemies would be too costly for the General. The wiser course of action was to accept Decree 1630 and then consider new options. Consequently, Nivar began to calm his officers. He ordered any preparations to march on the capital to cease and for the normal routine in the Brigade to resume. The General emptied his desk and unceremoniously drove out of the *16 de Agosto* compound. Soon after, the U.S. Ambassador sent a priority "immediate" message to Washington stating that Nivar had "permanently departed from the First Brigade."[81]

On November 8th, the Department of State's Bureau of Intelligence and Research published an assessment of the presidential decision of October 14th in Santo Domingo, entitled *President Balaguer Outflanks His Critics*. In the document, the Department's intelligence office stated that the President's reassignment of Generals Nivar and Pérez y Pérez had "effectively deflated foreign and domestic criticism of police counter-terror tactics ..." and "... enhanced Balaguer's position vis-à-vis his two leading military commanders." The State Department's conclusions were that the President's actions "again demonstrated Balaguer's manipulative ability and his mastery of the Dominican political environment...."[82]

One month later, the American Embassy in Santo Domingo also conducted an analysis of recent internal affairs in the Dominican Republic. It was concluded in the review that President Balaguer's orchestration of the events of October 14th had been nothing less than "a masterful political stroke."[83]

X

Nivar in the National Police

The pattern observed in the public life of Neit Nivar Seijas had been for him to ascend to a position of dominance, to suffer a setback of his own making, to pass through a period of despondency, and then to go on the offensive forcing his enemies to react to his new initiatives. October 14th, 1971, would be different, however. Even though he had lost the 1st Brigade, Nivar's depression was short-lived. The General's first act against Pérez y Pérez, albeit purely symbolic, was on the 15th of October. The majority of the seven police chiefs appointed by Balaguer since 1966 had been Armed Forces officers. Because selection came without warning, some of these designees took office still wearing their Army uniforms. All but Pérez y Pérez changed into National Police garb a few days afterward. Contrary to custom, Pérez y Pérez never adopted the gray police uniform. For the entire eight and one half months in the National Police, Pérez y Pérez wore the uniform of an Army major general. This non-traditional choice of Pérez y Pérez was the subject of criticism within the ranks of the police as well as among leftists. The former were irritated because career police officers resented outsiders filling the only general officer billet in their institution. The latter charged that Pérez y Pérez wanted to "militarize" what should have been a civilian law enforcement agency.

Nivar realized the public relations value in being perceived as the opposite of Pérez y Pérez. He had his tailors stay up most of the night of October 14–15 preparing the police chief-designate's first rebuke to his predecessor.[1]

At 10:00 A.M. of the following day, Nivar was sworn in at the Police Palace by the President. They were surrounded by Nivar's enemies (Generals Pérez y Pérez and Pilarte), his allies (Generals Alvarez Sánchez and Marmolejos), and neutrals (Admiral Jiménez, Commodore Amiama Castillo, and senior police colonels). He was wearing a custom-made uniform of a brigadier general of National Police.[2]

THE NIVAR PURGE

Traditionally, the assignment of a new head of the police meant a modest reshuffling of key personnel in the organization. Pérez y Pérez's appointment in January 1971, however, had had harsher results—high-ranking officers were involuntarily separated from the institution. But Nivar's arrival at the National Police was even more dramatic. He began his "housecleaning" with not just mere early retirements: Nivar placed select unwanted officers under arrest.

First, Nivar obtained authorization from the President to reestablish an additional deputy position in his organization. This non-controversial action was followed on October 17th with the appointment of his closest senior supporter in the National Police, Colonel Bisonó Jackson, to fill the new *Subjefe Ejecutivo* post.[3] The expected personnel transfers had barely begun, however, when Nivar was provided with a justification to embarrass Pérez y Pérez by arresting officers involved in the *La Banda* affair. In less than one week after Nivar took office, a new picture began to emerge concerning the murder of the five Héctor J. Diaz Club youths. Where, initially, it was thought that *La Banda* members were solely responsible for the atrocity, it soon became apparent that police personnel were directly implicated. There was sufficient evidence in the on-going investigation for Nivar to order the arrest of Lieutenant Núñez Peña and to direct that Lieutenant Colonel Guzmán Liriano not proceed to his new assignment in Barahona. Núñez was incarcerated in the *Torre del Homenaje* inside the *Fortaleza Ozama* (where Christopher Columbus had been imprisoned) and Guzmán Liriano was sent to Santiago to await the results of the investigation.[4]

At 11:20 A.M. on October 21st, an official police communiqué was released stating that the investigation revealed that one police officer and five police enlisted men were responsible for the murders.[5] All were in the Radio Patrol Department. Of special interest to the public was that the accused officer, First Lieutenant Virgilio Antonio Alvarez Guzmán, was the son of Nivar's friend and collaborator, Brigadier General Braulio Alvarez Sánchez.[6] Thus, Nivar had what he needed to order the arrest of former Radio Patrol commander Guzmán Liriano as well as the lieutenant and the five privates.

In a flamboyant and well-publicized manner, General Alvarez Sánchez personally turned over his son to General Nivar at police headquarters.[7] For the following few days, Dominican officers exclaimed that General Alvarez Sánchez had performed a "Moscardó," referring to the Spanish Civil War incident in which Nationalist Colonel José Moscardó refused to surrender the Alcázar in Toledo even after the Republican attackers informed Moscardó that if he did not capitulate, his son, who was a prisoner, would be executed. (The difference between Moscardó and Braulio Alvarez Sánchez was that Nivar, early on, had assured Alvarez Sánchez that his son would be protected by Nivar.[8])*

Although Nivar appeared to be focusing his attention only on Pérez y Pérez's old Radio Patrol Department, his purge actually affected many elements in the National Police. Nivar's main objective was to build a power base within his new command. He began on October 18th with the police intelligence service. The experienced chief of the Secret Department, Lieutenant Colonel Regalado, was sacked and moved to a post in the extreme northwest of the country. Major José Reyes Batista of the *Servicio Secreto* was arrested and jailed in the *Torre del Homenaje*, and numerous lower-ranking personnel were transferred out of the department. The new chief, Rolando Danilo Martínez Fernández, was a junior lieutenant colonel with little background in intelligence.[9] The real power within the Secret Department was not Martínez, however. Nivar placed an *hombre de confianza* in the headquarters of the intelligence service. Ramón Henríquez Figueroa, or "Moncho" as he was called, had experience in covert security work during the Generalissimo's regime and he had become a political intelligence operative within Nivar's inner circle during the post-Trujillo years. At first he was simply known as Nivar's *ayudante civil*, but, eventually, he was recognized as the dynamo that made things happen in the Secret Department.[10]

After the police intelligence service, the unit that Nivar most wanted to reshape was the Department of Special Operations. Not long after the General took over the National Police, he directed that the DSO be moved into Santo Domingo from the interior and that it be armed with mortars and machine guns. For many Dominicans in the capital, the first time that they had ever seen Department of Special Operations policemen was when they mounted guard around Nivar's headquarters building. The changes in the DSO's mission and weapons were contrary to everything its commander of five years had been taught by his U.S. Public Safety advisers. Lieutenant Colonel Pascual Féliz Fernández protested to General Nivar that the DSO was established to be a rural counterinsurgency police organization, not a military unit. Its method of opera-

---

In Hugh Thomas, The Spanish Civil War (p.203), Colonel Moscardó is quoted as saying to his son on the telephone:" ... commend your soul to God, shout Viva España and die like a hero. Goodbye my son, ... " In the mid–1950s, the Dominican officer corps had been well informed of the Moscardó incident because El Jefe was quite taken by the Spaniard's act of defiance. During Trujillo's visit to Spain in June 1954, Franco arranged for the Dominican to tour the Alcázar at Toledo where he was received by the then Lieutenant General Moscardó. After Trujillo returned to the Dominican Republic, a series of articles on the siege of Toledo, entitled "El Alcázar, Periódico Diario," began in the August 1955 issue of the Revista de las Fuerzas Armadas, the Dominican military magazine. When General Moscardó died, Trujillo ordered that representatives of the Armed Forces and National Police attend a special mass on April 18, 1956, for the defender of the Alcázar.

tions, he explained, was to patrol the countryside in small teams, to gather information from peasants, and to utilize as little firepower as possible. Lieutenant Colonel Féliz Fernández was backed up by U.S. Agency for International Development officials from the American Embassy, but Nivar was not swayed. He transferred Féliz Fernández to Montecristi and assigned Lieutenant Colonel Francisco Báez Maríñez to the Department of Special Operations in his place. (Báez had been General Alvarez Sánchez's intelligence chief when Alvarez Sánchez led the National Police in 1968.)[11]

The Duarte Department of the National Police did not give Nivar the same type of problem that he had had with the DSO. From his first day in the police, the *Cascos Negros* projected the military image that Nivar felt comfortable with due to his background. When he was sworn in at the Police Palace on October 15th, the Duarte Department, in black helmets and combat boots, and shouldering rifles, paraded in infantry battalion formation in honor of the new National Police chief. Nivar's only requirement was to replace the *Cascos Negros* commander, Lieutenant Colonel Virgilio Payano Rojas, with an individual he could rely on politically. Once again, Nivar selected an officer who had served in a sensitive position in the National Police under General Alvarez Sánchez. Command of the Duarte Department was given to Colonel Julio Carbuccia Reyes, a former Army officer and a close personal friend of Alvarez Sánchez.[12]

The assignment of commanders who controlled military-type units and the police intelligence service was of first priority for Nivar, but there were numerous other posts to fill that were important to the new chief of National Police. For political reasons, Nivar had to appoint provincial police commanders who would support him, and for economic reasons, he had to select allies to place in financially lucrative positions. No less important to Nivar was his need to embarrass openly his archrival. Pérez y Pérez's highly visible police public affairs officer, Lieutenant Colonel Francisco Graciano de los Santos, was sent to the COFA, the equivalent of "internal exile." Two officers who had been forced out of the police (*cancelado*) by Pérez y Pérez were returned to active status. Eventually, Colonel Bolívar Soto Montás became the police's spokesman and Lieutenant Colonel Juan Bautista Germán del Villar was appointed Nivar's adjutant with the new rank of colonel.[13]

Dominicans were only mildly interested in Nivar's elimination of Pérez y Pérez's influence in the National Police—what appealed to them more was Nivar's policy of moving legally against the thugs who had been in *La Banda*. On October 17th, "Macorís," the so-called "director general" of the "Anti-Communist and Anti-Terrorist" group, was formally arrested,[14] and, four days later, Nivar announced that he was going to

prosecute *La Banda* leaders. The General invited any citizen who had
been injured or attacked by members of *La Banda* to present his or her
complaint directly to Nivar so that the police chief could personally bring
the guilty to justice.[15] "Macorís" faced a judge on October 27th and Nivar
informed the nation that any individual issued an identification card by
the ex-"director general" would be investigated and, if appropriate, also
tried.[16] The height of the police chief's campaign against the former
members of the gang came on November 2nd when 33 jailed *La Banda*
thugs were legally charged with criminal acts, with conspiring to commit crimes, and with disrupting the peace.[17] These cases subsequently
were taken over by the judiciary system. When public interest was
diverted to other issues, a judge released the street fighters claiming that
there was a lack of evidence to convict them.[18]

Key police figures involved in *La Banda* fared similarly to the hoodlums. Although temporarily incarcerated, they escaped any long-term
punishment. Lieutenant Colonel Guzmán Liriano was expelled (*cancelado*) from the National Police on October 22nd for "extreme negligence," but he was not held in jail. He was quietly appointed the
Dominican consul in Ponce, Puerto Rico, in April 1972, and, after Pérez
y Pérez became the head of the Army in 1973, Guzmán Liriano returned
to active duty in that branch of the service as a lieutenant colonel. He
was given command of the Transportation Battalion and was eventually
promoted to Army colonel.[19]

Lieutenant Núñez Peña lingered on in the National Police—first in
a cell in the *Torre del Homenaje*, and then on normal status in the provincial police unit located in Neiba—before he was dismissed on April 21,
1972. Shortly after, he was appointed vice consul in Ponce. He never had
the opportunity to be reinstated like Guzmán Liriano, however; he committed suicide on June 29th, apparently because of problems with his
wife.[20]

General Alvarez Sánchez's son, Lieutenant Alvarez Guzmán, was
detained in San Cristóbal's Army compound where he was provided a
comfortable apartment. The 3rd Battalion commander in San Cristóbal,
Lieutenant Colonel Lachapelle Suero, was a member of General Nivar's
and General Alvarez Sánchez's clique; consequently, there were few
restrictions imposed on the lieutenant within the military installation or
in the town of San Cristóbal, which was the ancestral home of General
Alvarez Sánchez as well as General Nivar.[21] On October 12, 1972, General Alvarez Sánchez, the sub-secretary for army, appeared to recipro-
cate—Nivar's son, Neit Nivar Báez, was commissioned a second lieutenant
in Alvarez Sánchez's service. (After young Nivar donned the uniform of
an officer, he received, for the first time, military training in the fundamentals, such as how to salute.)[22] In the same month, a court lifted all

impediments to Lieutenant Alvarez Guzmán's freedom—the justification cited was ill health.[23]

The significance of Nivar's purge in the National Police was more than rearranging the organizational leadership of the institution so it would be responsive to the new chief rather than to Pérez y Pérez. Nivar had slightly altered the distribution of power in the capital by adding the DSO to his side of the equation. And, most of all, Nivar was viewed by many Dominicans as the people's champion who had stood up to *La Banda* and to those uniformed men who had created the hated police counterterror unit.

THE FIRST THREE MONTHS

General Nivar began his tour in the police as a popular national figure. Although his paid propagandists in the media were partially responsible for his good image, there was no doubt that a sizable number of Dominican citizens were truly convinced that the new chief of National Police was a different type of general. To fortify this favorable picture of himself, one of Nivar's first acts as head of the police was to go into the slum area where the five youths were murdered. In those surroundings, he publicly gave his word that counterterror operations would cease.[24] This gesture was followed by numerous statements in October geared to reduce tensions with the populace and to blunt attacks from political opposition groups. On the 20th, Nivar issued the open order that police units would act within the strict limits of the constitution; on the 21st, he pledged to eliminate police brutality; on the 28th, Nivar praised the press for cooperating with the police, thus causing a decrease in terrorism; and, on the 29th, he commented that policemen whose official conduct was questionable would be investigated to determine if they had "the necessary qualifications to serve the people."[25]

In November, the police chief continued his public relations campaign. Two of his statements reported by his radio station clearly reflected the work of his political advisers. On the 3rd, Nivar remarked that if disorders were to take place at the Autonomous University of Santo Domingo, he would not act unilaterally, but would provide assistance to university personnel. And, on the 30th, *Radio Clarín* stated that the General believed that "Dominican citizens should be allowed to own books advocating any ideology." The station went on to explain that the police chief's policy was that Communist literature would not be seized by the National Police.[26] It was obvious to those who knew Nivar that *Radio Clarín* was being very creative in its reporting. The General had no use for the "libertine" authorities (as he called them) at the university, nor for the right of Dominicans to own books Nivar considered "subversive."

Despite the questionable sincerity of the police chief's public remarks, they were proving effective. In October, political opponents of the government responded by expressing their approval of the new head of the National Police.[27] The most startling example of this change of attitude was the commentary made by former President Bosch on national television. After severely criticizing President Balaguer, Bosch declared "that General Nivar Seijas can end the state of terror in the country ... since the brigadier general assumed his post there has been peace."[28]

By the end of 1971, Balaguer was quite satisfied with the results of his October 14th decree. Nivar was no longer the strongman of the 1st Brigade, and the General had relaxed the pressure on the President that had been brought on by the employment of *La Banda*. The fact that Nivar had increased his popularity since he had been appointed chief of the National Police did not overly concern Balaguer because the conventional wisdom in the Dominican Republic was that no police chief could last six months without being tarnished politically.

Meanwhile, Pérez y Pérez quietly took over the 1st Brigade, and began his attempt to convert it from Nivar's autonomous politco-military instrument into a properly integrated element of the Dominican Army. This effort did not signify that the Brigade would become apolitical, however. Simply put, Pérez y Pérez's policy was that the Brigade should remain in politics, but in a low-key manner and, of course, it should support only Balaguer—thus it must cease being Nivar's private army.

On assuming command, Pérez y Pérez began the expected personnel changes. As his executive officer, the General brought in his friend, Colonel Julio César López Pérez. In 1956, Pérez y Pérez and López Pérez had served together in the 1st Regiment, *Generalísimo Trujillo*; they were promoted to captain in that unit on the same day.[29] They had both transferred to the Air Force in the early 1960s and participated in the 1965 civil war in that service's ground force. During the first segment of Pérez y Pérez's tour as head of the Armed Forces, López Pérez was chief of the lucrative *Armería*, a dependency of Pérez y Pérez's office. Nivar's military operations director, Lieutenant Colonel Romero Pumarol, was "exiled" to the National Police as an Army liaison officer; he was replaced by Lieutenant Colonel Rafael Cornielle Montero, a 1964 graduate of the U.S. Army's Command and Staff Course in the Canal Zone and a former member of the Dominican General Staff. Even though Cornielle had the necessary background, the new brigade commander did not relinquish military affairs totally to his S-3 as Nivar had done with Romero Pumarol.[30]

Pérez y Pérez was not able unilaterally to make all the personnel changes he desired during his first months in the Brigade. Lieutenant Colonel Lachapelle Suero remained in San Cristóbal as the 3rd Battalion commander and Lieutenant Colonel Reyes Pérez continued as the commander of the 1st Battalion at the *16 de Agosto* Military Camp. (The 2nd Battalion commander, the adroit Lieutenant Colonel Figueroa Carrión, though selected by Nivar made a smooth transition to Pérez y Pérez.) The same situation existed at the company commander level—many of Nivar's captains stayed on in the Brigade. The result was that Nivar retained his imprint on the 1st Brigade even after he had departed. The police chief recognized this advantage and exploited it thoroughly. Nivar continued to visit the homes of his former officers and to attend their weddings and funerals. He also did not change his practice of passing out money to Brigade enlisted men who were in need. Nivar's combination of charisma and money when dealing with commanders and soldiers of his old unit could not be matched by Pérez y Pérez. Thus, the cold, aloof new brigade commander never became popular within his organization while the old commander retained a great deal of the loyalty he had built up in his four and one half years in the 1st Brigade.[31]

In the Dominican Armed Forces of Trujillo, it was not uncommon for officers to be transferred from national-level positions to regimental or battalion commands. During the dictatorship, they accepted this reduction in authority, and they continued to accept it under Balaguer. Although the precedent existed, it could not be overlooked that Pérez y Pérez appeared out of place as the commander of an infantry brigade after spending four years as head of the military establishment. Despite what many observers considered an awkward situation, the highest-ranking officer in the Dominican Republic did the proper thing—he efficiently went through the paces of commanding his three battalions. He encouraged training and maintenance, he looked after the welfare of his troops, and he participated in the military civic action program. Plus, in keeping with Pérez y Pérez's no-nonsense approach to command, he called a halt to the constant visits of political, business, and press personalities to the Brigade's headquarters. He also altered the nature of the relationship with his U.S. adviser. Under Nivar, the American Army adviser was close to the General; in the case of Pérez y Pérez, the interchange became what could be characterized as "correct." Major Burdick kept his desk in General Pérez y Pérez's office after Nivar left the Brigade, but, two months later, when that U.S. officer completed his tour in the Dominican Republic, the adviser's desk was moved to the S-3 section.

As 1971 closed, the two rivals were in curiously different positions. With the help of the press, Nivar was portrayed as the protector of the common man's civil rights and the advocate of governance in accordance with the law. Left-wing parties, such as Juan Bosch's PRD, were sympathetic to Nivar and were willing to express this view openly. To many Dominicans, Nivar was more than another Army general temporarily assigned to the police—he was a central figure in national political affairs. In contrast, Pérez y Pérez had dropped from sight. He was not seen in the National Palace and he no longer was the subject of constant media attention. His military duties as an infantry brigade commander proved of little interest to the average Dominican. Ironically, in the beginning of 1972, Nivar would further eclipse Pérez y Pérez—not in the role of politician or police chief—but on Pérez y Pérez's new turf as a tactical ground force military commander.

THE COASTAL ROAD FIREFIGHT

The extraordinary events of January 12th, 1972, began simply enough as a routine bank robbery. On November 8, 1971, a Santo Domingo branch of the Royal Bank of Canada was held up by eight individuals. Two guards were disarmed, the equivalent of $62,000 was seized, and the thieves made their escape by automobile.[32] Later in November, General Nivar revealed to the public the names of the suspects. Their leader was Dr. Plinio Matos Moquete, a lawyer and head of the *Grupo Plinio* faction of the extreme-leftist MPD.[33] (Among Matos Moquete's past activities had been, reportedly, a plot to assassinate the U.S. ambassador.[34]) On the 2nd of December, Nivar issued a communiqué offering a reward for the capture of the bank robbers.[35] Beginning on January 4, 1972, the National Police put into effect a plan to isolate a section of Santo Domingo, and then to stage a large-scale search with the objective of flushing out the criminals.[36] Early on the 8th, the police, assisted by troops from the Armed Forces, cordoned off the business district and the main shopping area of the capital and launched a series of raids.[37] The dragnet was less than productive at first, but information was obtained from an accomplice of Matos Moquete that led directly to the bank robbers' safe house. (The source was the courier who delivered food to the hideout.) The house was a two-story wood and cement structure, 14 kilometers east of the capital, approximately 400 meters above the coastal Americas Highway, which was the principal road to the international airport.[38] During the early hours of January 12th, General Nivar and members of the National Police approached the building. What followed would start as a standard law enforcement raid, but would emerge as a joint military operation of the strangest type.

The area around the house was surrounded by Department of Special Operations policemen, then, at approximately 2:45 A.M., the courier was sent forward to knock on the main entrance of the building. When the door was opened and the presence of the police observed, four individuals fled from the house to a cave about 200 meters away. They hid in the cavern that was partially concealed by underbrush, but their hiding place was soon discovered after a barking dog drew attention to the cave opening.[39]

The Department of Special Operations assaulted the cavern at approximately 6:00 A.M., but the attackers were cut down by automatic weapons fire. Among the first killed was police Captain Virgilio Almánzar Fernández. Throughout the morning of the 12th, exchanges of gunfire took place between the DSO and the criminals without any significant results. (It was later learned that the 1,600-foot deep cave had been well stocked with weapons and ammunition.) At approximately 1:00 P.M., another assault was conducted, but the police suffered more casualties—another officer and additional enlisted men were dead. The government began to refer to the bank robbers as *guerrilleros*.[40]

While the firefight was underway near the cavern, a "military zone" had been created and sealed off, and a buildup of units had begun. The police's Duarte Department and the Army's 3rd Battalion provided troops from Santo Domingo and San Cristóbal, respectively. By 2:20 P.M., four AMX-13 tanks, two 105mm guns, and mortars utilized by the Army joined the task force that had reached a total of approximately 500 men. Overhead, the Air Force flew two helicopters and a Vampire jet. Under discussion was the possibility of the Vampire's firing rockets into the cave. A command post was established alongside the Americas Highway where "half track" armored personnel carriers, communications vehicles, and two and one half ton trucks were parked.[41]

General Nivar had been personally in charge on the ground since the operation began; however, after daylight, he nominally had to share that authority with Admiral Jiménez. Even though the Admiral was the head of the Armed Forces, there was little for him to do in the "military zone" except be available to the press. The coordination of troop movements and logistics support was under the direction of Lieutenant Colonel Héctor García Tejada from Army headquarters—he also had had the same responsibility for the cordon and raids in the capital three days earlier. (García Tejada was a 1964 graduate of the U.S. Army's general staff course in the Canal Zone.) Also seen near the action, standing on a tank, was General Lluberes Montás, the secretary of state of interior and police. Not to be left out, General Folch Pérez, the chief of staff of the Air Force, flew a helicopter in a circle over the conflictive area. Although General Checo's presence had not been noted by reporters on the scene, Nivar remarked during one of many press interviews that his ally, the chief of staff of the Army, had also been in the "military zone."[42] All had some marginal reason to be present except General Marmolejos, who held the title of commander of the San Isidro Air Base, but was nothing more than a political hack. He managed to have Nivar's station, *Radio Clarín*, report that he was "directing operations" in the area.[43]

By 3:00 P.M. on the 12th, the government was prepared to resume the offensive; this time, the attack would be conducted with mortar support. That assault eliminated any further resistance from the bank robbers. The last was killed at 4:15 P.M. (It was estimated that the first two died at approximately 6:00 A.M. and that the third at about 4:00 P.M.) A sweep from north to south, starting in the rough terrain above the cave and ending at the Americas Highway along the coast, revealed that the zone was cleared of fugitives. At 5:00 P.M., the operation was officially terminated.[44] When the four corpses were identified and their possessions screened, it was confirmed that they were not common criminals, but political activists of the extreme left. In the house and the cave were found rocket launchers, automatic weapons, ammunition, explosives, and field uniforms as well as the standard revolutionary warfare literature. Their leader, Matos Moquete, was not one of the dead, and there was no indication where he and the other members of his group were located.[45] The government operation was not without cost. There were a total of two officers and six enlisted men of the Department of Special Operations killed and six police enlisted men and one Army first lieutenant wounded. The Army lieutenant was a bodyguard of General Nivar.[46]

At the conclusion of the affair, it was inevitable that the question was asked why it required a large body of troops, tanks, artillery, and aviation to bring in four bank robbers. (Anti-regime critics would have been overjoyed to have learned that the tanks did not fire their guns because the firing pins were still locked up in an office safe where they had been placed during the Wessin y Wessin crisis, and that feeding the troops in the field had been resolved by the Combat Service Support Command's ordering 1,000 sandwiches from a restaurant.[47]) Predictably, student groups at the Autonomous University of Santo Domingo demonstrated against the government's actions. Rocks were thrown and store windows were broken, but the National Police soon had this outburst under control.[48] The public in general was not sympathetic to the students' cause— Matos Moquete and his gang had committed an ordinary bank robbery and eight policemen were dead because of their crime.

Balaguer played the issue out cleverly. The Papal Nuncio had requested a meeting with the President for the morning of the 12th. He and a commission were planning to propose a ceasefire and negotiations to establish a truce. Balaguer put off the appointment until the afternoon, thus providing Nivar with the extra time to finish the coastal road operation.[49] That evening the President posthumously promoted and decorated the fallen eight. The following day he and General Nivar led the formal funeral procession for the dead policemen.[50]

Undoubtedly, the hero of the January 12th incident was General Nivar. The press placed him physically with the DSO patrols during the pre-dawn phase of the operation, his bodyguard was wounded presumably when the lieutenant was near the General, and during daylight hours he continually was identified as being personally in command of the entire affair. When the operation was closing down, and many other flag officers were attempting to gain press coverage, Nivar's name continued to be cited first—before the secretaries of state and the service chiefs. And, in all fairness to the public relations-oriented chief of National Police, he deserved the attention because he was the officer who had taken charge. Nivar had truly exhibited initiative, courage, and determination.

In contrast, during the whole episode, there was one general whose name was never heard and one unit that was rarely identified. Pérez y Pérez was a non-person on January 12th, and, even though 1st Brigade soldiers had been in the zone of operations, the Brigade was seldom mentioned. It was understandable that the National Police would take the lead in investigating a bank robbery, and that initial patrolling to find the location of the criminals was best accomplished by the police's Department of Special Operations, but subsequent actions more correctly belonged to elements of the 1st Brigade. That unit had the cohesion, tactical training, crew-served weapons, and organic communications and transportation necessary to do the job quickly and efficiently. A minimum number of 1st Brigade troops, using fire and maneuver, would have made short work of four men holding out in a cave. But the 1st Brigade was introduced piecemeal and was under-utilized. The police bore the brunt of the operation while the Brigade was relegated to a secondary role. Pérez y Pérez, the principal ground force commander in the Dominican Republic, had been effectively squeezed out, and his rival had completely dominated the affair. For President Balaguer, the coastal road firefight had another dimension—the chief of National Police was beginning his fourth month in office more politically popular than ever.

NIVAR AS PRESIDENTIAL ASPIRANT

During the Trujillo dictatorship, there was a reluctance to use *El Jefe's* name in any place where a hidden microphone could pick up a conversation. From this apprehension there developed many strange security precautions—one was to identify, while speaking, President Trujillo or his office by silently passing one's hand diagonally across the chest signifying the presidential sash. Dominicans continued this custom during the Balaguer years more out of habit than fear. After General Nivar assumed command of the National Police, it became increasingly common to hear (and see) the statement that "Nivar dreams of the ..." and then, silently, a hand went across the chest.

On November 12, 1971, one of the first indications in print appeared suggesting that Nivar would be the government party's candidate for president in 1974. A column in the newspaper *El Nacional* pointed out that Nivar's popularity was growing and that the Police Palace and the presidency were "just one step apart."[51] Nivar was quick to repudiate the article. In a statement sent to the editor of the newspaper, Nivar unabashedly wrote that he was not involved in political activity, but was simply a " *militar de carrera,* " and that he was loyal to the chief of state, Dr. Balaguer.[52] After the events of January 1972 on the coastal highway, this type of news story became even more widespread, which was especially worrisome for anti-Nivar groups in the Armed Forces. If the President shared those officers' anxiety, he refused to reveal it to anyone.[53] The U.S. Embassy had informed Washington in the end of 1971 that Balaguer was "biding his time and waiting for the opportune moment" to undercut Nivar's growing political power.[54] Nothing was done until February 15th. The President's action, or lack of action, on that day was barely discernible, but it was highly unsettling for the General.

After Nivar took over the National Police on October 15th, 1971, he was quick to tell members of his clique that Balaguer and he had an agreement that the police assignment would only be until February 15th, 1972. The President never admitted that they had agreed to that date, although he probably had provided Nivar with some indication that a transfer after four months could be a possibility. It was not in Balaguer's interest, however, to release the General from the National Police while Nivar was immensely popular. For the President, it was essential that Nivar remain in his vulnerable post until he was politically damaged. Therefore, the 15th of February passed without any change of police chief. The General did not stop his requests that he be reassigned (his first choice was to return to the 1st Brigade), but the President remained evasive. February and March were good months for Nivar, and commentary that he would run for president continued unabated.[55] But the beginning of April would finally bring the bad fortune that Balaguer desired for his ambitious general.

On April 4th, almost exactly six months after Nivar was appointed chief of National Police, the Autonomous University of Santo Domingo exploded. The problem began when policemen attempted to search part of the campus for an MPD member who was suspected of clandestinely entering the country from Cuba. Resistance from students quickly turned to violence. General Nivar, consequently, ordered reinforcements into the university to restore order. He directed his Secret Department commander, Colonel Martínez Fernández, who was already on the campus, to take charge of the Duarte Department under Colonel Carbuccia Reyes and the Department of Special Operations under Lieutenant Colonel Báez Maríñez. In the ensuing confusion, elements of the police opened fire wounding ten students. (One, a young female, died two days later in the hospital.) Colonel Jorge Moreno's Military Police Battalion at *Fortaleza Ozama* was called in to augment the strained policemen who were struggling to control the rioting youths. Once the police had the upper hand, large numbers of students and some members of the faculty, to include the rector of the university, were arrested. The campus was then closed and occupied by the National Police with the assistance of military troops. University authorities denounced the government for committing an act of repression against opponents of the regime.[56]

All of these events had been played out numerous times in the Dominican Republic, but they were a new experience for Nivar as chief of the National Police. From the first day of the violence, Nivar was criticized by the press and leftist groups. During the two weeks that followed, the General attempted to restore his reputation with little success. In a press conference, a reporter (probably in Nivar's pay) asked if the General thought someone who wanted to discredit him was behind the incidents at the university. Nivar responded that it was a possibility, but this defense on the General's part never took root. Nivar also attempted to gain popular support by publicizing his efforts to determine who had ordered the police to begin firing. After a student claimed Lieutenant Colonel Báez was at fault, Nivar relieved the DSO commander and informed the public that Báez was under investigation. Even though General Lluberes Montás, the secretary of state of interior and police, declared on April 12th that, due to the circumstances, it was impossible to fix responsibility, Nivar, two days later, arrested Báez. (On May 5th, Nivar expelled Báez from the National Police.) Finally, by April 15th, the situation was stable enough for Nivar to return control of the university to its authorities.[57] The eleven days had been costly for Nivar the politician. The American Embassy reported to Washington that his "popular image" had been damaged and that he was seeking a transfer out of the police.[58] Rumors had spread that Nivar was to be sacked by the President,[59] which, of course, was the exact opposite from what Balaguer had in mind. When Nivar was asked at a press conference during the crisis how he felt about being the chief of police, he responded:

President Joaquín Balaguer with President Somoza and other officials, March 9, 1972. From left to right (seated) Maj. Gen. Enrique Pérez y Pérez, Commander, 1st Brigade; Rear Admiral Ramón Jiménez, Secretary of State of the Armed Forces; Anastasio Somoza, President of Nicaragua; and Balaguer, President of the Dominican Republic. Directly behind President Balaguer, from left to right (standing), are Brig. Gen. Eladio Marmolejos Abréu; retired Maj. Gen. Mélido Marte Pichardo; and chief of the Corps of Military Aides, Brig. Gen. Anselmo Pilarte. They are at the 1st Brigade observing a tactical demonstration in honor of Somoza. (March 9, 1972).

"Holding this position is not the most comfortable position for a military man."[60]

At the same time that General Nivar was attempting to extricate himself from the university quagmire, he was intriguing against his archrival. In contrast to Nivar, Pérez y Pérez had spent the period after the coastal road firefight engaged in the routine duties of a peacetime infantry brigade commander. The monotony was broken, however, by a tactical demonstration presented to visiting President Somoza on March 9th at the *16 de Agosto* Military Camp. The Nicaraguan head of state and President Balaguer sat in a specially erected reviewing stand with General Pérez y Pérez while a mock 1st Brigade infantry-tank assault took place to their front. Two Vampire jets provided what appeared to be close air support. Explosions on the objective (a hill defended by the "enemy") were simulated, offering up great amounts of noise and fireworks. Dominican 1st Brigade officers and U.S. Army advisers had worked together for a considerable amount of time so that the demonstration would impress the visiting dignitaries. From a showmanship point of view, the exercise was quite a success; therefore, it was decided to repeat the demonstration one month later for General George V. Underwood, the commander in chief of the U.S. Southern Command, headquartered in the Panama Canal Zone. The aftermath of the 1st Brigade program for General Underwood would provide Nivar with the opportunity he needed to embarrass Pérez y Pérez.

On April 11th, the same demonstration took place for the visiting American general. The performance went as smoothly as the Somoza exercise; however, General Underwood's speech following the demonstration became an instrument to be exploited by General Pérez y Pérez's enemies. The U.S. general's comments were intended to be diplomatic, and definitely not politically motivated, but in the internecine factionalism of the officer corps, the opposite interpretation developed. To the assembled group of Dominican flag officers, General Underwood described the exercise as "the best I have seen in my 35 years of military service" and called the 1st Brigade commander a "magnificent soldier." The following day a political opposition radio station broadcast an editorial entitled "The General." The commentator remarked: "Come on, general, we believe you have exaggerated a little bit…. Perhaps the firing moved you too much…. Continue inspecting troops, dearly beloved general, but avoid public statements."[61] The "magnificent soldier" attribute to Pérez y Pérez was not publicized by the Armed Forces,[62] but *El Caribe*, a respected newspaper, carried it on the front page.[63] Undoubtedly, Nivar was unhappy that Pérez y Pérez had been complimented, but it worked to Nivar's advantage because President Balaguer was irritated that General Underwood's speech sounded, at least to many Dominicans, like "the Pentagon" was endorsing Pérez y Pérez. Nivar made the most of that view with the President. The U.S. Embassy later reported to Washington that observers claimed that "Balaguer was greatly concerned" and that Pérez y Pérez "could represent a potential rival to Balaguer."[64]

Not content with criticizing Pérez y Pérez for allowing himself to be portrayed by the Americans as a possible competitor to Balaguer, Nivar went further by concocting the story that Pérez y Pérez was actually plotting to overthrow the government. During mid–April, Nivar and his allies began feeding Balaguer reports that Pérez y Pérez was in collusion with his friend the mayor of Santo Domingo, Manuel Antonio Jiménez Rodríguez, and Lluberes Montás in planning a coup d'état.[65] Nivar's motives for wanting to destroy Pérez y Pérez and Lluberes Montás were long established; however, in the case of Mayor Jiménez Rodríguez, the issues were less well known. Earlier in the month, Jiménez Rodríguez proposed that the city government take over the management of the national racetrack from a private firm. Reportedly, the company was owned secretly by Nivar. For that reason, and because the Mayor had been critical of Nivar's handling of the university crisis, Nivar was anxious to include Jiménez Rodríguez in the overall scheme against Pérez y Pérez and Lluberes Montás.[66]

From Balaguer's vantage point, there were numerous factors to consider. First, the President had allowed Nivar to be handled roughly during the university imbroglio, thereby hurting his presidential aspirations, but the General now needed some support to reestablish the balance of power within the military. Second, although the Pérez y Pérez-Lluberes Montás-mayor of Santo Domingo conspiracy was absurd, Pérez y Pérez needed to have his position weakened because the Underwood speech, on top of Nivar's setback at the university, had over-inflated Pérez y Pérez's status. And, third—according to the American Embassy—the President considered it advantageous to neutralize the Mayor. In a cable to Washington, Ambassador Meloy described Jiménez Rodríguez as a politician believed by Balaguer to be "a troublesome and irritating political opponent who, although posing no immediate or serious threat to his regime, represented an independent and therefore politically unacceptable power center in the [Dominican Republic]."[67] With those considerations in mind, the President, during the last week in April, took two rapid actions which startled the nation, and left the cunning Balaguer once again the preeminent manipulator of the Dominican officer corps.

On April 24th, the President promulgated a decree appointing General Pérez y Pérez secretary of state of interior and police; General Jorge Moreno replaced him as commander of the 1st Brigade. The outgoing secretary, General Lluberes Montás, was designated a military adviser to the president. Jorge Moreno's former position of commander of the Combat Service Support Command (which included the Military Police Battalion) at *Fortaleza Ozama* was given to General Pilarte. And, finally, Pilarte was relieved as the President's chief of the Corps of Military Aides and replaced by newly promoted Brigadier General Juan Tomás Reyes Evora.[68]

The significance of this decree was many-faceted. Nivar had been refused again the transfer he desired from the National Police, but, at least, his old brigade was given to a member of his faction, Jorge Moreno. Pérez y Pérez was removed from the strongest unit in the Dominican Republic, and appointed to a powerless cabinet position; however, nominally, he was police chief Nivar's superior. Pérez y Pérez's most eminent supporter, Lluberes Montás, was further debilitated by his loss of all authority and responsibility. The Military Police Battalion at *Fortaleza Ozama* was now under the control of Pilarte, a personal enemy of Nivar, while the Corps of Military Aides was turned over to Reyes Evora, a Nivar protégé.

Three days later, the President moved against the Mayor. On April 27th, Balaguer dispatched an official letter to the president of the Chamber of Deputies accusing Jiménez Rodríguez of plotting to replace the current constitutional regime with a military government. The President wrote that the Mayor had attempted to recruit various officers to join the conspiracy. The lower house of the legislature submitted the charges to the Senate where a resolution was passed dismissing Jiménez Rodríguez. He never had the opportunity to defend himself. These proceedings were all undertaken in less than a day. That evening the ex-mayor received political asylum in the Mexican Embassy and, on April 30th, he began his self-imposed exile in Mexico. Under Mexican protection, Jiménez Rodríguez blamed Nivar for his problems and accused the General of "having dangerous political ambitions."[69] The day after Balaguer sent his accusations to the legislature, he announced that no Dominican officers had joined the Jiménez Rodríguez plot, and Pérez y Pérez stated that if the ex-mayor had dared to talk to him about overthrowing the government "he would have shot or imprisoned" Jiménez Rodríguez even though he was a friend.[70]

THE LAST EIGHT MONTHS

Nivar and members of his faction were elated with the events of April 24th and 27th, while Nivar's clumsiness during the April 4th university crisis was fading from memory. Consequently, it was not yet in Balaguer's interest to release Nivar from the police. The General was unable to convince the President to transfer him from chief of the National Police to a position such as head of the Armed Forces or the Army. Despite Nivar's entreaties, Balaguer kept the General in that vulnerable post for eight more months. During that period, Pérez y Pérez did not attempt to exert authority over the National Police from the secretariat of interior and police. When he was asked at his first press conference what the relationship would be between Pérez y Pérez's office and the chief of the National Police, the General responded in a manner reminiscent of his numerous public statements during the 1970 electoral campaign that the Armed Forces would stay out of politics. On April 27, 1972, Pérez y Pérez claimed that he and Nivar were friends and that stories of friction between them were merely rumors.[71] Although this remark was believed by no one, Nivar was left alone to run the National Police in a manner that he (and the President) wished.

Nivar's other enemies also did not cause the police chief significant discomfort during his remaining eight months in the National Police. General Lluberes Montás had been damaged the most severely. His always reliable power base, the Special Forces Group, had a new commander who was not part of the closely knit Lluberes Montás brotherhood that had founded the Dominican airborne in 1960 after it was trained together in Spain. In fact, Captain Carlos Jiménez Fernández was not even airborne qualified until after he was appointed the commander of the Special Forces Group. It was understood at the San Isidro Air Base that Jiménez Fernández was in his new post to keep an eye on the old Lluberes Montás clique.[72] The President partially rehabilitated the paratrooper general on May 22nd when he designated Lluberes Montás the sub-secretary of state of the armed forces for air, with an office in the National Palace.[73] The position carried no command authority, but his appointment improved Lluberes Montás' image within the officer corps.

Colonel Cuervo Gómez devoted the remainder of 1972 to professionalizing the Armor and Artillery Battalions. He had established courses for officers and enlisted men in basic and advanced subjects at his new compound near Villa Mella. This effort was followed by field training exercises at the Sierra Prieta range north of Santo Domingo in August 1972, which involved AMX-13 tanks, 105mm Reinosa guns, and infantry from the 1st Battalion, 1st Brigade.[74] Although Colonel Cuervo Gómez was not drawn into politico-military affairs from May to December 1972, his units were now centered closer than before to key points in the capital. His only problem was that he had to cross the Presidente Peynado Bridge over the Isabela River to enter the heart of Santo Domingo. Consequently, the Colonel maintained troops armed with CETME assault rifles full time at the bridge.

General Ramiro Matos González in 1972 was the most dynamic and professional infantry officer at the San Isidro Air Base. Although opposed to Nivar, he was unlikely to initiate any action to impede Nivar's political activities. Consequently, the chief of National Police had no reason to concern himself with the Air Force's ground units unless an open confrontation involving the entire Armed Forces were to occur.

For different reasons there was minimal chance that the Military Police Battalion would take the lead against Nivar. General Pilarte and Nivar were personal enemies, but the new commander at *Fortaleza Ozama* was not an aggressive military or politico-military player. He had already made it known that he wished to retire from the Army.

The year 1972 saw a new development in the internal politics of the Armed Forces—Admiral Jiménez began to distance himself from Nivar, thereby giving up his neutral position. He was drawn toward the Pérez y Pérez faction initially because of a personal dispute he had had with Nivar, and then because of his concern with Nivar's growing dominance within the Armed Forces. Eventually, this slow change of attitude on the part of the titular head of the military establishment would solidify into a firm alliance with Pérez y Pérez and Lluberes Montás against Nivar. This anti-Nivar coalition became known as the "Triangle." Jiménez's contribution to the Triangle was not measurable in raw power, however. The Navy was militarily insignificant. And, in addition, there were factions within the maritime service opposed to Jiménez. The main clique outside Jiménez's coterie was that of Commodore Rivera Caminero. Jiménez's old mentor had been allowed to return to the Dominican Republic from the United States, and Balaguer had promoted him again to commodore; however, Rivera was not assigned to the Navy, and Rivera's main supporters were scattered—such as *Capitán de Navío* Manuel Olgo Santana Carasco who was on OAS observer duty along the Salvadoran-Honduran border and *Capitán de Fragata* Rolando Polanco y Polanco who had served a lengthy period as a naval attaché in Venezuela. Within Jiménez's faction was the chief of staff of the Navy, Commodore Manuel Logroño Contín, and, most important, Commodore Amiama Castillo. Amiama Castillo personified what Jiménez could offer the Triangle—he was intelligent, an excellent administrator, and a talented policy planner. He and Jiménez had strong links to Washington, which, in a Dominican crisis, would be invaluable. Finally, there were two anti-Nivar retired naval officers in key government positions who were also well connected with the United States, but were not part of a clique at the time. They were Commodore Enrique Valdez Vidaurre, the director of DNI, and Commodore Julio Rib Santamaría, the director general of Posts and Telecommunications.

The relative quiet of Nivar's enemies compared with the police chief's highly visible profile as the President's negotiator during labor strikes or as Balaguer's go-between with opposition political parties gave the impression that the General was gaining leverage at the expense of others in the Dominican Republic. On July 25, 1972, U.S. Ambassador Meloy dispatched a cable to Washington providing a political assessment. He stated that Nivar had "emerged as the virtually undisputed top military man in the country" and that "there are mounting indications he would like to succeed Balaguer when he eventually steps down from the presidency." The Ambassador followed with an important qualifier:

> Although Nivar's power has greatly strengthened in recent months, most observers believe that Balaguer is totally aware of Nivar's enhanced position, that he does not consider it a present threat, and that he is still in a position to cut Nivar down to size should he so choose.[75]

Among Dominicans, the Nivar ascendancy was reflected in a telling manner. In August 1972, the movie "The Godfather" (or "*El Padrino*") was shown to large, enthusiastic audiences in the capital. Widely heard throughout Santo Domingo was the remark that the Dominican Republic had its own Don Vito Corleone—it was General Nivar.

The Dominican "Godfather" had a personal style that was part coarse *Trujillista* military officer, part mafia boss, and part shrewd political operative. Three first-hand glimpses of General Nivar's behavior and surroundings during the height of his popularity are interesting to review.

On February 16, 1972, the Washington *Evening Star* published a story exclusively about General Nivar that induced some unexpected reactions from the police chief in the months that followed. The author of the article was the experienced Latin American specialist Jeremiah O'Leary. He had visited the Dominican Republic after Nivar had become firmly entrenched in the National Police, and he had developed some perceptive sources concerning the politico-military scene in Santo Domingo. O'Leary began his column with the headline "Police Strongman Follows Trujillo's Path to Power." Then these opening statements were made: "Fewer than 12 years after the death of Generalissimo Rafael Leonidas Trujillo, a new caudillo in the image and likeness of the slain dictator is beginning to emerge in this troubled land. He is Brig. Gen. Neit Nivar Seijas, 47, chief of the National Police, who was a young lieutenant in Trujillo's time and is now the most powerful military figure ... [in the Dominican Republic]." The article went on to comment that both Trujillo and Nivar were of humble birth from San Cristóbal. And that only Nivar's patron and "wary friend," President Balaguer, stood "between Nivar and the achievement of ultimate power." The substance of O'Leary's piece then followed. *La Banda*, the rivalry with Pérez y Pérez, and the crisis of October 14, 1971, were all cited. Also, the article addressed Nivar's wealth, his civilian advisers, his political power to include PRD approval of Nivar as police chief, and his relationship with the President. O'Leary concluded by writing: "If anything happens to Balaguer, the betting is that the poor boy from Trujillo's home town would take charge and stay in charge."[76]

When the published *Evening Star* story was read in the American Embassy in Santo Domingo, it was noted how closely the substantive segments of the piece followed, in abbreviated form, Defense Attache Office reporting. Later in the week, Nivar sent a message that he would like to meet with me as soon as possible at his Santo Domingo house. That evening, I arrived at the General's home and was ushered into a large room where the police chief, Salomón Sanz, and other members of Nivar's coterie were seated drinking scotch. Staring down at the group from the wall was a large oil painting of Trujillo in a generalissimo's uniform. With few words, Nivar handed me the O'Leary article translated into Spanish. My immediate concern was that Nivar was either outraged because O'Leary had become aware of closely held information such as the events at the 1st Brigade on October 14, 1971, or because the article claimed, and possibly the U.S. government agreed, that Nivar was a threat to the President. Consequently, to lessen the importance of the article, I made some remarks to the effect that O'Leary's work should not be taken seriously because he was not a qualified observer of Dominican affairs. Much to my surprise, Nivar looked crestfallen. It quickly became apparent that the General had not been angered by the article; moreover, the opposite had occurred—Nivar had been greatly pleased with O'Leary's comparison of him to *El Jefe.*

On March 8th, the opposition evening tabloid, *Ultima Hora,* featured a story about the O'Leary article suggesting that there was an "anti-Neit" campaign underway in the United States.[77] Thus, despite Nivar's satisfaction with the beginning and end of the article, the General was convinced by his advisers that he had to refute publicly the substantive portions of the piece. This action was first taken on March 9th when Nivar's station, *Radio Clarín,* broadcast a response to O'Leary. The General was quoted as saying: "It is obvious that this journalist was paid by persons who want to harm my public image." Then Nivar denied that he hesitated before accepting the President's orders on October 14, 1971, and he said that the O'Leary remarks concerning his wealth and political activities were not true. Relating to the PRD's satisfaction with his policies in the National Police, Nivar stated: "Why not ask the PRD about this? I am police chief of all the Dominican people, not of any particular group." Most of all, Nivar emphasized his loyalty to the President and his disinterest in replacing Balaguer in the presidency. Absolutely no reference was made to the dead dictator, Trujillo.[78] Further efforts were undertaken by the General and his associates to counter the O'Leary article, but, in truth, Nivar remained highly gratified with O'Leary's work because the article had identified him with *El Jefe.*

A physical description of the preliminaries to a one-on-one meeting with General Nivar in the Police Palace is a combination of the bizarre and the amusing. Arriving at the prearranged conference site required working through a maze of checkpoints and offices before a substantive conversation could begin. The initial phases of the odyssey were relatively simple. The uniform of a U.S. Army major was sufficient to gain access to the large headquarters building, with machine guns emplaced on the roof, only three blocks from the American Embassy. Policemen armed with rifles saluted and stepped aside. With the same ease, one was allowed to mount the stairs and arrive at the office complex of the chief of National Police without an escort. After the first door was opened, you passed through a waiting room where supplicants, hangers-on, and lower ranking members of Nivar's retinue were lingering. Then one entered the outer office of the police chief where a police field grade officer sat; he was one of the General's *ayudantes*. He opened the door to the chief's main office. Behind a large desk was an empty chair, and, on the wall, was an enormous National Police emblem. Nivar, however, was not in that formal setting. The aide ushered you through a door in the rear into what was commonly called in the Dominican Republic the "*privado*." Senior Dominican military officers normally had a desk and a cot in the *privado* for confidential meetings and for a place to sleep if their units were "*acuartelado*" (on alert in garrison). Instead of stopping at this point, which was usually the end of the labyrinth in most major headquarters, you were led down a narrow corridor to a medium-sized bedroom. A double bed dominated the room. Standing by the bed were three full colonels in deep discussion—the two Army officers were Pimentel Boves and Lachapelle Suero, and the National Police officer was Domingo Camilo Rosa. All were stationed, at that time, in the town of San Cristóbal. They nodded at you, a mere American major, and then the *ayudante* opened the last door. When you entered, you were surprised to see that you were in a bathroom. Next to a barber chair, by the sink, was Neit Nivar Seijas in uniform wearing dark glasses. After the customary military salutations were completed, the Chief placed one foot on the toilet bowl and began stating what Nivar wanted only you (and the U.S. government) to know.

Contrary to the just-described personal meeting in an official (albeit peculiar) setting, the non-official gathering of Nivar and his circle of followers was even less structured. Representative of the latter type of meeting was one set up by "Moncho" Henríquez of the *Servicio Secreto* at an apartment next to the Ecuadorian Embassy in Santo Domingo. (By 1972, Moncho was identified as a captain; later he would be called a police colonel.) There was no established beginning or end to the meeting and no formal agenda. Military and police officers in uniform and civilians came and went for hours and large quantities of scotch were continuously consumed. Despite this freewheeling atmosphere, business was successfully concluded. An example was when General Checo, the Army chief, sat down on a couch with Nivar and went over a list of personnel appointments. After Checo presented each name, Nivar indicated his approval or disapproval. Also, intelligence information was passed either by document or word of mouth. Moncho, as always in civilian clothes, was particularly active in this effort although the environment was not particularly conducive to an exchange of intelligence. As the night wore on, the police chief was becoming more intoxicated. Nivar's holstered pistol had slipped from his side to between his legs and he became unsteady on his feet. The General dropped into a chair at the head of a table and began eating the favorite dish of Dominicans—a *sancocho* or stew of goat meat, plantains and yucca. When the General finished eating, the meeting came to an abrupt end.

As the year 1972 drew to a close, an assessment of Nivar's politico-military situation revealed that the General had made more gains than loses since he had left the 1st Brigade. During his stewardship of the National Police, the most damaging experience in his public life had been the university crisis of April 1972. That campus incident had faded into the background, however, and Nivar's propaganda machine had striven to improve the police chief's standing as it related to the university. For example, during the second week in September, students participated in a series of demonstrations and protest marches—the Nivar response was a much publicized order by the police chief that the National Police was prohibited from firing on the demonstrators.[79]

The General's radio station had become the most listened to in the Dominican Republic,[80] and paid newsmen who did not work for *Radio Clarín* continued to attack Nivar's enemies as well as to enhance the police chief's image. In addition to Pérez y Pérez and Lluberes Montás, other Nivar opponents who were members of the government, such as Commodore Valdez Vidaurre, the director of the DNI, were targets of these press assaults.[81] Nivar's men also manipulated news stories to Nivar's advantage. When an Air Force sergeant major and a National Police sergeant were murdered on October 15th and 16th, respectively, and PRD headquarters was bombed on October 18th, a story was floated that anti-Nivar military personnel committed the crimes expressly to discredit Nivar.[82] Nivar also took the opportunity, whenever possible, to ingratiate himself with the legal opposition. On November 25th, the General informed reporters that he and the secretary general of the PRD, José Francisco Peña Gómez, "are personal friends" and that he (Nivar) "does not use his position to engage in politics."[83]

Despite Nivar's machinations, Balaguer continued to utilize the General as the President's political operative. The U.S. Embassy reported that, in the end of 1972, "Balaguer, frequently and effectively using police chief Neit Nivar Seijas as his instrument, further undermined opposition political organizations through skillful use of subornation and/or intimidation."[84] But no matter how useful Nivar could be to the President, Balaguer was not comfortable with the continuous flow of reports that Nivar aspired to the presidency. Even when the General would state publicly that he absolutely had no intention to run for president,[85] few believed him.

By the end of 1972, Balaguer realized that Nivar's continuation in the National Police was not proving beneficial to the President's interests. The plan to keep Nivar in the police until he was politically ruined had not succeeded; therefore, the President had to resort to one of his more conventional techniques—Pérez y Pérez's strength had to be increased.

In vintage Balaguer style, the President, without informing Nivar, issued Decree 3003 on Christmas night appointing Colonel José Ernesto Cruz Brea, a committed supporter of Pérez y Pérez, to the post of chief of the National Police. No position was cited for Nivar.[86] Four days later, on the 29th of December, it was announced in Decree 3020 that General Pérez y Pérez was designated the chief of staff of the Army in place of General Checo, a Nivar man. Again, no mention was made of Nivar.[87] The new year began with no change—Nivar remained unassigned.

XI

Pérez y Pérez Dominates the Ground Forces

In what seemed like an interminable length of time, Nivar was finally given a post. On January 4th, the National Palace announced that the General was appointed the secretary of state of the presidency with the temporary rank of major general.[1] One suggested reason for the delay was the necessity to reestablish legally the billet of secretary of state of the presidency in the cabinet—the position was last used by the Government of National Reconstruction during the 1965 civil war and was no longer on the statutes.[2] Nivar, and many other Dominicans, however, interpreted the late appointment to be a calculated slight on the part of Balaguer. The U.S. Ambassador stated the following in a cable to Washington:

> Although anxious to leave the politically vulnerable job as police chief, Nivar was reportedly humiliated by his unceremonious and sudden ouster and by the fact that he was not immediately given another assignment.[3]

The abrupt treatment by the President rankled Nivar, but that was not all that irritated the new secretary of state of the presidency. Again he had been denied the senior military post—secretary of state of the armed forces—or the second most prestigious (and potentially most powerful) position—chief of staff of the Army. Admiral Jiménez had been the Armed Forces chief since July 12, 1971, and General Checo had already been replaced as head of the Army. Therefore, Nivar's being deprived of either job was not because the incumbents were not due to be reassigned. To Nivar it was clear that the President categorically refused to allow him to lead the Armed Forces or the Army. Thus, once again, a dejected Nivar assumed a seemingly impotent position in the National Palace.

THE SECRETARY OF STATE
OF THE PRESIDENCY

Decree 3073, which designated Nivar secretary of state of the presidency, also outlined, very briefly, his responsibilities. Article 3 of the decree stated that the *secretario administrativo* and the *secretario técnico* in the National Palace would continue to operate as before—the only change would be that they were subordinated to the new secretary of state of the presidency.[4] The functions of those two officials, prior to Nivar's appointment, dealt with subjects such as revenues, comptrollership, economic statistics, planning, natural resources, internal and external commerce, legislative affairs, disaster relief, legal matters, correspondence, publications, and archives.[5] In short, Nivar was to be responsible for the management of Balaguer's civil executive offices—an activity that the General found tiresome.

At first, Nivar shared office space with General Juan de los Santos Céspedes, a FAD officer whose career had been in steady decline. The former pilot had been chief of staff of the Air Force, then he was reduced to sub-secretary of state of the armed forces (where he wrestled with projects such as what type identification or "dog tag" a soldier should wear), and, finally, he was relegated to the post of adviser to the President. Subsequently, a small separate office was arranged for Nivar near Balaguer's chambers. The General's principal staff officer was Lieutenant Colonel Bautista, formerly the Army's G-2. Colonel Bautista was a lawyer, and a competent administrator when he was on the General Staff.

Predictably, one of the first actions taken by Nivar was to establish a personal intelligence service. The General put the organization under "Moncho" Henríquez, who for obvious reasons was no longer in the Secret Department of the National Police. The service operated from its headquarters in a private home located on Rosa Duarte Street in the capital.[6]

Nivar initially involved himself with petty matters such as arranging a political luncheon for the President, issuing new passes to enter the National Palace, and sending Colonel Bautista out every morning to take the names of government employees who entered their office buildings late. When the General was chief of the President's Corps of Military Aides, he had supervision over the Presidential Guard and was responsible for Balaguer's personal security. He attempted to renew those activities from the secretariat of the presidency, but he faced an obstacle in Commodore Rivera Caminero, a strong-willed, long established opponent of Nivar, who had been designated the new head of the Corps of Military Aides on February 5, 1973. Nivar was forced to back off from

Dominican Armed Forces color guard at the 1st Brigade (1973). Cadets from all the services are carrying the flags. In front of them are Army personnel from the 1st Brigade.

dealing with the aides-de-camp and the Presidential Guard, but he was able to keep his hand in security matters.[7]

Although Nivar had a modest intelligence service and a wide range of contacts in the military and police establishments and in the private sector, he had no Armed Forces or National Police resources directly available to him. The General had been effectively checked, albeit temporarily, by the President. In contrast, General Pérez y Pérez began the new year as the preeminent land commander in the Dominican Republic.

PÉREZ Y PÉREZ AS GROUND FORCES LEADER

It was a decided advantage for the Pérez y Pérez faction that Cruz Brea commanded the National Police at the same time that his former superior, Pérez y Pérez, was chief of staff of the Army. The new police chief was an early and strong supporter of Pérez y Pérez and an implacable enemy of Nivar.

From a foreign observer's perspective in 1971, Colonel Cruz Brea was considered one of the three top field grade officers in the country. (The other two were Colonels Cuervo Gómez and Matos González.) Cruz Brea had been exposed to a civilian education in Chile and Mexico, and a military education in France. In 1965, he gained further international experience when he served as assistant military attaché in Washington. He was a doctor of laws (Santo Domingo—class of 1953), a student of political movements and modern warfare, and an armored cavalryman (Saumur—class of 1958). This extraordinary officer, as an Army major, joined General Pérez y Pérez's staff in the ministry of the armed forces in 1966, the day after Pérez y Pérez was sworn in as head of the military establishment. Cruz Brea remained with the General throughout Pérez y Pérez's full four years and seven months as secretary of state of the armed forces. In the first two years with the General, Cruz Brea was the director of the public information and civic action programs. Beginning in 1968, Cruz Brea, by then a lieutenant colonel, was appointed the chief of intelligence, J-2, of the secretariat of the Armed Forces. (The J-1, J-3, and J-4 sections were to be formed at a later date.) Cruz Brea gave military intelligence a sophistication normally not associated with that profession in the Dominican Republic. He was an exceptional analyst of politico-military affairs, he understood information-gathering operations, and he coordinated the normally fragmented Armed Forces intelligence services. Cruz Brea chaired the meetings of the G-2 (Army), A-2 (Air Force), and M-2 (Navy), and he established close liaison with DNI and National Police intelligence. When General Pérez y Pérez was transferred to the secretariat of interior and police, Cruz Brea continued as the J-2 under General Méndez Lara, and then Admiral Jiménez. Throughout this post-Pérez y Pérez period in the secretariat of the Armed Forces, Cruz Brea remained a member of the Pérez y Pérez faction.[8]

It was not surprising that Cruz Brea had sided with Pérez y Pérez rather than Nivar in the rivalry between the two generals. Cruz Brea's attitudes closely paralleled those of Pérez y Pérez and were the opposite from those of Nivar. As with Pérez y Pérez, Cruz Brea was intensely focused on his responsibilities, he lived unostentatiously, and his personal conduct was reserved. Nivar's freewheeling life style, his intrigues to ruin competitors in the officer corps, and his lack of military professionalism were distasteful to Cruz Brea. Also, Cruz Brea and Pérez y Pérez shared the view that Nivar's machinations with the political opposition for his own purposes were unacceptable. Cruz Brea and Pérez y Pérez believed that issues should be clearly defined, and actions related to those issues should be above board.

When Colonel Cruz Brea was appointed chief of the National Police in the end of 1972, it came as a complete surprise. His main goal for the distant future was to serve as the director of DNI. Becoming the police chief was never part of his plans. The President had met Cruz Brea many times in the National Palace, General Pérez y Pérez and Admiral Jiménez had spoken well of him, and his views on General Nivar were no secret. Consequently, it appeared useful to Balaguer to send Nivar a clear signal of presidential displeasure by designating Colonel Cruz Brea as Nivar's successor. Balaguer's message was apparently received—Nivar refused to attend the ceremony on December 26th when temporary Brigadier General Cruz Brea (still in Army uniform) was installed as the chief of National Police by the President.[9]

The appointment of a new police chief was always followed by officer transfers. What these personnel changes signified to the balance of power in the beginning of 1973 was that two key National Police units were moved like pieces on a game board from the Nivar group to the Pérez y Pérez group. Through Cruz Brea, Pérez y Pérez could now count on the Duarte Department and the Department of Special Operations in the event of an internal crisis in the capital. (The new commander of the *Cascos Negros* was Colonel Servio Tulio Cabrera Martínez. The DSO was under the command of Lieutenant Colonel Pascual Féliz Fernández.) The Secret Department of the police was also purged of Nivar men.

In addition to Cruz Brea's National Police, Pérez y Pérez had as allies most of the ground combat elements of the Air Force. General Matos González continued to exercise authority over the Air Force infantry at San Isidro Air Base. Less clear, however, was the loyalty of the airborne Special Forces Group after Captain Carlos Jiménez Fernández took command of the parachutists. As related earlier, the paratroopers believed that he was appointed their commander to break up the Lluberes Montás clique. Despite this perceived intention, the opposite appeared to have occurred. Even though Lluberes Montás commanded no troops, his charisma was very much felt at San Isidro. (To the delight of the airborne soldiers, the General would arrive at the air base driving his official black sedan—his chauffeur would be in the back seat.) "Chinino," as he was still known, was always hailed by his former men as the country's first paratrooper. This continual respect and affection were confirmed when Major Jiménez Fernández and a commission of parachutist officers presented the General, then a secretary of state, with the new blue beret to be worn only by active members of the Special Forces Group.[10] Consequently, even though Lluberes Montás was not in the Air Force chain of command, the assessment in the beginning of 1973 was that if he called for the Special Forces Group to support him, that "parachute battalion" would follow him against any other faction. Thus, when Pérez y Pérez took charge of the Army, he could rely on the key, non-Army ground force units in the capital.

As in all calculations relating to the distribution of power after the

1965 civil war in the Dominican Republic, the control of the capital was predominant. The new chief of staff could depend on Colonel Cuervo Gómez to provide the all-important tanks as well as the other armored vehicles and artillery of the Combat Support Command. The Military Police Battalion stationed at *Fortaleza Ozama* continued to be in the hands of Nivar's enemy, General Pilarte, and there had been no change in the political orientation of the Presidential Guard. For Pérez y Pérez, the main question concerning his Army was what would be the actions of General Marcos Antonio Jorge Moreno and the 1st Brigade in the event of an internal military crisis.

Jorge Moreno had been in the San Cristóbal Group and was Nivar's ally during the years that followed, but, in 1973, he appeared disengaged from the Pérez y Pérez-Nivar rivalry. Throughout his career he had glided in and out of jobs without too much effort. Jorge Moreno had been Trujillo's aide-de-camp and, after the fall of the dictator, in 1962, he served for six months as chief of staff of the Army with the temporary rank of brigadier general. When he was sent into exile later that year it was to the comfortable post of military attaché in Mexico City. Under Balaguer, he commanded *Fortaleza Ozama* until he was appointed the commander of the 1st Brigade. While in those command positions, Jorge Moreno was primarily thought of as a gentleman who enjoyed the good life. His courtly manner and nonabrasive style made him well liked by both civilians and military officers. Jorge Moreno's policy at the *16 de Agosto* camp was to move cautiously and avoid confrontation.

From Pérez y Pérez's point of view, it was not essential to engineer the removal of Jorge Moreno from the 1st Brigade. With Nivar outside the Armed Forces, Jorge Moreno posed no immediate threat to the new chief of staff. A sensible political approach for Pérez y Pérez was to treat the 1st Brigade as three separate battalions, rather than as an integrated, cohesive force under Jorge Moreno. Pérez y Pérez's policy would become apparent in February 1973 when the units of the Brigade were deployed to a combat zone.

General Pérez y Pérez did not have complete freedom to make major personnel changes in the constabulary Army that was spread throughout the interior of the country. His immediate predecessor, General Checo, had demonstrated a flabby management style, but the President had been pleased with Checo's approach to the Army in the provinces. Consequently, Pérez y Pérez had to accept Balaguer's first priority—political control of the population. For that reason, provincial commanders such as Colonel Jáquez Olivero (Checo's brother-in-law) and Colonel Almonte Mayer were retained in their posts despite their professional incompetence. As the commanders of Fort *General Benito Monción* in Mao and of Fort *Concepción* in La Vega, respectively, their primary function was to guarantee that the citizenry remained loyal, especially at the polls, to the President. In January 1973, Peña Gómez, the secretary general of the PRD, summed up Jáquez's role in the regime when he described the Colonel as the chief of *Balaguerismo* in northwestern Dominican Republic.[11] Almonte Mayer's real mission was also clearly revealed in May 1972 when he exclaimed in a public forum that "Dr. Joaquín Balaguer will remain in power as long as he lives since we, the military men, are in charge here."[12]

The new chief of staff was able to improve the caliber of some constabulary leaders, however. On January 21, 1973, he assigned Lieutenant Colonel Figueroa Carrión to command the 10th Battalion in Barahona in place of Lieutenant Colonel Morel Ramos. Earlier, Morel Ramos had caused difficulties when he overtly intervened in local politics.[13] Also, Pérez y Pérez retained Lieutenant Colonel Mota Henríquez as the commander of the 7th Battalion in San Francisco de Macorís—that provincial chief had the unlikely background of being one of Figueroa Carrión's bright Military Academy faculty members in 1958, and a 1963 graduate of the U.S. Army's Command and Staff Course in the Panama Canal Zone. Before Mota Henríquez, San Francisco de Macorís commanders were usually heavy-handed enforcers who were continually accused of harassing student groups and labor unions.[14]

For three years, there had been an organizational anomaly in the Army of the interior. Thanks to the U.S. government and the MAAG, one of the eight battalions outside the capital area was a tactical infantry unit, not a constabulary formation. In the end of 1972, the partially motorized 9th Battalion, under the competent leadership of Lieutenant Colonel Mélido González Pérez, was stationed in its entirety in Mao, and was capable of utilizing fire and maneuver against any objective in the 2nd Brigade's area of operations. The Dominican Army in the interior, on December 5, 1972, added a second such battalion to its roster. In less than one month from that date, General Pérez y Pérez took unofficial personal control of this unit—a battalion that was conceived over three years earlier when he was the secretary of state of the armed forces.

During 1969, there had been discussions between Pérez y Pérez and the American Embassy concerning U.S. support for two battalions in the 2nd Brigade's zone. Washington informed the Santo Domingo government that it would fund the project if the Army would reduce its overall personnel strength—an action the Dominicans were reluctant to implement. An agreement was finally reached and the terms were formalized in an April 18, 1969, memorandum of understanding. Thus, funds were made available for fiscal year 1970 to equip and train the 9th Battalion in Mao.[15] Despite assurances from Dominican leaders that the personnel reductions were to take place, the Armed Forces did not fully comply with the agreement. Consequently, the U.S. Department of Defense, in November 1969, indicated that further funding for the Dominican Army was in jeopardy.[16] The issue dragged on through 1970, requiring personal meetings between President Balaguer and Ambassador Meloy.[17] On December 4, 1970, the President sent the Ambassador a letter assuring him that the reductions in personnel would be carried out in accordance with the original 1969 agreement. In a further meeting between Balaguer and Meloy, a formula was arrived at which satisfied the Ambassador. Therefore, on December 11, 1970, the American envoy sent a cable to Washington recommending that the funds for the second battalion be released.[18] The recommendation was accepted. What followed was a debate as to where the new unit was to be located.

Original planning for the battalion clearly stated that it would belong to the 2nd Brigade, but Nivar, at the height of his power, began maneuvering to absorb the new battalion into the 1st Brigade. Both the President and the Ambassador opposed the Nivar initiative, but a suitable location for the battalion was still to be decided. Ambassador Meloy reviewed the issue carefully—in addition to his principal country team members, he also solicited the views of more junior officials in the embassy who he believed were well informed of Dominican politico-military and security assistance matters. The site agreed to by the President and the Ambassador was the town of Constanza in the *Cordillera Central*. Constanza was in the mountainous southwestern sector of the 2nd Brigade's area of responsibility, which placed it outside the populous Cibao Valley. The new unit's isolation from Santiago, where the 2nd Brigade headquarters was located, made it easier for Santo Domingo to exert authority over the battalion.

Military politics was not the only reason to establish the battalion in Constanza. It was an excellent area for training purposes as the American Embassy and the Dominican Armed Forces discovered in 1963. During the Juan Bosch administration, the 3rd Battalion had been trained in the mountains around Constanza by U.S. Army advisers. The instruction program concluded with an exercise on March 25th through the 29th, which was supported from the airfield in Constanza by FAD aircraft and paratroopers. President Bosch visited the field exercise and was briefed and escorted by the *Balaguerista* battalion commander, Major Pérez Aponte.[19] (Even after the 3rd Battalion was moved from the mountains to San Cristóbal, it retained the title *Batallón de Montaña* as an honorific.) It is interesting to note that when the 3rd Battalion was in Constanza, it was thought of as a national-level strike force to be inserted anywhere in the country where a counterguerrilla effort was needed.[20] General Pérez y Pérez followed the same concept insofar as the new battalion was concerned.

In the summer of 1971, officers and men began to arrive at Fort *Patria* in Constanza. The designation of 6th Battalion, *General Gregorio Luperón*, was transferred from the Army garrison in La Vega to the new formation in Constanza, and a new battalion commander was appointed. He was Major Carlos Antonio Castillo Pimentel, a 1959 graduate of the Military Academy, and third in the 1968 class of the *comando y plana mayor* course at the Officers School. Prior to his appointment, Castillo Pimentel had been a member of the Schools Command faculty at San Isidro. (He was a MAAG choice.) The new battalion numbered 800 men when it began a 15-month training program in September 1971. A permanent U.S. Army adviser was assigned to the battalion and a mobile training team from the Panama Canal Zone participated in a segment of the battalion's instruction. Completion of the program was recognized by the President on December 5, 1972. On that day, during a ceremony at the Constanza airfield, Balaguer presented the new 6th *Batallón de Cazadores* with its colors, and provided its officers and enlisted men with the authority to wear green berets. The President also promoted Castillo Pimentel to lieutenant colonel.[21] At the end of the month, General Pérez y Pérez assumed command of the Dominican Army and adopted the policy that he would be solely responsible for the deployment of the new battalion.

By the end of January 1973, Pérez y Pérez controlled, directly or indirectly, the majority of ground force units that could determine the outcome of an internal politico-military confrontation. This concentration of combat power would also provide the General with the counter-guerrilla capability the Balaguer government would require when ex-Colonel Francisco Caamaño Deñó returned to the Dominican Republic as an insurgent leader in February 1973.

XII

The Caamaño Dossier

From the end of the 1965 civil war until his return to the Dominican Republic in 1973, Colonel Caamaño had been the subject of much study and speculation. Politico-military analysts from various nations assessed his role in the Constitutionalist movement and his disappearance in Europe while in exile. The multitude of reported international sightings of Caamaño, from October 1967 to the beginning of 1973, provided the rebel leader with an aura of mystery that many found intriguing. For Balaguer's officer corps, however, the Caamaño question was deadly serious—the possibility of Caamaño's reemergence in the Dominican Republic, especially in front of armed leftist opponents of the government, was the single biggest threat to the institution's interests. This concern was felt by officers who belonged to all the old factions of the 1960s that were part of the Balaguer regime of the 1970s. Veterans of the CEFA, the San Cristóbal Group, the San Isidro Group, the Navy, and the National Police had in common their need to deny Caamaño the opportunity to regain a foothold in the country.

On the night of February 2, 1973, Cuban-trained and equipped Caamaño and his men landed on the south coast of the Dominican Republic for the purpose of launching a guerrilla war. Yet everything in Caamaño's formative years suggested that he would have been highly unlikely to commit himself to this Castro-style enterprise.

CAAMAÑO BEFORE EXILE

Francisco Alberto Caamaño Deñó was born into the Trujillo system. In the Armed Forces of the dictator, after the immediate Trujillo family, the most privileged individuals were the small group of generals who had been lieutenants with *El Jefe* in the U.S. Marine-led constabulary. The three most well known were Generals Fausto E. Caamaño, Antonio Leyba Pou, and Santos Mélido Marte Pichardo. To be the offspring of one of the three was a guarantee of career success as long as father and son remained loyal to Trujillo. The two Caamaños never wavered.

When General Fausto Caamaño was the sub-secretary—the highest-ranking officer in the Armed Forces after the Generalissimo and brother Héctor Trujillo—Caamaño's son was admitted, at age 17, to the naval academy. (Reportedly, young Caamaño was nicknamed "*El Loco*.") Two years later Francisco was commissioned. After General Caamaño was appointed Secretary of State of War, Navy, and Aviation, his son, who was 21, was promoted to *teniente de navío*, the equivalent of a captain in the Army. The promotion was considered unusual because Francisco had not held his previous rank of *alférez de navío* (first lieutenant) for more than a few months. He was the youngest captain in the entire Dominican Armed Forces. The new promotion was granted prior to young Caamaño's departure for the United States in 1954 to take company-level courses from the U.S. Marines in Coronado, California, and Quantico, Virginia. He had been forced to go abroad because Francisco's father wanted to extricate the junior naval infantry officer from a complicated love affair.[1] Curiously, Caamaño was the only major player of the early 1970s who had studied in the United States as a young officer. Wessin y Wessin, Nivar Seijas, and Pérez y Pérez had not had a powerful general for a father. They all became strong right-wingers, while, in contrast, U.S. Marine Corps-trained Caamaño, in 1973, led a Marxist-supported amphibious expedition against his country's elected government.

Subsequent to Caamaño's 1955 return to the Dominican Republic from the United States, he received routine naval infantry assignments for over three years. After his father retired, Caamaño was transferred to other services on numerous occasions. First he was moved to the Army, then to the CEFA, then to the National Police, and, finally, to the Air Force. During that period, "Franci," as he was called, gained a reputation for erratic behavior and a lack of sense of responsibility. Although after the 1965 civil war the members of the officer corps were generally biased against Caamaño, their many uncomplimentary stories about him were rarely disputed by Caamaño's admirers. Accounts of Caamaño's hard drinking were probably true, because Dominican officers, as a group, were notoriously heavy drinkers. More doubtful were some of the outrageous antics attributed to Caamaño such as, during drunken bouts, he would supposedly bite off the heads of live chickens. Whatever the truth, it is obvious that Caamaño, initially, was highly dependent on his father, and, subsequently, he had a bizarre career pattern, even for a Dominican officer.

In August 1961, the Trujillo family was close to being driven out of the country. On the 16th of that month, Ramfis promoted a large number of officers in an attempt to maintain the support of the officer corps. It is interesting to note that in the CEFA three officers on the promotion list who had begun their careers at approximately the same time were not equal insofar as their professional accomplishments. Major Cuervo Gómez of the Armored Battalion and Major Medrano of the Artillery Group were promoted to lieutenant colonel while Captain Caamaño, in supply, finally became a major. (He had been a captain since 1954.)[2] Other than being on the Navy, Army, and CEFA pistol teams, Caamaño had achieved very little that was noteworthy by the time the CEFA entered the Dominican political arena.

Major Caamaño, however, was not to have any role in the CEFA when that organization dominated the internal affairs of the country, because, in the beginning of 1962, he was transferred to the National Police. As a police officer, he participated in a series of events that leftist supporters of Caamaño were quite willing to forget. He became a member of the U.S.-created *Cascos Blancos* riot squad, which put down the anti-government demonstrations of July 1962.[3] In December of the same year, he led the National Police contingent which suppressed a religious cult at Palma Sola, 30 kilometers from the Haitian border, resulting in more than 45 deaths.[4] Dominicans called it the "Massacre of Palma Sola." Most embarrassing for the PRD was the fact that not only did Caamaño not oppose the overthrow of President Juan Bosch—he played an active part in preventing any uprising of the population in the capital in Bosch's support.[5] At the time, Bosch clearly considered Caamaño to be an enemy. On September 28th, 1963, three days after Bosch was ousted, the ex-president was deported on the frigate *Mella*. Police commander Caamaño was in charge of the armed detail responsible for guarding Bosch on the naval warship. During meals at sea, Bosch refused to eat with Caamaño, explaining that he would not sit at the same table with a son of General Fausto Caamaño.[6]

Being in the National Police during 1962–1964 was fortuitous for Caamaño, however. Washington believed that reforming and modernizing law enforcement was a high priority for the post-Trujillo Dominican Republic; consequently, U.S. assistance, through the Public Safety program of AID, provided extensive equipment and training for the National Police.[7] This policy enabled Caamaño to receive two promotions during his time in the police. By 1964, he was a full colonel commanding the Radio Patrol unit, one of the National Police's better assignments.

Caamaño's steady advancement in the police came to an abrupt halt on January 13, 1965, when he was taken into custody for plotting against the chief of National Police, General Belisario Peguero Guerrero. Apologists for Caamaño claimed that he and a professional police colonel, José Morillo López, were not staging a coup, but were attempting to inform the public of the police chief's corrupt and unethical practices,[8] while others maintain that Caamaño was involved in a simple, self-serving conspiracy.[9] Whatever the motivation, Caamaño proclaimed that the Radio Patrol was in a state of rebellion against General Peguero. President Reid Cabral (with Wessin y Wessin behind him) interceded by ordering the detention of Caamaño and Morillo. On January 18th, the two colonels were assigned as consuls to Jamaica—Caamaño was ordered to Kingston and Morillo to Montego Bay. Caamaño refused to accept the post; that ended his career in the police. He was transferred on February 13th to the Air Force without an assignment.[10] (Morillo, in one year, became chief of the National Police.)

Consequently, with the civil war only three months away, Caamaño had made enemies of the President and Wessin y Wessin, and had the support of no officer faction. There were few prospects for him at San Isidro, and it was likely that he would soon have his commission cancelled. It was not surprising, therefore, that when Caamaño learned on April 24th that a revolt had begun at the *16 de Agosto* Military Camp, he, as an individual, joined the rebellion. Although Caamaño brought no unit or following with him, from the 26th of April until September 3rd he held high office in the rebel government. Caamaño was the minister of the interior, then minister of the armed forces, and, finally, with the approval of Juan Bosch from Puerto Rico, president and commander in chief. When the civil war ended, it was Caamaño whom the world considered the leading military and political figure of the Constitutionalist movement. An evaluation of Caamaño's competence and political orientation by some of the individuals who had contact with him during the civil war reveals many disparate views.

The president of the Government of National Reconstruction, Antonio Imbert Barrera, believed that Caamaño was demented,[11] and the American ambassador in Santo Domingo, William Tapley Bennett, dismissed Caamaño as unstable and a "light-weight thinker."[12] Lieutenant General Bruce Palmer, the first commander of U.S. troops in the Dominican Republic, was unimpressed with Caamaño's mannerisms and appearance, and focused on the Dominican's instability as a youth.[13] But special presidential envoy and former ambassador John Bartlow Martin, after a meeting with Caamaño during the 1965 crisis, wrote: "He [Caamaño] was not crazy. And he had command presence, crowd presence."[14] Washington's representative during negotiations, the astute and experienced Ambassador Ellsworth Bunker, related that Caamaño, during meetings, was calm and outwardly friendly.[15]

In an effort to determine Caamaño's political beliefs, Ambassador Martin's words in 1965 are most significant:

> In all my time in the Dominican Republic, I had met no man whom I thought might become a Dominican Castro—until I met Caamaño.... It

makes little difference when Castro 'became a Communist.' It would make little difference when Caamaño became one.[16]

As to Caamaño's ideology in 1965, some participants had no doubts. Predictably, Wessin y Wessin was convinced Caamaño was a Communist.[17] The Brazilian commander of the Inter-American Peace Force, General Hugo Panasco Alvim, shared this position.[18] The CIA chief in Santo Domingo, David Atlee Phillips, provided a different perspective, however. In his memoirs, Phillips wrote that Caamaño was "Not a Marxist, he was brave and not unduly clever; soon he began to welcome the counsel of hard-core Marxists from various groups."[19] Tad Szluc, the *New York Times* reporter in Santo Domingo, who had had discussions with Caamaño, explained in his Pulitzer Prize-winning account of the civil war that Caamaño, unlike Castro, was politically unsophisticated. Szluc remarked that Caamaño seemed to have few ideological beliefs; however, the journalist did concede that, from the beginning, Communist groups had infiltrated the Constitutionalist movement.[20] A comprehensive U.S. Army Command and General Staff College study of the civil war sums up the majority view of the key Americans in the Dominican Republic at the time:

> Few, if any, U.S. officials thought Caamaño a Communist, although there existed from the outset speculation—soon to become conviction—that his newfound leadership within the Constitutionalist movement was more nominal than real...[21]

Observers had generally agreed that Caamaño demonstrated courage while leading the rebels under fire. His ability to organize the defense at the Duarte Bridge also had been the subject of favorable comment by many. Constitutionalist officers, such as Lieutenant Colonel Hernándo Ramírez and Major Núñez Nogueras, stated, after the civil war, that Caamaño's tactical aggressiveness had injected into the rebellion the will to win.[22] A Cuban-born, Jesuit priest, José A. Moreno, claimed that Caamaño's military leadership extended beyond Constitutionalist officers and enlisted men. Moreno had lived with the irregular insurgents in the *comandos* during the revolt and, from that vantage point, he maintained that the armed, civilian opponents of the Reid government looked to Caamaño as their military leader.[23] General Palmer was less impressed (especially after the combat action of June 15th) with Caamaño's tactical ability.[24] There appears, however, little doubt that the rebel commander had gained the respect, militarily, of the diverse groups participating in the uprising.

Caamaño in Europe

On January 23, 1966, Caamaño arrived in Great Britain. In keeping with Article 8 of the Act of Dominican Reconciliation, he had been "reincorporated" into the Armed Forces and given a legitimate assignment.[25] Caamaño held the rank of colonel (this time his commission was in the Army), and he was appointed military attaché to his country's embassy in London. Caamaño—like his opponent Wessin y Wessin—assumed that the exile was to be short-lived. Caamaño had reasoned that when a constitutional chief of state succeeded provisional president García Godoy, there no longer would be an impediment to his recall, thus making the posting in London a temporary one.[26]

Since Caamaño did not expect a long stay in Great Britain, he was able to cope with his isolation and idleness during his first months in London. From the outset, Caamaño was disinterested in performing the duties of a military attaché; it came as no surprise that his involvement with the British Army was minimal. Many Latin American officers accredited to non-Iberian language countries tended to gravitate toward their own Hemispheric groups rather than to develop extensive contacts with host government officials.[27] But Caamaño also found no comfort in the Latin American military community in London. Considering Caamaño's leftist political associations during the months preceding his diplomatic appointment, it is doubtful that many of his Latin attaché counterparts in Great Britain would have been interested in too close a personal or professional relationship with him. Added to his loneliness brought on by his lack of military colleagues was the fact that he was physically separated from his children, and then from his wife, who had moved to Spain. Yet, despite his unhappiness in London, Caamaño, initially, found outlets unrelated to his position as a military attaché. For example, he accepted invitations to speak to three university student groups (Oxford, Cambridge, and London School of Economics), he met with left-wing personalities, and he provided press interviews.[28] Caamaño's attempt to present a positive attitude can be seen on March 25, 1966, when he granted an interview to Uruguayan journalist Carlos Núñez of the weekly *Marcha*. During the discussion with Núñez, Caamaño was quoted as saying: "I can return [to the Dominican Republic] whenever I deem it convenient, in accordance with the pledge the government made to me. That is what was agreed upon when I left the country, and President García Godoy repeated it to me a short time ago through an emissary."[29]

Since Caamaño had little association with British or Latin American military personnel, and he was intellectually not compatible with many of the civilian leftists he met in London, Caamaño's contacts with other exiled Constitutionalists became especially important to him. His uncle, police Captain Alejandro Deñó Suero, joined him in London as his *ayudante*.[30] This relative was followed on March 18th by former CEFA Captain Pedro José Guerra Urbí, who was appointed assistant military attaché.[31] Both Deñó Suero and Guerra Urbí had fought on the Constitutionalist side. Caamaño also met often with Dominican rebel officers in exile in other countries of Europe. Easily accessible to Caamaño was his former G-3, operations officer, Captain Héctor Lachapelle Díaz, who was the Dominican military attaché across the English Channel in Belgium. In May 1966, Caamaño and Lachapelle Díaz traveled to Rome to meet with Constitutionalists Lieutenant Colonel Pedro Alvarez Holguín from Paris, Lieutenant Colonel José Caonobo Fernández from Madrid, Major Manuel Núñez Nogueras from Bonn, and Colonel Emilio Ludovino Fernández who was assigned to the embassy in Rome. While in Italy, Caamaño made a strong statement to the press that the June 1st elections were essential for the Dominican Republic.[32] Privately, he was convinced that Juan Bosch would be elected, and he assumed that he would be appointed minister of the armed forces.[33]

Bosch, however, was decisively defeated by Balaguer, leaving Caamaño, according to a London observer, in a state of "shock and disbelief."[34] (Ironically, Bosch had no intention of appointing Caamaño the head of the Armed Forces. On May 31st, in private, he made it clear that if he won the presidency, he would select a non-controversial minister, who, unlike Caamaño, would be acceptable to the majority of the officer corps.[35]) Caamaño no longer could rely on the elections as a means for his recall; however, he still thought it likely that the new government would bring him home in the spirit of political reconciliation. Ten days after President Balaguer was inaugurated, he issued Decree 38 allowing numerous Armed Forces officers assigned abroad to return to the Dominican Republic. Even though the Dominican naval attaché in London was on the list, Caamaño was not included.[36] It is at this point that Caamaño's hopes for the future seemed to evaporate and his anxiety began to grow.[37]

During Caamaño's second winter in London, he met with Juan Bosch. After their January 1967 exchange of views, Cuban propaganda emphasized that the ex-president was forced to leave the country because of U.S. pressure, and that Caamaño was the leader of the Dominican armed popular movement.[38] Two months later, Caamaño met secretly in Paris with Dominican representatives of the MPD and the Fourteenth of June Revolutionary Movement. The French government reported that Caamaño was traveling incognito and without the knowledge of the Constitutionalist officers in France.[39] That spring, Caamaño told a Santo Domingo newsman in London that he was "eager to return to the Dominican Republic," and then he launched into an attack on the

United States—the Organization of American States, according to Caamaño, was "serving as the exclusive instrument of U.S. interests."[40] In the summer, Balaguer clearly reaffirmed his position that Caamaño was a threat to peace if he were allowed to return to the country.[41] For Caamaño, it was during this period that various themes began to gel: He was inspired by Che Guevara's guerrilla campaigns, and he was not optimistic that the radical leftist parties of the Dominican Republic could succeed.[42] Added to these thoughts was Caamaño's own continued depression brought on by his fear of perpetual exile. Caamaño, thus, began to realize that he had to set a new course for himself.

By August 1967, Caamaño probably had already taken steps to collaborate with the Cubans. During that month, PRD leaders Francisco Peña Gómez and Emanuel Espinal visited London. Upon their return to the Dominican Republic, Peña Gómez publicly reported that they had "found a new Colonel Caamaño." Peña Gómez claimed that Caamaño was devoting his time to studies, that he was lean as a result of a physical training program, that his will power had not been affected by exile, and that he was "confident in his future." Then Peña Gómez relayed a message from Caamaño that sounded very much like the rallying cry of an aspiring national leader who was attempting to expand his base of support and to provide the populace with a common enemy:

> Colonel Caamaño asked us to cordially greet the Dominican people and all his comrades in arms both Constitutionalists and anti–Constitutionalists because his heart does not harbor hatred or rancor. He knows better than anyone else that in the Dominican Revolution the only victors were the North Americans who imposed their will on us by force of arms.[43]

There were various conflicting accounts as to what the Cuban government and Caamaño agreed upon prior to his disappearance. The same ambiguity existed concerning the details of his actual defection in The Hague on October 24, 1967. As on many occasions in the past, Caamaño departed for the continent on October 21st[44] to visit with Constitutionalist officers assigned to Dominican embassies in Europe and to spend time with his family in Spain. His first stop was the Netherlands where Lachapelle Díaz had been transferred from Belgium. During the evening of October 24th, Caamaño told his host in The Hague, Lachapelle Díaz, that he was going to take a walk alone—he never returned.[45]

One version of what subsequently occurred was prepared by the U.S. State Department's Bureau of Intelligence and Research. This "Intelligence Note" for the Secretary of State, entitled *Missing Dominican Rebel Leader May Be in Cuba*, dated December 8, 1967, reported that Caamaño left The Hague on October 25th for Cologne. Five days after, he met with unknown Constitutionalist officers near Bonn. An unidentified official of the Cuban Embassy in Bonn also attended the meeting. The Intelligence Note continued that Caamaño, on November 1st, was allegedly driven to Frankfurt-am-Main where he departed by air for Mexico "and perhaps on to Cuba." (This information was characterized by the Department of State as "unconfirmed but plausible.")[46]

A second version was obtained from a Cuban intelligence officer who defected to the United States in March 1969. According to him, the Cuban intelligence service planned the defection of Caamaño, code name *Operación Estrella*, in Havana and Paris. Caamaño traveled from The Hague to Paris for approximately one day without a Cuban escort. He had cut off his moustache and was wearing a wig. A personal meeting between Caamaño and Cuban intelligence operatives took place in Paris. From that city, he was transported to Prague, using a false passport, and then he was taken to Cuba.[47]

A third version, written by Hamlet Hermann Pérez, who was with Caamaño in Cuba, was published in 1983. According to Hermann, Caamaño did not take a walk alone in The Hague, but was accompanied by an unidentified Constitutionalist to a restaurant. Once inside, a Cuban agent assisted Caamaño in disguising himself with a wig and makeup. Then Caamaño traveled overland to Prague where he boarded a flight for Havana.[48]

For one month, Caamaño's absence was not noted by the Dominican government. Captain Lachapelle Díaz's excuse for his failure to report immediately Caamaño's disappearance was that Caamaño had vanished during an earlier visit to Lachapelle Díaz's home. After two weeks, according to Lachapelle Díaz, Caamaño surfaced in Paris.[49] And since Caamaño infrequently was in his embassy office in London,[50] the ambassador and his staff in England were not concerned with Caamaño's whereabouts. This attitude of indifference changed, however, on November 23rd. On that day, the public finally became aware of Caamaño's disappearance after the Santo Domingo daily *Listín Diario* published the story that he was missing. The newspaper had acquired the information from contacts in Europe.[51] From then until Caamaño's return to the Dominican Republic in February 1973, his location was the subject of rumor, speculation, and, in the officer corps, apprehension.

CAAMAÑO GOES TO GROUND

For the remainder of his life, Francisco Caamaño Deñó refused to allow the Dominican people to know where he was located or what he was planning. Dominican military intelligence, however, was convinced that he was alive and was reasonably sure that he was in Cuba. Military intelligence in Santo Domingo was correct, but for over five years the leaders of the Dominican Armed Forces and their intelligence services had a wide assortment of raw data to ponder.

During the last days of November 1967, Caamaño's relatives, Constitutionalist officer colleagues, and PRD party figures all addressed the Colonel's disappearance, but none claimed that they knew where he was in hiding. His wife, from Spain, stated that Caamaño had been expected in Madrid for a visit; however, he had failed to appear.[52] One of the Colonel's brothers, speaking for his father, retired General Fausto Caamaño, and the rest of the family, denied that Caamaño had returned to the Dominican Republic, but they disbelieved that he was in a Communist country.[53] Constitutionalist officers in Europe attempted to determine Caamaño's whereabouts; however, they maintained that they had been unsuccessful. The case was turned over to the Dutch police, which acquired the collaboration of its French and Spanish counterparts.[54] Initially, PRD reaction in Santo Domingo was shrill. The party's secretary general, Peña Gómez, exclaimed publicly that the Colonel's disappearance would create an "international scandal" and set off internal violence.[55] PRD ex-President Juan Bosch, however, took a cryptic approach, which would become his theme on the subject: Caamaño was alive and had acted with a specific purpose in mind, but his location was unknown.[56] President Balaguer was even more detached; his comments on the issue for the next five years would be marked by a note of indifference. His first remarks on the Caamaño matter were that he knew only what the press had published on the subject.[57]

Immediately following the initial reports that Caamaño had vanished was the speculation that he had defected to Cuba. This option was raised in various political camps. Right-wing Falangists in Spain put forth this possibility,[58] as well as left-wing Dominicans in Paris.[59] The rumors took on a more alarmist tone when a report from Brazil (which was obtained from a "highly reliable source" in New York City) stated that Caamaño was in Havana organizing a coup d'état to be launched in the Dominican Republic on either the 24th or the 31st of December.[60] When Balaguer was asked what the possibilities of a *golpe* were, he curtly dismissed the idea.[61] But before 1967 ended, the gossip concerning the Colonel's whereabouts extended beyond Cuba—he was placed in Venezuela,[62] in Central America, in Eastern Europe, in Paris, and in the Dominican Republic covertly preparing for a guerrilla war.[63]

For the officer corps, the specter of Caamaño would dovetail with the already established north coast invasion syndrome. Caamaño's disappearance gave rise to the apprehension that a guerrilla army under the Colonel—a force in being—was prepared to invade the Dominican Republic. This new fear was coupled with the old Trujillo era experience that the country's external enemies would strike along the Atlantic shore as they had done at Luperón in 1949 and at Maimón and Estero Hondo in 1959. The first manifestation of this anxiety involving Caamaño was seen in the beginning of 1968. On February 25th, the Air Force began reconnaissance flights in the vicinity of Puerto Plata on the north coast. During the following five days, ships and more aircraft were deployed to the general location, and the 2nd Battalion, 1st Brigade, and elements of the 4th Brigade, were moved from the capital to the Estero Hondo-Luperón-Cambiaso-Maimón-Puerto Plata region. (Nivar made a well-publicized appearance to "inspect" the Army's troops.) This military activity was undertaken in reaction to fragmentary reports sent from the area that Caamaño had landed or was about to land.[64] To prevent panic from setting in, Balaguer, on March 4th, informed the nation that the whole affair had been nothing more than a pre-scheduled field training exercise. He stressed that: "There is no evidence that an armed expedition is being prepared against our country."[65] But the military deployments were not routine, mock war games—they were genuine operational responses to what was believed, at the time, to be credible intelligence. And it was not an isolated episode—it would be the first of many false alarms linking Caamaño with a maritime invasion of the north coast.

In 1968, Dominican military intelligence was the recipient of a continuous flow of Caamaño sightings. These reports began before the north coast scare and continued, unabated, through the year. On January 20th, one account placed Caamaño not in the Western Hemisphere, but back in Europe. Allegedly, he and Juan Bosch, in Madrid, were planning to create a new Dominican leftist political party.[66] In the month that followed, imprecise information became available that, in actuality, Caamaño was in Cuba.[67] The President, once again, felt it necessary, on February 26th, to inform the public that there existed no solid evidence as to the location of the Colonel.[68] Balaguer's attempt to calm the country had a short-lived effect, however. Three days later, the secretary general of Balaguer's own political party was quoted in the press as saying that Caamaño was in Cuba.[69] Added to the confusion was the comment on March 10th by a prominent Cuban exile in Miami,[70] and the statement on March 11th by the Dominican leftist Fourteenth of June Revolutionary Movement that, indeed, the Colonel was in Cuba.[71] The Balaguer government immediately attempted to downplay those reports.[72] And from the legal opposition PRD, on March 11th, Juan Bosch's theme was repeated: "[We do] not know Caamaño Deñó's whereabouts or his political plans."[73]

By mid–March 1968, it was conceded by the government that the intelligence service of the secretariat of the Armed Forces was having difficulty answering the many questions concerning the Caamaño disappearance.[74] In April, the raw reports reached the exotic when Communist China, North Vietnam, and Algeria were placed on the list of Caamaño sightings.[75] It was in May that Dominican military intelligence finally received a substantive report from a seemingly reliable source. According to documents found on an insurgent's body in western Venezuela, Army intelligence officers of that country determined that Caamaño had succeeded the dead Che Guevara as Fidel Castro's guerrilla warfare organizer for Latin America. Caamaño allegedly was responsible for the direction of insurgent operations to include the management of funds, the disposition of weapons, and the control of agents. This report indicated that Venezuela and Colombia were Caamaño's most active enterprises.[76] Added to this report was information acquired by the Secret Department of the National Police that Caamaño was training Dominicans from the MPD and the Fourteenth of June Revolutionary Movement in Cuba. Names of trainees were provided.[77] Although there were many reasons for discounting the segment of the report that stated that Caamaño had replaced Che Guevara, the possibility that Caamaño was in Cuba, working with Castro's international revolutionary warfare department, seemed likely. Caamaño's potential as a troublemaker began to grow.

Balaguer did not change his public information policy, however. On May 8th, the President commented that he gave little importance to the Venezuela report, and he emphasized that he did not know if Caamaño was in Cuba. (He also insisted that ongoing troop movements were only training exercises—in May the country was in the midst of another north coast scare.)[78] However, one week later, on May 15th, Balaguer announced that, by executive order, Caamaño was declared a deserter and was cashiered from the Armed Forces.[79] The significance of the President's designating Caamaño a deserter was that Balaguer's position before May 15th had been that the government had no basis to declare Caamaño a deserter without first knowing the circumstances surrounding his disappearance. (Wessin y Wessin carped from Miami that Balaguer should have taken that action against Caamaño ten days after the Colonel left his post in London without permission.[80])

During the remainder of 1968, the geographically diverse sightings of Caamaño continued. For example, he supposedly participated in insurgent activity in Venezuela, he was with guerrillas in the mountains of Colombia, he was killed in the jungles of Guatemala, he passed through Jamaica, and he died while he was secretly in the Dominican Republic.[81]

Even though many observers in 1968 found it difficult to give too much weight to the Caamaño affair, the chairman of the Subcommittee on Inter-American Affairs of the U.S. House of Representatives, who had completed a trip throughout the Caribbean Basin, thought differently. Congressman Armistead I. Selden's official report, dated November 2, 1968, stated the following:

> Numerous rumors about Caamaño's presence in different Latin American countries, as well as behind the Iron Curtain, have circulated.... Many of them center on one location: Cuba.... If Caamaño is indeed in Cuba, and if he should choose to press his opposition to the existing order in the Dominican Republic, his return to that country, perhaps in the guise of an insurgent leader, could serve as a rallying point for those dissident elements in the old 'Constitutionalist' movement which are unhappy with the Balaguer administration. In the rather tenuously balanced political environment of the Dominican Republic, such a development could have seriously disturbing consequences.[82]

In the beginning of 1969, the President gratuitously threw out the offer that Caamaño could return to the Dominican Republic to participate in the 1970 electoral campaign. Balaguer's proposal on January 12th was curious since Caamaño was still classified as a deserter and, once again, the country was going through another north coast alarm.[83] Two days later, it was reported that Caamaño had participated in a December 20–31, 1968, gathering entitled the "Congress of Integration of Latin American Guerrillas" in Santander Department, Colombia.[84] On February 7th, a convoluted plot was aired in which alleged Communist Spaniards living in San Francisco de Macorís, northeast of the capital, were reportedly planning to overthrow the government in conjunction with a Caamaño-led armed landing from Cuba. Fidel Castro supposedly controlled the conspirators in the Dominican interior by clandestine radio.[85] The report of Caamaño and the Spanish Communists of San Francisco de Macorís was quickly forgotten, but the possibility that Caamaño could return specifically for the presidential elections generated some speculation. A small group of militant young leftists associated with the PRD refused to believe that their future "military liberator" would involve himself in a bourgeois electoral process,[86] while a handful of ex-Constitutionalist officers residing in the Dominican Republic discussed the possibility of Caamaño's becoming their legitimate candidate.[87]

Talk of Caamaño in the electoral campaign did not staunch the flow of international sightings of the former colonel. In April, he was reported to be in the Netherlands,[88] in May the French Sureté allegedly notified Santo Domingo that he was in Paris,[89] and in August and September he was being pursued by the police in Argentina.[90] In that South American country, he was supposed to have been first in Mendoza, then in Cordoba, and finally in Santa Fe. According to Argentine sources, Caamaño had been one of the organizers of the May riots in Cordoba, which resulted in 20 deaths and over 100 injured.[91] These reports were not based on strong evidence, but information concerning Caamaño, obtained from a Cuban defector in 1969, probably was accurate.

In late March 1969, a Cuban intelligence officer in Paris, Orlando Castro Hidalgo, defected to the United States government. Dominican military intelligence became aware of Castro Hidalgo's debriefing no later than July 1969. The Cuban claimed that Caamaño traveled to Cuba via Paris and Prague in October 1967, and had remained on the island since that date. Caamaño was not designated the replacement for Che Guevara, and there was a suggestion that there was not a high opinion in Cuba of Caamaño's ability.[92]

From 1970 forward, there was a reduction in the number of Caamaño sightings, but there were no changes in the policies of Caamaño, Bosch, or Balaguer. The ex-Colonel still remained totally silent—he provided no explanation for his disappearance and made no comment on the disclosures of the Cuban defector. Former President Bosch was interviewed in Paris by a Chilean journalist in March 1970. In answer to questions concerning Caamaño, Bosch replied: "Caamaño has gone to some part of the world, but for very well defined reasons.... Neither I nor anyone in my party has any contact, direct or indirect, with Caamaño. We know absolutely nothing. We know nothing about what he is doing or thinking."[93] As for President Balaguer, he continued to brush aside questions on Caamaño with the equivalent of "all I know is what I read in the newspapers."[94]

A surprise statement about Caamaño came from Fidel Castro on January 7, 1971. On that day in Havana, Castro definitively told Emilio Herasme Peña, the Dominican secretary general of the professional journalists' union, that he knew where the Colonel was located; however, he said it must remain a secret. Castro was quoted: "I must abstain from commenting on that because possibly the enemies of the revolutionaries may be interested in knowing where he is. Really, I am not willing to cooperate with the enemy by giving information." Castro also made it clear to the newsman that there would be a "second revolution" in the Dominican Republic and he implied that Caamaño would be its leader.[95]

Citing the Castro interview, General Perdomo Rosario, the new commander of the 2nd Brigade, on January 29th, instructed the press that his command was prepared to prevent Caamaño from invading the country through the north coast.[96] (Perdomo Rosario had some reason to feel confident because the U.S. MAP-supported 9th Battalion in his zone had received all its equipment and had completed its training.) One week later Wessin y Wessin boasted on television that he was willing to face Caamaño if there was an invasion.[97]

The Dominican Republic was not invaded in 1971, nor in 1972, and the Caamaño sightings continued, though at a much slower pace. (The

Soviet Union was added to the list.[98]) The last Caamaño report, dated a few days before January 19, 1973, was received by the intelligence service of the secretariat of the Armed Forces. It stated that Caamaño had died in Santiago, Cuba, of unknown causes. According to the unidentified source, Caamaño had gone through strenuous training as a guerrilla, but his relations with the Cuban government had deteriorated. The Castro regime, the report stated, would not support a Caamaño operation and would not allow the Colonel to leave the island.[99] The secretary general of the PRD, Peña Gómez, insisted on January 20th that Caamaño was alive, but he refused to explain how he knew that this was the case.[100]

Despite the many sightings and rumors to the contrary, the evidence indicates that after Caamaño vanished he lived exclusively in Cuba. His activities on the island, however, are not fully accounted for except that a segment of his stay was devoted to preparing for rural guerrilla operations in the Dominican Republic.[101]

XIII

The Critical First 12 Days of the Caamaño Expedition

Under the cover of darkness, at 7:30 P.M., on February 2, 1973, Francisco Caamaño Deñó and the eight members of his guerrilla band, in an auxiliary-powered sailboat, dropped anchor in the Bay of Ocoa more than one mile off the southern coast of the Dominican Republic. They were approximately 50 air miles west of Santo Domingo. The original plan of the former amphibious operations-trained, naval infantry officer called for everyone to disembark in a rubber raft at the same time; however, when they attempted to load the raft, it was determined that the craft was unable to hold the entire group and its equipment. Caamaño, therefore, ordered that the landing be undertaken in two, rather than one, increments. He and four of the guerrillas were able, in the raft, to reach Caracoles Beach without incident. Caamaño then sent one of the four back to the sailboat in the rubber craft to bring the remainder of the team ashore. The boat handler, however, lost his way in the moonless night and was beached; once on land, he began walking east on the coastal highway. At 10:00 P.M., the insurgents on the mother ship decided that they had waited long enough for the raft—they weighed anchor and prepared to run the sailboat aground; however, they could not get the vessel under way. The four guerrillas, therefore, abandoned the sailboat and swam toward the coast. They were able to link up with Caamaño at Caracoles Beach, but much of the group's equipment was left behind. Early in the morning of February 3rd, Caamaño and seven of his band moved inland, while the solitary ninth man, who had piloted the ill-fated rubber raft, arrived in the capital via the coastal highway.[1] Thus began the long-awaited Caamaño expedition.

FEBRUARY 4–7

For the Dominican officer corps, the beginning of the Caamaño affair took place one day later. The Army 3rd Brigade's six-man Caracoles Post, led by a noncommissioned officer, reported early on February 4th that peasants had observed strangers departing the beach in a northerly, inland, direction, and that a sailboat, which they had never seen before, had been left unattended in the area. When Dominican officers inspected the boat, they identified it as a 42-foot, two-mast Chris Craft Comanche, named the *Black Jak*.[2] A rapid review of the items in the vessel revealed 10 maps of the Dominican Republic, 260 rounds of .223 caliber ammunition, one grenade manual, five grenade fuses, a complete medical kit, a military compass, five sticks of dynamite, a portable Sony radio, six suitcases, clothes to include elements of military uniforms, books, and Dominican money.[3] Of special interest were a photograph of Caamaño, a 1971 budget of the Dominican Republic, a document containing the 1961 Dominican Army order of battle, a photograph of two youths in Cuban military uniform, and a map with

Guerrilla leader ex–Col. Francisco Caamaño Deñó. This photograph was taken in the Dominican hills in early February 1973. (*La Noticia*)

notations representing an area of operations near Testero Mejía mountain, northwest of the town of San José de Ocoa. A clearly visible sign had been posted on board the vessel—it read in Spanish that the boat was rigged to explode. (The claim that explosives were rigged was false.)[4]

During the afternoon of February 4th, an Army sergeant and his patrol reported that eight men in military fatigues carrying weapons (the AR-15 rifle was identified) and backpacks were sighted near El Pilar, west of San José de Ocoa. The leader of the group of men told the sergeant that he was a colonel in the 4th Brigade and that they were on a topographic mission. Army headquarters had also received fragmentary reports, originating from peasants, that a small group of uniformed men were heading north with mules, equipment, and weapons.[5]

Although the leadership of the Armed Forces could not determine what had occurred during the *Black Jak*'s arrival, there was no doubt that armed opponents of the government had infiltrated into the country. The Dominican Army had not had a 4th Brigade for three years and no topographic mission was authorized at the time in the San José de Ocoa area. The main preoccupation of General Pérez y Pérez and Admiral Jiménez was whether the Caracoles Beach landing was a feint to induce the Armed Forces to commit the preponderance of military resources to the southern area, thus leaving the north coast vulnerable to the main effort.[6]

Based on the information received on February 4th, the Armed Forces and National Police were placed on full alert. The first tactical deployment ordered was the dispatch of one company of the Army's 3rd Battalion, stationed in San Cristóbal, and one company of the police's Department of Special Operations, located outside Santo Domingo, to the San José de Ocoa area. In addition, the 6th *Cazadores* Battalion in Constanza was given the task of defending the principal national telecommunications facility built on top of Alto Bandera mountain in the *Cordillera Central*. The Navy ordered all available vessels to commence patrolling, and the Air Force was directed to begin reconnaissance operations.[7]

Early on February 5th, before the full significance of Caamaño's presence in the Dominican Republic was understood by the people of Santo Domingo, General Cruz Brea, the chief of National Police, operating on his own authority, took one of the most important actions of the campaign. He ordered the National Police discreetly to cut off entrances to the capital from the interior of the country, thus preventing a potential guerrilla concentration in the mountains from easily linking up with the far more dangerous leftist extremist groups located in the urban areas of Santo Domingo. This initiative on the part of the police chief reduced the possibility that Caamaño could establish a second front in the critical capital area.[8]

Later in the day, the National Police began more visible security measures in Santo Domingo. The Autonomous University of Santo Domingo was surrounded, causing the rector to suspend classes. The houses of Juan Bosch and PRD secretary general Peña Gómez were searched although they were not present—both had gone into hiding. Radio stations owned by opponents of the regime were temporarily closed down without explanation.[9] Newspapers continued to operate and foreign news services such as *EFE* of Madrid and *Agence France-Presse* of Paris were not impeded, however. The U.S. Embassy reported to Washington that, as of 6:00 P.M., February 5th, "Santo Domingo remains calm, if tense."[10]

After a lengthy meeting between the President and senior leaders of the military and security establishments (including General Pérez y

Pérez, Admiral Jiménez, General Cruz Brea, and DNI director Valdez Vidaurre[11]), the government released an official communiqué through the public relations office of the secretariat of the Armed Forces. The Dominican people were informed by radio and newspaper that on the morning of February 4th a "group of guerrillas from Cuba" landed at Caracoles Beach, in the Province of Azua, "for the purpose of initiating subversive activities in different parts of the country." A description of the sailboat was then provided. This information was similar to the earlier internal Army report, plus the communiqué stated that the vessel was registered in New York. A list of items on board the *Black Jak* was then given. The communiqué also claimed that a large number of documents were found which implicated "Juan Bosch and other political leaders in the preparation of this conspiracy against the public peace." The communiqué ended by informing Dominicans that the Armed Forces, acting under the instructions of the President, would prevent a repetition of April 24, 1965 [the beginning of the civil war], and that the "authorities maintain control in all provinces of the republic." The communiqué was dated February 5, 1973.[12] The official communication had not cited Caamaño's name nor indicated that the guerrillas, according to the captured map, were probably planning to operate northwest of San José de Ocoa.

The area Caamaño chose in the Dominican Republic for irregular warfare had certain advantages for him. The San José de Ocoa region had been politically difficult for Dominican governments. In December 1963, there had been sporadic rebel activity in that area as part of a nationwide rural insurgency campaign led by Manuel Tavárez Justo of the Fourteenth of June Political Group,[13] and in February 1967 there were serious guerrilla problems in the same general location. Dominican military intelligence had determined that Orlando Mazara, a Communist Chinese-trained leader of the Fourteenth of June Revolutionary Movement, had been able to operate with some popular support in 1967 near San José de Ocoa before he was brought down. Limited anti-government sentiment still lingered in 1973 among the peasants of the region.[14] The terrain also had appeal. The San José de Ocoa area was in the foothills of the *Cordillera Central*, the highest mountain range in the Caribbean. Mobility for regular Dominican troops was difficult, and targets of opportunity for guerrilla raids were available. (The most significant potential objective was the before mentioned telecommunications center atop Alto Bandera peak.) If Caamaño's arrival in the San José de Ocoa area was the main insurgent effort, it could only mean that he was preparing to establish a rural insurgency concentration or *foco* in that zone with the purpose of creating a rallying point for insurrection in the capital. This concept of operations followed the classic Cuban experience of 1956–1958 in which Fidel Castro operated in the Sierra Maestra while urban insurgency grew in Havana.

A review of the situation later on February 5th convinced General Pérez y Pérez and Admiral Jiménez that stronger measures in the vicinity of San José de Ocoa were required. A joint task force of approximately 400 men was established; its mission was to locate the guerrillas rapidly and destroy them. The hastily assembled unit initially consisted of elements of the Army's 1st Brigade and 6th Battalion, and the police's Department of Special Operations. Troops from the 2nd and the 3rd Battalions of the 1st Brigade were assigned to a provisional mixed battalion, and men from the 6th Battalion made up the second provisional battalion.[15]

Brigadier General Perdomo Rosario was given command of the task force. Supposedly, he was already in charge of operations in the zone that Caamaño had traveled through—from Caracoles Beach, north, past the villages of Las Charcas, Los Quemados, and El Cercado, to the San José de Ocoa area—because, as the sitting commander of the 3rd Brigade, this entire region was in his jurisdiction. Perdomo, however, did not have a reputation for military professionalism. To compensate for this inadequacy, Colonel Pompeyo Ruiz Serrano was designated the principal general staff officer of the task force. Ruiz Serrano was a 1963 graduate of the Command and Staff Course in the Canal Zone and, in 1965 during the civil war, he was the operations officer that planned the successful sweep in the northern sector of Santo Domingo. After the conflict, he had been the founding director of the Officers School. The commander of the 1st Brigade mixed battalion was Lieutenant Colonel Francisco Matos Gutiérrez. Before his assignment to the task force, Matos Gutiérrez was the commander of the 1st Battalion, 1st Brigade; however, when he joined the counterguerrilla operation, he was given command of troops only from the 2nd and the 3rd Battalions. One possible explanation for this anomaly was that Pérez y Pérez wanted to hold the 1st Battalion back as a national reserve, but he did not want the commanders of the 2nd and the 3rd Battalions to lead troops in the combat zone because of their affiliation with Nivar. Whatever the reason, soldiers from the 2nd and the 3rd Battalions were to be led in the San José de Ocoa area by the commander of the 1st Battalion. In contrast to the 1st Brigade mixed battalion command issue, the 6th Battalion element sent to the task force was under the leadership of the actual commander of the entire battalion—Lieutenant Colonel Castillo Pimentel. Finally, the DSO policemen in the task force were commanded by their long-time commanding officer, Lieutenant Colonel Féliz Fernández. He had participated in the December 1963 counterinsurgency effort as a first lieutenant, and during the May 1967 operations in San José de Ocoa he, as a captain, had led the DSO.[16]

The command post of the task force was placed in the San José de Ocoa police station, and troops were trucked rapidly into the zone of operations, which was between Testero Mejía mountain and San José de Ocoa. (Organic mortars were left in garrison.)[17] The Air Force increased its reconnaissance flights of OH-6A helicopters and P-51 fighters over the area. Admiral Jiménez's concern that a second landing was highly probable caused him to make a formal request to the American government for the U.S. Navy to patrol the waters off the Dominican north coast. Washington's response to the Admiral was that reports would be sent to him of "any and all suspicious ships and craft"; however, the U.S. government declined to "initiate special surveillance" at that time.[18]

During its first hours of existence, the task force had received little new intelligence information; the last significant report had come earlier from the sergeant who had talked with Caamaño on February 4th in the vicinity of El Pinar. Poor visibility limited the use of the helicopters, and the P-51s were even less effective. As early as February 5th, there had been a communications breakdown between the task force headquarters in San José de Ocoa and the field units patrolling the countryside. Adverse weather and difficult terrain also caused logistics problems of which the paucity of food was paramount. One positive development was that the Dominican Army rapidly recognized the need to gain the full support of the peasantry; therefore, civil affairs teams were immediately dispatched to the villages to explain the Army's presence and to provide assistance through civic action. (Also understood was the importance of maintaining the loyalty of the enlisted men; consequently, on February 5th, a commission of officers was sent to various installations to ensure support for the government.)[19]

The first armed contact with Caamaño's group took place during the night of February 5–6. It occurred near the hamlet of La Ciénaga, alongside the Testero Mejía peak, approximately 13 kilometers northwest of San José de Ocoa, when troops from the 1st Brigade mixed battalion engaged in a firefight with guerrillas. The initial report from the Army patrol was that one enlisted man was killed and one was wounded; a guerrilla was believed wounded.[20] A more complete report subsequently sent from the field stated that three soldiers from the mixed battalion were dead and three were wounded. The task force claimed four guerrillas killed, but no bodies were found.[21]

The number of casualties was not released to the public. Instead, at 10:00 P.M., February 6th, the secretariat of the Armed Forces issued a communiqué stating that government forces had the guerrillas surrounded on the slope of Testero Mejía mountain. Admiral Jiménez's communiqué continued that it was hoped that the guerrillas would surrender to obviate any loss of life.[22] In the outskirts of San José de Ocoa, however, rumors were circulating among the peasants that there had been a major firefight in the hills and individuals had been killed or hurt. The accredited newsmen in the area attempted to track down the story. As a group, they approached General Perdomo Rosario in the hopes that he would, at least, provide some insight on how the military operation was developing. Sitting in his jeep, surrounded by six bodyguards, Perdomo showed little interest in military affairs, but wanted only to share baseball stories with the newspapermen.[23] The correspondent from the respected *Listín Diario*, consequently, had to turn elsewhere for his story and, by the night of February 6th, the real situation was exposed. *Listín Diario*'s journalist had discovered the truth—three were dead and three were wounded. But before *Listín Diario* had the opportunity to publish the story, the French news service *Agence France-Presse* took the *Listín Diario* account and (after crediting *Listín Diario*) broadcast it to the world.[24]

The discovery that the guerrillas were not trapped, and, moreover, that they had killed three Dominican soldiers left the public in a sober mood. General Pérez y Pérez's immediate actions were to increase the size of the task force to 600 men, to provide further communications support for field units, and to order M-79 grenade launchers to be brought forward from the *16 de Agosto* Military Camp to the San José de Ocoa area.[25] (One hundred 1st Brigade enlisted men and seven officers had completed U.S. Army training with the new 40mm M-79s on May 2nd, 1972.[26]) The chief of staff of the Dominican Army, however, knew that these steps alone would not solve the problems that had developed in San José de Ocoa.

It became evident to General Pérez y Pérez that the main difficulty in the task force lay with its commander. General Perdomo was not exercising command vigorously enough, and there was a breakdown of operational control within the task force. The former problem was apparent because government troops were not aggressively pursuing the guerrillas. In the latter case, confusion reigned in Perdomo's organization. The command post in the town of San José de Ocoa was too far from the zone of operations. Orders were carried by messenger, and, at times, eight hours lapsed before the orders were received by the maneuver elements. Perdomo was not aware of the location of most of the 1st Brigade units, and the 6th Battalion commander would not obey the General's orders unless they were approved in the capital. Lieutenant Colonel Castillo Pimentel refused to deploy his troops in designated blocking positions until he received a concurrence from Santo Domingo, a decision that resulted in the February 5–6 night escape of the guerrillas. Even though Pérez y Pérez was partially responsible for instituting this direct link between Santo Domingo and the 6th Battalion for political reasons when the *Cazador* unit was established, Castillo Pimentel had taken his semi-autonomy too far when he ignored the task force commander during a combat operation. And this unacceptable situation was aggravated by Perdomo's apparent disinterest in exerting his command authority over the 6th Battalion.[27]

During the morning of February 7th, troops from the 1st Brigade mixed battalion again made contact with the guerrillas in the Testero Mejía peak area. There was a firefight, but the insurgents slipped away leaving one more government soldier wounded. There was no evidence that there had been guerrilla casualties.[28] It then became obvious to the President, in addition to General Pérez y Pérez, that the regime's campaign was adrift. Perdomo Rosario once again had failed. As when he was the CEFA tank commander in the opening days of the 1965 civil war, and chief of National Police in the second half of 1970, he was not up to the job. In the late morning of February 7th, Balaguer, Pérez y Pérez, and Armed Forces secretary Jiménez boarded a helicopter and flew to San José de Ocoa. The presidential party arrived at noon, and, after 45 minutes of discussion in the task force, the group returned to the capital.[29] Balaguer had relieved General Perdomo of command and appointed Brigadier General Juan René Beauchamps Javier as his replacement. In addition, the President selected Brigadier General Ramiro Matos González to be task force chief of operations. Balaguer made the final decision on the leadership of the ground forces in San José de Ocoa, but the personnel nominees were undoubtedly selected by Pérez y Pérez.

The key man in the campaign was to be General Matos González. The FAD infantry officer had distinguished himself in 1963 during counterinsurgency operations in the vicinity of Las Manaclas, located in the *Cordillera Central*, and had maintained his reputation as a counterguerrilla expert during the ten years that followed.[30] Even Cuba's propaganda outlet, *Prensa Latina*, acknowledged this fact.[31] The President had designated Matos chief of operations, but he would become much more. In reality, Matos' role was to be the tactical commander within the area of operations.

Overall command of the military zone was given to General Beauchamps Javier, a respected, no-nonsense, officer who could be expected to get the job done. As theater commander, he was a choice few could challenge. And in the execution of their new mission, Beauchamps and Matos were no strangers. In 1968, when Beauchamps was in charge of the Army's North Zone as commander of the 2nd Brigade, and Matos was head of the Air Force's North Command, they had worked successfully together during a regional emergency.[32]

The defeat of the guerrillas was not the President's only consideration; he also had to take into account the politics of the officer corps before he made any military appointments. Balaguer's new lineup provided him with the following mosaic:

- Admiral Jiménez would continue in the cabinet as secretary of state of the armed forces. He would be useful in dealing with the American Embassy and the press.
- General Pérez y Pérez would remain the chief of staff of the Army; from that position, he could run the conflict militarily at the national level. His iron hand would direct the employment of all ground forces in the zone of operations, in the highly important capital, on the north coast, and in the east. Pérez y Pérez could also keep an interfering Nivar at bay.
- General Beauchamps' ambiguous political leanings, beginning in 1968 when he was the 2nd Brigade commander in Santiago, would partially mollify Nivar. Since then, Beauchamps had kept up a working relationship with Nivar. But, above all, military requirements would come first with Beauchamps.
- General Matos would be loyal to the chain of command, he would be disinterested in promoting himself politically, and he would focus solely on defeating the guerrillas.
- General Cruz Brea would efficiently support Pérez y Pérez in the capital and in the mountains (where the police DSO would be invaluable), and he would be an obstacle to Nivar's exploiting the former police chief's connections in the National Police.
- Colonel Cuervo Gómez would provide the President with the tanks in Santo Domingo, and he would deny Nivar access to the armored vehicles.
- General Folch Pérez, the FAD chief and experienced pilot, would devote his full attention to keeping his aging aircraft flying. (His disinterest in his airborne and infantry troops[33] was a positive factor politically.)
- General Lluberes Montás was in limbo as sub-secretary of state of the armed forces for air, but he was available to re-enter the scene if a need arose—either because of guerrilla developments or Nivar intrigues.

In sum, Balaguer had a senior Armed Forces team that was capable of defeating Caamaño, and he had effectively excluded Nivar from the biggest military operation since the Dominican civil war of 1965.

The relief of General Perdomo was followed by other key personnel changes in the task force. Colonel Ruiz Serrano, the principal staff officer, and Lieutenant Colonel Matos Gutiérrez, the commander of the 1st Brigade mixed battalion, were sacked. Colonel Héctor García Tejada, the G-3 of the Army General Staff, was assigned to the task force on February 7th as deputy operations officer, but he quickly was moved from the operations staff to commander of the 1st Brigade mixed battalion. Although Castillo Pimentel had come close to being relieved, he was allowed to remain in command of the 6th Battalion.[34]

At the same time, command and control problems were streamlined in the San José de Ocoa area. A forward command post was established close to the maneuver units. The main command post in the town of San José de Ocoa took over combat service support functions—logistical sluggishness caused by the difficult terrain and poor organization was soon rectified.[35] One example lay in the difficulty feeding the troops' patrolling in the mountains. The normal operating procedure for the Dominican Army in the field was to live by local purchase, but this system had rapidly grinded down and rations had to be hastily prepared in Santo Domingo. The serious food re-supply problem was temporarily resolved with the shipment of 2,000 rations, prepared by commercial companies, to the area of operations. Also, the secretariat of the Armed Forces requested that the U.S. government provide an emergency allocation of C-rations to feed 500 personnel for five days.[36]

By February 7th, the military and police intelligence services began to develop a hazy preliminary picture of the enemy situation from established sources in the Dominican Republic. Fragmentary information suggested that, according to a 1971 plan, Cuban-trained guerrillas, in January 1972, were to be infiltrated into the hills to operate in concert with the extreme-leftist urban group, the *Comandos de la Resistencia*. The government's success during the January 12, 1972, coastal road firefight, however, caused the insurgent campaign to be postponed until February 1973, because the four bank robbers killed by the National Police had been key members of the *Comandos de la Resistencia*. (A document found with their corpses mentioned a "*Comandante* Román" who was training in Cuba for the purpose of establishing a rural guerrilla operation in the Dominican Republic.) Current intelligence information, related to the Caracoles landing, indicated that there had been two infiltrations—the first entered the capital and the second went into the San José de Ocoa area. The objective of the insurgents was to overthrow the Balaguer government. The initial phase was the preparation for terrorist operations in Santo Domingo to include spreading confusion, assassinating military and police officials, and assaulting Armed Forces installations. An assessment of the intelligence at hand revealed that planned violence in the capital was the main threat to the government. It was believed that once disturbances began, it would be difficult to control the population because too many individuals in the poorer sections of the city had easy access to weapons. Consequently, potential chaos in Santo Domingo had to be addressed immediately.[37]

In the evening of the same day that Balaguer visited the command post in San José de Ocoa, he addressed the nation from his office in the National Palace. He began by remarking that it had only been hours since he had returned from the location where "subversive activities involving the guerrilla group ... are now taking place." Balaguer then stated that the insurgent operation was "an attempt to force the government into concentrating in that area the greatest number of military units possible so as to leave the capital city and other areas of the country with insufficient defensive units." He followed by pointing out that "we are virtually certain that the group that landed on Caracoles Beach comprised ten persons. Two of the group, dressed in civilian clothes, calmly traveled to Santo Domnigo. The other eight, dressed in olive drab uniforms, headed toward Las Charcas, Azua Province." The President described what peasants had reported concerning the guerrillas' movement north into the hills. Balaguer then spoke of Cuban involvement and revealed to the public, for the first time, the existence of a captured map with notations on it: "The group, composed of personnel specially trained in Cuba and other communist countries purposely left a strategic map on Caracoles Beach showing the various mountainous areas where they planned to carry out their operations." These comments were followed by implicating Caamaño, whose photograph was found in the sailboat. Balaguer stressed that the map and the Caamaño picture were part of a deception plan. Then the President cryptically stated that "on the same Sunday [February 4] that the landing at the Ocoa beach was revealed, a well-known opposition leader traveled to Santiago and met with some of his closest friends and other elements that are known to have participated in the 24 April 1965 revolution. Moreover, according to proof obtained by the government, one of the opposition leaders declared that the so-called *Aguila Feliz* [Happy Eagle] Operation had to be implemented before next Saturday [February 10]. Because of all these indications that there is a plot to disturb public peace and lead the country to the situation existing on 24 April 1965, the government feels compelled to take emergency measures to protect the threatened order. Regardless of how drastic they may seem, these emergency measures are aimed solely at preventing a disaster similar to the one that occurred in 1965." Subsequently, Balaguer remarked, "I must also warn the instigators of the subversive plot that the government is fully aware of their plans and knows every detail of what is being planned. And it has decided to act strongly and mercilessly." After emotionally speaking of the national flag, the "constitutional emblem," and the Dominican people, the President closed his 15-minute address.[38]

In the Balaguer speech, he had implied that Juan Bosch and the PRD leadership were in collusion with the guerrillas, but had not provided any evidence of this conspiracy other than to cite the unexplained operation, code-named *Aguila Feliz*. But for the President to link Bosch with the guerrillas had historical significance. Balaguer, in his address, had emphasized that the guerrilla landing and trek into the mountains constituted a diversionary action to allow anti-regime elements to strike elsewhere, thus bringing on the same situation that had existed on April 24, 1965. On that date, a small, localized revolt in Bosch's name had brought on a massive insurrection in Santo Domingo. The President did not explain what he meant by "emergency measures," but an interpretation of the indicators available to Balaguer could only mean that "emergency measures" were for the defense of the capital.

Since February 4th, Santo Domingo had been amazingly quiet. On the 5th, the state-owned university had been surrounded and Juan Bosch's and Peña Gómez's houses had been raided, but no violence had ensued. The rector of the university had sent students home without incident, and the PRD leaders went into hiding. During the following day, there had been some arrests, but nothing untoward developed. That evening Bosch released two written communiqués attacking the regime without revealing his location. He claimed that the PRD was not involved with the guerrilla landing and he denounced the government's "criminal plan." On the following day, the U.S. Embassy reported that "as of noon today (February 6), the situation in the capital remains relatively calm."[39] The Director General of Telecommunications, Lieutenant Colonel Leoncio García y García, met with representatives of the National Broadcasters Association on the same day. They reached an agreement to allow the resumption of radio programming as long as political and labor union material would be temporarily suspended. This proviso was strongly attacked by the press—Balaguer's response was to reduce tensions by transferring García y García to the postal service as its new chief, and by softening the agreement with the National Broadcasters Association.[40] (The Lieutenant Colonel was a former Trujillo bodyguard; Balaguer had appointed him the administrator of the international airport in 1966 when García y García was a captain. His move from the airport to the telecommunications directorate had taken place as recently as December 1972.) On the 6th of February, the search for Bosch and Peña Gómez continued without success, and the former president issued a third statement in which he maintained that the case against him was a "product of President Balaguer's imagination."[41] By February 7th, speculation among knowledgeable Dominicans was that Balaguer knew where Bosch was hiding, but he preferred not to find him.[42] This relaxed attitude in the capital changed markedly after Balaguer's evening address.

Santo Domingo's citizens awoke on February 8th to discover that they were under a form of martial law. The evening before, the President gave the order to the chief of National Police and the secretary of state of the armed forces to secure the capital. Police units were directed to engage in stepped up house searches and to broaden the number of detentions of potential terrorists. Patrolling and road checks were to be expanded. Armed Forces personnel were to be placed at key points throughout the city, to include the entrances of all radio stations. Also, they were to augment National Police mobile patrols. The Armored Battalion was instructed to post five AMX-13 tanks at the exits of the Autonomous University of Santo Domingo campus, to send two more tanks to the Duarte Bridge, and to display armored vehicles in poorer neighborhoods as a show of force. Infantrymen were to join the police already assigned to the university and the bridge. The COFA staff was to be increased. (According to Operation Plan 1–72, dated January 24, 1972, which had been prepared for the defense of the capital, the city was subdivided into eight zones with Armed Forces and National Police units given responsibility for each zone. Coordination was effected from the COFA.)[43] The President had made it clear what he meant by "emergency measures."

A U.S. Defense Attache Office, Santo Domingo, appraisal of the situation, prepared on the 8th of February, concluded that even though legal rights may have been infringed upon in some instances, the President's February 7th decision to deny the use of the capital to extreme-leftist allies of the rural guerrillas was a skillful military maneuver. The government had survived the immediate problem, but it remained vulnerable to the outcome of events in the foothills of the *Cordillera Central*.[44]

FEBRUARY 8–15

By the 8th of February, a rudimentary picture began to emerge as to the identities and capabilities of the guerrillas in the San José de Ocoa area. There had been numerous reports from the hill country that the guerrillas numbered eight men. The President and the military and police chiefs believed that two additional individuals had entered Santo Domingo, but this information was not adequately confirmed. There was wide agreement, by February 8th, that the head of the expedition was Caamaño. Initially, his photograph on the *Black Jak* pointed that way, and an analysis of the handwriting on the sign displayed in the sailboat matched samples of the former colonel's handwriting.[45] Descriptions of the leader of the eight, by peasants and the patrol sergeant, did not fit exactly with the image remembered by Dominicans of the 1965 portly Caamaño, but the thinner guerrilla chief in the San José de Ocoa hills could be Caamaño after a physical fitness program.[46] Another member of the eight insurgents was more easily identified by eyewitnesses. The fact that one guerrilla was missing his left arm and three fingers from his right hand indicated that he was, most assuredly, Heberto Geordano Lalane José, a Fourteenth of June Revolutionary Movement activist who had been disfigured by the explosion of a homemade bomb in his hands while he was preparing to participate in the anti-government disturbances of 1963.[47] The press had come upon the rumor that a third member of the insurgent group was named Hamlet German.[48] This suspect was probably Hamlet Alberto Hermann Pérez, a civil engineer and former professor at the Autonomous University of Santo Domingo.[49] He had been implicated in insurgent activities in the San José de Ocoa area when the guerrilla leader Orlando Mazara was killed in February 1967.[50]

From the outset, the guerrillas left a trail of evidence during their foot march north into the hills. The uniforms of the insurgents were described by peasants as green fatigues, but of a lighter color than the Dominican (and U.S.) Army olive green. A soft work cap, not unlike the type used by various foreign armed forces, was recovered on February 5th. Peasants reported that each guerrilla was carrying two weapons. The U.S.-made AR-15 and M-14 rifles were identified.[51] On February 4th, at the village of El Cercado, the insurgents had purchased two mules to carry provisions[52] but, after the first firefight, the mules were abandoned.[53] From that point on, the guerrillas began to discard their equipment at an ever-increasing rate. During the night of February 7–8, the insurgents left behind shaving gear, a French-English dictionary, and a book of poetry.[54] The following day, the amount of material found was greater and more significant. Recovered were a new twenty piece dentist's kit, one Polaroid camera and film, one set of armorer's tools, two large straw bags used in the Dominican Republic to load mules, one large bag of rock salt, one large bag of spaghetti, one pair of sneakers made in France, numerous bags of candy and gum, rope, one German butane gas re-filler for lighters, and cans of food such as sardines, tomato paste, and cereal. Also found were torn parts of a uniform with what appeared to be bloodstains.[55]

The gear recovered in the countryside revealed that the intention of the guerrillas was to remain in a rural setting for some time. The large bag of rock salt was to be used to preserve food. And a complete dentist's kit, candy, and a Polaroid camera indicated that the guerrillas probably were planning a civic action program in the interior.

On the 8th, there was also further clarification from an unexpected quarter concerning the guerrillas: Juan Bosch, in hiding, sent the U.S. Embassy, through intermediaries, a written explanation of his current political position, in which was included the statement that the guerrillas had actually landed on the shore of the Bay of Ocoa on February 2nd, and that only one insurgent had proceeded to the capital, not two as reported by President Balaguer. Bosch maintained that he had learned this information on February 3rd (a day before the Dominican Armed Forces), but he and the PRD were not involved in the expedition.[56]

With the new commanders leading the government forces, the pursuit of the guerrillas was stepped up during the night of February 7–8. Troops swept across the crest of Testero Mejía mountain, but made no contact with the insurgents. The headquarters of the task force did not know where the guerrillas were located, but it was estimated that the insurgents had moved northwest towards Las Cuevas. Consequently, government troops near the top of Testero Mejía peak were re-directed toward Las Cuevas.[57] The Air Force flew helicopter reconnaissance missions, in which General Matos González personally participated, and aircraft dropped leaflets over suspected insurgent areas of concentration calling for the surrender of the guerrillas to save lives.[58] On February 9th, task force units took up new positions. They were deployed in a wide ring, approximately 20 kilometers in diameter, geographically centered on Las Cuevas hill. The 6th Battalion was in the north and northeast, the 1st Brigade mixed battalion was in the south and southeast, and the police DSO was in the north and northwest. The concept of operations was to drive the fleeing guerrillas into DSO blocking positions in the northwest; they then would be surrounded and destroyed.[59]

While the situation in the San José de Ocoa area was far from being resolved, the capital was very much under the control of the security forces. The one major act of violence, the assassination of a policeman, occurred not in Santo Domingo, but in Santiago. (There had been two bomb explosions in the capital, but there was little damage.)[60] Residents of Santo Domingo finally received official notification on February 8th of the task force casualties on Testero Mejía mountain. The public affairs officer of the Armed Forces, Lieutenant Colonel Fidel Báez Berg, announced that three soldiers of the 2nd Battalion, 1st Brigade, were dead (Privates Pedro Regalado Pérez Sánchez, Gumersindo Moreta Santana, and Desiderio Fermín Monc-ión Veras), and three were wounded. He further claimed that two guerrillas had been killed, but he admitted that their bodies had not been recovered.[61]

In the capital, the decision had been made to direct military operations from the secretariat of the Armed Forces rather than from the Army General Staff,[62] but there was no joint organization to exercise operational control at the national level. As the Caamaño venture progressed, however, there was an attempt to rectify this inadequacy by forming an embryonic joint general staff. Admiral Jiménez appointed the well-trained Army Colonel Romero Pumarol to the new post of operations officer, J-3, and a central war room was established. Although the secretary had taken these positive steps, Jiménez had neglected to designate a J-4 to consolidate armed forces logistics. The Admiral could have utilized the capable and experienced Colonel Felipe Rivas Perdomo, the chief ordnance officer of the armed forces, as the joint logistics coordinator; however, Jiménez assigned him to non-related duties, such as checking on bank guards. This omission would have adverse consequences.[63] In contrast to J-3 and J-4 matters, the intelligence function was in a sounder state. There had been a J-2 Section in being for seven years, although its current chief, Lieutenant Colonel Franco Benoit Liriano, had only been in his position since the end of 1972. Colonel Benoit did not have the intellectual strength and breadth of knowledge of his predecessor, the newly promoted Brigadier General Cruz Brea; but Benoit, a former CEFA artilleryman, was one of the more promising officers of his generation, and he was a 1971 Canal Zone staff college graduate.

It was in Colonel Benoit's office, on the ground level of the National Palace, that the first physical evidence linking the guerrillas to Cuba was noted. The equipment left behind on the beached *Black Jak* did not arrive in the J-2 Section until February 10th. The Army's representatives in the Caracoles Beach area had relinquished control of the sailboat to Navy personnel stationed in the nearby *Las Calderas* Naval Base. The captured material on board was sent up Navy channels before it eventually was deposited on the floor of Colonel Benoit's section. After a close analysis of each item, the conclusion was reached that the guerrillas probably traveled from Cuba to various points in Western Europe and Mexico. There they purchased new clothing and equipment from commercial establishments, and rendezvoused somewhere in the Caribbean. Possibly, while in the Caribbean, they acquired their weapons and ammunition.[64] The single most significant find among the guerrillas' effects was a small can of anodyne ointment with the acronym "MINSAP" printed on it. MINSAP is the abbreviation for the Cuban *Ministerio de Salud Publico*, the Ministry of Public Health. Everything else had apparently been thoroughly sanitized so that no connection could be made with a Communist country. The ointment can, which was no wider than a silver dollar and approximately one inch in depth, had been stuck under the lining of a personal first aid kit found inside a suitcase. Evidently, it had not been seen when the first aid kit was screened prior to the commencement of the clandestine mission.[65] In addition to labels in the new clothing, items of special interest were an Orly Airport, Paris, receipt, dated January 23, 1973, found in a jacket; a bank statement in German, dated January 22, 1973, found in a coat made in West Germany; and plastic wrappers in Italian, used to enclose medical equipment.[66]

The ammunition containers revealed sophisticated preparation. These heavy-duty plastic pouches were in a different color for each type of ammunition (7.62mm, .223 caliber, .30 caliber carbine), and were hermetically sealed. Spare parts for the U.S.-made AR-15 rifle were also found. Small-sized metal and wood disks with a hole in the middle, and little sheets of thin metal were included with the equipment, but it would not be until later that it was understood exactly how they were utilized to fabricate hand grenades.[67]

The 9th of February passed without any action between government forces and the guerrillas. General Pérez y Pérez flew into the area of operations where he met with General Matos González. He then visited 6th Battalion troops in the vicinity of the village of La Horma, almost directly north of San José de Ocoa. Admiral Jiménez accompanied him on the flight from the capital and went to the task force's main command post in town, where he issued new press guidelines restricting the movement of reporters within the boundaries of the officially designated military zone.[68] The following day, information was received that three armed individuals had approached peasants in an effort to purchase food. The strangers, who were able to buy a small amount of rice, appeared to be suffering from hunger and fatigue. Later, the local inhabitants observed that the three were joined by five other armed men in a hut on the side of a hill, northeast of Las Cuevas.[69] Troops were ordered into the area adjacent to the hill (which was designated Hill 922), and close air support was requested; however, the poor visibility prevented the Air Force from flying any missions over the target.[70] Early on the 11th, the insurgents again sought out peasants for the purpose of buying food. This information and more discarded AR-15 spare parts were also passed to the Army.[71]

At approximately 2:30 P.M., February 11th, 6th Battalion troops sighted the guerrillas at Arroyo Rincón near Hill 922. Platoon-sized units of the *Cazadores* Battalion attempted to encircle the insurgents; a firefight began in which the 6th Battalion utilized automatic weapons and M-79 grenade launchers, but, by 4:30 P.M., the guerrillas had escaped. Army troops were ordered to prepare ambush sites northwest of Arroyo Rincón in an attempt to block the fleeing insurgents.[72]

The guerrillas had left behind at Arroyo Rincón eight knapsacks. In one was found a diary indicating that the group had departed the French island of Guadeloupe on January 26, 1973, aboard the *Black Jak*. Also discovered in the knapsacks were 35 solid explosives shaped in the form of a cylinder. They were approximately four inches in length and each had a hole in the top of the cylinder block. With the explosives were 35 hand grenade-type fuses. If these explosives were wrapped in the metal sheets and disks found earlier on the sailboat, and then the fuses were inserted into the holes, the insurgents would be armed with 35 crude, but functional, hand grenades. In addition to these homemade munitions, there was included one factory-fabricated fragmentary grenade with "R.F." stamped on it. Also, there were three packages, consisting of three Penguin aerial signal flares each, bought from the Laurentian Trading Post, 1952 Bank Street, Ottawa, for $2.82 a package. Numerous pouches of 7.62mm, .223 caliber, and .30 caliber carbine ammunition were in the knapsacks, as well as various types of medicines. Among the material were three overlays or templates of a map of the Dominican Republic printed with symbols reflecting the Dominican military order of battle, and numerous overlays with distance estimates marked on them. Last, there were copies of 1972 and 1973 Dominican magazine articles, which summarized the events of 1971 and 1972.[73]

Once again the guerrillas had eluded government troops. A problem that the task force faced on February 11th was its inability to move troops rapidly in the *Cordillera Central*. The FAD had set up a temporary air facility for helicopters on San José de Ocoa's sports playing field, but the OH-6A and Alouette II helicopters, which used the air strip, were designed for command and control and individual, not unit, transportation. There was no alternative because the OH-6As and Alouette IIs were the only helicopters available to lift members of the 1st Brigade and the 6th Battalion in the mountainous zone of operations. (The one Alouette III was designated for presidential use.) The weather had also been difficult. In addition to the fog and rain that restricted the utilization of the helicopters, the inhospitable climate had been hard on the Dominican soldier. The low temperature was an uncommon experience for the infantryman who mainly lived in the tropical lowlands. And the Armed Forces did not have on hand the warm clothing necessary to protect the troops from the cold.

To resolve these issues, Admiral Jiménez turned to the U.S. government. On February 11th, he asked the American Embassy, on an emergency basis, to provide the Armed Forces with 1,000 field jackets. This solicitation was rapidly processed through the U.S. Southern Command to Washington.[74] The Armed Forces secretary followed up his request with a second one—he informed the Embassy that the Dominican Air Force urgently required two Iroquois UH-1D transport helicopters and that the Army needed ten AN/PRC-25 radios. The Admiral added to these items 4,350 rounds of 40mm ammunition to be used by M-79 grenade launchers.[75] The U.S. government was favorably disposed to everything on Jiménez's lists except the helicopters, which were considered too costly. (The UH-1D was no longer available; it was the UH-1H that was under consideration by Washington.)[76]

During the morning of February 12th, Balaguer made his second trip to the San José de Ocoa area. With General Pérez y Pérez and Admiral Jiménez, the President, in his Alouette III, flew over the terrain where the recent military activity had taken place. Then, at approximately noon, he landed in San José de Ocoa, and, after two hours, he returned to the capital.[77] Contrary to Balaguer's first visit on February 7th, the President made no public announcement,[78] but it soon became evident that there was to be an increase in the task force's troop strength. On the same day, 60 paratroopers of the Special Forces Group were trucked into the area of operations from San Isidro Air Base.[79] (This unit would be the first non-U.S.-supported combat maneuver element to join the task force.) On alert to follow were 300 members of the 1st Battalion, 1st Brigade. With its arrival, the total task force strength would rise to 1,000.[80]

After the departure of the 1st Battalion, Santo Domingo would be held in check principally by the National Police. The policemen were to be assisted by the contingent of 1st Brigade soldiers who had remained at the *16 de Agosto* Military Camp, by the Military Police Battalion stationed at *Fortaleza Ozama*, by Air Force infantrymen at San Isidro, and by a handful of sailors. The armored vehicles from the tank battalion would provide psychological support. The zones in the city under COFA coordination would have to be adjusted to take into account the fact that many of the Army and FAD participants were to be sent to San José de Ocoa. This new deployment was not considered a risk to the capital because the President and his security advisers had concluded that, by February 12th, the urban situation was well under control.[81] What did preoccupy the Armed Forces leadership was the traditional Dominican military concern that the primary enemy incursion would be somewhere on the 144 mile Atlantic coastline. To meet such an eventuality, General Pérez y Pérez and Admiral Jiménez would have to rely mainly on the 9th Battalion located in the northern town of Mao. Early warning for the MAP-supported battalion would depend upon fixed-wing aircraft flying out of the *Coronel Piloto Juan Antonio Minaya Fernández* Air Base in Santiago and five Navy vessels: the sea-going tug *Macorix*, the former U.S. Coast Guard cutter *Restauración*, and three coastal patrol boats *Betelgeuse, Aldebarán,* and *Bellatrix.*[82]

Even though the Armed Forces continued to be absorbed with the defense of the north coast, the Caamaño expedition had generated protective measures against external threats on all the country's frontiers. On the government's first day of the crisis, General Pérez y Pérez directed that the commanders of the 2nd and 3rd Brigades instruct their subordinate unit leaders on the border to inform their Haitian counterparts of the possible existence of guerrillas in the Dominican Republic. The Dominican Army officers were to request that Haiti's frontier posts deny entry to any fleeing insurgents.[83] In the east, on February 9th, a small boat was sighted at Uvero Alto, approximately 33 air miles southeast of Miches. The 4th Battalion, which was the Army constabulary unit responsible for the eastern sector of the Dominican Republic, dispatched troops; they were able to round up six people. It was subsequently determined after interrogation that those arrested were involved only in smuggling Dominicans into Puerto Rico.[84] On the same day, an Air Force P-51 fighter observed a tanker in the Mona Passage off the village of Macao. According to the pilot, he requested that the vessel identify itself and he received no answer. The P-51 then sprayed the tanker with gunfire. Eventually, it was learned that the ship was the *Vestalif* of Norwegian registry. It was leased to Shell Oil and was in transit to Venezuela. The Oslo government followed up with a diplomatic note demanding an explanation; the President quickly offered an apology for the incident. The issue was soon forgotten because there had been no casualties or serious damage to the *Vestalif.*[85]

The lack of solidarity in the officer corps since the fall of Trujillo quite naturally brought into question what would be the reaction within the institution to the landing of Caamaño. The past history of military disloyalty to various post-1961 governments, and of the internecine factionalism that led to the 1965 civil war, caused the press, as well as the security apparatus, to focus on officer fidelity. The first suggestion of treachery in the officer corps was a February 6th radio report that unidentified officers in the National Police had been arrested in connection with the Caracoles Beach landing. Colonel Bolívar Soto Montás, the police public affairs officer, denied that any "colonel or any other police officer" was under arrest or investigation.[86] In fact, an Army lieutenant colonel had been apprehended on the 6th as a precautionary measure. Lucas Fernández Sánchez had been identified as having been in contact with a Marxist before the arrival of the guerrillas, but he was cleared of any wrongdoing. He had merely been pursuing a woman related to the leftist.[87] Fernández Sánchez was a jovial, overweight officer who had spent most of the Balaguer years working in public relations at Army headquarters. He would have been a most unlikely collaborator with Caamaño or with any revolutionary group. (In the end of June 1973, Fernández Sánchez was released from jail and retired.[88] An indication of his non-involvement with the guerrillas was revealed when he received a good-paying government job shortly after retirement.[89])

In Madrid on February 7th, Wessin y Wessin told the Spanish press that he believed the arrival of the guerrillas was nothing more than disinformation "organized by the Balaguer government itself in order to destroy the political opposition."[90] Of significance was that he did not call on his followers, who were mainly ex-CEFA members, to take any action for or against the regime. One former CEFA officer, however, was denounced as a traitor, but within a few hours he was exonerated. On February 7th, the Santiago newspaper *El Sol* printed that Lieutenant Colonel Luis García Recio had landed with the insurgents. *Agence France-Presse*, in turn, broadcast this story internationally.[91] García Recio's main fault was arrogance, not leftist leanings. When he was on the Army General Staff in 1971 he had tangled with General Nivar, and was sacked. After numerous meaningless jobs, on January 17, 1973, he reluctantly departed for Ecuador as the military attaché. On the same day that *Agence France-Presse* released its broadcast, the secretariat of the Armed Forces informed the public that it had confirmed that García Recio was in the Dominican embassy in Quito, not in the San José de Ocoa hills.[92]

If there were any support for the guerrillas from the officer corps, it would most likely have come from Constitutionalist officers. Insignificant individuals, such as cashiered police officer Jorge Marte Hernández, were placed in protective custody,[93] but the opposite occurred with the major Constitutionalist leaders in country. The former second-ranking man in the rebel military had been the ex-naval infantryman, Manuel Montes Arache. On September 21, 1971, he was allowed to return to the Dominican Republic after over five years abroad. He then made many attempts to be placed on active duty. (One of his gestures to curry favor within the Armed Forces was his co-sponsorship in December 1971 and December 1972 of a commemorative mass for Ramfis Trujillo.) Montes Arache finally regained full active status on February 8th—the government announced that not only was the *Capitán de Fragata* back in uniform, he was also placed in charge of coordinating street patrols in Santo Domingo.[94] Unlike the Montes Arache case, the regime did not exploit for propaganda purposes the presence in the Dominican Republic of the third most important Constitutionalist. Héctor Lachapelle Díaz continued his normal duties in the 2nd Brigade, but reporters did not focus on his activities as they had that of Montes Arache. Two of the regime's security services, however, could not be faulted for the same omission.[95]

On February 12th, the most vivid example of pledging loyalty came to light when a communiqué was issued by the "Reserves of the Armed Forces and National Police." One hundred and eight retired personnel, from the rank of lieutenant general to sergeant, issued a statement condemning the "subversive" group in the "mountainous zone" of San José de Ocoa, and announcing support for the government of President Balaguer. The first name on the communiqué was Fausto E. Caamaño, the insurgent chief's father.[96]

Contrary to rumors from the countryside, there had been no contact between task force troops and the insurgents on February 12th and 13th.[97] Even though the location of the guerrillas was not clear, in the capital the secretariat of the Armed Forces released a communiqué during the evening of the 13th stating that the insurgents were surrounded, and that only the inclement weather prevented the government from capturing them. The secretary of state of the armed forces guaranteed that the guerrillas' lives would be spared if they were to surrender.[98] In the field, General Matos González redeployed the combat elements of the task force in a northwestern direction. By February 14th, he had integrated the FAD Special Forces Group and the newly arrived Army 1st Battalion into the overall maneuver plan of the task force.[99] At the main command post, General Beauchamps had assured that communications equipment and food were reaching the tactical units. He ordered that the number of security personnel at the sensitive telecommunications complex on Alto Bandera mountain be increased. And he prepared to absorb 250 more soldiers, bringing the task force strength to 1,250. Troop morale was assessed to be good on February 14th.[100]

The 14th of February was the first day since military operations began in the mountains that there was favorable weather. The hills were free of mist and the sky was clear.[101] Aircraft could resume reconnaissance missions, and the Air Force hoped to provide close air support with its P-51s and with an OH-6A helicopter's utilizing a specially mounted 7.62mm gun.[102] Search operations through 5:00 P.M. on the 14th had disappointing results, but prior to nightfall the guerrillas were sighted by government troops, although their numbers could not be determined and no exchange of gunfire took place.[103] On the following day, after dark, troops in an ambush position, approximately one kilometer from the village of Nizaíto, alongside the road that ran from San José de Ocoa in the south to Constanza in the north, opened fire in the direction of a moving silhouette in the brush. There were numerous bursts in response from the insurgents before the guerrillas were able to disengage.[104]

Despite the fact that the insurgents were still free, the picture that had formed of the guerrillas by February 15th, through a combination of peasant reports and military sightings, was an optimistic one for the government. First, the guerrillas, who were traveling as a group, had not added any recruits—their number remained the original eight and at least one was wounded. Second, they were operating in an area where little that is eatable grows, and they were desperate to acquire food. And, third, they had taken a frantic, serpentine route in an attempt to shake off their pursuers. The information posted on the Armed Forces' "enemy situation" maps, through February 15th, indicated that after the guerrillas escaped the encirclement on Testero Mejía peak, they turned northwest toward Las Cuevas, then they changed direction many times before they finally moved east. The group crossed the San José de Ocoa-Constanza road between the villages of Valle Nuevo and La Nuez, where they ran headlong into the ambush of February 15th.[105] Caamaño was still thought to be the chief of this harried band, according to scattered reports that originated mainly from the cities.[106] On the 16th of February, it would be confirmed that the ex-colonel was indeed the guerrilla leader, and that it had taken only twelve days to break the back of his rural guerrilla expedition.

XIV

The Death of Caamaño and the Aftermath

The last hours of former Colonel Francisco Caamaño Deñó's life were spent leading the equivalent of a squad of light infantrymen. On his final day of existence, Caamaño—the 1965 commander in chief of the Constitutionalist army—was responsible for the maneuvering of only seven men in a desperate attempt to save their lives.

FEBRUARY 16–28

The chain of events that led directly to the death of Caamaño began three minutes after midnight on the 16th of February. At that moment, according to the guerrilla Hermann Pérez, the sound of a truck was heard on the San José de Ocoa-Constanza road.[1] Although conflicting accounts exist, the best evidence indicates that what subsequently occurred was the result of a chance encounter between the insurgents and the Army vehicle, rather than a preplanned ambush on the part of Caamaño and his men.[2] The guerrillas were in the process of crossing the road in their effort to evade government troops nearby. The two-and-one-half ton truck, which was organic to the 2nd Battalion, was traveling north toward the military encampment at Nizaíto.[3] The insurgents opened fire and threw a hand grenade at the vehicle. Even though all soldiers who were riding in the truck were wounded and the vehicle was damaged by 43 direct hits,[4] the action had been worse than useless—it was a deadly mistake. The government forces were able to pinpoint the exact location where Caamaño and his group had left the San José de Ocoa-Constanza road after the firefight, and the task force determined that the guerrillas were moving in a northeasterly direction.[5]

After a five-hour hike in the dark, the guerrillas made camp at daybreak in a heavily wooded area known as Arabia.[6] That patch of land is situated between Alto Bandera mountain and the village of La Nuez,

221

and it is approximately 25 kilometers, in a direct line, from the town of San José de Ocoa.[7] Caamaño spread his men out on a hillside covered with dense foliage. The guerrillas took measures to conceal themselves from overhead flights and Caamaño posted a lookout to give warning of anyone approaching their positions on foot. Believing that they were secure, the insurgents took off their boots and planned to rest until daylight ended.[8]

While the guerrillas either slept, cleaned their weapons, or ate what little rice remained, elements of the task force deployed around Arabia. Troops from the 1st Brigade moved forward while paratroopers from the Special Forces Group prepared to block the insurgents.[9] Shortly before 11:00 A.M., soldiers from the 1st Brigade sighted the guerrilla encampment and opened fire, pinning down the insurgents. The surprised guerrillas threw themselves flat on the ground, but they were still highly vulnerable; 40mm grenades, fired from the 1st Brigade's M-79s, began to land and explode next to the prone rebels. Caamaño then gave the order to withdraw—five of his men succeeded in disengaging, but he and two others failed to escape.[10] There are many versions of what then occurred.

The official position was concisely put forward in an Armed Forces bulletin released at 9:00 P.M. on February 16th, after General Pérez y Pérez and Admiral Jiménez met with the President in the National Palace.[11] The communiqué announced that at 3:30 P.M., on February 16th, in San José de Ocoa's Nizao area, there was an "exchange of fire" between the "group of expeditionaries," who, on the "morning of Saturday, February 3rd, landed at Caracoles Beach"; and the joint forces of the Army's 1st Brigade and *Cazadores* group, and the Air Force's and National Police's special forces. As a result of the "confrontation," the following were killed: Wellington Ascanio Peterson Pietersz, Heberto Geordano Lalane José, and ex-Colonel Francisco Alberto Caamaño Deñó. Then the announcement provided the names of four members of the 1st Battalion, 1st Brigade, who had been wounded. The communiqué ended by stating that the pursuit of the remaining guerrillas continued and that contact was expected soon.[12]

Over the years, numerous, different accounts would circulate as to how Caamaño died. Less than 24 hours after the communiqué was released, one of the first of these versions was provided by an alleged eyewitness. Although his description of the event cannot be fully confirmed, there is overall historical value in his account. According to the Dominican military source of the information, Caamaño and Peterson Pietersz were taken alive by government troops. Lalane José was dead. Caamaño had received a leg wound and he was led to believe that he would be taken to the capital as a political prisoner. A senior Dominican officer asked the guerrilla leader a series of questions. Caamaño, in reply, stated that his landing in the Dominican Republic had been a matter of many years' planning. He had felt that the political situation in the Dominican Republic was ready for a popular revolt. Caamaño had had contact with elements of the PRD, and, in fact, that party had provided him with the Dominican currency that he had for the operation. Caamaño claimed that the initial objectives were either to enter Santo Domingo or to stage a long-term rural insurgency. Events that developed during his arrival in the Dominican Republic made Caamaño decide against entering the city. Caamaño chose to follow the rural insurgency course of action in the San José de Ocoa area; however, he believed that the capital was prepared to provide him immediate support. The guerrillas had had some peasant assistance, but during their last contact with government troops they were operating alone. After this debriefing, the senior Dominican officer surprised Caamaño by asking him what was his last wish. A startled Caamaño responded by uttering a vulgarity and making an anti-government remark. Then the senior Dominican officer ordered that Caamaño be shot. He was executed by an unidentified military man who was chosen to be the executioner because the individual had lost a family member during the 1965 civil war. Peterson Pietersz was also executed.[13]

In an evaluation of this information, it must be understood that the interlocutor would have been more likely to lie about the Caamaño connection with the PRD than about the manner in which Caamaño had died. Concerning the former matter, it was not uncommon for members of the officer corps to attempt to persuade U.S. observers that the PRD was a serious Communist threat. The execution of captured guerrillas, however, was accepted by some in the Dominican Armed Forces. It is doubtful that the source of this account thought he was passing on unusual information when he reported that Caamaño was taken alive and then summarily executed.

When Admiral Jiménez presented the press with his communiqué on the night of February 16th, he informed the reporters that they could send representatives the next morning to the mountains to view the corpses of the guerrillas prior to burial. Early on the 17th, the Air Force flew three newsmen (a reporter from *El Caribe*, a photographer from *Listín Diario*, and a camera man from CBS) to a stretch of flat land northwest of La Nuez known as the *llanura* de Nizao. At 7:30 A.M., Admiral Jiménez and Generals Pérez y Pérez and Beauchamps displayed the three corpses which were laid out near the San José de Ocoa-Constanza road, and answered a few questions. They did not give details of the combat action, however. The Dominican officers stated that the guerrillas were surrounded at the Arabia area and, according to General Pérez y Pérez, Caamaño fought to the "last bullet." General Beauchamps remarked that the guerrillas engaged in "battle" with his men.[14] The newspapermen noted that Caamaño and Lalane were easy to identify. The *El Caribe* reporter personally had known Caamaño since they were boys in grammar school, and Lalane was missing an arm and three fingers. They were all dressed in olive green field uniforms, sweaters, and no boots. Caamaño had three bullet wounds and was underweight.[15] The press representatives were shown Caamaño's AR-15 rifle, the corpses in the process of being fingerprinted, and the truck that had been shot up on February 16th, and then, after two hours, they were returned to Santo Domingo. Contrary to their original expectations, they were told that they could not witness the burial.[16] After all civilians departed, the bodies of the three were not buried, but were set on fire.[17]

After almost eight years of being a threat to the officer corps, Caamaño was dead. The defeat of rural and urban guerrilla leaders during or subsequent to armed combat, such as the elimination of Manuel Tavárez Justo in 1963, of Orlando Mazara in 1967, and of Otto Morales in 1970, did not have the same impact as did the permanent removal of Caamaño from Dominican affairs in 1973. Support for revolutionaries like Tavárez, Mazara, and Morales was usually not found outside radical leftist circles. Former Colonel Caamaño's potential political base, however, was far broader. Because of Juan Bosch's absence in 1965, Caamaño, as president of the rebel government, was the recipient of Bosch's political mantle during the civil war. This legacy meant that Caamaño, in theory, could lay claim to the PRD, the best organized party in the country. Each of the other parties, to include Balaguer's *Partido Reformista*, was held together solely by its leader. In the PRD this was not the case. It was through excellent organization that the PRD retained followers among the better-than-average educated Dominicans who wanted governmental and social reform in the post–Trujillo era. And, most important, the well-organized PRD continued to have support in low-income neighborhoods of Santo Domingo. The *barrios* not only provided the PRD with a following of union and non-union workers; the poorer sections of the capital also were heavily populated with unemployed veterans of the 1965 civil war who had fought under Caamaño. Added to these PRD members and adherents were the regular officers and enlisted men who had either embraced, or found themselves swept up in, the Constitutionalist rebellion, and, after the war, were excluded from the Armed Forces. It was never determined if Caamaño could have welded together those various groups into a viable political movement, but it is certain that the Dominican officer corps feared that eventuality. After the 16th of February, that anxiety disappeared.

In mid–February, before the death of Caamaño, the embryonic joint general staff at the secretariat of the Armed Forces began to wither away. First, Colonel Romero Pumarol, the J-3, was moved to the task force; thus, during the height of operations, there was no operations officer at the national level. Second, the well-established J-2 Section ceased to have a mission that was directly related to the anti-guerrilla campaign in San José de Ocoa, and, third, the war room was closed. Finally, a J-4 never was appointed; consequently, no joint logistics policy was ever formulated. Reports from the field were not sent through staff officers, but were normally transmitted personally to the Admiral. He, on an impromptu basis, assigned tasks to members of the secretariat, but no orderly coordination or integrated planning was practiced at the joint level.[18]

The demise of the joint general staff did not result in the transfer of its functions, as limited as they were, to one of the service staffs, such as the Army General Staff. During the first days of the anti-guerrilla campaign, General Pérez y Pérez's headquarters remained outside the stream of events, because there was an attempt to concentrate everything in the fledgling joint general staff. This situation did not change, even when General Pérez y Pérez began to eclipse the Admiral in the management of the counterguerrilla effort. Specifically, the G-1, Colonel Angel Urbano Matos, conducted normal personnel business without involvement in the San José de Ocoa affair. The G-2, Lieutenant Colonel José Peral Brea, provided intelligence officers and enlisted men to the field, but maintained only moderate interest in the activities of the guerrillas. The G-3 Section ceased operations almost entirely. Colonel García Tejada, the chief of the section, had been sent to the task force, and his work in the General Staff was taken over as an additional duty by the G-4, Lieutenant Colonel Vidal Reyes. The acting G-3 attempted to provide some support to the San José de Ocoa zone of operations, but his responsibilities were never clearly defined. The chief of the Civil Affairs Section, G-5, became the administrative staff officer for the task force commander in the field; therefore, his office in the General Staff was closed. These officers, as well as the sub-chief of the General Staff, Colonel Valenzuela Alcantara, were competent and knowledgeable, but they were not given the opportunity to coordinate the anti-guerrilla campaign. A key member of the Special Staff, the *intendente general* or quartermaster general, Lieutenant Colonel Martín de los Santos Florentino, did have an important role to play in confronting the Caamaño expedition, but this officer had assumed his post less than three weeks before the insurgent landing, and he had absolutely no experience or training as a logistician. His lack of ability had already caused serious supply problems for the task force.[19]

Since there was no national general staff-type organization coordinating activities in support of the San José de Ocoa operation, the task force headquarters had to absorb broader responsibilities. Nominally, the S-3, operations officer, was General Matos González; however, he had become a full-time field commander. Because of his absence from the forward command post, Army Colonel Escarramán Mejía became the acting operations officer. Earlier assignments and the Inter-American Defense College course in Washington made him an acceptable choice. The other principal staff officers were *Capitán de Fragata* Oscar Padilla Medrano, and Air Force Lieutenant Colonels Manuel Sánchez Cuevas and José Isidoro Martínez González. Although Padilla Medrano was in the Navy, he had graduated from the U.S. Army Command and Staff Course in the Panama Canal Zone in December 1970. Sánchez Cuevas had had extensive exposure to the Air Staff at San Isidro and, as with Escarramán Mejía, he was a graduate of the Inter-American Defense College. As for Martínez González, his main experience had not been on a staff, but as an airborne infantry commander. Initially, his most valuable contribution stemmed from his familiarity with small unit tactics through U.S. special operations training.[20]

At the time of Caamaño's death, the task force forward command post was situated in Peravia Province, north of San José de Ocoa, with easy access to the road leading to Constanza. It was set up in a small farmhouse where Colonel Escarramán and operations and intelligence officers performed the duties of a battle staff. In San José de Ocoa, the main command post, located in the town police station, housed the logistics and personnel management teams that controlled the service support tail of the task force. The Army had established a motor park and a supply point, and the Air Force had expanded its helicopter maintenance facilities, in the same urban area as the main command post. Supplies were moved to encampments positioned in an arc, north of the town of San José de Ocoa—in Las Cuevas, Nizaíto, and La Horma. The main supply route was the San José de Ocoa-Constanza road. It was in this sprawling area, officially designated a "military zone," that General Pérez y Pérez, and to a lesser degree, Admiral Jiménez, devoted the majority of their time. The cockpit of President Balaguer's current military establishment had moved physically from Santo Domingo to the foothills of the *Cordillera Central*.

The attitude in the task force's forward command post, on February 18th, was that the anti-guerrilla campaign was virtually over. Because Caamaño had been killed, it was believed that all that remained was to consolidate the victory. Since the 16th, it was estimated that the five fugitives were in the vicinity of Mono Mojao hill, not too distant from where Caamaño fell. Elements of the 6th Battalion were directed to surround that terrain and close with the guerrillas. The eastern sector of the sus-

pected insurgent position was blocked by paratroopers of the Special
Forces Group, who had been lifted into place by helicopters. The road
from San José de Ocoa, north to the village of Valle Nuevo, was patrolled
by units of the 1st Brigade, and a sweep of the area west of the road, also
conducted by 1st Brigade troops, was undertaken to catch any guerrillas
who were able to slip through the 6th Battalion encirclement.[21]

An assessment of the operational effectiveness of the task force in
the aftermath of the Arabia engagement was generally positive. The
troops were among the best trained in the Dominican Republic, and
most of their officers in key positions were efficient. Communications
and re-supply were considered satisfactory. The feeding problems were,
at least temporarily, resolved, and troop morale was high. Cross-country
mobility, however, remained difficult because of the rugged terrain. Helicopters were in continuous use, although they had limited lift capacity
and the weather had been poor. (A common sight in the sky over the
San José de Ocoa area was the movement of soldiers with their legs hang-
ing out of the small OH-6A rotary aircraft.)[22]

Prior assumptions about the guerrillas had been confirmed after
the events of February 16th. First, Caamaño and his men were suffering
from a lack of food. The three undernourished corpses were physical
proof of that supposition. Second, the insurgents' equipment was in
poor condition. The captured weapons—the AR-15, a U.S.-made .30 caliber M-1 carbine, and a West German-made 7.62mm G-3 rifle—as well as
the dead guerrillas' boots and clothing, showed this to be the case. And,
third, some peasants had collaborated with Caamaño. Interrogations
had revealed that this was true; however, it proved to be less extensive
than feared.[23]

On February 18th, a visitor's observation of the San José de Ocoa
area revealed that normal commerce continued in town and its environs. Although roadblocks existed on the main arteries, civilians moved
in and out of San José de Ocoa with little restriction and public transportation was not impeded. There was no overt evidence of serious
disaffection; however, the population remained suspicious and tense.[24]

In the capital, the official announcement on February 16th of the
death of Caamaño was accompanied by a heightened security presence.
Key communications and administrative buildings were provided extra
guards and increased joint Armed Forces-National Police patrols were
visible throughout the city. The government made a point of letting the
public know that the former Constitutionalist leader, Montes Arache,
was in charge of the patrolling effort in the volatile northern sector of
Santo Domingo. The night of February 16–17 passed without incident in
the near empty streets of the capital.[25] Except for the sound of some sporadic gunfire after dark on February 18th, the city continued to be calm.

Consequently, on February 19th, twenty-five percent of Army troops in Santo Domingo were granted passes, and, on the 21st, a significant reduction in overt military posture took place. At first light, the tanks positioned around the university and the Duarte Bridge were returned to their garrison, and the mobile patrols throughout the capital were reduced in number. The National Police's Duarte Department remained at the entrances to the university campus and military sentinels were still posted in front of radio stations and official buildings, but the government had sent a clear message: Because the situation was under control, the government could relax its grip on Santo Domingo.[26]

On the day before the tanks were removed from the capital, the regime was embarrassed from a totally unexpected quarter. The problem began on February 19th, when a Dominican in Havana presented himself to the Cuban news service *Prensa Latina* and claimed that he was Wellington Ascanio Peterson Pietersz. He provided documentation indicating that his father was Dutch and his mother was Dominican, and that he was a student who had resided in Cuba for five years. This information was broadcast internationally from Havana on the 20th, and, on the same day, confirmed by the secretariat of the Armed Forces in Santo Domingo. Admiral Jiménez's public relations office released a communiqué, dated February 20th, conceding that indeed there had been an error. The fingerprints taken of the corpse on the 17th of February, north of San José de Ocoa, were reviewed and the dead guerrilla was then identified as Alfredo Pérez Vargas, not Peterson Pietersz. Subsequently, Pérez Vargas' mother admitted that the photograph of the corpse was that of her son.[27] Pérez Vargas had been a Navy enlisted man who had fought on the Constitutionalist side in 1965, and he had been a member of the Fourteenth of June Revolutionary Movement.[28]

Running parallel in public interest with the story about the incorrect identification of the dead insurgent was the request made to the President by retired General Caamaño that his son's remains be returned to the family for proper burial. Balaguer replied that the matter had been forwarded to the secretariat of the Armed Forces so that by "common accord" between Admiral Jiménez and General Caamaño, an appropriate date could be selected to follow through with the request.[29] Responses of that vague nature continued, thus never allowing the issue to be closed.

In the San José de Ocoa hills, optimism for a rapid conclusion to the counterguerrilla operation began to evaporate soon after February 21st. The cordon, deployed following the death of Caamaño, continued to tighten, but it produced no results. In addition, there were confusing sightings outside the encirclement of a possible insurgent presence near La Horma, and as far away as Jarabacoa; these reports proved to be false.

By February 23rd, there still had been no contact with the guerrillas. Under consideration was the possibility that they had backtracked to Testero Mejía peak to acquire food that the insurgents had cached. Another view in the task force was that the five had not gone a great distance, but had remained in the general area where Caamaño was killed.[30]

While the search for the guerrillas was on, Dominican officers continued in their attempt to resolve the myriad of difficulties that had surfaced since the task force was established. The rations obtained from the U.S. government were turned over to the Armed Forces and were integrated with local rations for distribution on February 19th. The unfamiliar rations and bad water caused some stomach disorders, but these were isolated cases. As of that date, the warm clothing, requested from the United States, was still not available. (One thousand field jackets would arrive on February 28th.) Movement on the highways and roads had not been a serious problem because Washington had provided numerous trucks to the Army's Transportation Battalion. There were sufficient vehicles in that unit to support properly the task force, including the Air Force's paratroopers. New tires were issued to the 1st Brigade for use on its organic vehicles which enhanced ground mobility within the task force.[31]

Personnel issues had not been overly problematic for General Beauchamps. There had been some minor incidents such as the arrest of three Army enlisted men—one for malingering, one for firing his rifle without orders, and one for refusing to go on patrol—but, overall, troop discipline and morale remained good.[32] General Pérez y Pérez was of the opinion that the proper level of personnel strength had not yet been reached; therefore, although some soldiers were returned from San José de Ocoa to their barracks, a larger number was sent to the task force. As of February 23rd, the total strength in the military zone had reached 1,400 men.[33]

Civil affairs and public information had not been neglected. On February 21st, the Army announced that, when the situation permitted, it planned to build a school in the mountain community of Piedra Colorada.[34] And, on the next day, the Air Force dropped leaflets in the mountainous areas around La Nuez, La Horma, and Nizaíto, guaranteeing the lives of any guerrillas who surrendered.[35] Admiral Jiménez personally took the lead in the government's public relations campaign by inviting newsmen to *Las Calderas* Naval Base on February 23rd to see Caamaño's boat, the *Black Jak*. The secretary, accompanied by his public information officer and his intelligence staff chief, Lieutenant Colonels Báez Berg and Benoit Liriano, respectively, briefed members of the press and then allowed them to board the vessel, inspect it, and take pictures. Jiménez showed the reporters Caamaño's handwritten sign found on the *Black Jak* that warned of explosives, and then, for comparison, the Admiral provided an example of the ex-colonel's handwriting on a pre-1965 official document. Jiménez refused to answer questions concerning the alleged information linking the Caamaño landing to Juan Bosch or Cuba, but he did mollify the newsmen somewhat by stating that the press would be able to increase its representation in the San José de Ocoa area in the coming week.[36]

On February 23rd, the number of Dominican troops killed in action rose to a total of four. One of the wounded soldiers, sent from San José de Ocoa to the Air Force hospital at San Isidro for treatment, died of his injuries on that day. Corporal Juan Ramón Lora Cepeda, of the 1st Battalion, was riding in the truck on the San José de Ocoa-Constanza road on the night of February 15–16 when the engagement with Caamaño and his men began. The corporal was wounded during the firefight.[37] The military press office in the National Palace announced his death and notified the public that on February 25th, which was Armed Forces Day, a mass would be held at *Fortaleza Ozama* for the four deceased soldiers. The co-sponsors of the mass were the secretariat, the three services, the police, and the official veterans organization.[38]

After seven days of uncertainty, the guerrillas' possible position began to be reported by peasants. At 5:30 P.M., on February 23rd, the insurgents were sighted at Mono Mojao hill, and, the following morning, they were seen in the vicinity of the mountain village of Los Limoncillos, east of the San José de Ocoa-Constanza road, approximately seven kilometers from La Nuez. Further information, placing the guerrillas in the same area, was reported on the 26th. The significance of this information was that peasants had talked directly with the insurgents. It appeared that the guerrillas were attempting to recruit local inhabitants as guides.[39] The 6th Battalion was ordered to encircle the suspected insurgent position. The task force was convinced that the guerrillas were bottled up and that they could be engaged and destroyed with ease.[40]

Instead of closing rapidly with ground troops; however, the order was given for the Air Force to overfly the area, and then to prepare a plan to strafe the insurgents. At San Isidro, the FAD had maintained ten P-51s and four Vampire jets armed and on alert for utilization in the counterguerrilla operation. For most of February, the poor weather and a lack of an appropriate target had precluded the use of these aircraft.[41] The FAD fighter pilots were, at last, given their chance on Dominican Independence Day.

In keeping with the dismal unit reputation established in the opening days of the 1965 civil war, the P-51 squadron, in February 1973, would once again fly a useless ground support mission, although in the San José de Ocoa hills there would be no political repercussions, caused in 1965 by countless non-combatant deaths in the streets of Santo Domingo. The first strike was late on the national holiday, the 27th of February. Two P-51s attacked an area marked on FAD maps as Los Almendros de Arabia. On the following morning, four P-51s repeated the operation. The infantry, with the aid of peasant guides, then searched the area, but no evidence of a rebel presence was discovered.[42] Six years later, former guerrilla Hermann Pérez would write that the P-51 air strikes were useful because he and his group could tell where the Armed Forces thought they were vis-à-vis where they actually were located.[43]

By the end of February, the task force reached its maximum strength of approximately 1,500 men.[44] At that time, the 1st Brigade contributed a total of 680 troops (15 from Headquarters Company, 306 from the 1st Battalion, 195 from the 2nd Battalion, and 164 from the 3rd Battalion). The 6th *Cazador* Battalion sent 468 men, the Special Forces Group was represented by about 200 paratroopers, and the Department of Special Operations was made up of approximately 100 policemen. The remainder of the 1,500, from various units in the Armed Forces, was assigned to the headquarters of the task force. The Army component of the task force was made up of troops drawn from ten different rifle companies; however, company, as well as battalion, designations had lost their meaning in the San José de Ocoa area.[45]

The lack of organizational integrity became even more evident in the end of February when a new concept of operations for the task force was adopted. It was the third approach since the beginning of the counterguerrilla campaign. Initially, the tactical maneuver was the classic "hammer and anvil" method: Through exerting pressure, the guerrillas were to be driven into ambush sites. Secondly, after the "hammer and anvil" failed, an encirclement with all sides closing in was attempted. When the guerrillas continually escaped and their location remained undetermined, it was decided, in the end of February, to initiate the zone system. The third concept was to divide the area of operations into zones and sub-zones. Within each sub-zone patrolling was undertaken, from small base camps, outwardly, as spokes of a wheel from its hub.[46]

With the implementation of the new concept of operations, clearly defined command and control lines had quickly disappeared. Subordination was not from the task force through a chain of command, such as through battalion, company, and platoon, but from the task force directly to the sub-zone. The officer designated to command the sub-zone was responsible for maintaining cohesion within his unit—former association with established battalions and companies was no longer significant. And the commander of this new entity was either a colonel, a lieutenant colonel, or a major; consequently, it was not uncommon for colonels to be seen leading platoon-size units.[47]

The new, unusual organization for combat required additional field grade officers to be placed in front of troops; therefore, officers in staff positions were re-assigned to the zones and sub-zones. Colonel García Tejada, who had left the task force headquarters earlier, was joined by Colonel Romero Pumarol and Lieutenant Colonel Martínez González. Also among the small unit leaders were Colonel Julio César López Pérez, Lieutenant Colonel Darío Morel Ramos, and Majors Juan de Dios Aranda y Martín, Manuel de Jesús Checo Jáquez, Pedro Díaz Mena, Jaime Osell, Nabucondonosor Páez Piantini, Julio Ramón Solano Hernández, Ramón de Jesús Rodríguez Landstoy, and Aris Burgos Villa.[48]

When March 1973 began, the Dominican Armed Forces had adopted a new concept of operations for the task force and had instituted a new command and control system in the field. To oversee these innovations was the almost perpetual physical presence of the secretary of state of the armed forces and the chief of staff of the Army in the San José de Ocoa hills. What was lacking was the location of the five guerrillas.

MARCH 1–21

The new month brought no change in the task force's inability to establish contact with the insurgents. On the 1st and 2nd of March, government units failed to locate the guerrillas[49]; this induced much speculation within the officer corps. In the capital, it was suggested that task force troops were moving too cautiously in an attempt to avoid casualties,[50] while in the task force, it was believed that the insurgents went undetected because the guerrillas were paying large sums of money to peasants for protection.[51] Although there was no firm evidence, intelligence officers in the forward command post estimated that the guerrilla group was still in the old zone of operations centered on Mono Mojao hill, with its most likely position being the Arabia area where Caamaño had been brought down.[52] This lack of success in the field was eclipsed, however, by Dominicans' learning the identity of the member of the insurgent band who had landed in the Bay of Ocoa and then entered Santo Domingo on February 3rd. The circumstances in which his name was revealed were nothing less than curious.

On March 3rd, the leftist-oriented evening tabloid, *Ultima Hora*, released a story stating that the newspaper had conducted an interview with Carlos Toribio Peña Jáquez on the 1st of March. Peña Jáquez admitted that he was one of Caamaño's men who had come ashore at Caracoles Beach. On arrival, he alleged that he was sent on a special mission to various cities, including Santo Domingo, by the former colonel. Peña Jáquez then went on to claim that the press photographs of the corpses were not those of Caamaño and Lalane José, although Pérez Vargas' body had indeed been correctly identified. Peña Jáquez told the newspaper that the *Comandos de la Resistencia* was the urban group that the guerrillas were to contact in the Dominican Republic. He provided many isolated details, such as Caamaño did not carry an AR-15 rifle, and that he wore a beret, not a cap, but Peña Jáquez begged ignorance to questions of a broader nature, maintaining that he was a mere "soldier" in the expedition. *Ultima Hora* closed the article without revealing where Peña Jáquez could be located.[53]

The Secret Department of the National Police followed up the *Ultima Hora* story by inviting the director, Virgilio Alcántara, and the chief editor, Gregorio García Castro, of the newspaper, to police headquarters. In government files it was known that Peña Jáquez was an office machine repairman, that he had fought on the Constitutionalist side during the 1965 civil war, and that he had links to the Fourteenth of June Revolutionary Movement.[54] The intelligence service of the National Police was convinced that the *Ultima Hora* story was an attempt to project the illusion that Caamaño was still alive, thus generating urban support for the guerrillas in the San José de Ocoa area.[55] It was with this concept in mind that the Peña Jáquez affair would take a new, unexpected turn.

General Cruz Brea had always been an advocate of psychological warfare. Because he felt that there was a need to counterbalance the Peña Jáquez press interview, the National Police chief directed that measures be taken to create doubts in the mind of the public as to the credibility of Peña Jáquez's statements. One means utilized by the National Police was the release of a communiqué on March 5th stating that Peña Jáquez had been a Secret Department informant.[56] In the communiqué, the police contrived the account that Peña Jáquez was infiltrated into "subversive" groups so that he could report on plans in Cuba directed against the Dominican Republic. The communiqué continued that Peña Jáquez had fulfilled his mission when he separated himself from the Caamaño band after the landing at Caracoles Beach and traveled to Santo Domingo where he reported to the government security services. He provided them with a description of the arrival of the nine guerrillas, to include their *"nombres de guerra"* and other undisclosed "information of great value for the authorities." The police speculated in the communiqué that Peña Jáquez, subsequently, was pressured by "communists"; therefore, to save his life, he provided the anti-government interview to *Ultima Hora.* At the end of the communiqué, the following guerrilla cover names were listed: "Román," "Freddy," "Sergio," "Juan," "Braulio," "Eugenio," "Julio," "Rolando," and "Felipe." "Felipe" was identified as Peña Jáquez.[57] (Seven of the names were to be confirmed. "Julio" and "Rolando" were not used—the correct names were "Ismael" and "Armando."[58])

The police attempt to discredit Peña Jáquez was not the final word on the issue. On March 8th, Peña Gómez, the PRD secretary general, from hiding, demanded that the regime display the bodies of Caamaño and the other two guerrillas to resolve who was telling the truth. Peña Gómez stated "Even if former Colonel Caamaño Denó were truly dead, if the government does not answer the questions raised by Peña Jáquez's statements, the Dominican masses will continue seeing Caamaño's ghost in the mountains as the Mexican peasants saw Emilio [sic] Zapata riding on his white horse through the fields, demanding land and freedom for his people."[59] (The PRD leader appeared more inspired by the closing scenes of the Marlon Brando film *Viva Zapata!* than by the actual memory of Caamaño held by Dominicans.)

Within the task force, at midday on March 5th, the situation was categorized as bad; it was feared that the inability to find the guerrillas would have an adverse effect in the capital. There had not been a useful report on the location of the insurgents for one week. The government had arrested two peasants for reportedly collaborating with the guerrillas, but no information of value had been obtained from them. In the forward command post, the best estimate was that the insurgent group had not left the area north of San José de Ocoa and east of the road to Constanza.[60]

The frustration felt by members of the task force was shared by the media; newsmen complained that the government's last press conference had been as long as 17 days ago. (Apparently, they did not consider the visit to *Las Calderas* Naval Base to be a genuine press conference.) Reporters cornered Admiral Jiménez leaving the President's office at noon on March 5th and pressed him for anything concerning military operations. The secretary exclaimed that he had "nothing new" and that a press conference would be called as soon as he acquired something worth passing on to them.[61]

Since the Dominican Army had been deployed in the field against the Caamaño expedition, the public had received numerous media reports concerning the activities of the 1st *Duarte* Battalion, the 2nd *Sanchez* Battalion, the 3rd *Mella* Battalion, and the 6th *Cazador* Battalion. All were U.S. equipped and trained (although their American Army trainers were not allowed to accompany them into the San José de Ocoa hills). The unit that also had received the same preparation, but through all of February had remained out of the news, was the 9th *Santiago Rodríguez* Battalion, garrisoned in the northern town of Mao. On March 1st, Dominicans learned that the 9th Battalion was attempting to locate three suspected guerrillas, rumored to have been seen between the municipalities of Monción and San José de las Matas. They were allegedly carrying rifles and packs. The commanders in the task force operating in the San José de Ocoa area had been ordered not to talk to reporters, but Balaguer's politico-military chieftain of Valverde Province recognized no such restraint. Even though Colonel Jáquez Olivero was the fort commander, not the battalion commander, in Mao, he introduced himself to the press as the head of the 9th Battalion and informed the newsmen that he "would crush any attempt to establish a guerrilla base" in the region he controlled.[62] The actual military deployment of the 9th Battalion under its real commander, Lieutenant Colonel González Pérez, was as follows: Approximately 130 troops were on patrol in the hills north and south of their installation, and 200 men in Mao were designated a national reserve force for use, if necessary, on the north coast.[63]

Members of the extreme left had yet to play any role in the support of the Caamaño expedition. They were quick to blame Juan Bosch and his party for contributing to the death of the ex-colonel by inaction, and they accused Bosch and Peña Gómez of cowardice because they remained in hiding, but radical leftists had taken no significant measures themselves.[64] During the first week in March, there was the possibility that this inactivity could change. The security services received reports that the MPD was planning to kidnap a foreign diplomat or a high Dominican official. One report specifically stated that a U.S. military attaché was targeted. The main purpose of the kidnapping was to spare the lives of the guerrillas operating in the San José de Ocoa zone by exchanging them for the hostage. Other objectives of the kidnappers were to create problems between the Dominican regime and the foreign government involved and to develop tension and agitation in the capital, thus easing counterguerrilla pressure in the hills. The President did not want a repeat of March 24, 1970, when the U.S. Air Attaché was kidnapped and exchanged for 20 political prisoners; however, the government did not have the resources to increase markedly the protection of all foreign diplomats in Santo Domingo. Nevertheless, precautions were taken (especially with military attaches), and the extreme left continued to maintain a low profile.[65]

On March 6th, information at last became available concerning the fugitives. According to a peasant, three insurgents on March 4th entered his store in the vicinity of the village of Carmona and purchased rice, beans, sugar and meat. Upon departure, the three moved in an easterly direction. The peasant gleaned that one of the guerrillas was a cousin of Colonel Caamaño,[66] making it most likely that he was Claudio Caamaño. If true, it would mean that of the nine who had come ashore at Caracoles Beach, possibly six had been identified.

Claudio Caamaño Grullón was a first lieutenant in the National Police prior to the 1965 civil war. He joined the Constitutionalist rebellion and became his cousin's G-2 with the rebel rank of major. After the war, he was reinstated in the police with his regular rank and sent to Chile for security forces training. He departed on schedule for South America, but he never returned to resume his career as an officer in the National Police.[67]

The government was relieved that it finally had a guerrilla sighting and that it was within the San José de Ocoa area. This information indicated that the insurgents had failed to re-establish themselves outside the zone of operations. The task force promptly directed that troops be deployed to the east in an effort to contain the fleeing guerrillas. The lack of helicopter support made this shift in direction difficult, but it was accomplished.[68]

Soon after the report was received from Carmona, the task force was informed that a peasant was in custody who could describe how he had been forced to act as a guide for the insurgents.[69] On March 7th, the local inhabitant told his story to Dominican military intelligence officers. The peasant explained that at approximately 10:30 P.M. on March 4th, four armed men ordered him to take them from Carmona, where they had bought provisions, to the path that leads to the Nizao River. They tied the end of a rope around the peasant's waist and used it as a leash. He was told that they would kill him if he attempted to escape. From March 4th to early March 7th, the group traveled through the area of La Cieneguita-Montenegro-El Yayal. On the 7th, they released the guide and began moving toward La Vigía. The four identified themselves only as "Juan," "Sergio," "Freddy," and "Ismael." Physical descriptions of the four revealed no unusual characteristics. Freddy claimed that he had three children and Sergio stated that his father was named Plutarco. The men were dressed in uniform-type olive green clothes. Three wore hooded overcoats. They had rifles, but the peasant could not identify them, and each had a knapsack and a small bag containing rice, sugar, codfish, and oil. The insurgents claimed that they wanted to fight to help the peasantry. Promised were hospital care and land that was in the hands of the rich. The guerrillas commented that government troops had passed near them, but the insurgents remained undetected. The reason, according to the rebels, was that the Army concentrated its search on the high ground, while the guerrillas moved in the valleys.[70] (Six years later, the guerrilla Hermann Pérez described how they, in hiding, were so close to the soldiers that they heard the troops remark that they were members of the 1st Battalion, and that they were under the command of Colonel Romero Pumarol.)[71]

The peasant did not know what the insurgents' future plans were, but it was obvious that the rebel group had been reduced to four men, and that they were in the vicinity of the Peravia-La Vega provincial boundary line, traveling east toward the Duarte Highway. That thoroughfare, which was roughly parallel to the San José de Ocoa-Constanza road, was the principal artery in the Dominican Republic. The Duarte Highway's main terminals were the capital in the south, and the nation's second largest city, Santiago, in the north.

As stated before, the U.S.-supported 9th Battalion in the northern region had been designated the national reserve strike force to be deployed in the event of an insurgent landing along the north coast. The ability to accomplish this tactical mission was partially altered when 9th Battalion troops were sent into the hills in response to the rumored presence of guerrillas south of Mao. (The "guerrillas" proved to be only coffee thieves carrying sacks.) The unit's combat capability as a maneuver battalion was further decreased when its strength in Mao was reduced to less than a rifle company. One hundred and thirty personnel and their vehicles were attached to the task force in the San José de Ocoa area, and troops were sent to augment the north coast guard posts in the vicinity of Maimón and Estero Hondo.[72] Thus, the 9th Battalion in the north had begun to appear less like a tactically structured mobile reserve and more like any other constabulary unit in the Dominican Army.

Although the task force, led by Generals Beauchamps Javier and Matos González, and the Santo Domingo police, under General Cruz Brea, were the focal points in confronting the Caamaño expedition, the constabulary Army played a vital role in shoring up the Balaguer regime in the interior. The President had empowered local military commanders to be practically autonomous pro-consuls in their provincial areas. Operating extra-legally, these officers arrested potential agitators and opposition party leaders. In addition, they ordered their locally stationed troops to engage in a variance of population control methods which successfully prevented the development of secondary pockets of insurgency.[73]

During the Caamaño affair, Balaguer's provincial military leaders were Brigadier General Estrella Sahdalá in Santiago; Colonels Jáquez Olivero, Almonte Mayer, and Medina Sánchez in Mao, La Vega, and Dajabón, respectively; and Lieutenant Colonel Mota Henríquez in San Francisco de Macorís. In the South Zone, Brigadier General Perdomo Rosario was in San Juan de la Maguana and Lieutenant Colonel Figueroa Carrión was in Barahona. The sole commander of the East Zone was Colonel Grullón Hierro, whose headquarters was in San Pedro de Macorís.

Although each provincial area had its unique features, the constabulary units generally operated in much the same manner during February and March 1973. An example of how the Army functioned in the interior after the Caracoles Beach landing was announced can be found in the actions of the 10th Battalion, 3rd Brigade. That battalion was headquartered in the southern coastal town of Barahona, west of the Bay of Ocoa. (It did not have jurisdiction over the counterguerrilla area of operations—that zone initially was the responsibility of the 8th Battalion, 3rd Brigade.)

After the news arrived of the maritime incursion, there was an attitude of confusion among anti-government elements in the four provinces of Baoruco, Pedernales, Barahona, and Independencia, which made up the 10th Battalion's sector. It was suspected by the population that the guerrilla report was a trap of the government to induce the opposition to surface. (This was an old Trujillo trick.) Early on, it was determined by the local security services that collusion between anti-regime groups and the newly arrived guerrillas did not exist. Within the town of Barahona, however, it was assessed that there were second level leftists who had the potential to initiate agitation. In contrast, in the rural areas there was little sympathy for the guerrillas.[74]

Upon receipt of orders from higher headquarters on February 4th, all 10th Battalion personnel reported for duty and were placed on alert. In Barahona, low-level members of the PRD who were considered capable of committing acts of violence were apprehended, along with members of the extreme left. (At the height of the crisis, there were approximately 20 prisoners, including common criminals, in the National Police/Army jail.) The leaders of the PRD in Barahona, however, were not arrested because they were respectable members of the community, such as businessmen and professionals. Nevertheless, they were placed under surveillance. The small number of troops available in the 10th Battalion required the commander to call veterans back to active duty. The former servicemen who worked for government organizations, such as 60 men from the Barahona sugar mill, were given the responsibility to guard government-owned property. Since the sugar harvest had begun, there was concern that terrorists would attempt to burn the cut cane. The missions of patrolling the beaches, establishing roadblocks, and augmenting rural posts were given to regular troops of the Battalion. Urban patrolling and guarding key buildings, such as radio stations, were shared with the National Police. There was also effective collaboration between the local representatives of the military and police intelligence services. To maintain security of the Barahona airfield (the major air installation in the South Zone), the Battalion's two "half track" armored personnel carriers, with mounted .50 caliber machineguns, were stationed alongside the runway. They were in communication with the control tower; if the tower was not satisfied with the identity of an approaching aircraft, the armored vehicles were to open fire.[75]

As events progressed, numerous reports were received of guerrillas being sighted. Most of this information referred to three unidentified men in military garb. Patrols and intelligence personnel investigated each report and determined them false. It was suspected that misinformation was being planted at different locations to strain the security forces; however, this possibility was never confirmed. In addition, an alleged guerrilla landing was reported at Enriquillo, down the coast from Barahona, and more than one boat was sighted without lights. All this information also proved of no value. The policy of Lieutenant Colonel Figueroa Carrión, the battalion commander, was not to report guerrilla sightings to the 3rd Brigade in San Juan de la Maguana or to Army headquarters in Santo Domingo, until he thoroughly investigated each case. The reason was that the government was deploying troops every time a peasant claimed he had seen an insurgent. The result was increased tension between the population and the security forces over false alarms.[76]

Initially, the civilian community accepted the "state of emergency" well. The Lions Club and the Rotary Club met with the military and police , and, willingly, provided assistance. The management of the Barahona sugar mill also was anxious to help. The same attitude was evident in the countryside. There was smooth cooperation between the soldiers—many came from the region—and the peasants. As the "state of emergency" continued into its second month, however, the urban civilian sector began to feel the strain. Leaders of the government party, the *Partido Reformista*, complained more than legal opposition leaders, because the restless population was becoming critical of the Balaguer regime's restrictions. The consequence was heightened irritation among workers. It was evident by the second week of March that a continued government clampdown would have an overall negative effect on the towns in the 10th Battalion's area of responsibility. By that time, the Battalion was facing an uneasy calm in Barahona.[77]

Internal problems were few. Logistical support for the Battalion's widespread, subordinate elements (4 companies, 12 detachments, and 20 posts) continued at the same level of effectiveness as before the national crisis. Trucks to transport troops were placed on loan from government agencies, such as the sugar mills and the Forestry Directorate. Because armored vehicles could serve no useful purpose in urban areas or in the countryside, the two L-60D light tanks at battalion headquarters remained in garrison. Air Force personnel were operating from the Army installation in support of a fixed-wing trainer aircraft that flew reconnaissance missions over the south coast.[78] (The 10th Battalion headquarters building and the adjacent airfield had, at one time, been the FAD *Capitán Piloto Rafael Dávila Quesada* Air Base.)

After March 7th, the receipt of useable information on the fleeing guerrillas halted. For one week, the situation remained unchanged. To compensate for this lack of developments, there were attempts by the government to shape public opinion through staged events. For example, on March 7th, it was announced that the Chamber of Deputies had given the President a vote of confidence for his handling of the Caamaño affair[79]; on March 10th, General Matos took time off from the campaign to engage in civic action handouts for peasants in the *Cordillera Central*[80]; and on the same day, General Beauchamps informed the press that a new road in the mountains would be constructed for local use.[81] Even Juan Bosch inadvertently helped the Balaguer regime's image by furtively coming out of hiding to request that the PRD change its policies and then, in a craven manner, he hastily went underground again.[82] None of these occurrences, however, could alter the fact that the last overt success for government troops was on the 16th of February when Caamaño and two of his men were cornered.

At last, on March 15th, contact was established with the guerrillas; however, the circumstances were far from favorable for the regime. At 2:30 P.M., a five man patrol, made up of 1st Brigade troops, was fired on by individuals who were concealed in a high-ground position on La Yautía hill, less than eight kilometers west of the Duarte Highway. The soldiers came under fire when they moved into a clear, unprotected area. Two were killed. The guerrillas were able to escape without revealing their identities or number.[83] At 9:30 that evening, the Armed Forces public information office reported that a sergeant and a private from the 3rd Battalion, 1st Brigade (Carlos Alberto Pérez and Carlos Antonio Deñó de la Rosa, respectively) had been killed during an exchange of fire at La Yautía, in the jurisdiction of the town of Bonao. Guerrilla casualties, the government conceded were unknown.[84] In the U.S. Embassy cable to Washington on the 16th, it was emphasized that the communiqué was "the first officially reported contact between the insurgents and members of the security forces since February 16 when Francisco Caamaño and two of his colleagues were killed."[85]

The firefight had taken place between Bonao and Villa Altagracia. The latter town, on the Duarte Highway, was almost a suburb of Santo Domingo. Earlier, General Cruz Brea, thinking of the security of the capital, had expressed concern that the insurgents would attempt to come out of the hills at Villa Altagracia. He warned that under urban cover they could easily infiltrate into Santo Domingo and join extreme leftist groups in the city.[86] The proximity of the guerrillas to built-up areas alongside the Duarte Highway created a new set of problems that General Beauchamps tried to resolve by taking four actions. He re-positioned the bulk of his maneuver elements in the Bonao-Piedra Blanca area, he set up roadblocks on the Duarte thoroughfare, he moved his command post facilities to La Yautía, and he established a military base and encampment at Los Mogetes, near Villa Altagracia.[87] A new phase in the counterguerrilla campaign was about to begin.

Although the shifting of troops from the *Cordillera Central* to lower terrain adjacent to the Duarte Highway seemed uncomplicated, logistics and personnel functions in support of the task force began to feel the strain. When the concept of operations was changed to the zone system in the end of February, base camps in the new zones and sub-zones had to be organized to provide essential materiel for the troops, such as food and ammunition. Many of those isolated areas could only be supplied by helicopter. Consequently, rotary-wing aircraft were operating in reduced numbers when the new deployment of the task force took place in mid–March. The 1,000 field jackets had arrived from the United States in the last days of February, as well as boots purchased on an emergency basis from the Republic of Korea. The footgear, however, proved incapable of standing up to constant wear in rough terrain. Although feeding the troops had improved since the first days of the campaign, by the middle of March Dominican soldiers again began to complain that sufficient food was not available. Enlisted men resorted to buying provisions directly from peasants—in many cases they paid with IOUs. Even worse, when a shipment of rations finally arrived, it was found to have spoiled. These conditions made it necessary for General Pérez y Pérez to relieve the Army's quartermaster general of responsibility for the supply of food—this function was temporarily assigned to retired General Marte Pichardo, the head of the President's civilian program to provide meals for the needy.[88]

The personnel level of the task force continued at 1,500 despite the request to General Pérez y Pérez from various sectors to reduce it. One Army General Staff officer went so far as to state seriously that the troops could not remain continuously in the field for more than 60 days because it was impossible for the Dominican soldier to be without a woman beyond that length of time.[89] Whatever the reason, disturbing personnel problems began to surface. On March 15th, four enlisted men from the 6th *Cazador* Battalion were arrested and imprisoned in *Fortaleza Ozama*. They were charged with failing to act aggressively in the field the day before.[90] By the 20th, it was noted that troop morale was beginning to decline. Rumors began to circulate that the firefight that took place on March 15th was, in reality, Air Force paratroopers' firing in error on the Army, causing the two 1st Brigade fatalities. Officer negligence was blamed. Also, the story was being spread that officers were hoarding food while enlisted men went without rations.[91]

The failure of the task force to bring the counterguerrilla operation to a close, coupled with the Pérez y Pérez decision to maintain the task force personnel strength at 1,500 men, were issues which brought about the first significant military policy recommendation to be offered by the U.S. MAAG to the Dominican Army during the Caamaño affair. Up until March 16th, American Army unit advisers had discussed the ongoing operations with their Dominican counterparts, but, since the advisers did not have the authority to participate in the campaign, suggestions were only provided on an unofficial basis, friend to friend. On March 16th, however, General Pérez y Pérez's U.S. Army adviser met with the chief of staff in Pérez y Pérez's private office in Army headquarters, and presented him with direct advice on the future conduct of the campaign. (The author was present in his capacity as a military observer.) The American officer recommended that the task force should return part of its troops to their garrisons and then adopt the tactics of the U.S. Army in Vietnam. The adviser explained that a smaller body of men could patrol selected areas in the operational zone, and a mobile reaction force could be positioned to exploit any contact made by the patrols. General Pérez y Pérez allowed the American to complete his remarks and then the chief of staff responded politely, but firmly, that a solution used in Vietnam was not appropriate for the Dominican Republic. He continued that 1,500 troops would remain in the field until the last guerrilla was eliminated. General Pérez y Pérez had, in effect, meant that he would not adopt a less than successful foreign approach, but would conduct operations in the Trujillo manner—pile on more and more Dominican soldiers until the guerrillas were snuffed out.

Pérez y Pérez's rejection of the MAAG advice came at the same time that an increase in anti-U.S. sentiment was developing within the officer corps. This attitude had taken form as a result of the perceived lack of support that the military and police had received from the United States during the security operations of February and March 1973. Senior Dominican officers understood that foreign aid had to be regulated by a civilian Congress, but what was not understood by many in the Dominican military was why Washington had been quick to support Far Eastern countries threatened by insurgency, but, in the case of the Dominican Republic, only 600 miles from U.S. borders, assistance had been slow in materializing. Some members of the Dominican military leadership were asking why a small amount of equipment, such as helicopters, could not be diverted from Vietnam to the Caribbean to allow the Dominicans to eliminate the rural guerrillas before a potentially explosive urban situation erupted. Also questioned was why had the U.S. government charged the Dominican Republic for items such as C-rations when the same food could be purchased locally for less money.[92]

The criticism of U.S. security assistance policy seems hardly justified when one considers that the task force was made up of five Army battalions and one National Police unit that had been equipped and trained by the United States at no cost to the Dominican government. Nevertheless, it must be recognized that during the third week in March, there were ample reasons for apprehension among the heads of the military and police establishments. This anxiety was revealed on March 17th when the Armed Forces secretary, the Army chief of staff, and the National Police chief voiced their concerns to the President. They explained that because the Armed Forces were taking longer than expected to end the rural guerrilla campaign, anti-regime elements of the urban population were emboldened to take action. Reports had been received that the extreme left had begun to believe that there would be value in staging student demonstrations, strikes, and acts of terrorism in the cities. The senior officers requested that the President provide additional funds to be utilized in an effort to avert the possibility of urban warfare in conjunction with the guerrillas in the interior. Balaguer was not convinced, however.[93]

During the difficult days immediately following the death of the two 1st Brigade soldiers near the Duarte Highway, an almost forgotten general would make his move to re-establish himself at the center of power. Neit Nivar Seijas, it was widely rumored, had fallen into disfavor since the guerrillas had landed. The U.S. Embassy reported to Washington that "General Nivar seems to have been relegated to a back seat since the invasion. Balaguer's rather cool greeting of Nivar on TV after the President's Feb. 7 speech, in contrast to the relatively effusive (for Balaguer) embrace given to Brig. General Salvador Lluberes Montás, is widely interpreted here as a conscious effort further to downgrade Nivar."[94] The slights to Nivar were many. He had not accompanied the President to the field, he had been publicly identified as a non-participant in military planning,[95] and his close collaborators had been excluded from the task force. None of the key officers in the operational zone, except for Colonel Romero Pumarol, were Nivar men, and Romero Pumarol undoubtedly was already seeking a new patron. Most significant was the absence of Nivar's old 1st Brigade battalion commanders, especially since they had participated in a field training exercise in the San José de Ocoa hills on June 12th through June 18th in 1971. The only compensation for the Nivar clique was that in 1973 many of the majors in the San José de Ocoa area had been associated with Nivar when they were captains in the 1st Brigade. (Examples were Majors Aranda y Martín, Checo Jáquez, Díaz Mena, Osell, Páez Piantini, and Solano Hernández.)

During the Caamaño affair, Nivar, on three occasions, privately requested that the President appoint him commander of the counter-guerrilla campaign, but Balaguer rejected Nivar each time by telling the General that he was needed in the capital. On March 16th, Nivar changed his tactics and began overtly to agitate against the military and police leadership. He was strongly critical of the conduct of operations in the San José de Ocoa and Bonao areas. Specifically, Nivar blamed General Pérez y Pérez for constantly interfering in the internal activities of the task force. Nivar also attacked the chief of National Police by criticizing General Cruz Brea for mishandling security in the capital, for treating the left with a heavy hand, and for publishing communiqués that contained poorly prepared and false information. Moreover, Nivar accused the government's intelligence services, including the DNI, of failure to perform adequately during the crisis brought on by the arrival of the Caamaño expedition.[96]

In the fourth week of March, a rumor began to circulate that Pérez y Pérez had had an accident while in a helicopter.[97] This technique was an old Nivar gambit—its purpose was to facilitate the removal of the targeted individual from his post. The press tracked down Pérez y Pérez at the new Los Mogotes military encampment on the 23rd and asked him for confirmation of the story. The General responded that there had been no accident and that he was in excellent health. He attributed the incorrect story to his "enemies."[98]

The President's policy was not to involve himself in the day-to-day direction of military operations either in the San José de Ocoa area or in the capital. He was quite willing to delegate that authority to the senior members of the officer corps whom he had appointed.[99] But when the issue was controlling Nivar's political ambitions or preventing the generals from raiding the treasury, Balaguer preferred to personally take charge. The President blocked Nivar by firmly telling him that it was absolutely essential that the General remain by his side in Santo Domingo. And, in turn, Balaguer deflected Pérez y Pérez and his allies by insisting that the Armed Forces and National Police must make do with the money that had already been allocated to their agencies because the budget already committed the additional funds they sought for public works construction projects.[100]

Thus Nivar was not given the opportunity to utilize the anti-guerrilla campaign to enhance his political fortunes. In addition, the members of the Pérez y Pérez clique were put on notice that, even though they had a free hand tactically to finish off the guerrillas, they would not be allowed to exploit the insurgency for the purpose of acquiring supplemental funds to build up the Armed Forces. It was understood that if the Pérez y Pérez group failed to end operations rapidly, Nivar was in the wings, waiting to take over the reins of command. Above all, it was made eminently clear that even though the President was disposed to let others deal with the details of the campaign, Balaguer was still in overall control.

XV

The End of the Campaign

Just when the virulent factionalism of the officer corps appeared to be overshadowing the military aspects of the counterguerrilla effort, tactical developments in the operational area gained the nation's attention. In a period of six days, two guerrillas would be killed in action, one insurgent would be captured, and the body of a fourth rebel who had died in the hills would be discovered.

MARCH 22-27

During the night of March 22nd, the fleeing guerrillas ran headlong into an ambush set up to block access to the Duarte Highway corridor. In a heavily wooded area, near the village of Los Mogotes, 1st Brigade troops killed one insurgent and wounded another[1] in what, six years later, former guerrilla Hermann Pérez would characterize as the "*emboscada final.*"[2] The injured rebel managed to stay alive until approximately 5:00 the following morning, when he was finished off.[3]

On the same day, the Armed Forces secretary invited newsmen to the temporary military encampment at Los Mogotes to view the corpses. The reporters saw two undernourished bodies dressed in tattered, olive green military-style clothes and worn-out combat boots. Admiral Jiménez then made available the insurgents' belongings. They consisted of two rifles (a Belgian FAL and a West German G-3), eight ammunition clips with 7.62mm rounds, two blankets, an overcoat, a spoon, and some personal trinkets.[4] The press was not shown the various charts that the guerrillas had been carrying. One sheet was a map of Santo Domingo; it was marked with key points, which included the headquarters of the Army, the National Police, and the Navy.[5] As of midday, neither corpse had been identified.

Lieutenant Colonel Báez Berg, the Armed Forces' public relations officer, had staged the press conference for the approximately 20 national and international reporters in an area replete with military trappings. In addition to the expected attendance of Admiral Jiménez (in a new camouflage uniform) and General Pérez y Pérez, the task force commanders, Generals Beauchamps Javier and Matos González, and representatives of their staff, Army Colonel Escarramán Mejía, Air Force Lieutenant Colonel Martínez González, and Navy *Capitán de Fragata* Padilla Medrano, were present. Also on hand were flag officers not directly involved in the San José de Ocoa-Villa Altagracia operation—General Folch Pérez and Commodore Logroño Contín, the chiefs of staff of the Air Force and Navy, respectively, and Commodore Amiama Castillo, a sub-secretary of state. The backdrop to the press gathering was the continuous movement of helicopters, military vehicles, and troops, giving the newsmen the sensation that they were in a combat zone.[6] Conspicuously absent were General Nivar and members of his faction.

Shortly after nine o'clock that evening, the secretariat of the Armed Forces released a communiqué. It stated that at 11:00 P.M. on the 22nd and at 5:00 A.M. on the 23rd, in the hills of Los Mogotes, located in the jurisdiction of Villa Altagracia, there had been combat action between members of the military and what remained of the guerrilla group that had landed at Caracoles Beach. Two insurgents were killed. From fingerprints, one had been identified as Juan Ramón Payero Ulloa. The Armed Forces had suffered no casualties. The communiqué closed with the statement that the last two guerrillas were being pursued through the mountains close to the area where the firefights had taken place.[7]

When the newspaper *Ultima Hora* of March 24th went on sale that evening, Dominicans read that the unidentified dead guerrilla was Mario Galán.[8] (It would later be confirmed that the *Ultima Hora* source was correct—the second corpse was indeed that of Mario Galán. His complete name was Mario Nelson Galán Durán.[9])

Payero Ulloa had been a leftist student organizer, then a member of the Fourteenth of June Revolutionary Movement.[10] Galán Durán had been studying medicine at the Autonomous University of Santo Domingo before joining the Constitutionalists during the 1965 civil war. He too was connected with the Fourteenth of June Revolutionary Movement.[11]

An Armed Forces review of the guerrilla situation, as of March 23rd, concluded that of the nine original guerrillas, five were confirmed dead. They were Caamaño, Lalane José, Pérez Vargas, Payero Ulloa, and Galán. Peña Jáquez was hiding somewhere in the capital, thereby leaving three. The two on the run in the countryside were tentatively identified as Hermann Pérez and Caamaño Grullón. The ninth apparently had dropped out, at least by March 4th—one fragmentary piece of information suggested that that unidentified individual had been wounded and had to be eliminated because he could not keep up with the others.[12]

In the task force headquarters, it was assessed that the two insurgents, thought to be Hermann Pérez and Caamaño Grullón, had succeeded in reaching the east side of the Duarte Highway, and were making every effort to enter Santo Domingo. The maneuver elements of the task force intensified search operations on both sides of the highway from Piedra Blanca, north of Villa Altagracia, to the outskirts of the capital, south of Villa Altagracia. They were being aided by Dominican Air Force police dogs obtained earlier from the United States. In addition, General Pérez y Pérez directed the Military Police Battalion at *Fortaleza Ozama*, commanded by Major Félix Bautista de Oleo, to throw a heavy roadblock across the Duarte Highway in the vicinity of Herrera, a western suburb of Santo Domingo.[13]

Within the capital, the security posture was increased. The National Police had received information that radical leftist groups, to include the *Comandos de la Resistencia*, were planning urban terrorist acts in conjunction with a general strike to take place on March 26th and 27th.[14] In Santo Domingo, police patrols were augmented and the entire Military Police Battalion was deployed. The expanded COFA, which had monitored security activity in the capital since the Caamaño expedition was first detected, continued to function at full capacity.[15] But, as the officer corps braced itself for a renewed anti-government effort in Santo Domingo, the capture of the insurgent Hermann Pérez on March 25th in Villa Altagracia, signaled that the threat of rural guerrillas' entering the capital was nearing an end.

Hermann Pérez, traveling alone, attempted to move surreptitiously from a cane field bordering the Duarte Highway to the highway itself by mingling with a crowd of villagers who had formed on the road when a serious, multi-automobile accident took place outside Villa Altagracia. The gaunt, emaciated stranger, dressed in torn, olive green, military-style clothes, looked highly suspicious to the civilian guards of the state-owned Catarey sugar mill, who had congregated near the accident. The guards, armed with shotguns and revolvers, stopped Hermann Pérez and asked for his name. Without hesitation, the fugitive informed the sugar mill security employees that he was the guerrilla Hamlet Hermann. He asked that he be guaranteed that his life would be spared. (Six years later he would write that he requested "prisoner of war" status.) Hermann Pérez also told the guards that he had not eaten for three days, and that he only had a machete—his rifle, he claimed, had been discarded in the hills.[16] Hermann Pérez was turned over to a police lieutenant and escorted to the local National Police detachment. Shortly after, he was taken into custody by Air Force Captain Pou Castro,[17] who had been part of Admiral Jiménez's and General Pérez y Pérez's entourage in the field.

Since the National Police had been the first agency in Santo Domingo to be notified of the insurgent's capture, General Cruz Brea was the first senior officer to arrive on the scene in the Villa Altagracia area. The police chief had the opportunity to converse at length with Hermann Pérez. It was the general's impression that the captive had a strong intellect and that he was capable of organizing an anti-regime movement at the highest levels. Their conversation was interrupted by the arrival of the Armed Forces secretary. Admiral Jiménez informed General Cruz Brea, Captain Pou Castro, and the police officers and men present that Balaguer had ordered that the captured guerrilla not be harmed. The Admiral explained that Hermann Pérez's mother and aunt had pleaded that the life of the captive be spared. The prisoner's aunt, Doctor Altagracia Pérez Peña, was the President's sub-secretary of education and a family friend of Balaguer.[18]

Hermann Pérez then was transferred to the temporary military encampment at Los Mogotes where he was interrogated by various military officers until the following morning. On March 26th, at 3:30 P.M., four members of the press were granted permission to see the prisoner and to ask a limited number of questions.[19] Attending this press conference were Admiral Jiménez and Generals Pérez y Pérez and Beauchamps. Hermann Pérez stood before the newsmen in handcuffs and provided them with brief responses to their questions: He had been treated well by his captors; former Colonel Caamaño had led the group; the members of the expedition used cover names—his was "Freddy"; and one guerrilla, known as "Braulio," had died of exposure and was buried near Los Limoncillos between Arabia and Mono Mojao hill.[20] Then there was some friendly banter between Hermann Pérez and a reporter from the newspaper *El Caribe*, who had known the rebel as a chess and baseball player at the university.[21] That evening, the *Ultima Hora* tabloid (which had not been selected to send a representative to the press conference) published a story stating that the remaining guerrilla was Caamaño's cousin, and his alleged cover name was provided.[22] (*Ultima Hora* printed the wrong *nom de guerre* for Claudio Caamaño Grullón.)

Before the reporters met Hermann Pérez at Los Mogotes, the secretariat of the Armed Forces, on March 26th, released a terse communiqué announcing his capture. The document stated that at approximately 8:00 P.M., March 25th, between Villa Altagracia and the Catarey sugar mill, members of the mill's guard service had apprehended "Hamlet Herman [sic] Pérez," one of the two guerrillas who had survived earlier firefights with the military. His request that his life be spared, and how he had been armed, were included in the communiqué.[23]

The next morning, the handcuffed Hermann Pérez accompanied General Matos González and a detail of troops by helicopter to the spot where the prisoner had informed his interrogators that "Braulio" had been buried on February 21st. Hermann Pérez explained that the suffering "Braulio" had been left behind with his weapon because he could not continue the cross-country pace. When the guerrillas returned for him on February 21st he was dead.[24] The partially decomposed body of the insurgent was found under some rocks at the location indicated by Hermann Pérez. By the corpse's side was his U.S.-made .30 caliber carbine loaded with a clip of ammunition.[25] ("Braulio" would later be identified as Ramón Euclides Holguín Marte. He had been a peasant member of the PRD in the interior.[26])

After the prisoner and his military escort returned to the Los Mogotes encampment, Hermann Pérez was loaded on a helicopter for the second time that day (March 27th). He was transferred to San Isidro Air Base where an in-depth interrogation was scheduled for the week that followed.[27]

On the 26th of March, General Pérez y Pérez reversed his policy that 1,500 troops would remain in the field until the last guerrilla was neutralized. Despite the fact that the insurgent, assumed to be Claudio Caamaño Grullón, was still at large in the countryside, the chief of staff ordered that all Army troops, except approximately 350 men, be returned to their garrisons. The mission of the 350 personnel was to continue the search for the last guerrilla, principally in the hills surrounding Villa Altagracia.[28]

The withdrawal of most of the 1st Brigade and all of the Special Forces Group, and the partial evacuation of the temporary military camp at Los Mogotes, began almost immediately. All troops returning from the task force were granted two days' rest, and soldiers throughout the nation were issued passes wherever possible. The Air Force and Navy, countrywide, reduced their readiness postures to 50 percent on alert. By March 27th, it was evident that the general strike would not materialize; therefore, National Police presence in Santo Domingo was cut back, and only 50 percent of the Military Police Battalion was placed on standby. In the North Zone, the same force reductions were taking place. Roadblocks were dismantled and increased urban patrolling was discontinued. The 9th Battalion was returned to its garrison in Mao, and all rifle companies, but one, of the 6th Battalion were sent back to their installation in Constanza. The *Cazador* company still in the field was assigned to the counterguerrilla operation in the vicinity of Villa Altagracia.[29] The South and East Zones had no organic tactical maneuver elements, but their constabulary troops had been on a heightened state of readiness since the beginning of the Caamaño affair—they were returned to normal duty status when the capital and the North Zone received their orders to stand down.

In Santo Domingo, during the evening of March 27th, Admiral Jiménez, with General Pérez y Pérez present, informed newsmen that the counterguerrilla operation was "practically terminated."[30] The Armed Forces secretary conceded that one insurgent probably remained in the *Cordillera Central*, but, he added, "one man alone does not constitute a guerrilla war."[31] In the headlines the following day, the press, citing the Jiménez interview, announced that the anti-guerrilla war was over. Assuredly, this was the political message that the President, through Admiral Jiménez, wanted to send. On March 3rd, Balaguer had made it clear to his commanders that he was impatient to terminate the Caamaño enterprise.[32] It was doubtful, however, that General Pérez y Pérez personally would consider the Caamaño affair closed until the last guerrilla was permanently *hors de combat*.

MARCH 28-APRIL 16

March 28th began in what appeared to be one more day in the country's step by step return to normalcy—in Santo Domingo, the Military Police Battalion and the COFA received orders to revert to their pre-crisis operational status.[33] But, that evening, an act of violence would usher in a new state of anxiety in the city, and would provide General Nivar with an opportunity to advance his political interests: The chief editor of *Ultima Hora*, Gregorio García Castro, was assassinated in front of witnesses on a street in the heart of Santo Domingo. Recently, he had been questioned by the police's Secret Department concerning the published interview of the insurgent, Peña Jáquez. Plus, his newspaper had identified the guerrillas Mario Galán and Caamaño Grullón. García Castro also was well known for attacking government policies in his *Ultima Hora* column. Although some members of the officer corps found García Castro's writings highly irritating, he was not an extremist. The U.S. Embassy described him as "a moderate 'leftist' long associated with nationalistic causes,"[34] and Balaguer had been his friend when they both were in exile in New York City during 1962.[35]

The reaction to the murder was predictable: outrage on the part of the press and an immediate presidential order to the police to open an investigation. On the night of March 28th, Nivar spent two hours at the funeral home publicly grieving, an action that, of course, was published in the morning news.[36] Balaguer, on the 29th, elevated government involvement in the issue further—he promulgated Decree 3295, appointing a three-man "Special Commission" to investigate the assassination.

The members of the body were General Nivar, presiding; General Cruz Brea; and Dr. Juan Arístides Taveras Guzmán, the nation's attorney general. In the decree, all the intelligence services of the Armed Forces and the National Police, as well as the police's criminal investigative department, were directed to cooperate with the commission. The results of the commission's work were to be reported to the President.[37] García Castro's burial took place on the same day as the decree was released. Attending were the leaders of every major media outlet as well as a large number of working newsmen. Nivar was able to have printed in the press coverage of the funeral that he was a "good friend" of the deceased newspaperman.[38]

The internal workings of the Special Commission were far from harmonious, principally because of the Nivar-Pérez y Pérez rivalry. For Nivar, Cruz Brea represented Nivar's enemy, Pérez y Pérez, not the institution of the National Police. In private, Nivar railed against Pérez y Pérez and his clique, claiming that Cruz Brea had threatened him by brandishing a hand grenade on the police chief's belt, and that Captain Pou Castro, a Pérez y Pérez follower, was a madman who wished to eliminate him (Nivar). (For years, Cruz Brea had worn a small, Swedish-made grenade on his pistol belt, and Pou Castro had been the leader of Pérez y Pérez's counterterror squad.)[39] Outbursts between Nivar and Cruz Brea eventually reached public attention; one example was a shouting match outside the President's office in the National Palace.[40] The President realized that he had to make an adjustment to curtail the adverse publicity related to the Special Commission. It was essential that Nivar remain on the board because the President needed his reputation to blunt attacks against the government concerning the García Castro murder. In contrast, Cruz Brea was new on the national scene, without a personal following of his own. Consequently, of the two, Cruz Brea would have to go, but Nivar could not be allowed to gain a total victory. The solution was Balaguer's Decree 3298, issued on the night of April 2nd: General Cruz Brea was placed on 15 day leave and his replacement as acting chief of National Police would be, contrary to Nivar's recommendations, General Lluberes Montás.[41]

In mid-morning, April 3rd, Lluberes Montás was sworn in as acting police chief and Cruz Brea departed National Police headquarters after informing reporters that he planned to travel to the United States for medical reasons. A new decree was issued that day assigning Lluberes Montás to the vacant seat on the Special Commission. That evening, the press was able to learn from sources in the government that the assassins of García Castro were an officer and two enlisted men from the Secret Department of the National Police.[42] They were subsequently identified as First Lieutenant Juan María Arias Sánchez and Corporals

Miltón de la Cruz Lemus and José Rafael Pérez Pereyra. On April 5th, Lieutenant Colonel Carlos Peguero de la Cruz, chief of the Secret Department, was relieved of his post—Cruz Brea had appointed him.[43] The American Embassy reported to Washington that the murder of García Castro had "touched off a power play between Balaguer's two most powerful generals"—Nivar and Pérez y Pérez—and that "few observers believe that Cruz Brea will return to his police position."[44]

General Nivar, on April 9th, announced that the Special Commission had presented its findings to the President.[45] The U.S. Embassy characterized the report as "... apparently incomplete and somewhat contradictory...,"[46] but the Special Commission did accuse the police lieutenant and corporals of murdering García Castro. According to the report, there was no evidence that others were involved.[47] In a segment of the testimony provided to the commission, an unidentified individual took a swipe at Cruz Brea. It was claimed that the general had attempted to impede a portion of the investigation in an effort to protect the police, however, this allegation was denied by Cruz Brea and was never acted on. The President, however, did follow up on the accusation levied against the three members of the *Servicio Secreto*. On April 10th, they were cashiered from the National Police and turned over to a civilian court for trial. A pre-trial hearing was initiated two days later.[48]

By April 16th, the García Castro affair had run its course. In Decree 3387, General Lluberes Montás was confirmed as chief of National Police and Colonel Cruz Brea was returned to the Army in his permanent rank.[49] Soon after, Cruz Brea was appointed an Army inspector with a desk directly across from General Pérez y Pérez's office in Army headquarters, and the sacked chief of the Secret Department, Lieutenant Colonel Peguero de la Cruz, was transferred to a Santo Domingo police zone as an inspector.[50]

The politico-military impact of the changes that had occurred in the wake of the March 28th murder had proven insignificant. General Nivar had succeeded in temporarily discrediting a Pérez y Pérez man, but in the balance of power Nivar had gained little. In appointing Lluberes Montás to the police, Balaguer had forced Nivar to contend with a member of the anti-Nivar "Triangle," who, unlike Cruz Brea, had a viable faction of his own at San Isidro. Nivar, while on the commission, had been able to exert enough pressure to have Lieutenant Colonel Caonobo Reynoso Rosario, a *Nivarista*, designated the new chief of the Secret Department. This attempt, on the part of Nivar, to gain a foothold in the police intelligence service did not have long lasting results, however. On May 28th, Lluberes Montás transferred Reynoso Rosario to a meaningless position in the interior and replaced him with General Pérez y

Pérez's former Secret Department chief, Colonel Luis Arzeno Regalado.[51]

The events that transpired concerning the García Castro assassination had not influenced counterguerrilla activities in Villa Altagracia. In the last days of March, search operations were conducted in the cane fields and hills throughout the area. It was confirmed that the fugitive was indeed Claudio Caamaño Grullón and that his cover name was "Sergio." He was assumed to be hungry and exhausted. In addition to the patrols on the ground, Air Force helicopters flew reconnaissance missions and dropped leaflets requesting Caamaño Grullón to surrender. Aiding in the latter effort was the guerrilla's father, retired Major César Caamaño, who, on a loudspeaker, pleaded with his son to turn himself in to government forces.[52]

By the beginning of April, it was apparent that Caamaño Grullón was not likely to be found near Villa Altagracia, and that the threat in the capital was minimal. Consequently, on April 2nd, Balaguer issued the statement that the police encirclement of the Autonomous University of Santo Domingo would be terminated, and he authorized a further troop reduction in the field. On April 3rd, Colonel Robinson Brea Garó, the sub-chief of police, and Colonel Cabrera Martínez, the commander of the Duarte Department—whose *Cascos Negros* had the responsibility for closing off the campus—transferred control of the university to its rector.[53] On the same day, General Pérez y Pérez directed that the 350 troops searching for the insurgent be cut back to 40 men from the 1st Brigade. Their new mission was to maintain contact with peasants in the vicinity of Los Mogotes.[54] After eleven days, this detail, under the command of Captain Pedro Burgos Deschamps, was ordered to retire to its 1st Brigade barracks.[55] With its withdrawal, the San José de Ocoa task force's last remaining formation in the field had returned to garrison.

APRIL 17-JULY 3

Contrary to what the officer corps expected, Caamaño Grullón did not follow the Duarte Highway corridor into the capital. Instead, the last rural guerrilla headed to the southwest, in the direction of Haina on the coast, and then turned east, toward Santo Domingo.[56] At 10:00 A.M. on the 17th of April, he entered the Mexican Embassy unopposed and requested political asylum.[57]

While the search was on for Caamaño Grullón, Hermann Pérez was held captive at San Isidro Air Base. According to Hermann Pérez years later, he, at San Isidro, was subjected to a vigorous interrogation through

April 1st. During that ordeal, his interrogators utilized techniques emphasizing psychological pressure rather than physical torture. Then military officers supervised his preparation of a statement explaining the events that led up to the landing on the south coast.[58] At San Isidro, Hermann Pérez revealed that there had been extensive Cuban involvement in all phases of the Caamaño expedition up to the insertion of the guerrillas at Caracoles Beach on February 2nd. After reviewing the results of the interrogation, Admiral Jiménez and General Pérez y Pérez recommended to the President that the evidence be presented to the Organization of American States as proof of Cuba's act of aggression against the Dominican Republic. Balaguer, however, stated that the government would not take the issue to the OAS. Moreover, the President further directed that only a limited amount of the information relating to Cuba would be given to the public.[59] On April 19th, Hermann Pérez's statement was completed.[60] It was an altered version of what the prisoner had actually described to his interrogators. Details concerning Cuban involvement in the preparation of the operation had been deleted from the manuscript.[61] Before the statement was released, Balaguer, on April 24th, made his position clear concerning Cuba in his response to a question asked by a member of the visiting U.S. National War College. The President explained that there was no firm evidence that the Castro government was behind the Caamaño invasion.[62]

On the 7th of May, the Armed Forces secretariat distributed photostatic copies of 20 hand-written pages to the press. The document contained the Hermann Pérez statement.[63] After an analysis in the Political Section, the U.S. Embassy, on May 9th, dispatched a summary to Washington with the following comments:

> Hermann's statement is notable for its vagueness and lack of precision. While admitting, for example, that the guerrillas were in fact trained in Cuba, Hermann explicitly stated that the Cuban government was opposed to any invasion of the D.R. emanating from Cuban soil and refused to provide any assistance for such an adventure. Similarly, Hermann's treatment of the PRD is also open to various interpretations. While repeatedly suggesting links between the PRD and the Caamaño group, he does not reveal that the top PRD leadership was in any way directly involved in the operation. The absence of any direct allegation regarding the involvement of Juan Bosch and José Francisco Peña Gómez with the guerrilla operation is particularly noteworthy. Thus, while implying that the PRD was aware of the guerrillas' plans, Hermann provided no indication that the PRD either approved of the action or was committed in any way to support it.[64]

The Embassy concluded its comments by stating that "the very vagueness of Hermann's declaration will provide the GODR [government of Dominican Republic] maximum flexibility…" in dealing with Cuba and with the opposition PRD.[65]

Parallel chronologically with the events related to Balaguer's refusal to incriminate Cuba of complicity in the Caamaño guerrilla enterprise, was his handling of Juan Bosch and the PRD. From the beginning of the Caamaño affair, the government had indicated that undisclosed information existed implicating the ex-president and his party with the guerrillas. As late as April 17th, Admiral Jiménez was quoted as saying that "at the right moment" the necessary proof would be made available linking Bosch with the Caamaño invasion.[66] But, while the Hermann Pérez statement was being prepared, Balaguer changed his policy. On April 23rd, General Lluberes Montás, as chief of police, announced that there were no charges pending against Bosch,[67] and, four days later, an Armed Forces communiqué was released stating that the President had ordered that full personal protection be granted to Bosch because he was not considered to have been involved in the Caracoles Beach operation.[68] After some empty rhetoric,[69] the ex-president, on May 4th, came out of hiding and, three days later, Peña Gómez followed him.[70]

Within the officer corps, there was disagreement with Balaguer's decision not to accuse Cuba before the international community of participation in the Caamaño expedition. The same sentiment existed among the officers concerning the President's disinterest in pursuing the Juan Bosch and PRD issue.[71] Even though there was unhappiness with Balaguer's policy, it is significant that the officer corps was willing to accept the little doctor's judgment. Officers at all levels knew that Cuba had played the major role in preparing Caamaño and his men for their insurrectionary enterprise. As for Bosch and his party, the Dominican military had repeatedly heard the government make public allegations—from the description of the material found aboard the *Black Jak* at Caracoles Beach to the end of the counterguerrilla operation—that the ex-president and the PRD were in league with Caamaño and his men. Yet when Balaguer let the matter pass in the end of April and the beginning of May 1973, the officer corps docilely fell in line behind the President. The officers never would have acted so passively from 1962 to 1965. Their lack of action in 1973 was more reminiscent of their subservient conduct in the era of Trujillo, than of the turbulent years between the end of the Trujillo regime and the beginning of Balaguer's first elected presidency.

Balaguer's desire not to allow international attention to focus on the Caamaño affair precluded the Armed Forces from staging a national-level victory ceremony similar to the ostentatious displays common during the Trujillo years. There were to be no parades through the streets of Santo Domingo and Santiago, nor mass formations of troops and bands assembled in sports arenas. Balaguer did allow, however, one event that he normally presided over at the beginning of each new year. He would promote deserving officers and enlisted men in the National Palace with only essential members of the media present. The recipients of the promotions were to be a handful of junior officers and a limited number of sergeants and corporals. No one above the rank of captain was to be formally honored.

The modest ceremony began at 7:20 P.M. on May 18th in the upper-floor chamber where the President normally received official visitors. First, in a departure from the standard New Year's gathering, Balaguer offered his sympathies and embraced a family member representing each of the six soldiers killed in action. He also handed out a grant of financial assistance as a survivor's benefit to each of the six relatives.[72] Then, he began the promotions. A general order had been cut, effective May 15th, placing four men on an officers' promotion list. First Lieutenants Francisco Israel Vasquez Cuevas and Raúl Almonte Lluberes of the 1st Brigade and 6th Battalion, respectively, were advanced to captain in the Army. Additionally, Second Lieutenant Francisco Abréu Jaime was promoted to first lieutenant and Sergeant Obdulio Antonio Batista Rodríguez was commissioned a second lieutenant. Both were in the 1st Brigade.[73] (At the ceremony, a fifth Army lieutenant, Ramón Hernández Hernández, was added to the group.[74]) The President pinned the insignias of rank on the five officers and then handed out sergeant's stripes to 14 men and corporal's stripes to 26 soldiers. All were in the Army except for three Air Force sergeants.[75] Silently looking on were the national-level military leaders, Admiral Jiménez and General Pérez y Pérez; the two field commanders, Generals Beauchamps Javier and Matos González; and three members of the task force staff, Colonel Escarramán Mejía of the Army, Lieutenant Colonel Martínez González of the Air Force, and *Capitán de Fragata* Padilla Medrano of the Navy.[76] Conspicuous by his absence was General Nivar Seijas.

By mid–May, Balaguer was especially anxious to bring the Caamaño episode to a close. After the release of the Hermann Pérez statement on May 7th, the Armed Forces leadership believed there was little more to be gained by holding him for interrogation. It was understood by the military that the President intended to deport the prisoner; however, it had not been decided where Hermann Pérez would be sent. Armed Forces leaders preferred Spain because they had confidence in Franco's security services. Hermann Pérez, however, had indicated that he wished to go to Mexico. In addition, the ex-guerrilla had made it clear to his captors that he wanted official Dominican protection from the time he left prison at San Isidro Air Base until his arrival abroad. Hermann Pérez had expressed his fear of assassination by radical leftist groups, as well as from ultraconservative members of the Armed Forces.[77] The time had also arrived to send Caamaño Grullón on his way. While sitting in the

Mexican Embassy, he had made his views known to the Dominican public. The "solitary guerrilla,"[78] as he was called in the press, had drawn attention to himself as the rebel who had outwitted the Armed Forces in the hills. It was understood that after the required, time-consuming interchange between the Dominican foreign ministry and its counterpart in Mexico City, Caamaño Grullón's destination would be Mexico because that was the country that had granted him political asylum.

During the evening of May 17th, the government announced that Hermann Pérez and Caamaño Grullón had been granted safe conduct to depart the country. The President had instructed the Armed Forces to implement the order although the official communiqué did not indicate the destination of the two ex-guerrillas.[79] Ten days later, Caamaño Grullón left Santo Domingo for Mexico City aboard a Spanish *Iberia* airliner.[80] The following day, he spoke to the press in the Mexican capital; his photograph appeared that evening on the front page of *El Nacional* in Santo Domingo.[81] On June 3rd, Hermann Pérez followed. He also departed on an *Iberia* flight; with him were his wife and four children.[82] They were met at Mexico City's international airport by Caamaño Grullón. Subsequently, the two former guerrillas were separately interviewed by a Dominican *Ultima Hora* correspondent.[83] On the 4th, Caamaño Grullón flew to Havana and, in five days, Hermann Pérez also took up residence in Cuba.[84] Only Peña Jáquez remained.

The last member of the Caamaño expedition had been an enigma from the start. As related above, when Peña Jáquez first broke his silence, he claimed to have been sent to Santo Domingo on a special mission after arriving at Caracoles Beach. Then, as already stated, the National Police, in a March 5th communiqué, maintained that Peña Jáquez was a government secret agent who had contacted the authorities after he came ashore. On March 27th, however, the National Police chief explained that he had no idea where Peña Jáquez was and that the alleged informant had betrayed the police.[85] In Hermann Pérez's May 7th statement, he supported Peña Jáquez's position that he was dispatched by former Colonel Caamaño to carry out specific missions in the capital,[86] but, before Caamaño Grullón left for Cuba, Caamaño Grullón denied that Peña Jáquez had been sent on any mission. Caamaño Grullón said that Peña Jáquez was considered a casualty of the disembarkation operation at Caracoles Beach and was written off on February 3rd as a combat loss.[87]

When César Herrera, the presidential press secretary, on May 18th, was discussing with newsmen the safe conducts issued the night before for Hermann Pérez and Caamaño Grullón, he led the reporters to believe that if Peña Jáquez were to acquire diplomatic asylum, he too would be able to exit the country without problem.[88] On May 25th, Admiral Jiménez went one step further by informing correspondents that if Peña Jáquez surrendered to the Armed Forces, he would receive the same guarantees of safety granted to Hermann Pérez.[89] Approximately one week later, Peña Jáquez, from hiding, made contact with representatives of the Catholic Church. Under the auspices of Archbishop Hugo Polanco Brito, arrangements were made with the Embassy of Chile for Peña Jáquez to receive political asylum.[90] At 8:00 P.M. on June 7th, Peña Jáquez, accompanied by the Archbishop, entered the Chilean Embassy, and the following day the Dominican foreign ministry confirmed that the Allende government had granted political asylum to Peña Jáquez.[91] His safe conduct was not issued until July 2nd; the day after, he and his wife and four children departed on a Venezuelan commercial aircraft for the first leg of their trip to Chile.[92] In an interview with a reporter from *El Nacional* before Peña Jáquez's departure, he admitted that the reason that he had traveled to Santo Domingo on the night of the landing at Caracoles Beach was because he had lost his way and decided to walk towards the capital.[93]

Thus, all nine members of the Caamaño expedition were accounted for—six were dead and three were in exile. And, after the fall of the Allende government, Peña Jáquez, along with Hermann Pérez and Caamaño Grullón, was a resident of Cuba.[94]

THOUGHTS ON THE GUERRILLA ENTERPRISE

The extent of official Cuban involvement in the Caamaño expedition has been the subject of contention over the years. What is clear is that by 1973 Castro had de-emphasized his policy of exporting revolution in Latin America through guerrilla movements, in favor of opening diplomatic and trade ties with numerous countries in the Western Hemisphere.[95] What has not definitively been established was the nature of Castro's actions as they specifically related to Caamaño. From the left, the view has been presented that the Cubans wanted to hold Caamaño back because conditions were not favorable for a successful guerrilla campaign in the Dominican Republic, but when Caamaño, who insisted on "liberating" his country, could no longer be restrained, he was cut loose by Castro. Despite pessimistic indicators, the Cubans had some hope that Caamaño would succeed.[96] In contrast, from the right, it has been postulated that Castro sent Caamaño to certain defeat so that the Cuban leader could permanently rid himself of his unwelcome Dominican guest.[97] This latter position was partially fortified by the information provided by a Cuban intelligence officer who defected to the United

States in 1969. He claimed that Caamaño was personally not well thought of in Cuba; therefore, plans to utilize him in a foreign operation were suspended.[98]

Although it cannot be determined whether Caamaño acted with the full backing of Castro, it is apparent that the Caamaño expedition at least had some form of doctrinal support from the Cubans. In what appears to be an almost slavish copy of Castro's experience of 1956-1958, Caamaño attempted to establish a rural insurgency in the *Cordillera Central* for the purpose of creating a rallying point for an uprising in Santo Domingo. This plan was a replica of what evolved in Cuba when Castro created a " *foco*" (or rural strategic base) in the Sierra Maestra, which allowed for the expansion of the urban insurrection in Havana. The *foco* strategy advocated that a small, proficient cadre of guerrillas would form a nucleus of revolutionary activity in a rural area. This central concentration would expand with peasant recruits who would be politically indoctrinated and militarily trained. From this *foco*, the impetus would be provided for an urban insurrection to grow and then, eventually, to triumph by bringing down the government.[99]

By 1973, the conventional wisdom in Latin America was that the *foco*, as a guerrilla war strategy, was dead. Many failures of the *foco*, of which the 1967 defeat of Che Guevara in Bolivia was the most famous, had led revolutionaries to declare that the time of the *foco* had passed.[100] Even Juan Bosch, an individual with little interest in military affairs, categorically stated in January 1972 that the *foco* was the wrong form of revolutionary warfare for the Dominican Republic.[101]

Despite this widespread negative attitude toward the *foco*, Caamaño's men were quick to parrot what they had learned in Cuba. From the Mexican Embassy in Santo Domingo, Caamaño Grullón remarked that the objective of their expedition was to establish a *foco*, which "would gradually obtain the support of the masses."[102] When Caamaño Grullón and Hermann Pérez were interviewed in Mexico City, they stressed that their first goal was to make contact with the peasantry for the purpose of creating a "*foco guerrillero*." Caamaño Grullón stated emphatically that "we were and are committed *foquistas*."[103]

Thus, there is little doubt that the Caamaño strategy was to be based on a Cuban strategy. The method of implementing that strategy was also to follow a Cuban model. It was known as the "war of the flea."

When Hermann Pérez was under interrogation, he informed his captors that fundamental to the training they received in Cuba was the concept of the "war of the flea."[104] *The War of the Flea* is the title of a book written by Robert Taber, a U.S.-born newspaperman who fought with the Castro forces at the Bay of Pigs. In this work, begun in 1964, Taber explained that the Cuban style of revolutionary warfare had been based on a plan of attrition with the ultimate objective of causing the political disintegration of the target government. To gain this political goal, it was essential to convince the people of the nation that their country was on the verge of collapse. The first phase in creating that ambience was to discredit the military by projecting the image that the uniformed services were both impotent and repressive. Once that impression was established, the armed forces would find it difficult to alter the way in which they were perceived by the population. To attempt to reverse their impotence, they would become more ruthless; if they curbed their ruthlessness, they would be portrayed as weak.

According to Taber, Cuban doctrine called for guerrilla groups initially to chip away at the government (such as fleas harassing a dog). Decisive actions were to be avoided. The element of surprise and the pursuit of limited objectives were the tactical guidelines during this preliminary period. Concurrent with that effort was a strong propaganda program to exploit the government's inability to cope with the insurgents. The guerrillas would have the advantage in that they could strike where they desired with a minimum of logistical burden. The government, in contrast, would need to defend everywhere; it would have to protect key installations, army outposts, and urban centers simultaneously. To maintain the sense of normalcy, the government would utilize excessive manpower and expend great sums of money. The Cuban concept in the initial phase, however, insists that the guerrillas must not operate in large units and that their equipment must be simple and, if possible, drawn from the arsenals of the government. Thus, the guerrillas must remain mobile, must not have a complicated organization, and must obtain their intelligence and logistical support from the population. After the armed forces are viewed to be powerless and the guerrillas continue to survive, new phases of the insurgency can begin, which will culminate in political victory.[105]

The implementation of the "war of the flea" concept was supposed to follow the establishment of the *foco*, but the *foco* strategy did not take hold in the Dominican Republic. Consequently, with the failure of the *foco*, Caamaño never had the opportunity to test the "war of the flea" model. Taber's concept, however, proved viable less than a decade later when guerrilla groups supported by Cuba introduced it into Central America.

While Cuban advisers shaped the strategy and concept of operations that Caamaño was prepared to implement, he, apparently, was responsible, or had a major say, in the selection of Dominican personnel, the choice of armament, and the location where the *foco* would be established. First, of the guerrillas selected by Caamaño for the expedition, one- third were not physically fit for a military campaign. Lalane José was missing his left arm and three fingers from his remaining limb, Holguín Marte had one leg shorter than the other as a result of an accident, and Peña Jáquez was middle aged and had a weight problem.[106] Second, the caliber of the rifles carried by the group was not standardized. At least the 7.62mm and the .30 caliber carbine ammunition could be replenished from Dominican Armed Forces stocks, but Caamaño's AR-15 was not used in the Dominican Republic; consequently, .223 rounds were not available. Finally, the decision to establish the *foco* in the high ground, northwest of San José de Ocoa, initially appeared sensible because of the easily defendable terrain and the availability of targets such as the Alto Bandera telecommunications facility, but one factor was not considered. Nothing edible grew in that area. If the guerrillas were to be denied access to the peasantry, they could not live off the land.

Caamaño's weak preparation for the expedition was followed by his clumsy and ill-timed implementation of the plan. From the beginning, Caamaño and his eight colleagues were at a decided disadvantage. The first major objective of the campaign was to develop the *foco* in the mountainous region near San José de Ocoa. To complete this phase, the fundamental prerequisites were a successful clandestine landing, followed by the unobserved infiltration of the guerrilla group north to the future base camp. Caamaño never had the luxury of operating on his own terms, however. The disembarkation at Caracoles Beach miscarried; the *Black Jak* and its contents were discovered; the route of Caamaño's journey north, past numerous villages, was reported by peasants and an Army patrol; and the guerrilla band's arrival in the Testero Mejía peak area, the proposed site for the *foco*, was not accomplished covertly. Consequently, Caamaño lost his opportunity to lay the foundation for an insurgency war in the Dominican Republic.

Hermann Pérez, Caamaño Grullón, and, later, Fidel Castro himself, remarked that the operation failed because the Caamaño expedition did not have sufficient time to develop the first phase properly.[107] Instead, the guerrillas were forced to engage in combat only three days after they completed their landing at Caracoles Beach. Caamaño never regained his equilibrium. In a frantic effort to elude the Army, his group began abandoning food, equipment, and ammunition. For Caamaño, this rout ended on February 16th when he and two of his guerrillas were killed. Caamaño Grullón admitted in Mexico that six days after the death of his cousin, the remaining members of the band decided that the rural guerrilla campaign was lost and their only alternative was to flee to the safety of the capital.[108] Thus, in record time, one of the most poorly mounted invasions in the history of irregular warfare was obliterated.

In conclusion, it is evident that an outdated Cuban strategy and flawed Caamaño tactics contributed to the destruction of the expedition. What next must be evaluated is the effectiveness of the Dominican officer corps in bringing about that defeat.

MILITARY PERFORMANCE
OF THE GOVERNMENT

To my knowledge, the only purely military critique of the 1973 Dominican counterguerrilla operation was a report I wrote, as the American Embassy's army attaché, at the close of the campaign. It was entitled *Dominican Rural and Urban Ground Force Counterinsurgency Operations —A Military Assessment.*[109] The document opened with an introduction and background data; then the government's four major strategic decisions were described and evaluated. After this information, an assessment was undertaken of Dominican military organization and of each of the principal general staff functional areas in the following order: intelligence, operations (which included communications), logistics, personnel, and civil affairs.[110]

The first substantive statement of the report was: "The Dominican ground forces successfully engaged a guerrilla band in the beginning of 1973. During its operations, a potential rural insurgency was destroyed and a dangerous urban insurrection averted with a minimum of bloodshed and no undue stress on the average citizen."[111] Subsequently, the report declared that the most significant decision made by the government was "the rapid establishment of military control in the capital.... The result was that the highly volatile population of Santo Domingo (the sole scene of the 1965 Civil War) did not have the opportunity to be exploited by anti-Government extremists. In denying to the opposition the capital as an urban warfare battlefield, the Administration guaranteed itself ultimate victory."[112]

The study then stated that a professional critique of the operation surfaced some failings that could spell serious trouble for the Dominican Republic if it were to face a more grave threat than it did in 1973. These problems were that the Dominican national defense organization was poor; that the Army refused to follow fundamental practices in organizing for combat; that the emphasis on countersubversion instead of combat intelligence resulted in poor intelligence operations; that the logistical system of the Armed Forces was extremely bad; that the ground forces did not have adequate air mobility; and that the morale of the enlisted men declined in the end of the operation.[113]

The first problem area was military organization at the national level. Joint control from the secretariat of the Armed Forces was characterized as "woefully inadequate." This subject was concluded by the statement that Admiral Jiménez "gave up partial leadership by sharing overall command with General Pérez y Pérez." The subsequent discussion of Army headquarters revealed that "the Army Chief of Staff became closely involved with operations, but the Army General Staff stayed outside" the entire process.[114]

The second deficiency concerned task force organization. These strong words are quoted from the report: "The organization of the rural counterguerrilla task force for combat was one of the worst examples of military professionalism observed in the operation. Instead of utilizing an already established staff and adding established units to tailor a task force capable of accomplishing the mission, the whole situation was patched together without use of a base. The major tactical unit in the Dominican ground forces is the Army 1st Brigade. That unit has a typically structured S-1 through S-4 staff and three tactically organized battalions. Neither the 1st Brigade staff nor a complete battalion entered the area of operations."[115]

The third difficulty centered on rural intelligence operations. The critique described the problem as follows: "The Dominican military establishment has always had great confidence in the peasant supporting the Armed Forces with intelligence information. Initially, this attitude proved correct because peasants did report the first locations of the guerrillas to the Government. As the operation progressed, however, there was surprise in noting that peasants were collaborating with the guerrillas. This development occurred for a variety of reasons: The guerrillas were paying large sums of money and, more interestingly, there was evidence of some political sympathy for the Caamaño group." At that point in the report, remarks were made concerning 1967 insurgency activities in the San José de Ocoa area. The document continued: "Since that time, that sector of the country has always been difficult for the Government. Despite this uncooperative spirit on the part of a few peasants, the overall intelligence situation favored the task force rather than the guerrillas, even though there were long periods without the receipt of any intelligence on the location or activities of the guerrillas. Where the difficulty arose was in the weak system of collection and, more importantly, in the slowness of the Government's response to information. The first failing (poor collection) was a result of the fact that the Dominican Armed Forces emphasized countersubversion rather than combat intelligence, and the second failing (poor response) was the lack of air and ground mobility within the zone of operations."[116]

The fourth weakness was in the area of logistics. Since this was a major problem, the paragraph entitled "Logistics" will be quoted in its entirety:

It was in the field of logistics that the Dominican ground forces exhibited its most serious deficiencies. Both at the national planning level and at the combat service support level there was evidence of mismanagement and inefficiency. A view of the various sub-areas of logistics during the operation reveals the following: a. Control and Planning. At no time was a Logistics Officer (J-4) appointed in the Secretariat of the Armed Forces. The position of Chief Ordnance Officer of the Armed Forces existed at the opening of operations, but that capable officer was given various non-related functions by his superior, Admiral Jiménez, ... rather than being designated logistical coordinator for the country's military operations. Within the Army General Staff, the G-4 (who is also competent) was denied an overall coordinating role for Army logistics matters. In the areas of POL and transportation, his influence was felt, but other important sections of logistics such as rations, ammunition, and clothing were not considered his responsibility. The officer who should have assumed authority for combat service support matters in the field was the Quartermaster General, but that job was filled by a political appointee who had never been to a military school, much less a logistical course. By Dominican standard procedures, this incompetent should have been responsible for the functions of re-supplying food and clothing, but even fundamental supply work was beyond him. Eventually, the critical requirement of ration planning was taken from the Quartermaster General and assigned partially to Major General Melido Marte Pichardo, a retired general who normally is the President's security coordinator. Throughout the entire operation there was no logistics plan in effect. Assets were sent to the operational area immediately after they were obtained, and priorities were not established.

b. Rations. The most critical logistical sub-area was food. The troops entered the zone of operations without a well established ration re-supply program (despite earlier U.S. Army adviser efforts to establish this system), and at no time did the task force overcome this problem. Expedients were purchasing C rations from the U.S. Government, assembling locally made food into packages, buying from peasants, and finally confiscating from peasants. In some cases, troops went three days without food other than what they could gather from the land. Although there is no doubt that the difficult terrain strained re-supply, attempts to alleviate the problem by stockpiling in the area of operations and establishing alternate means of distribution other than helicopter were insufficient.

c. Transportation. Ground mobility to the town of San José de Ocoa was adequate primarily because of the numerous vehicles provided to the Dominicans by the U.S. Government at the recommendation of U.S. Army advisers. At that point, transportation became almost ineffective. Instead of purchasing large numbers of mules and hiring load bearers, the small number of observation-type helicopters was overloaded with personnel and material. Utilization of helicopters for that purpose and for the continuous movement of general/flag officers from the capital to the area of operations resulted in the eventual breakdown of air transportation. Helicopters were rarely available for tactical support; at one point, only one effective helicopter was serviceable in the entire task force.

d. Maintenance. Ground transportation did not suffer seriously from maintenance failures; however, in the case of the more sensitive rotary aircraft, the lack of maintenance eventually paralyzed the air support to the ground forces.

e. Clothing. The troops of the task force went into the area of operations without warm clothing. The San José de Ocoa area is a sector of the country that is unfamiliar to the majority of Dominican soldiers who come from the lowlands. Consequently, adverse climate conditions required emergency measures to clothe properly the troops. Since the Armed Forces had no warm uniforms on hand, field jackets were purchased commercially from Miami and from the U.S. Government. The normal poor condition and lack of standardization of uniforms in the Dominican Army and Air Force caused confusion: Troops from the same organization were dressed in a variety of clothing. Therefore, there was difficulty in identifying who was with the Government and who was a guerrilla. (For two years, recommendations had been made by U.S. Army advisers for the Dominican Army to standardize its field uniform.)

f. Ammunition, POL, and Construction. These three areas were not problems. The reasons are that there were few firefights, vehicles were not utilized extensively in difficult terrain, and no engineer construction work was necessary. POL [petroleum, oils, lubricants] were obtained from civilian oil companies.

g. Medical. Since there were only six KIA and nine WIA in the Government forces, medical resources were not strained. Stomach disorders did develop, however, as a result of strange food and water. Medical officers were with the task force, and casualties were evacuated to fixed hospitals.[117]

The fifth inadequacy was the Dominican Army's weak airmobile capability. The army attaché's report emphasized that the lack of helicopters that could transport troops impacted negatively on the entire conduct of operations.[118]

The final problematical area, under "Personnel," was described as follows: "The morale of the troops was high in the beginning of the operation. The Army 6th Battalion and the police Department of Special Operations exhibited exceptionally good morale because of their prior training and experience in the area of operations. Air Force Special Forces troops had good *esprit de corps* as a result of their parachutist training. Eventually, the lack of food, clothing, and tangible operational results brought serious strain on the enlisted men. This manifested itself with disciplinary problems, complaints against the officers, and a lack of aggressive spirit in the operational area. The situation was beginning to reach serious proportions when, fortunately, the large scale operation terminated."[119]

An assessment of the Air Force's performance during the counter-guerrilla campaign can be summed up in two sentences: First, the FAD helicopter mission was critical; but, because of the limitations cited above, the effectiveness of the helicopters was less than satisfactory. And, second, P-51 close air support contributed nothing to the operation.

The Navy did not receive overly favorable public comments for its activities during the Caamaño affair. Most heard was the criticism that the naval service had failed to intercept the guerrilla mother ship, *Black*

Jak, when it entered the Bay of Ocoa. Although this carping was unjustified, it could not be denied that the country's principal naval base, *Las Calderas,* was located on the eastern entrance to the bay. In his annual report to the legislature, Admiral Jiménez made a special effort to bring attention to the fact that the Navy had engaged in intense patrolling from February to June 1973. The report singled out seven vessels that had been involved. They were the corvette *Juan Alejandro Acosta,* the former U.S. Coast Guard cutter *Restauración,* the Sewart boats *Proción, Aldebarán,* and *Bellatrix,* and the two tugs, *Caonabo* and *Macorix.*[120] In reality, as in the past, individual naval officers, such as the Armed Forces secretary himself, had made more of a contribution than the Navy as an institution.

Thirty years later, the army attaché's assessment appears unduly harsh to the very author who prepared it. The 1973 critique was influenced by the curriculum of the staff college at Fort Leavenworth, while General Pérez y Pérez, in 1973, was following a line of reasoning that combined a vague U.S. Army structure with Trujillo era politico-military techniques. When Caamaño landed, the officer corps was facing its greatest challenge since the 1965 civil war; however, the Dominican Armed Forces of 1973 was not the same institution that it had been eight years before. It had received generous U.S. support, but that was not the main difference. What was most important was that Balaguer's Dominican Republic was stable and its officer corps was under the President's control—two conditions that had not existed when the civil war began four turbulent years after the death of Trujillo. Thus, Balaguer's military cohorts in 1973, with all their shortcomings, ended up with total victory in an incredibly short period of time by Hemispheric standards. Other Latin American insurgencies have spanned the careers of their officer corps.

XVI

The Last Years of the Rivalry Between Nivar and Pérez y Pérez

The end of the potentially most dangerous rural guerrilla campaign since the U.S. Marine occupation caused little change within the Dominican officer corps.

CAREER DEVELOPMENTS AND POLITICS

Generals Nivar and Pérez y Pérez remained at their posts and their relationship with the President continued unaltered. Also at the national level, Admiral Jiménez retained the Armed Forces portfolio in the cabinet and the Air Force and Navy were still led by the same chiefs of staff. And General Lluberes Montás began conducting business in the Police Palace in a manner that suggested that he would be serving a full term in the National Police.

The two task force commanders returned to their pre-February, routine duties more quickly than expected. As early as April 18th, the public was informed that General Beauchamps Javier was presenting diplomas to the enlisted graduates of an English language course, at his old post as head of the Schools Command.[1] Also in the press, on April 23rd, General Matos González was photographed welcoming visiting members of the U.S. National War College as part of the protocol duties of the sub-chief of staff of the Air Force.[2]

Even those general officers whose military reputations were under a shadow because of ineffectiveness in the field, or because they were not called up with their units, suffered no damage to their careers. General Perdomo Rosario returned to the 3rd Brigade after he was relieved from command of the task force and resumed his duties as brigade commander and chief of the South Zone. No post-campaign problems surfaced for General Jorge Moreno either. Even though his 1st Brigade saw the most action in the task force, he received no diminution in his trappings of authority at the *16 de Agosto* Military Camp for not being selected to lead his men in the hills. Balaguer's positive public attitude toward his general officers continued as if Caamaño had never landed.

The experience of some of the colonels who had been part of the San José de Ocoa operation was different. It was widely recognized that Colonel García Tejada had been successful as a troop leader. At the termination of hostilities, he was rewarded by his appointment to command the 6th *Cazador* Battalion in place of Lieutenant Colonel Castillo Pimentel, who had been partially responsible for the failure to trap the guerrillas during the opening days of the campaign.[3] There is no doubt that internal military politics played a part in Colonel García Tejada's selection, however. He was a known member of the Pérez y Pérez faction. The importance of membership in an Armed Forces clan can also be seen in the case of two other colonels, who fared far differently from the new 6th Battalion commander after the Caamaño affair was over. Colonel Romero Pumarol had done well as a troop leader in the task force, but after the completion of the campaign, he was not assigned to a post comparable to that of García Tejada.[4] Romero Pumarol had formerly been a *Wessinista*, then a *Nivarista*, but, unfortunately for him in 1973, he had yet to become a Pérez y Pérez follower. For Colonel Ruiz Serrano, the aftermath of San José de Ocoa was inauspicious. He was relieved as the task force's principal general staff officer along with his commander, but unlike General Perdomo Rosario, he was not given a worthwhile assignment. Shortly after, he was forced into retirement.[5] Ruiz Serrano, in 1973, did not have a patron to protect him.

A review of the fortunes of those three colonels during and immediately after the counterguerrilla campaign provides an interesting insight into Dominican officer politics, but none of those accounts can compare, at the time, with the startling development in the career of Colonel Guarién Cabrera Ariza. This notorious Air Force colonel's background—from his polo playing days with Ramfis to his murder of two civilians in a restaurant on April 11, 1971—was described earlier.[6] Despite his dismal record, Cabrera had the distinction of being the only colonel promoted to brigadier general at the close of the counterguerrilla operation. And he had absolutely no involvement in the Caamaño affair at any level. Cabrera's promotion to general officer and his appointment as sub-secretary of state of the armed forces for air on April 26, 1973, was completely the President's doing. Balaguer's advancement of this useless wastrel immediately after the defeat of the guerrillas almost appears to be a calculated slight directed at every professional member of the officer corps.

A small number of thoughtful officers were concerned with the low morale evidenced among enlisted men during the final phase of the counterguerrilla operation. The increase in disciplinary problems and the disrespect shown to junior troop leaders were considered indicators of possible trouble ahead for the officer corps. The problem was partially alleviated by the President's promoting 40 enlisted personnel, but it was recognized that other efforts had to be made to ensure the future allegiance of the common soldier.[7] One mode adopted by the secretariat of the Armed Forces was the utilization of special traveling commissions. These groups, made up of field grade officers from the three services and the police, were sent to installations throughout the country for the purpose of addressing joint enlisted audiences. The subjects of the commissions' speeches were loyalty to the government, caution against anti-regime propaganda, and patriotism. These presentations were generally received without any reaction from the troops.[8]

Before the memory of the Caamaño expedition faded completely, General Pérez y Pérez made an effort to remove nonproductive senior officers from the ranks of the Army and, at the same time, fill positions from his own following. In October, information leaked out that he was attempting to retire four generals who were universally considered deadwood.[9] Three of these officers, Méndez Lara, Pérez Guillén, and Pilarte Núñez, were clearly too old for an active command, and the fourth, Perdomo Rosario, was a proven incompetent. The Army chief of staff was only partially successful, however. He was able to retire Pérez Guillén in April 1974 and Méndez Lara in June of the same year, but the President balked at removing Pilarte from command of *Fortaleza Ozama* and Perdomo from chief of the provincial South Zone. Pérez y Pérez did gain advantage by having Colonel Cuervo Gómez of the Combat Support Command promoted, in the end of 1973, to brigadier general, and Colonel Cruz Brea appointed, in the beginning of 1974, to commander of the Armored Battalion. Then, most importantly, General Lluberes Montás, on April 25, 1974, was returned to the Air Force as chief of staff, an action which gave the paratrooper officer direct command of the country's airborne and FAD infantry. (He was replaced in the police by Rafael Guzmán Acosta, a neutral career policeman.)[10] Thus, Pérez y Pérez entered the national election period in a strong politico-military position vis-à-vis Nivar.

During the presidential campaign of 1974, it was reported that Nivar aspired to be Balaguer's running mate; however, when Balaguer selected the civilian incumbent, Nivar blustered to his confidants that he did not need the vice presidency because if Balaguer were to die in office it would be Nivar who would determine who would be the next president of the republic.[11] Instead of being a candidate in 1974, Nivar joined Pérez y Pérez in repeating their performance during the 1970 electoral contest. Nivar actively involved himself in political activity, while Pérez y Pérez did nothing overtly, but allowed the Army to engage in blatant electioneering. Evidence of military support for Balaguer's candidacy was seen throughout the Dominican Republic. Provincial Army chieftains such as Jáquez Olivero and Almonte Mayer were highly visible in the interior as they had been four years before. In Santo Domingo, detachments such as Army Captain Marte Hoffiz's mobile column of armed vehicles raced through the streets of the capital flying *Reformista* Party banners. At the *16 de Agosto* Military Camp, a photograph of Balaguer was placed on the wall behind each 1st Brigade soldier's bed in the platoon bays. Common in constabulary units was the practice of fixing a small picture of the President on the wooden stock of each soldier's rifle. Even professional commanders such as General Cuervo Gómez could not resist—he had a large mural portrait of Balaguer painted on the outside of a barracks in the center of his garrison at Villa Mella. Behind the scenes, there were other instances of Armed Forces' backing for Balaguer. The COFA was activated as it had been for earlier elections; however, in 1974, there was no attempt to convince observers of political impartiality. Assigned to take charge of the augmented Center was the old San Cristóbal Group activist, General Braulio Alvarez Sánchez. The COFA's written operations plan for the security of the capital during elections was bound in the colors of the *Reformista* Party, and it was entitled "*Operación Victoria.*" The plan had two purposes: First, it would be used to ensure order while voting was taking place, and second, it could be utilized if "special actions" were needed in the unlikely event that Balaguer began to lose at the polls.

The President's candidacy needed no emergency implementation of *Operación Victoria*, however. On the day before the elections, the PRD coalition pulled out of the race because of reported governmental repression directed against the opposition during the campaign. Only one small party, headed by a *Trujillista* ex-admiral, remained to challenge Balaguer. The President won reelection with approximately 85 percent of the vote.[12]

THE POLITICO-MILITARY CRISIS OF 1975

In the beginning of 1975, the "Triangle" had experienced two years of ascendancy over the Nivar faction. General Pérez y Pérez, the senior member of the group, led an Army that was increasingly under his personal control. He had the unswerving loyalty of General Cuervo Gómez and Colonel Cruz Brea; he could rely on them for armor. The 1st Brigade's commander, Jorge Moreno, was a figurehead only—two thirds of his combat units would respond directly to the Army chief of staff. Pérez y Pérez could also depend on the Military Police Battalion at *Fortaleza Ozama* and the country's strategic reserve, the 6th *Cazador* Battalion. The second Triangle member, General Lluberes Montás, was the master of San Isidro Air Base, a fact that gave the anti-Nivar forces undisputed power in the eastern sector of the capital. The last individual to make up the Triangle was Admiral Jiménez. Although he contributed no military clout (other than the weak Navy), he did have certain assets: Jiménez's position as head of the Armed Forces offered psychological leverage, his close links with Commodore Valdez Vidaurre of the national intelligence service (DNI) were invaluable, and his contacts with the Americans, both in the U.S. Embassy and in Washington, enhanced his image.

While the Triangle flourished, Nivar's power was slowly being drained away. He had been isolated from his Armed Forces base by Balaguer in the beginning of 1973 and, after, he was the witness to his politico-military emasculation by his enemies. Over the course of one year, Generals Pérez y Pérez and Lluberes Montás systematically transferred his supporters in the Army and the National Police to unimportant posts or forced them into retirement. On occasion, a dejected Nivar approached Balaguer with the proposal that the General succeed the President after Balaguer retired from public life; however, the little doctor consistently avoided giving a favorable response to Nivar. Observers then began to report that Balaguer would refuse to see Nivar for lengthy periods; they noted that this would cause the secretary of the presidency to fall into what was described as a "deep depression," at which point he would talk of retiring from both the Army and the government.[13]

It was at this low ebb in Nivar's fortunes that Balaguer would once again find it useful to rehabilitate his dissatisfied general. On March 17, 1975, the young editor and government critic of *El Nacional*, Luis Orlando Martínez Howley, was assassinated near the Autonomous University of Santo Domingo, an action that set off a strong anti-regime reaction similar to what had occurred in the wake of the March 28, 1973, murder of Gregorio García Castro. Despite the appointment of an investigative commission, antagonism directed against the regime and the National Police refused to subside; therefore, the President found it necessary to take further steps to appease the public.[14] The Triangle realized that the police chief had to go, but what its members had not anticipated was the return of Nivar.[15]

The May 7th announcement of Nivar's appointment as chief of police came without prior consultation with senior members of the officer corps. They learned of the news at the same time as did ordinary citizens, and were stunned that their old nemesis had once again been placed in the center of Dominican national affairs.[16] It is surprising that long-time players in the politics of the military such as Pérez y Pérez, Jiménez, and Lluberes Montás were unprepared for Balaguer's move.

The equilibrium of power had been out of balance for over one year; consequently, a presidential adjustment was merely a matter of time. And Balaguer's established style, as was vividly displayed on October 14, 1971, was simultaneously to increase the strength of a weak faction in the officer corps and to quiet opponents in the street by changing police chiefs. The lack of recognition of Balaguer's balance-of-power doctrine on the part of Pérez y Pérez and his allies was a temporary failing, but the form of their response to the Nivar appointment was a serious, inexplicable miscalculation.

From the evening of May 7th to the following morning, numerous meetings of the chiefs of staff and the Armed Forces secretary and their factions took place. The Triangle's first overt act was to refuse to attend the May 8th installation of Nivar at the Police Palace even though the President was to officiate. Instead of appearing with Balaguer and Nivar, Pérez y Pérez and Jiménez participated in a ceremony at San Isidro in which Lluberes Montás was awarded honorary pilot's wings. The Air Force event took place at 10:00 A.M. while the eight minute presidential stay at police headquarters started at 11:40 A.M.[17]; thus there was ample time for the representatives of the high command to attend both ceremonies. This gesture of dissidence (which was publicized in the press) was followed by an unprecedented act of defiance by Balaguer's military leaders. A letter of resignation, dated May 9, 1975, was prepared and signed by Admiral Jiménez, General Pérez y Pérez, General Lluberes Montás, and Commodore Logroño Contín. Sub-secretary Amiama Castillo presented the letter to the President shortly after 9:00 P.M.[18] A translation of the entire letter reads as follows:

> We respectfully bring to the attention of Your Excellency our decision to resign, effective immediately, our positions of Secretary of State of the Armed Forces, Chief of Staff of the Army, Chief of Staff of the Navy, and Chief of Staff of the Air Force, respectively, because we are not in agreement with decisions that have been taken recently.[19]

Much to the amazement of the four officers, Balaguer accepted the resignations without any objection. They then took one more step in ratcheting up the crisis—early on May 10th, they called a press conference in the secretariat and, at 11:30 A.M., they released their resignation letter to the media[20]; by this action, they officially informed the entire nation that the high command was attempting to pressure the commander in chief into rescinding a direct order that the leaders of the Armed Forces opposed.

The controversy had reached a remarkable point in Balaguer's relationship with his general officers. Since 1966, Pérez y Pérez had been the President's quiet bulwark against the extremes in the officer corps: Threats to Balaguer from right-wing, ex-CEFA Wessin y Wessin followers

or from left-wing, Constitutionalist Caamaño supporters had been eliminated by Pérez y Pérez. He was a general upon whom Balaguer could
totally rely. Jiménez had been an articulate Balaguer spokesman with
foreign officials and in the cabinet and, since the Caamaño affair, he had
delivered exhortations to the officer corps to remain loyal to the President.[21] The only signer of the resignation letter that, in the past, Balaguer had had reason to doubt was the ex-*Wessinista* Lluberes Montás,
but, in every crisis, he had proven faithful to the President. The popular paratrooper had become a staunch Balaguer man. And, lastly,
Logroño Contín, the steady ex-sailor turned naval officer,[22] was a politically uncomplicated member of the Jiménez clique who, independently,
would never oppose his superiors. Interestingly, Nivar, despite his numerous humiliations at the hands of the President, could never bring himself to stand up publicly to Balaguer as Pérez y Pérez and his allies had
done on the 9th and 10th of May.

Up until the morning of May 10th, Balaguer had maintained his
normal work schedule and had remained silent concerning the opposition expressed by his leading flag officers.[23] Before the press conference
in the Armed Forces secretariat terminated, however, he sprang into
action. For the next three days, the diminutive commander in chief dominated politico-military affairs in a manner far beyond the capacity of any
of his generals or their naval counterparts.

The President first promulgated four executive orders. Decree 850
designated a pilot, Colonel Renato Malagón Montesano, to be the new
chief of staff of the Air Force; number 851 appointed Commodore Rivera
Caminero to his old post as head of the Navy; and Decree 852 brought
back Colonel Mario Imbert McGregor from retirement to fill the position of Air Force sub-chief of staff.[24] The last decree, number 852, was
the most striking—Balaguer named himself the secretary of state of the
armed forces.[25] Then the President, with an augmented military escort
in combat gear, drove to the air base at San Isidro where he personally
read the decree appointing the newly promoted General Malagón to
command the Air Force. From the air base, the presidential entourage
moved to naval headquarters located at the *27 de Febrero* Navy Base at the
mouth of the Ozama River. In the midst of his retainers as well as naval
officers, Balaguer swore in Commodore Rivera Caminero as chief of staff
of the Navy.[26] The only part of Balaguer's work that remained was to
replace General Pérez y Pérez.

During May 10th, a rumor began to circulate that Pérez y Pérez had
seized control of the 1st Brigade and had deployed it immediately outside the capital.[27] This story had no foundation, but it gained a certain
amount of credence because the brigade's commander, General Jorge
Moreno, was not with his unit but was with the President at the naval

base, and Pérez y Pérez could not be found for comment. Although there was no real threat to the government, highly visible security measures were taken throughout the Santo Domingo area. First, all troops on May 10th were placed on alert in their barracks (*acuartelado*). Second, the Presidential Guard was directed to defend the palace grounds. And, third, the President ordered Nivar's Department of Special Operations, armed with automatic weapons and dressed in camouflage uniforms, to surround the National Palace building.[28] It was in this atmosphere that the President began the second phase of his plan to defuse the military crisis.

A steady stream of officers of various ranks began to arrive at the National Palace during the afternoon of May 10th. Shortly after 8:00 P.M., Balaguer returned to his office and received these visitors for approximately four hours. The press was made available to record the names of the callers. Among the first identified by reporters were General Guzmán Acosta, the ousted police chief, and General Nivar, accompanied by an exceptionally large and well-armed escort. They were followed by Generals Jorge Moreno of the 1st Brigade; Valdez Hilario, the then ambassador to Haiti; Beauchamps Javier, the former San José de Ocoa task force commander; Alvarez Sánchez, the sub-secretary of state of the armed forces for army; and Marte Pichardo, the President's security coordinator.[29] These orchestrated visits were valuable to Balaguer for two reasons. They provided the public with images of military leaders pledging loyalty to the President, and they were linked with the preparation of two documents, which were completed on May 11th and issued as official communiqués from the Armed Forces and from the National Police.

The military establishment's proclamation consisted of only one paragraph of text. It stated that the Armed Forces "support the measures adopted and those that might be adopted in the future by our commander in chief ... Dr. Joaquín Balaguer...."[30] It was signed by 22 generals and commodores and 37 field grade officers and their naval equivalents. The new chiefs of staff of the Air Force and Navy, General Malagón and Commodore Rivera Caminero, respectively, had signed, but General Pérez y Pérez's name was absent. The Army's three brigade commanders, the heads of the combat support and logistics commands, and twenty battalion commanders had signed. Also committed were the chiefs of the Air Force's five major commands, and the commanders of the Navy's three naval bases and three geographic zones.[31] The presence of some of the signatures was predictable, such as those of Alvarez Sánchez, Checo, Marmolejos, Lachapelle Suero, and Jáquez Olivero. They were all long-time *Nivaristas*. But what was noteworthy was the number of Pérez y Pérez followers who had also affixed their signatures to the document. Among them were General Cuervo Gómez and Colonels Cruz Brea, García Tejada, Guzmán Liriano, and López Pérez. Even Commodore Amiama Castillo, who had been with the Admiral at the May 10th press conference and had carried the resignation letter from Jiménez to the President the night before, had signed his name.[32]

The National Police communiqué was equally terse. In one sentence, the police leaders committed themselves to the "unconditional and invariable" support for the President's past, present, and future actions. General Nivar was the first on the list. He was followed by the signatures of a police general (Bisonó Jackson was chief of the Corps of Military Aides) and 26 field grade officers. The commanders of the three key police organizations—the Duarte Department, the Special Operations Department, and the Secret Department were included.[33]

It is highly doubtful that Pérez y Pérez would have used force at any time before May 11th to resist the appointment of Nivar to the National Police. Even more improbable would have been Pérez y Pérez's use of troops after that date, when the public read the communiqués. To have done so, Pérez y Pérez would have had to convince his faction, and its allies, to confront Balaguer personally. As Nivar had realized on October 14th, 1971, it was one thing to have a showdown with a military opponent, but it was quite another to threaten physically a Balaguer-led coalition of factions.

On May 12th, the third phase of the President's artful plan was implemented. That morning, without prior warning, he issued Decrees 854 and 855—General Alvarez Sánchez was appointed head of the Army and General Beauchamps Javier was designated Balaguer's replacement as secretary of state of the armed forces. Early in the afternoon, Balaguer administered the oath of office in the National Palace, and then the vice president accompanied the two generals to the secretariat building where they were installed in their new posts.[34] Although there was a large group of officers from all the services present, members of the Triangle did not attend. The officer corps knew that they had not been assigned to new positions and that Jiménez and Logoño Contín had been reduced to their permanent ranks of commodore and *capitán de navío*, respectively. (Pérez y Pérez and Lluberes Montás retained their permanent ranks of major general and brigadier general.)

It appeared that Balaguer had completed the last phase of his plan; however, the President had one final act to play out. On June 2nd, he brought Pérez y Pérez and Jiménez back into the fold by appointing them to the cabinet. The portfolios of interior and police and of foreign affairs were given to the general and the commodore, respectively.[35] They were sworn in on the following day. After the ceremony, Jiménez was uncharacteristically closed mouthed, while Pérez y Pérez, who normally had little to say in public, was effusive with the press. He stated that the reasons for the May 9th resignations had "totally disappeared" and that the Armed Forces thought of the President as their "father." When asked by reporters what would be his principal goal as secretary of state of interior and police, Pérez y Pérez listed three objectives—the first was "to serve Dr. Balaguer with loyalty."[36] Thus ended the politico-military crisis of 1975.

In the months that followed, Balaguer tidied up loose ends caused by the bizarre events of May 8th through May 12th. Jiménéz's rank of rear admiral was restored and Lluberes Montás was designated the director of the financially lucrative autonomous agency that ran the state-owned flour mills. The post of sub-secretary of state of the armed forces for army, left vacant by Alvarez Sánchez's advancement, was filled by General Matos González. (Since the beginning of 1975, the highly professional ground force officer had been serving in the Army rather than in the FAD.) The odd man out was the least political of the four who had resigned. Logoño Contín never regained his flag rank. He retired as a *capitán de navío* and died soon after.[37]

The distribution of power after the May 1975 affair clearly favored Nivar. He lost no time in reshaping the National Police by replacing opponents with officers from his faction. The first to be relieved of command was Colonel Luis Arzeno Regalado, Pérez y Pérez's former police intelligence chief. Others were to follow.[38] As key allies, Nivar could rely on General Alvarez Sánchez, head of the Army; General Jorge Moreno, commander of the 1st Brigade; General Marmolejos, commander of *Fortaleza Ozama*; and Colonel Lachapelle Suero, a powerful battalion commander at the *16 de Agosto* Military Camp. In contrast, the Triangle had been broken up. Pérez y Pérez had lost considerable leverage because he commanded no troops as interior and police secretary, and few of his followers continued in important posts. The President, however, did not give Nivar total dominancy. In the Army, Balaguer retained General Cuervo Gómez as commander of the nation's armor and artillery and he would not allow a change in the command of the Presidential Guard. After May 1975, however, there was a modification in the Air Force's role in the President's balance-of-power scheme. General Lluberes Montás had been removed from the equation, and, even though his Spanish airborne school classmates were still on active duty, their influence was greatly diminished. The absence of a paratrooper in a position of authority was further aggravated with General Matos González's transfer to the Army. For the first time since 1967, the Air Force was led only by pilots, a fact that reduced the significance of the FAD ground forces.

What was unusual in the changes of May 1975 was Balaguer's reintroduction of personalities who were linked with neither faction. The

President had allowed Rivera Caminero to return to the country two years after the civil war, but he was not assigned to an important post because, according to some observers, Balaguer did not trust the former Armed Forces secretary.[39] If the President had any doubts concerning the commodore, they were pushed aside on February 5, 1973, when Balaguer selected the naval officer to head the Corps of Military Aides. In that position, Rivera Caminero would be a useful check inside the President's military household on the new secretary of state of the presidency, General Nivar. Balaguer proved correct because Nivar's attempts to co-opt the Presidential Guard and the President's aides-de-camp/bodyguards in the National Palace were blocked by Rivera Caminero. Balaguer's motivation in May 1975 was less subtle. When the commodore took over the Navy, which he had commanded twice before, his first order of business was to dismantle Jiménez's well-established clique and replace it with Rivera Caminero men who had been out of favor for many years.

Even more dramatic than the return of Rivera Caminero to the Navy was the reintegration of Colonel Mario Imbert McGregor into the Air Force. The pilot had been involuntarily retired in the wake of the Wessin y Wessin coup plot of 1971 while his superior, Lluberes Montás, was retained on active status. The events of May 1975 gave Balaguer the opportunity to rehabilitate Imbert McGregor, and thus impress upon the members of the officer corps that their careers were in his hands. As with Trujillo before him, Balaguer, and only Balaguer, could determine each officer's future.

The End of the Nivar-Pérez y Pérez Rivalry

There was no ultimate victor in the Nivar-Pérez y Pérez struggle. The rivalry merely faded away as a result of Balaguer's failure to win the presidential elections of 1978. Even though all the factions of the active duty military establishment supported the President's reelection, the May 16th vote went decidedly against Balaguer. Generals Nivar and Beauchamps Javier, as police chief and Armed Forces secretary, respectively, stopped the ballot-counting process with only 25 percent of the votes tabulated, but foreign and domestic pressure forced them to resume the count.[40] Balaguer showed little enthusiasm for defying a large sector of Dominicans, as well as the government of the United States, by falsifying the outcome of the elections.[41] Nivar talked of launching a coup d'état; however, Pérez y Pérez (who had been commanding the 1st Brigade since November 4, 1977) refused to take any type of action without Balaguer's approval.[42] The President declined to grant any such authorization; therefore, the results of the election stood.

For the remaining three months of Balaguer's term, the Nivar-Pérez y Pérez competition would not play a significant role in Dominican politico-military affairs. Instead, officers were more focused on what the future would hold for them under the PRD government of President-elect Antonio Guzmán. Guzmán made every attempt to appease the members of the officer corps, such as promising them that there would be no dismissals and no involuntary retirements, and that officers who were no longer on active duty (read Constitutionalists) would not be given commands. The *Balagueristas*, in turn, went out of their way to give the impression that they were a unified force. The most blatant demonstration of solidarity was at a May 20th press conference when Nivar and Pérez y Pérez, for public consumption, embraced each other as old friends.[43]

Projecting an image of strength was not sufficient to suppress officer corps anxieties, however. During Balaguer's last weeks in the presidency, he made a series of organizational adjustments, legislative changes, and personnel appointments for the purpose of providing officers with a sense of security that they believed they would require under a PRD government. Undoubtedly, Balaguer knew that the new president would be able to circumvent these eleventh hour initiatives (especially if Guzmán was backed by the U.S. Embassy); however, Balaguer agreed to engage in some last minute mischief. Two possible reasons were that, first, Balaguer was bitter in the way the PRD conducted itself during the elections,[44] and, second, he was willing to make a parting token gesture, no matter how futile, to please his followers in uniform. Among Balaguer's final actions was the change of subordination of the Department of National Investigations (DNI) from the presidency to the secretariat of the Armed Forces. This new arrangement prevented the PRD from gaining access to the files of the country's primary security service. Another Balaguer reorganization was the transfer of General Marte Pichardo's meals-for-the-needy program from the office of the presidency to the Armed Forces; this would deny the PRD a valuable political tool as well as a source of graft. In addition, the outgoing president directed that junior officers and enlisted men receive an immediate raise in pay.[45]

Balaguer submitted to the legislature a new organic law of the Armed Forces; its most controversial article stipulated that an officer could not be transferred from a military post by civilian authorities until he completed two years in that position. This proposed regulation, in effect, guaranteed that any officer appointed before Guzmán became president on August 16th would be frozen in his position until mid–1980.[46] On the 20th of July, 1978, Balaguer revealed his legacy to the president-elect: Pérez y Pérez was appointed chief of staff of the Army, Nivar was designated commander of the 1st Brigade, Lluberes Montás was assigned chief of staff of the Air Force, and Jorge Moreno was selected to fill a new post, "coordinator of the Armed Forces" (which was changed on August 1st to "chief of staff of the Armed Forces"). Other veteran *Balagueristas* were not forgotten. Promotions were handed out to the politically faithful less than a month before Guzmán took office. The most prominent were Alvarez Sánchez, Checo, Jáquez Olivero, and Marmolejos, who were all promoted to permanent major general.[47]

Despite Balaguer's efforts, President Guzmán, on his inauguration day, launched a purge of the *Balagueristas*. The new president took advantage of the perceived backing of the large, distinguished U.S. delegation, which was in Santo Domingo for the inaugural ceremonies, to issue decrees that ignored the laws and regulations put together by Balaguer. Guzmán made sweeping personnel changes on his first day as president. Nivar was removed from the 1st Brigade and appointed the Dominican delegate to the Inter-American Defense Board in Washington, D.C. Lluberes Montás was relieved as chief of staff of the Air Force by a seasoned pilot. And Amiama Castillo, who, for many years had been kept away from a command by Balaguer, was promoted and designated head of the Navy.[48] The changes in national leaders were followed by the forced retirement of numerous older officers whose principal value was loyalty to Balaguer. Among the first to be sent home were Major Generals Marte Pichardo, Jáquez Olivero, Estrella Sahdalá, and Pilarte.[49] Moreover, the new president did not stop after he promulgated the initial August 16th decrees. Many field commanders were dismissed and continuous retirement orders were issued removing such Balaguer activists as Major Generals Checo and Marmolejos and Brigadier General Pimentel Boves.[50]

One anomaly in the 16th of August decrees was the retention of Pérez y Pérez as head of the Army. There was some speculation that the new president had not removed the chief of staff because Pérez y Pérez had refused to join the coup d'état that had been forming during the electoral period.[51] Nevertheless, in an unexpected move on September 30th, President Guzmán sacked Pérez y Pérez in an apparent attempt to further root out Balaguer supporters in the government. The ex-Army chief of staff was offered, as compensation, the ambassadorship in Madrid.[52] The General appeared ready to accept the posting, but the assignment fell through, allegedly because the government of Spain refused *agrement*. Guzmán then proposed that Pérez y Pérez go to London as military attaché.[53] On November 10th, the President and the General met for fifteen minutes. A furious Pérez y Pérez refused the post in Great Britain and complained that he was being treated shabbily.[54] (It could not have been lost on Pérez y Pérez that he was being assigned to the same exile position as Caamaño in 1966.) Pérez y Pérez angrily repeated a statement that he had made on other occasions—he "would leave his country only as a corpse."[55] The next day, Pérez y Pérez was retired. On January 9, 1979, Pérez y Pérez's ally, Lluberes Montás, was offered the same London posting. When he refused, he also was retired.[56] The Balaguer balance-of-power doctrine had ended and the Nivar-Pérez y Pérez politico-military rivalry had disappeared.

XVII

A Final View

The political passing of Balaguer in 1978 ended the Nivar and Pérez y Pérez groups, but it did not alter the officer corps' compulsion to organize into cliques. As early as the May 1978 election period, new factions were forming (e.g., the "19th of May Group"),[1] and new leaders were being identified (e.g., Colonel Ramón Rodríguez Landestoy).[2] The changing dynamic in the officer corps did not indicate that there were no longer members of the post-Trujillo era clans in the Armed Forces, however. In 1978, most of the senior and mid-level officers on active duty had been associated with at least one of the various cliques during the previous fifteen years. Of interest is how they fared after the departure of President Balaguer.

THE OFFICER CORPS FACTIONS: EPILOGUE

The San Cristóbal Group of the early 1960s developed into the powerful Nivar faction of the next decade. Although Nivar's group seemed indestructible, by mid–1978 it was in complete disarray. The main reason was that its leader was in exile. Nivar's appointment as the Dominican delegate to the Inter-American Defense Board took effect on August 24th. After his arrival in Washington, he also became the vice chairman of the body.[3] By agreement under the Board's charter, the vice chairman's position rotated alphabetically, by country. When it was the Dominican Republic's turn, its senior delegate, with governmental approval, could be designated vice chairman. If Santo Domingo declined, the post would pass to the next country, in alphabetical order, until a nation accepted the posting. The United States was exempt because Washington always provided the chairman.

Because the vice chairman's responsibilities were mainly ceremonial, the only prerequisite for the post was that he be at least the equivalent of a major general. (In contrast, to be the director of the Inter-American Defense Board's International Staff did require experience in general staff management and in strategic planning.[4] In both those functions, Nivar would have been unable to fulfill his duties, unless, as was his practice, he found a qualified surrogate to do the actual work.) Nivar's tour in Washington was uneventful (although he did manage to fall down a flight of stairs and break some bones), while President Guzmán, in the Dominican Republic, continued to lash out against the exiled general. In March 1979, Nivar's brother, Pericles Nivar Seijas, and Nivar's son, Neit Nivar Báez, were forcibly retired from the officer corps.[5] On February 27th of the following year, the President completed the job by retiring Nivar while he was still assigned to the Board. Decree 1569 stated that Nivar's separation was due to length of service; consequently, he was awarded a pension.[6]

Shortly after his return to Santo Domingo, Nivar founded the right-wing *Partido Acción Nacional* (PAN). The General's plan was to run for the presidency in 1982; however, he left open the possibility that he would join a coalition with Balaguer if the ex-president chose to enter the race. While on campaign, Nivar, on February 7, 1982, suffered a heart attack and died on the way to the hospital. He was only 57 years old.[7] In December 1984, Colonel "Nivarito" Nivar Pellerano was asked what had become of the various members of his uncle's retinue. Colonel Nivar (who was then the J-2) replied that they had all abandoned the General before his death—he had "died alone."[8]

In the mid–1960s, many of the senior members of the San Cristóbal Group retired before they could become part of the Nivar faction. Those who did continue on active duty beyond 1966, and others who joined the 1st Brigade commander's coterie after the San Cristóbal Group name was no longer used, for the most part had successful careers. As indicated above, many became general officers, such as Alvarez Sánchez, Checo, Jáquez Olivero, Marmolejos, Jorge Moreno, Lachapelle Suero, Grullón Hierro, Bisonó Jackson, Medina Sánchez, García y García, Reyes Evora, and Martínez Fernández. And almost all ended up financially well off, if not rich. These advantages were offset by the fact that after Balaguer lost the elections, they were systematically retired from the Armed Forces and National Police. After the purge, only one dedicated *Nivarista*, Lachapelle Suero, was allowed to reach national-level command.

Contrary to the Nivar experience, the retirement of Pérez y Pérez did not totally bring down his senior followers. Major military commanders who had been part of the Pérez y Pérez group, such as Generals Cuervo Gómez, Matos González, Cruz Brea, and García Tejada, remained on active service and rose in importance within the Armed Forces. Less prominent individuals who were close to the General were not as fortunate, however. One officer who was retired in the wake of Pérez y Pérez's departure was his old friend from their days in the *Generalísimo Trujillo*

Regiment, Brigadier General López Pérez. Also, Colonel Guzmán Liriano, of *La Banda* fame, and the notorious Colonel "Polanquito" Polanco González were given pensions when Pérez y Pérez was retired.[9] (Curiously, the controversial ex-chief of Pérez y Pérez's counterterror squad, Joaquín Pou Castro, was allowed to stay on until he retired as a brigadier general. In later years, he was accused of being implicated in the 1975 Luis Orlando Martínez Howley assassination case.[10])

Initially, Pérez y Pérez's life in retirement was very much the opposite from that of Nivar. Instead of seeking political power, Pérez y Pérez devoted his efforts to improving his cattle business and his agricultural lands. After Balaguer regained the presidency in 1986, he had occasion to call on Pérez y Pérez to assist him in government.[11] In May 1996, one such event proved an embarrassment for the President. Three days before the May 16th presidential elections, Pérez y Pérez was brought out of retirement to lead the National Police. Balaguer realized that the appointment was a political mistake when his opponents created a furor over Pérez y Pérez's harsh methods. The President, therefore, replaced the General after only 27 days in office.[12] On October 29th of the same year, Balaguer's successor retired Pérez y Pérez once again.[13] Less than a month later, accusations were made that Balaguer and eight of his officers were responsible for the murder of Martínez Howley. Pérez y Pérez's name was included in the accusation; however, Pérez y Pérez was not arrested nor indicted, as were some of the other *Balaguerista* officers.[14] The notoriety of the case may have been one reason that Pérez y Pérez took up residency in southern Florida.

As stated earlier, the San Isidro Group was an oversimplified term used mostly in the 1965 civil war to describe Dominican military aviation, the Air Force infantry, and the CEFA, which were all located at installations in San Isidro. At the time of the 1978 elections, the foremost representative of the FAD's ground forces continued to be Pérez y Pérez's ally, General Lluberes Montás. He, however, never regained that stature after his January 18, 1979, forced retirement, and he was unable to pass on his mantle of leadership to any member of his clique. After Lluberes Montás' removal, a pilot, not a paratrooper, would always dominate San Isidro.

The pilots at San Isidro entered the post-Balaguer era with mixed feelings. On February 27, 1980, one of their own, Mario Imbert McGregor, was designated the secretary of state of the armed forces; he was the first pilot to wear three stars since Ramfis.[15] Also, many older air generals were retired (e.g., de los Santos Céspedes, Folch Pérez, and Malagón Montesano[16]); this made room for the younger aviators to move up. The new administration spoke often of improving the technical ability of the officer corps; however, the fliers did not have access to modern, technically advanced airplanes. Eventually, the much-prized P-51s were sold off to private buyers such as air museums. Pilots were relegated to flying aging transports and helicopters.[17]

Of all the factions of the 1960s, the evolution of the CEFA officers was the most interesting. They could be placed in two broad categories: Those who remained loyal to Wessin y Wessin after Balaguer became president in 1966, and those who transferred their allegiance from Wessin to Balaguer at that time. Many of the first grouping suffered imprisonment, and later were subjected to harassment and surveillance. Wessin himself was not allowed to return from exile to the Dominican Republic until May 28, 1978. His following in the military establishment had vanished, and his political party, the PQD, had failed miserably in the May 16th elections.[18]

Three of the senior *Wessinistas* who turned their backs on Wessin and joined Balaguer made a wise career choice. Wessin's successor in the CEFA, the incompetent Elio Osiris Perdomo Rosario, continued on active duty despite his numerous major failures. When he died of a heart attack in November 1976, he was commanding the 3rd Brigade.[19] Juan René Beauchamps Javier also gained considerably by throwing in his lot with Balaguer. Two years after his success in confronting the Caamaño expedition, the President appointed him secretary of state of the armed forces. On December 30, 1977, he was promoted to lieutenant general, a rank not used since the Trujillo era. When Balaguer lost the 1978 elections, Beauchamps, expectedly, was replaced in the cabinet, but, unlike Pérez y Pérez, he was quite willing to go abroad. He was offered the ambassadorship to Argentina.[20] The third ex-*Wessinista* who thrived under Balaguer was the above-mentioned Lluberes Montás. (He was in the CEFA before the airborne was transferred to the FAD in 1963.) His extraordinary advancement on September 6, 1967, from lieutenant colonel to chief of staff of the Air Force, with the rank of brigadier general, would not have occurred if he had not openly shifted his loyalty from Wessin to Balaguer.

Of special interest is the development of the CEFA officers who started together as faculty members at the Military Academy before the end of the Trujillo regime and eventually served Wessin, before pledging their loyalty to Balaguer. By the end of the 1960s, Manuel Antonio Cuervo Gómez, Pedro Medrano Ubiera, Ramiro Matos González, Téofilo Ramón Romero Pumarol, Héctor Valenzuela Alcantara, and Jesús Manuel Porfirio Mota Henríquez had been identified as the nucleus of a future professional Armed Forces.[21] Even though they faced difficulties in an officer corps that was suspicious of members who had received foreign advanced training, they ultimately were successful. All became general officers. (Medrano had no real opportunity to function as a brigadier general, however; he died at the age of 50.[22]) Two were able to hold the three most important posts in the Armed Forces. At different times, Generals Matos González and Cuervo Gómez were appointed commander of the 1st Brigade, chief of staff of the Army, and, finally, as lieutenant generals, secretary of state of the armed forces.[23] It is significant that two of the most talented men in the officer corps received their most important postings during PRD administrations rather than in the Balaguer years.

The PRD's ascendancy to power contained surprises for the naval officers' faction. Rivera Caminero fully expected to be retained on active duty because he had opposed the coup plotting that had preceded the August 16, 1978, inauguration. The new president, however, not only removed him as head of the Navy—he also retired him involuntarily on January 9, 1979. (Rivera Caminero died in November. It was remarked that Guzmán never forgave him for ordering the bombardment of the capital on April 27, 1965.)[24] The appointment of Amiama Castillo as Navy chief was also unexpected because he was known to be unsympathetic toward the PRD. After waiting in the wings as a flag officer for eight years almost to the day, he was given his own command. For the Navy, this meant that the Jiménez/Amiama Castillo clique displaced the Rivera Caminero clique.

What the officer corps, as well as knowledgeable Dominicans, was most unprepared for was the retention of Admiral Jiménez as foreign minister in a PRD cabinet. Guzmán's decision not to dismiss the naval officer proved beneficial for the country's international image. Jiménez played an important role in the 1978 OAS foreign ministers conference and worked untiredly as the head of the OAS committee charged with ending the Nicaraguan conflict. The government of Colombia nominated the well-known Admiral to be the next secretary general of the OAS. In the balloting, he came in second, losing to the incumbent. After four and one half productive years in the foreign ministry, Jiménez, in January 1980, resigned and entered retirement.[25] He was the prime example of how senior naval officers in the Dominican Republic could contribute significantly as individuals, even though their branch of the Armed Forces had little impact on politico-military affairs.

The return of Constitutionalist officers to Dominican soil was a fascinating process to observe. As stated earlier, it was Balaguer who authorized the first two Constitutionalists to come home—they were *Capitán de Fragata* Montes Arache and Captain Lachapelle Díaz. The two officers were reintegrated into the Armed Forces, and the President exploited, for propaganda purposes, Montes Arache's presence in Santo Domingo during the Caamaño campaign. As we have seen, former Colonel Caamaño and his cousin, ex-First Lieutenant Caamaño Grullón, chose to reappear in the Dominican Republic as guerrilla fighters in 1973. The slow-to-learn Caamaño Grullón tried a second time; on June 6, 1975, he and two others were clandestinely put ashore along the southern coast. This guerrilla farce ended with Caamaño Grullón's arrest, trial, and imprisonment. Balaguer released him in August 1977.[26]

Under PRD presidents, many Constitutionalists returned and were given government posts; however, attempts were made not to alarm the officer corps by the nature of the Constitutionalists' assignments. The first to arrive was Major Manuel Núñez Nogueras. He was promoted to lieutenant colonel and assigned to President Guzmán's Corps of Military Aides.[27] Montes Arache was made sub-chief of staff of the Navy and eventually reached the rank of rear admiral. Lachapelle Díaz, under PRD administrations, served as the Army's public relations officer and its logistics staff officer (G-4). On August 17, 1984, he was promoted to brigadier general by President Salvador Jorge Blanco and assigned to the Military Academy, where he had been stationed in 1963 before he was cashiered for coup plotting. In 1985, he was the director of that institution of learning.[28] Colonel Emilio Ludovino Fernández was dropped from the Armed Forces while serving as the military attaché in Rome, but he continued on in the Dominican Embassy as a civilian. When Admiral Jiménez resigned as foreign minister in January 1980, Fernández was appointed to succeed him. He subsequently was designated secretary of state of industry and commerce. Fernández left government in 1982 and assumed a party leadership position in the PRD.[29] Other Constitutionalist officers were allowed to fill governmental positions. For example, Colonel Rafael Yeges Arismendy was director general of price controls, former Lieutenant Colonel Servando Boumpensierre Morel was director general of passports, ex-Lieutenant Colonel Jorge Marte Hernández was an official in the state-owned water works, Colonel Jorge Percival Peña was a pilot for the national airline, and ex-Captain Mario Peña Taveras was ambassador to Guatemala. In contrast, key leaders of the rebellion, such as Lieutenant Colonels Miguel Angel Hernándo Ramírez and Pedro Alvarez Holguín, ended their foreign exile, but declined to participate in the public sector.[30]

The Constitutionalist faction had returned to the Dominican Republic, but it is obvious that the PRD presidents consistently bowed to the majority of the officer corps by denying the Constitutionalists command of the Army, Air Force, and Navy or of key troop units. And with Balaguer's victory at the polls in 1986, the window of opportunity once again was closed for the Constitutionalist faction.

BALAGUER AND THE OFFICER CORPS IN RETROSPECT

In the Trujillo era, the officer corps was an integral part of the regime. The Generalissimo used it to perpetuate the dictatorship, principally as his instrument of repression. It had no independent voice, and it was easily controlled, to the point that the officers accepted the leadership of Trujillo and his family without question. Nothing changed when Balaguer became Trujillo's figurehead president in 1960. The "compliant intellectual,"[31] as he was described, steered clear of any substantive involvement with the officer corps in deference to the Trujillos.

After the fall of the Trujillo family in 1961, the Dominican Republic went through a period of chaos; the Armed Forces attempted to fill the political vacuum, but they failed principally due to factionalism and greed. The turmoil reached its zenith during the 1965 civil war—a struggle that could only be brought to a halt by the intervention of U.S. troops. Foreign occupation of Santo Domingo allowed elections to be held on June 1, 1966. Balaguer won—what remained to be seen was how he would control his disruptive and self-indulgent officer corps.

The initial image of the President and his military commanders was not an optimistic one. In public appearances, Balaguer's diminutive stature, head cocked to the side, and hands clasped in front of him starkly contrasted with the tall officers in full uniform who flanked him and appeared to overwhelm the new commander in chief. Nothing could be further from reality, however. The Balaguer technique gave the President total control over the members of the officer corps. He was their puppetmaster, and they never failed to respond. Balaguer played individuals and factions against each other, he deployed units around the politico-military center of gravity—Santo Domingo—in such a manner that a balance of power was maintained, he prevented professional officers from establishing an elite clique, he bought loyalty through corruption, and he retained a quiet linkage to the defunct Trujillo regime.[32]

The result was that Balaguer was able to bring about what only the U.S. Marine occupation and Trujillo had been able to accomplish. From 1966 to 1978, Balaguer dominated the officer corps to such an extent that the military could not impose its will on the President, and he was able to limit the officer corps to activities within the parameters he had laid out.

Balaguer's overt relationship with his officers diminished their stature in the eyes of the public. The President adopted the practice of moving senior officers to new assignments (or to no assignment) without warning; of appointing flag officers to posts which, to observers, seemed to be a demotion; and of attending official functions with generals' and commodores' performing what appeared to be the duties of orderlies. It was often asked why these degradations did not cause officers to resign in protest. The probable reason was that Trujillo had utilized the same methods and, since the Balaguer regime's benefits compensated for the humiliations, the senior officers willingly fell in line.

By 1971, the officer corps, as well as the nation, was stabilized. The President had little to fear from within the institution, although threats from outside the active duty officer corps still lingered on. In mid-year, the Wessin y Wessin faction was crushed by a counter-coup, thereby, for practical purposes, eliminating any danger from ultra right-wing officers. The leftist challenge from Constitutionalist officers was also neutralized after the Caamaño expedition was defeated in 1973. Consequently, the President had no viable external opponents from the right or from the left and, internally, the officer corps was controlled through guile. In the later case, the Balaguer technique was best exemplified by his manipulation of the Nivar-Pérez y Pérez rivalry.

An interesting question concerns the nature of Balaguer's true opinion of Nivar and Pérez y Pérez. In the ex-president's memoirs, published in 1989, Balaguer made no mention of Pérez y Pérez and only cited Nivar's name once in a cursory manner concerning military opposition to the results of the 1978 presidential elections.[33] In a year-by-year obituary section at the end of the autobiography, Balaguer recorded General Marte Pichardo's 1984 death and identified the old veteran as an "*aviador y militar.*"[34] Nivar had died on February 7, 1982, but his name was conspicuously absent from the numerous 1982 obituary listings in the book.[35]

Balaguer never compared Nivar and Pérez y Pérez in public statements, and he rarely evaluated them for the record in private conversations. One example of the latter can be found in a Department of State document, dated May 4, 1967. On April 27, 1967, Balaguer spoke of the two officers to U.S. Ambassador John Crimmins. The President's comments to the American envoy provide a rare opportunity to note Balaguer's views of the two officers early in his presidency. On May 4th, the U.S. Embassy dispatched a message to Washington containing the information obtained during the April 27th discussion.[36]

According to the cable, Balaguer stated that Nivar was "an able career officer who is loyal." This phrase was followed in the message by quoting the President's exact words: "*I think* he will carry out my instructions." (The italics are the author's.) Balaguer then claimed that he owed a debt to Nivar for Nivar's prior loyalty and service. The President conceded that "Nivar is [a] focus of anti-Trujillista sentiment" and that Nivar "is interested in building up his position, but he does not have decisive influence either with [Balaguer] or in [the] military." Balaguer added that Nivar had been removed from the National Palace to stop accusations that Nivar was attempting to exploit his earlier closeness to the President. Ambassador Crimmins then provided his own assessment:

> [The President] throughout this portion conversation gave clear impression he fully aware Nivar's ambitions and controversy surrounding him, and that he has clear idea of how far he prepared permit Nivar to go.[37]

In the next paragraph of the telegram, Ambassador Crimmins provided Balaguer's thoughts on Pérez y Pérez; they were more complimentary than the remarks Balaguer had just made in the meeting concerning Nivar. The embassy message reported that the President said that Pérez y Pérez

> is loyal and responsive to him and noting that, among other things, Pérez' legal training has endowed him with broader outlook than that of most military officers, of whom Pérez appears [to] be one of the best.... Pérez is unpopular in military, perhaps partly because of professionalism of his approach ('he is severe').... [His] supervision has considerably reduced contraband and profiteering potential previously available to and abused by opportunistic officers.[38]

There are ample indications that Balaguer maintained essentially the same opinion of the two generals throughout his public life.

Undoubtedly, Balaguer cared little for the officer corps as an institution, but he realized that no one could govern a post-Trujillo Dominican Republic without including the military, with all its faults, in the political fabric of the state. As the little doctor had said many times, "We do not live in Switzerland." Thus, he needed instruments like Nivar and Pérez y Pérez as principal actors in his balance-of-power scheme. Even though Nivar was a devious conspirator and Pérez y Pérez was a ruthless enforcer, Nivar also was an indefatigable and effective political manager working in support of his president, and Pérez y Pérez was an accomplished military leader, loyal to his commander in chief. Nivar and Pérez y Pérez were important individually for Balaguer, and they were indispensable corporately to him as Armed Forces intramural antagonists.

Chapter Notes

CHAPTER I

1. Bruce J. Calder, *The Impact of Intervention: The Dominican Republic during the U.S. Occupation of 1916–1924* (Austin: University of Texas Press, 1984), 54–55, 61 (hereafter cited as Calder, *U.S. Occupation*); Captain Stephen M. Fuller, USMCR, and Graham A. Cosmas, *Marines in the Dominican Republic, 1916–1924* (Washington, D.C.: History and Museums Division, Headquarters, U.S. Marine Corps, 1974), 45–49 (hereafter cited as Fuller, *Marines*); Howard J. Wiarda, *Dictatorship and Development: The Methods of Control in Trujillo's Dominican Republic* (Gainesville: University of Florida Press, 1968), 43 (hereafter cited as Wiarda, *Control*).

2. Marvin Goldvert, *The Constabulary in the Dominican Republic and Nicaragua: Progeny and Legacy of United States Intervention* (Gainesville: University of Florida Press, 1962), 13 (hereafter cited as Goldvert, *Constabulary*); Wiarda, *Control*, 28.

3. Sumner Welles, *Naboth's Vineyard: The Dominican Republic, 1844–1924* (Mamaroneck, New York: Paul P. Appel, Publishers, 1966), Vol. II, 810 (hereafter cited as Welles, *Naboth's Vineyard*).

4. Robert D. Crassweller, *Trujillo: The Life and Times of a Caribbean Dictator* (New York: The Macmillan Company, 1966), 29, 32, 36, 47 (hereafter cited as Crassweller, *Dictator*); Goldvert, *Constabulary*, 14–15; Teniente de Navío Ernesto Vega y Pagán, *Biografía del Generalísmo Doctor Rafael Leonidas Trujillo Molina, Benefactor de la Patria y Padre de la Patria Nueva, Comandante en Jefe de las Fuerzas Armadas de la Nación* (Ciudad Trujillo: Editorial Atenas, 1956), 42.

5. Major Brian J. Bosch, Memorandum, Subject: *The Plight of Military Professionalism in the Dominican Republic* (Defense Attaché Office, Santo Domingo, Jan. 9, 1973), 2–3 (hereafter cited as Bosch, *Professionalism*).

6. Charles D. Ameringer, *The Caribbean Legion: Patriots, Politicians, Soldiers of Fortune,*

1946–1950 (University Park: The Pennsylvania State University Press, 1996), passim.

7. Dominican Republic, Secretaría de Estado de las Fuerzas Armadas Dominicanas, *Revista de las Fuerzas Armadas* (Jun. 1959), 18–19 (hereafter cited as *Revista*).

8. *Revista* (Jul. 1961), 12.

CHAPTER II

1. Troy S. Floyd, *The Columbus Dynasty in the Caribbean, 1492–1526* (Albuquerque: University of New Mexico Press, 1973), 18–20, 69, 77, 244-fn. 42.

2. Wiarda, *Control*, 47–50; Manuel Ortega, *The Political and Socio-Economic Role of the Military in Latin America*, Appendix F: *Dominican Republic* (Coral Gables, Florida: Division of Research, Center for Advanced International Studies, University of Miami, 1969), F-14-F-16 (hereafter cited as Ortega, *Military Role*)

3. Howard J. Wiarda, *The Dominican Republic: Nation in Transition* (New York: Frederick A. Praeger, 1969), 67–69.

4. *Revista* (Jan. 1954), 18–21.

5. Neill Macaulay, *The Prestes Column: Revolution in Brazil* (New York: New Viewpoints, 1974), 25–29, 235; Alfred Stepan, *The Military in Politics: Changing Patterns in Brazil* (Princeton, New Jersey: Princeton University Press, 1971), 82 (hereafter cited as Stepan, *Brazil*); Louis A. Pérez, Jr., *Army Politics in Cuba, 1898–1958* (Pittsburgh: University of Pittsburgh Press, 1976), 126, 145–150, 165; Colonel Ramón M. Barquín, *Las Luchas Guerrilleras en Cuba: De la Colonia a la Sierra Maestra* (Madrid: Editorial Playor, S.A., 1975), Vol.I, 167–170; Brian J. Bosch, *The Salvadoran Officer Corps and the Final Offensive of 1981* (Jefferson, North Carolina: McFarland & Company, Inc., Publishers, 1999), 8 (hereafter cited as Bosch, *Salvadoran Officer Corps*).

6. G. Pope Atkins and Larman C. Wil-

son, *The United States and the Trujillo Regime* (New Brunswick, New Jersey: Rutgers University Press, 1972), 92 (hereafter cited as Atkins and Wilson, *Trujillo Regime*).

7. Adrian J. English, *Armed Forces of Latin America: Their Histories, Development, Present Strength and Military Potential* (London: Jane's Publishing Company, Limited, 1984), 226 (hereafter cited as English, *Armed Forces*); Lt. Col. Robert J. Icks, *Tanks and Armored Vehicles* (New York: Duell, Sloan and Pearce, 1945), 239, 244, 254–255; *Jane's Armour and Artillery, 1979–1980*, edited by Christopher F. Foss (London: Jane's Publishing Company, Limited, 1979), 284 (hereafter cited as *Jane's Armour*); *Revista* (Jan.-Apr. 1958), 11, 35; *Revista* (May-Jun. 1958), 21; *Revista* (Apr. 1959), 6,9.

8. English, *Armed Forces*, 226–227; *Jane's Armour*, 12; *Revista* (Sep. 1959), 19; *Revista* (Oct. 1959), 9, 13; Armin Halle, *Tanks: An Illustrated History of Fighting Vehicles* (Greenwich, Connecticut: New York Graphic Society, 1971), 135.

9. Major Brian J. Bosch, *Order of Battle Summary, Foreign Ground Forces* (U.S. Embassy, Santo Domingo: U.S. Department of Defense Intelligence Information Report, DD Form 1396, Jul. 28, 1971), 16–17 (hereafter cited as Bosch, *Order of Battle*); *Jane's Armour*, 426; *Revista* (Apr. 1959), 5; *Revista* (Oct. 1959), 11.

10. Coronel Teófilo Ramón Romero Pumarol, "En las Fuerzas Armadas Dominicanas, Esto Fué lo Primero," *Revista* (Jun. 1972), 60; *Revista* (Jan. 1960), 45.

11. *Revista* (Jan.-Apr. 1958), 4, 78; *Revista* (Feb. 1959), 55; *Revista* (Apr. 1959), 29; *Revista* (Jun. 1959), 18.

12. U.S. Congress, Senate, Committee on the Judiciary, Subcommittee to Investigate the Administration of the Internal Security Act and Other Internal Security Laws, *Communist Threat to the U.S. Through the Caribbean: Testimony of Brigadier General Elias Wessin y Wessin*, 89th Congress, 1st Session, Oct. 1965 (Washington, D.C.: Government Printing Office, 1965), 109 (hereafter cited as *Testimony, Wessin y Wessin*); *Revista* (Jun. 1959), 21; *Revista* (Jan.-Jun. 1988), 8–9.

13. *Revista* (Jul.-Aug. 1963), 48; *Testimony, Wessin y Wessin*, 171, 190; interviews.

14. *Revista* (May-Jun. 1958), 13.

15. U.S. Department of the Army, U.S. Army School of the Americas, Letter, subject: *Freedom of Information Act Report-Command and Staff Graduates* (Dec. 9, 1998) (hereafter cited as USARSA Letter).

16. John Bartlow Martin, *Overtaken by Events: The Dominican Crisis from the Fall of Trujillo to the Civil War* (Garden City, New York: Doubleday and Company, Inc., 1966), 126–127, 254–255, 484–485 (hereafter cited as Martin, *Events*).

17. *Revista* (May-Jun. 1964), passim; T.D. Roberts, et al., *Area Handbook for the Dominican Republic* (Washington, D.C.: Foreign Area Studies, The American University, 1966), 394; *Listín Diario*, Feb. 27, 1964, 10 (hereafter cited as *Listín*); *Listín*, Jan. 28, 1965, 4; *Listín*, Feb. 18, 1965, 1.

18. Piero Gleijeses, *The Dominican Crisis: The 1965 Constitutionalist Revolt and American Intervention*, translated by Lawrence Lipson (Baltimore: The Johns Hopkins University Press, 1978), 128–129 (hereafter cited as Gleijeses, *Crisis*).

19. Gleijeses, *Crisis*, 248–250; Lawrence A. Yates, *Power Pack: U.S. Intervention in the Dominican Republic, 1965–1966* (Fort Leavenworth, Kansas: Combat Studies Institute, U.S. Army Command and General Staff College, 1988), 43 (hereafter cited as Yates, *Power Pack*); Willard L. Beaulac, et al., *Dominican Action-1965: Intervention or Cooperation?* (Washington, D.C.: The Center for Strategic Studies, Georgetown University, Jul. 1966), 27–30 (hereafter cited as Beaulac, *Action-1965*); interview.

20. *Testimony, Wessin y Wessin*, 249–250.

21. Theodore Draper, *The Dominican Revolt: A Case Study in American Policy* (New York: Commentary, 1968), 191–193 (hereafter cited as Draper, *Dominican Revolt*); *National Reconstruction Government Radio*, Sep. 4, 1965; *Dominican Armed Forces Radio*-San Isidro, Sep. 6, 1965; Gleijeses, *Crisis*, 410-fn. 106; *Testimony, Wessin y Wessin*, 168–181.

22. *The New York Times*, Sep. 3, 1966, 22 (hereafter cited as *NY Times*); *The Washington Post*, Sep. 7, 1966, A25 (hereafter cited as *Washington Post*); *Radio Continental*, Sep. 7, 1966.

23. U.S. Department of State, U.S. Embassy, Santo Domingo, airgram, Oct. 25, 1970, 6 (hereafter cited as U.S. Emb. airgram); Dominican Republic, Centro de Enseñanza de las Fuerzas Armadas (CEFA), *Libro Blanco de las Fuerzas Armadas y de la Policía Nacional de la República Dominicana* (Santo Domingo: Editora del Caribe, C. por A., 1964), 94–95.

24. U.S. Emb. airgram, Oct. 25, 1970, 6; Martin, *Events*, 542.

25. U.S. Department of State, U.S. Embassy, Santo Domingo, telegram, Jun. 1, 1964 (hereafter cited as U.S. Emb. telegram); Gleijeses, *Crisis*, 130; *Radio Comercial*, Sep. 2, 1964.

26. Interview.

27. *Revista* (May 1975), 54, 56; U.S. Emb. telegram, Jul. 27, 1964.

28. Gleijeses, *Crisis,* 131–132.

29. Gleijeses, *Crisis,* 248–249, 394-fn. 62; Beaulac, *Action-1965,* 11, 27.

30. Interview.

31. Beaulac, *Action-1965,* 14.

32. Gleijeses, *Crisis,* 195–197; José A. Moreno, *Barrios in Arms: Revolution in Santo Domingo* (Pittsburgh: University of Pittsburgh Press, 1970), 210–211 (hereafter cited as Moreno, *Barrios*).

33. Moreno, *Barrios,* 210–211.

34. Hamlet Hermann, *Francis Caamaño* (Santo Domingo: Editora Alfa y Omega, 1983), 28, 32–33, 38, 40, 71 (hereafter cited as Hermann, *Caamaño*); *Emisoras Nacionales,* Jan. 19, 1965; Abraham F. Lowenthal, *The Dominican Intervention* (Cambridge: Harvard University Press, 1972), 196-fn. 24 (hereafter cited as Lowenthal, *Intervention*); Martin, *Events,* 667.

35. Martin, *Events,* 667.

36. Lowenthal, *Intervention,* 205-fn. 31; Gleijeses, *Crisis,* 151.

37. Gleijeses, *Crisis,* 151.

38. Gleijeses, *Crisis.*, 164, 378-fn. 229, 379-fn. 241; Ramón Alberto Ferreras, *Guerra Patria* (n.p., 1966), 101 (hereafter cited as Ferreras, *Guerra*)

39. Interview.

40. USARSA Letter; *Revista* (Nov.-Dec.196 4), 16–17; Draper, *Dominican Revolt,* 44–48.

41. Gleijeses, *Crisis,* 246.

42. Gleijeses, *Crisis,* 246–248.

43. Gleijeses, *Crisis,* 103–104, 130, 190, 391-fn. 15.

44. Gleijeses, *Crisis,* 152; Abraham F. Lowenthal, "The Dominican Republic: The Politics of Chaos," in *Reform and Revolution: Readings in Latin American Politics,* edited by Arpad von Lazar and Robert R. Kaufman (Boston: Allyn and Bacon, Inc., 1969), 42; interview.

45. Gleijeses, *Crisis,* 146; Lowenthal, *Intervention,* 78; Martin, *Events,* 649; Ortega, *Military Role,* F36; Ferreras, *Guerra,* 100.

46. G. Pope Atkins, *Arms and Politics in the Dominican Republic* (Boulder, Colorado: Westview Press, 1981), 16–17 (hereafter cited as Atkins, *Arms and Politics*); Dominican Republic, "Act of Dominican Reconciliation," in *Testimony, Wessin y Wessin,* Appendix VI, 265–269; Dominican Republic, "Institutional Act," in *Testimony, Wessin y Wessin,* Appendix VI, 269–275; Santo Domingo Domestic Service, Sep. 28, 1965 (hereafter cited as SDDS); Gleijeses, *Crisis,* 279; General Bruce Palmer, *Intervention in the Caribbean: The Dominican Crisis of 1965* (Lexington: The University Press of Kentucky, 1989), 112 (hereafter cited as Palmer, *Crisis of 1965*).

47. SDDS, Jan. 6, 1966; *Washington Post,* Jan 23, 1966, A16; *Radio Continental,* Jul. 12, 1966; *Listín,* Apr. 1, 1966, 17.

48. Interview.

49. USARSA Letter.

50. Valentina Peguero, "Trujillo and the Military: Organization, Modernization and Control of the Dominican Armed Forces, 1916–1961," Ph.D. diss. Columbia University, 1993, 211 (hereafter cited as Peguero, "Trujillo and the Military"); *The Military Balance, 1973–1974* (London: International Institute for Strategic Studies, 1974), 62; English, *Armed Forces,* 231; Nelson Arciniegas, "Trayectoria de la Fuerza Aérea Dominicana," *Revista* (Jun. 1974), 51–73 (hereafter cited as Arciniegas, "Fuerza Aérea").

51. *Revista* (Aug. 1952), 32; *Revista* (Jun.-Jul. 1954), 76–77.

52. English, *Armed Forces,* 233.

53. *Revista* (Jun. 1974), 8; *Revista* (Aug. 1956), 60; interview.

54. Arciniegas, "Fuerza Aérea," 73; Ortega, *Military Role,* F43.

55. *Testimony, Wessin y Wessin,* 157, 161; Gleijeses, *Crisis,* 192–193; Beaulac, *Action-1965,* 21.

56. *Testimony, Wessin y Wessin, 250.*

57. *Revista* (Aug. 1959), 47–49; *Revista* (Jul.-Aug. 1968), 30–31; *Revista* (Jun. 1974), 10.

58. *NY Times,* Feb. 12, 1966, 12; U.S. Emb. telegram, Mar. 16, 1966; interview.

59. U.S. Emb. telegram, Feb. 5, 1966.

60. U.S. Emb. telegram, Feb.11, 1966.

61. Ian Bell, *The Dominican Republic* (Boulder, Colorado: Westview Press, 1981), 214–215 (hereafter cited as Bell, *Dominican Republic*).

62. *Revista* (Aug. 1952), 32.

63. *Jane's Fighting Ships, 1972–1973.* Edited by Raymond V. B. Blackman (New York: McGraw-Hill Book Company, 1972), 80–81 (hereafter cited as *Jane's Ships*); Robert Erwin Johnson, *Guardians of the Sea: History of the United States Coast Guard, 1915 to the Present* (Annapolis: Naval Institute Press, 1987), 404–405; English, *Armed Forces,* 229–230.

64. Atkins and Wilson, *Trujillo Regime,* 96; interview.

65. *Revista* (Mar.-Apr. 1964), 8; interview.

66. *Revista* (Nov. 1972), 8, 10; *Revista* (Mar. 1975), 57–59.

67. *Revista* (Sep. 1968), 25–26; *Revista* (Nov. 1972), 10.

68. Beaulac, *Action-1965,* 26–27; *El Caribe,* Jan. 19, 1962, 2; *Revista* (May 1975), 57.

69. *Revista* (Nov. 1972), 7–8; Atkins, *Arms and Politics,* 139.

70. *Revista* (Jan.-Apr. 1958), 79; *Revista* (Nov. 1972), 9–10; interviews.

71. Gleijeses, *Crisis*, 390-fn. 2.
72. Interview.
73. Atkins, *Arms and Politics*, 76–77.

CHAPTER III

1. Interviews.
2. Bell, *Dominican Republic*, 212.
3. Interviews.
4. Interview.
5. Interviews.
6. U.S. Emb. airgram, Dec. 8, 1968, 29; interviews.
7. U.S. Emb. telegram, Sep. 7, 1966; *Washington Post*, Sep. 3, 1966, A14.
8. U.S. Emb. airgram, Sep. 11, 1966, 6; U.S. Emb. airgram, Jun. 13, 1968, 7; U.S. Emb. telegram, Sep. 7, 1966; *NY Times*, Sep. 3, 1966, 22; *Washington Post*, Sep. 7, 1966, A25; *Radio Continental*, Sep. 7, 1966.
9. Major Brian J. Bosch, *New Armor Order of Battle and Political Significance* (U.S. Embassy, Santo Domingo: U.S. Department of Defense Intelligence Information Report, DD Form 1396, Feb. 22, 1971), 2 (hereafter cited as Bosch, *Armor*); U.S. Emb. telegram, Oct. 3, 1969; *Radio Comercial*, Sep. 18, 1969; *Agence France-Presse*, Oct. 4, 1969 (hereafter cited as *AFP*).
10. Bosch, *Order of Battle*, 17.
11. Bosch, *Professionalism*, 6–8.
12. *Revista* (Aug.-Sep.-Oct. 1970), 13–14.
13. *Revista* (Mar.-May 1967), 40; *Revista* (Feb.-Mar.-Apr. 1970), 31; USARSA Letter; Lt. Col.(ret) William C. Camper, Letter, Apr. 24, 1999, 2 (hereafter cited as Camper, Letter); interviews.
14. *Revista* (Aug. 1971), 6–10; U.S. Emb. telegram, 28 Apr. 1970; Atkins, *Arms and Politics*, 89; *El Caribe*, May 1, 1970,1.
15. *Revista* (Jun. 1974), 12; *Revista* (Jul.-Aug. 1957), 44; SDDS, Aug. 8, 1966; U.S. Emb. airgram, Sep. 22, 1969, 2; interviews.
16. Bosch, *Professionalism*, 8.
17. Calder, *U.S. Occupation*, 238–239; Fuller, *Marines*, 46, 48; Welles, *Naboth's Vineyard*, Vol. II, 908.
18. Germán E. Ornes, *Trujillo: Little Caesar of the Caribbean* (New York: Thomas Nelson and Sons, 1958), 142–143 (hereafter cited as Ornes, *Little Caesar*).
19. Gleijeses, *Crisis*, 88–89, 107, 117–118.
20. *Revista* (Mar.-Apr. 1957), 54.
21. Interviews.
22. Interviews.
23. Howard J. Wiarda and Michael J. Kryzanek, "Dominican Dictatorship Revisited: The Caudillo Tradition and the Regimes of Trujillo and Balaguer," *Revista/Review Interamericana*, Vol. 7, N0.3 (Fall

1977), 431; Jeremiah O'Leary, "Dominican Politics. Police Strongman Follows Trujillo's Path to Power," *The Evening Star* (Feb. 16, 1972), A10 (hereafter cited as O'Leary, "Strongman"); U.S. Emb. airgram, Dec. 20, 1970, 3; interviews.
24. *Revista* (Jul. 1971), 6–8; Bernard Diederich, *Trujillo: The Death of the Goat* (Boston: Little, Brown and Company, 1978), 244, 248 (hereafter cited as Diederich, *Trujillo*).
25. *Revista* (May-Jun. 1958), 13.
26. Diederich, *Trujillo*, 136, 140–141, 142, 155, 188, 192.
27. *Listín*, Apr. 20, 1971, 1; *Listín*, Jan. 22, 1973, 10A; interviews.
28. *Revista* (May-Jun. 1958), 13.
29. Diederich, *Trujillo*, 165.
30. *Radio Comercial*, Jul. 15, 1972; Ornes, *Little Caesar*, 141.
31. Arciniegas, "Fuerza Aérea," 53.
32. Atkins, *Arms and Politics*, 81, 119; *Listín*, Jan. 11, 1972, 13; *Revista* (Aug.-Sep.-Oct. 1979), 110.
33. Interviews.

CHAPTER IV

1. *Revista* (Nov.-Dec. 1964), 20.
2. *Revista* (Nov.-Dec. 1964), 21–22.
3. Bosch, *Salvadoran Officer Corps*, 17.
4. El Salvador, Estado Mayor General de la Fuerza Armada, "Historia del Estado Mayor General de la Fuerza Armada," *Revista de la Fuerza Armada* (Jan.-Feb.-Mar. 1979), 4.
5. *Revista* (Nov.-Dec. 1964), 27; Bosch, *Salvadoran Officer Corps*, 22–23.
6. Mayor Eduardo Ernesto Mendoza Morales, "Reseña Histórica, Escuela de Comando y Estado Mayor 'Dr. Manuel Enrique Araujo,'" *Revista Docente*, No. II (Sep. 1995), 12–13.
7. *Revista* (Nov.-Dec. 1964), 28–29; Rafael Meza Gallont, *El Ejército de El Salvador* (San Salvador: Imprenta Nacional, 1964), 35–36 (hereafter cited as Meza Gallont, *El Salvador*).
8. *Revista* (Nov.-Dec. 1964), 30; Meza Gallont, *El Salvador*, 28–32.
9. Tte. Coronel Luis Ney García Recio, "La Academia Militar 'Batalla de las Carreras' y su Aporte al Ejército Nacional," *Revista* (Oct. 1968), 23–24.
10. *Revista* (Jan.-Feb. 1963), 6.
11. Martin, *Events*, 323.
12. Arturo R. Espaillat, *Trujillo: The Last Caesar* (Chicago: Henry Regnery Company, 1963), 24 (hereafter cited as Espaillat, *Last Caesar*).

13. *Revista* (Aug. 1971), 15.
14. *Revista* (Mar.-May 1967), 27; *El Caribe,* May 13, 1963, 3.
15. *Revista* (Aug. 1971), 6.
16. Atkins and Wilson, *Trujillo Regime,* 89–90.
17. Crassweller, *Dictator,* 364; *NY Times,* Jun. 18, 1958, 2.
18. Larman C. Wilson, *United States Military Assistance to the Dominican Republic, 1916–1967* (paper prepared for delivery before the Seminar on the Dominican Republic, Center for International Affairs, Harvard University, Apr. 20, 1967, n.p. 1967), 70 (hereafter cited as Wilson, *Assistance*).
19. U.S. Department of State, "Military Assistance Agreement Between the United States of America and the Dominican Republic. Mar. 8, 1962," *United States Treaties And Other International Agreements* (Washington, D.C.: Government Printing Office, 1950–1975), Vol. XV, 701–707; Thomas E. Weil, et al., *Area Handbook for the Dominican Republic* (Washington, D.C.: Foreign Area Studies, The American University, 1973), 207–208; *Revista* (Oct.-Dec. 1962), 56.
20. Wilson, *Assistance,* 70–75; Yates, *Power Pack,* 185.
21. USARSA Letter.
22. Lt. Col (ret) Ildefonso Lombraña, Jr., personal papers, section one, 7–10 (hereafter cited as Lombraña papers).
23. Bosch, *Order of Battle,* 3.
24. Lombraña papers, passim; Wilson, *Assistance,* 75; Martin, *Events,* 145.
25. U.S. Emb. telegram, Jan. 25, 1966.
26. U.S. Department of State/U.S. Department of Defense telegram, May 4, 1966.
27. U.S. Emb. telegram, May 7, 1966.
28. U.S. Emb. airgram, Mar. 24, 1966, 11; U.S. Emb. airgram, Jun. 13, 1968, 2; *Washington Post,* Oct. 16, 1966, L4.
29. Camper, Letter, 1.
30. *Revista* (Mar.-May 1967), 44–49; Capitán Carlos Antonio Castillo Pimentel, "Escuela para Oficiales y sus Proyecciones Futuras," *Revista* (Sep. 1968), 15 (hereafter cited as Castillo, "Escuela para Oficiales").
31. *Revista* (Mar.-May 1967), 48; USARSA Letter.
32. *Revista* (Mar.-Apr. 1977), 127–129.
33. Camper, Letter, 1–2.
34. Castillo, "Escuela para Oficiales," 17–23.
35. Liliano Angulo, "Escuela para Oficiales Celebra 3ra Promoción," *Revista* (Dec. 1968), 16.
36. Camper, Letter, 2; *Revista* (May-Jun.-Jul.-Aug. 1969), 13–14; Mayor Porfirio Alejandro Díaz, "Que es el Comando de Escuelas, Ejército Nacional," *Revista* (Jul. 1971), 97–99 (hereafter cited as Díaz, "Comando de Escuelas").
37. Camper, Letter, 2.
38. *Revista* (Sep.-Oct. 1963), 39; *Revista* (Nov.-Dec. 1963), 4–5; *Revista* (Sep.-Oct. 1964), 28; *Revista* (Nov.-Dec. 1964), 16–17.
39. Díaz, "Comando de Escuelas," 103.
40. U.S. Department of the Army, U.S. Army School of the Americas, "Diagrama Histórico de la Escuela de las Américas," *Adelante* (Summer 1988), 21–22.
41. U.S. Emb. airgram, Apr. 14, 1968, enclosure 4.
42. U.S. Emb. airgram, Apr. 14, 1968, 5–6; U.S. Emb. airgram, Dec. 21, 1967, 1.
43. U.S. Emb. airgram, Apr. 14, 1968, 5–6; U.S. Emb. airgram, May 31, 1970, 3; U.S. Emb.telegram, Apr. 5, 1972.
44. U.S. Emb. airgram, Jan. 15, 1969, 4.
45. Lt. Col (ret) Stanley A. Castleman, Letter, Dec. 16, 1999, 2 (hereafter cited as Castleman, Letter).
46. U.S. Emb. telegram, Jul. 27, 1964.
47. U.S. Emb. airgram, Sep. 6, 1967, 2.
48. *Jane's Ships,* 82.
49. Nelson Arciniegas, "Ingeniero Naval Contreras Peña Ofrece Declaraciones a Revista Militar," *Revista* (Mar. 1971), 32; Liliano Angulo, "Marina de Guerra, Una Profesión Honorable," *Revista* (Sep. 1972), 37–40; *Revista* (Feb. 1972), 17–20; *Revista* (Nov. 1972), 76.
50. U.S. Emb. telegram, Jul. 8, 1972.
51. U.S. Emb. telegram, Jul. 14, 1972.
52. *Revista* (Jul. 1972), 22–24.
53. Martin, *Events,* 122.
54. Tad Szulc, *Dominican Diary* (New York: Delacorte Press, 1965), 23, 78 (hereafter cited as Szulc, *Diary*); Hermann, *Caamaño,* 71–72.
55. Martin, *Events,* 664.
56. *Listín,* Sep. 9, 1972, 1,4; U.S. Emb. airgram, Oct. 7, 1971, 9.
57. SDDS, Dec. 3, 1965.
58. U.S. Agency for International Development, Office of Public Safety, *Weekly Progress Report, Dominican Republic.* Mar. 4, and May 27, 1966; *Listín,* May 12, 1971, 14; U.S. Emb. airgram, Oct. 7, 1971, 10.
59. Bosch, *Order of Battle,* 4–12.
60. Interviews.
61. Bosch, *Order of Battle,* 17.
62. Bosch, *Order of Battle,* 16–17.
63. Bosch, *Order of Battle,* 13–16.
64. Bosch, *Order of Battle,* 4, 14, 16.
65. Bosch, *Order of Battle,* 2.
66. USARSA Letter.
67. *Revista* (Nov.-Dec. 1963), 4.
68. Howard J. Wiarda, Editor, *Materials for the Study of Politics and Government in the Dominican Republic, 1930–1966* (Santiago,

Dominican Republic: Universidad Católica Madre y Maestra, 1968), 69.
  69. *Revista* (Jan. 1971), 43.
  70. *Revista* (Aug. 1956), 58.
  71. *Revista* (Aug. 1952), XV.
  72. *Revista* (Jul. 1971), 8; *Listín,* Aug. 5, 1971, 1.
  73. U.S. Emb. telegram, Jun. 25, 1971; U.S. Emb. telegram, Apr. 5, 1972; Castleman, Letter, Dec. 16, 1999, 4; English, *Armed Forces,* 230–231; Arciniegas, "Fuerza Aérea," 62–68.
  74. U.S. Emb. telegram, Sep. 30,1970; Ortega, *Military Role,* F43; Bosch, *Order of Battle,* 3.
  75. U.S. Emb. airgram, Feb. 25, 1970, Annex I to first enclosure, 2.
  76. *La Noticia.* Mar. 1, 1974, 4; *Revista* (Nov. 1970), 70–71; *Revista* (Feb. 1972), 17–19; *Revista* (Mar. 1972), 42; *Revista* (Jul. 1972), 22–24; *Revista* (Nov. 1972), 76; *Revista* (Dec. 1974), 123–127; *Jane's Ships,* 82.
  77. U.S. Emb. airgram, May 31, 1970, 2.

CHAPTER V

  1. Interview.
  2. Segundo Teniente Diógenes Noboa Leyba, *Revista Militar* (Oct. 1948), 13.
  3. Interview.
  4. Peguero, "Trujillo and the Military," 208–209; interview.
  5. Albert C. Hicks, *Blood in the Streets: The Life and Rule of Trujillo* (New York: Creative Age Press, Inc., 1946), 103–113.
  6. English, *Armed Forces,* 233.
  7. Martin, *Events,* 417–438; *Testimony, Wessin y Wessin,* 116.
  8. U.S. Emb./Defense Attaché Office telegram, Apr. 20, 1971; interview.
  9. Interview.
  10. SDDS, May 12, 1971; *Listín,* May 7, 1971, 15.
  11. U.S. Emb. telegram, Apr. 19, 1971.
  12. *Revista* (May 1975), 53.
  13. *Revista* (Apr.-May 1966), 34.
  14. *Revista* (Sep.-Oct. 1956), 28.
  15. *Revista* (Aug. 1952), 27–29.
  16. *Revista* (Sep.- Oct. 1963), 11.
  17. *Revista* (Mar.-Apr. 1968), 60; *Revista* (Jul.-Aug. 1968), 12.
  18. *Revista* (Dec. 1972), 82.
  19. Interview.
  20. SDDS, Jun. 23, 1966; *Listín,* Jun. 23, 1966, 1.
  21. Martin, *Events,* 108.
  22. Wiarda, *Control,* 122.
  23. *Revista* (Oct. 1968), 91.
  24. *Revista* (May-Jun.-Jul.-Aug. 1969), 68.

  25. *Revista* (Nov.-Dec. 1964), 7; *Testimony, Wessin y Wessin,* 249.
  26. USARSA Letter.
  27. *Revista* (Apr. 1972), 80–82; *Revista* (Jun. 1972), 58–60; *Revista* (Jul. 1972), 65–68; *Revista* (Sep. 1972), 6–9; *Revista* (Dec. 1972), 11–12.
  28. Lyle N. McAlister, *The "Fuero Militar" in New Spain, 1764–1800* (Gainesville: University of Florida Press, 1957), 5–10, 13–15, 88–89.
  29. U.S. Emb. airgram, May 10, 1970, 6.
  30. *AFP,* May 4, 1970; *Listín,* May 5, 1970, 4; *Listín,* May 26, 1970, 3; interview.
  31. *Revolutionary Nationalism Network,* May 5, 1970.
  32. *Latin America Political Report* (Latin American Newsletters, Ltd., Nov. 17, 1978), LAPR XII, 354.
  33. *El Caribe,* May 2, 1962, 7; *Listín,* Jan. 10, 1964, 4; *Listín,* Feb. 6, 1964, 4; U.S. Emb. airgram, Apr. 1, 1964, 6; *Listín,* Jan. 26, 1967, 10; *Listín,* Jan. 27, 1967, 5; *Listín,* Apr. 12, 1971, 1,4; *Listín,* Apr.13, 1971, 1; *Listín,* Sep. 3, 1971, 5; *Listín,* Sep. 17, 1971, 13; *Revista* (Jun. 1974), 8; Castleman, Letter, Sep. 14, 2000, 1.

CHAPTER VI

  1. Interviews.
  2. *El Caribe,* May 12, 1975, 16; *El Caribe,* Feb. 8, 1982, 1.
  3. U.S. Emb. telegram, Mar. 16, 1966; Bosch, *Professionalism,* 9; Atkins, *Arms and Politics,* 71; *Listín,* Feb. 12, 1966, 4; *El Caribe,* Feb. 16, 1967, 7; *El Caribe,* Feb. 12, 1966, 8; U.S. Defense Intelligence Agency, *Biographic Sketch, Neit Nivar Seijas,* Apr. 1979, 4 (hereafter cited as DIA *Bio Sketch, Nivar*); U.S. Defense Intelligence Agency, *Biographic Sketch, Enrique Pérez y Pérez,* Sep. 1978, 3 (hereafter cited as DIA *Bio Sketch, Pérez y Pérez*).
  4. *Revista* (Jan. 1954), 20; *Revista* (Apr.-May 1956), 58; *Revista* (Jan.-Apr. 1958), 78, 80; *Listín,* Feb. 8, 1982, 13; DIA *Bio Sketch, Nivar.* Apr. 1979, 4.
  5. *Revista* (Jan. 1956), 57; *Revista* (Jan.-Apr. 1958), 12; *El Caribe,* Feb. 12, 1966, 8; *El Caribe,* Jan. 12, 1962, 10; *Listín,* Feb. 12, 1966, 4; U.S. Defense Intelligence Agency, *Biographic Data, Enrique Pérez y Pérez.* Jul. 1970, 3 (hereafter cited as DIA *Bio Data, Pérez y Pérez*).
  6. U.S. Emb. airgram, Oct. 25, 1970, 5; *El Caribe,* Feb. 12, 1966, 8; *Revista* (Feb. 1959), 56; *Revista* (Apr. 1959), 31; *Revista* (Oct. 1959), 31.
  7. Interview.
  8. Peguero, "Trujillo and the Military," 256; *NY Times,* Jul. 3, 1959, 6; Espaillat, *Last Caesar,* 144; Crassweller, *Dictator,* 347.

9. DIA *Bio Data, Pérez y Pérez,* Jul. 1970, 3.

10. *El Caribe,* Feb. 12, 1966, 8.

11. U.S. Emb. airgram, Oct. 25, 1970, 6; *Testimony, Wessin y Wessin,* 112; *El Caribe,* Jan. 5, 1962, 6; *El Caribe,* Jan. 12, 1962, 9; *El Caribe,* Jan. 18, 1962,1, 4; *El Caribe,* Jan. 25, 1962, 9; *Radio Caribe,* Jan. 17, 1962; U.S. Defense Intelligence Agency, *Biographic Data, Neit Nivar Seijas,* Jan. 1967, 2, 3 (hereafter cited as DIA *Bio Data, Nivar*).

12. *El Caribe,* Jul. 17, 1962, 7; *SOA Graduates,* Jul. 16-Nov. 30, 1962 (Washington, D.C.: School of the Americas Watch, n.d); U.S. Emb. telegram, Mar. 16, 1966; DIA *Bio Sketch, Pérez y Pérez,* Sep. 1978, 3; *El Caribe,* Feb. 12, 1966, 8; U.S. Emb. airgram, Jul. 15, 1966, 8–9.

13. *El Caribe,* Dec. 10, 1962, 16; Lombraña papers, section one, 2.

14. *El Caribe,* Feb. 6, 1963, 12; interviews.

15. U.S. Emb. airgram, Oct. 25, 1970, 6; Dominican Republic, Centro de Enseñanza de las Fuerzas Armadas-CEFA, *Libro Blanco de las Fuerzas Armadas y de la Policía Nacional de la República Dominicana* (Santo Domingo: Editora del Caribe, C. por A., 1964), 94–95; *Listín,* Oct. 15, 1971, 4; *El Caribe,* Apr. 14, 1964, 8; DIA *Bio Data, Pérez y Pérez,* Jul. 1970, 4; interviews.

16. U.S. Emb. airgram, Oct. 25, 1970, 8; Gleijeses, *Crisis,* 149.

17. Interviews.

18. U.S. Emb. telegram, Jan. 25, 1964; U.S. Emb. telegram, Apr. 5, 1964; U.S. Emb. telegram, Apr. 14, 1964; U.S. Emb. airgram, Apr. 22, 1964, 4; U.S. Emb. telegram, Aug. 10, 1964; *Listín,* Apr. 14, 1964, 10; *El Caribe,* Apr. 14, 1964, 1; *AFP,* Apr. 12, 1964; *Radio Comercial,* Aug. 28, 1964; *Radio Comercial,* Sep. 2, 1964.

19. U.S. Emb. telegram, Apr. 14, 1964.

20. U.S. Emb. airgram, Jul. 1, 1964, 1.

21. Gleijeses, *Crisis,* 149.

22. U.S. Emb. airgram, Sep. 30, 1964, 6; U.S. Emb. telegram, Oct. 2, 1964; *Revista* (May-Jun. 1964), 34; *Listín,* Sep. 29, 1964, 2; *Listín,* Oct. 2, 1964, 1; *Listín,* Oct. 3, 1964, 1; *Listín,* Oct. 4, 1964, 2, 4; U.S. Emb. airgram, Oct. 7, 1964, 3.

23. U.S. Emb. airgram, Feb. 3, 1965, 2; *Listín,* Jan. 28, 1965, 1, 2, 4; *El Caribe,* Jan. 28, 1965, 1; *El Caribe,* Jan. 29, 1965, 1, 8.

24. U.S. Emb. airgram, Apr. 20, 1965, 6; *Listín,* Apr. 13, 1965, 1,4; *Radio Comercial,* Apr. 13, 1965.

25. Gleijeses, *Crisis,* 176, 382-fn.4.

26. U.S. Emb. telegram, May 21, 1965; Yates, *Power Pack,* 116; Major Lawrence M. Greenberg, *United States Army Unilateral and Coalition Operations in the 1965 Dominican Republic Intervention* (Washington, D.C.: Analy-sis Branch, U.S. Army Center of Military History, 1987), 50–51; Martin, *Events,* 694; Dan Kurzman, *Santo Domingo: Revolt of the Damned* (New York: G.P. Putnam's Sons, 1965), 270 (hereafter cited as Kurzman, *Revolt*); Danilo Brugal Alfau, *Tragedia en Santo Domingo (Documentos para la Historia)* (Santo Domingo: Editora del Caribe, 1966), 258; *Washington Post,* May 16, 1965, 1; *Washington Post,* May 18, 1965, 9A; interviews.

27. Interview.

28. U.S. Emb. telegram, May 26, 1965; DIA *Bio Data, Pérez y Pérez,* Jul. 1970, 1.

29. U.S. Emb. telegram, Nov. 21, 1965; Palmer, *Crisis of 1965,* 114; SDDS, Oct. 21, 1965; *El Caribe,* Feb. 12, 1966, 8; *Prensa Latina,* Oct. 19, 1965; *AFP,* Oct. 23, 1965; *AFP,* Oct. 29, 1965; DIA *Bio Sketch, Pérez y Pérez,* Sep. 1978, 3; interviews.

30. U.S. Emb. telegram, Jan. 6, 1966; U.S. Emb. telegram, Jan. 7, 1966; SDDS, Jan. 6, 1966; *El Caribe,* Jan. 7, 1966, 10.

31. *AFP,* Jan. 8, 1966; *Radio Pueblo,* Jan. 7, 1966.

32. U.S. Emb. telegram, Jan. 10, 1966.

33. U.S. Department of State telegram, Oct. 28, 1965.

34. U.S. Emb. telegram, Nov. 2, 1965.

35. U.S. Emb. telegram, Jan. 31, 1966.

36. U.S. Emb. telegram, Feb. 3, 1966.

37. U.S. Emb. telegram, Feb. 5, 1966.

38. *Listín,* Feb. 5, 1966, 1.

39. *El Caribe,* Feb. 7, 1966, 12; *Radio Comercial,* Feb. 7, 1966.

40. U.S. Emb. telegram, Feb. 9, 1966; U.S. Emb. telegram, Feb 28, 1966.

41. U.S. Emb. telegram, Feb. 11, 1966.

42. U.S. Emb. airgram, Feb. 23, 1966, 5.

43. U.S. Emb. airgram, Feb. 10, 1966, 3.

44. *Latin America* (Latin American Newsletters, Ltd., May 16, 1975), LA IX, 149.

45. U.S. Emb. telegram, Mar. 19, 1966; Atkins, *Arms and Politics,* 72.

46. U.S. Emb. telegram, Feb. 28, 1966; *AFP,* Feb. 28, 1966; *El Caribe,* May 12, 1975, 16.

47. U.S. Emb. telegram, Mar. 16, 1966.

48. *Radio Continental,* Mar. 2, 1966.

49. U.S. Emb. telegram, Mar. 16, 1966.

50. *Revista* (Apr.-May 1966), 5.

51. *Radio Comercial,* May 19, 1966.

52. U.S. Emb. telegram, Oct. 12, 1965; U.S. Emb. airgram, Oct. 25, 1970, 6–7; Joaquín Balaguer, *Memorias de un Cortesano de la "Era de Trujillo"* (Madrid: G. del Toro, 1989), 401 (hereafter cited as Balaguer, *Memorias*); Atkins, *Arms and Politics,* 72; *Listín,* Oct. 15, 1971, 4; DIA *Bio Data, Nivar,* Jan. 1967, 2.

53. Balaguer, *Memorias,* 158; Jonathan Hartlyn, *The Struggle for Democratic Politics in*

the Dominican Republic (Chapel Hill: The University of North Carolina Press, 1998), 110 (hereafter cited as Hartlyn, *Democratic Politics*).

54. U.S. Emb. telegram, Jul. 27, 1966.

55. DIA *Bio Data, Nivar,* Jan. 1967, 1; interviews.

56. U.S. Emb. airgram, Oct. 25, 1970, 7; interviews.

57. U.S. Emb. telegram, Aug. 11, 1966; *Washington Post,* Aug. 10, 1966, A6.

58. *Prensa Latina,* Sep. 11, 1966.

59. U.S. Emb. telegram, Dec. 9, 1966.

60. U.S. Emb. telegram, Feb. 16, 1967; *El Caribe,* Feb. 16, 1967, 1,7; *Radio Comercial,* Feb. 16, 1967; *Radio Continental,* Feb. 17, 1967.

61. U.S. Emb. airgram, Mar. 12, 1967, 4.

62. U.S. Emb. telegram, May 4, 1967.

63. SDDS, Mar. 21, 1967; SDDS, Mar. 23, 1967; *Listín,* Mar. 23, 1967, 1, 4; Balaguer, *Memorias,* 233.

64. *Radio Comercial,* Mar. 28, 1967; U.S. Emb. telegram, Apr. 10, 1967; interviews.

65. U.S. Emb. telegram, Mar. 21, 1967.

66. Balaguer, *Memorias,* 239.

67. U.S. Emb. telegram, May 4, 1967.

68. U.S. Emb. telegram, Apr. 9, 1967; *El Caribe,* Apr. 8, 1967, 1.

69. *Washington Post,* Oct. 16, 1966, L4.

70. U.S. Emb. telegram, Apr. 9, 1967.

71. U.S. Emb. airgram, Oct. 25, 1970, 2.

72. U.S. Emb. airgram, Oct. 25, 1970, 4; U.S. Emb. airgram, Jun. 4, 1967, 1–2.

73. *Revista* (Jul. 1960), 1; *Revista (*Nov. 1960), 13; *Revista (*Jun.-Jul. 1954), 88; *Listín,* Sep. 7, 1967, 4; *Listín,* Mar. 13, 1969, 5; Aliro Paulino, Jr., *La Noche que Trujillo Volvio,* 4th ed. (Santo Domingo: Mundo Diplomático Internacional, 1966), 96; Bosch, *Order of Battle,* 5.

74. *El Caribe,* Apr. 11, 1967, 1; interviews.

75. U.S. Emb. airgram, Oct. 25, 1970, 2–3.

76. *Revista* (Jan.-Feb. 1971), 33–34.

77. U.S. Emb. airgram, Oct. 25, 1970, 2–3; interviews.

78. Interviews.

79. Lombraña papers, section two, 1, section three, 7, 9; interview.

80. U.S. Emb. telegram, Dec. 19, 1967; U.S. Emb. airgram, Dec. 28, 1967, 4.

81. U.S. Emb. airgram, Jun. 13, 1968, 5.

82. U.S. Emb. airgram, Sep. 19, 1968, 4.

83. U.S. Emb. airgram, Sep. 19, 1968, 4.

84. U.S. Emb. airgram, Jun. 13, 1968, 8.

85. U.S. Emb. airgram, Jun. 13, 1968, 5.

86. U.S. Emb. telegram, Jan. 3, 1969.

87. Camper, Letter, 3; interview.

88. Camper, Letter, 3; interview.

89. U.S. Emb. airgram, Oct. 25, 1970, 2; interview.

90. SDDS, Sep. 6, 1967.

91. U.S. Emb. telegram, Sep. 6, 1967.

92. SDDS, Jun. 25, 1968; SDDS, Jul. 9, 1968.

93. U.S. Emb. airgram, Sep. 22, 1969, 1–2.

94. SDDS, Mar. 13, 1970; *Radio Comercial,* Mar. 19, 1970.

95. *Radio Comercial,* Apr. 14, 1970; U.S. Emb. telegram, Apr. 15, 1970.

96. U.S. Emb. airgram, Oct. 25, 1970, 5; interview.

97. U.S. Emb. telegram, Aug. 11, 1966.

98. Interview.

99. U.S. Emb. airgram, Oct. 25, 1970, 6; *Radio Comercial,* Dec. 31, 1969; *Listín,* Dec. 31, 1969, 1, 4; *El Caribe,* Jan. 1, 1970, 11.

100. *Radio Universal.* Dec. 31, 1969; *Radio Comercial,* Jan. 3, 1970.

101. Interview.

102. U.S. Emb. telegram, Apr. 28, 1970; *Listín,* Dec. 24, 1969, 12A; *Radio Comercial,* Jan. 12, 1970; *Radio Comercial,* Apr. 1, 1970; *Radio Comercial,* Apr. 8, 1970; *Radio Comercial,* Apr. 9, 1970; *Radio Comercial,* Apr. 17, 1970; *El Caribe,* May 4, 1970, 11.

103. *Radio Comercial,* Jan. 31, 1970.

104. *Reuters,* Apr. 8, 1970.

105. U.S. Embassy, Santo Domingo, *Briefing Paper, Dominican Republic, 1961–1971,* 4.

Chapter VII

1. U.S. Emb. airgram, Oct. 25, 1970, 1, 4.

2. U.S. Emb. airgram, Oct. 25, 1970, 4–5.

3. Bosch, *Armor,* 1–2, 4.

4. U.S. Emb. airgram, Oct. 25, 1970, 3–4; interviews.

5. U.S. Emb. airgram, Oct. 25, 1970, 7.

6. *Radio Continental,* Oct. 5, 1969.

7. *Listín,* May 10, 1971, 7A; *Listín,* Jun. 22, 1971, 15; *Radio Comercial,* Jun. 7, 1971; U.S. Department of Defense, U.S. Southern Command, *Biographic Data, Neit Nivar Seijas,* Sep. 1974, 4 (hereafter cited as USSOUTH-COM *Bio Data, Nivar*); interview.

8. U.S. Emb. airgram, Oct. 25, 1970, 9.

9. U.S. Emb. airgram, Oct. 25, 1970, 8–9.

10. U.S. Emb. telegram, Dec. 18, 1970.

11. Interview.

12. *Listín,* Dec. 23, 1970, 10A; interviews.

13. *Radio Comercial,* Aug. 5, 1969.

14. Carlos María Gutiérrez, *The Dominican Republic: Rebellion and Repression,* translated by Richard E. Edwards (New York:

Monthly Review Press, 1972), 52, 125–126 (hereafter cited as Gutiérrez, *Repression*).
15. U.S. Emb. airgram, Oct. 25, 1970, 11; interview.
16. U.S. Emb. telegram, Dec. 18, 1970.
17. Bosch, *Armor*, 2–3.
18. *Radio Comercial*, Jan. 2, 1971; *Listín*, Jan. 1, 1971, 1.
19. *Revista* (Jul. 1971), 6–10; *Listín*, Jul. 13, 1971, 4; *Listín*, Mar. 16, 1970, 2; interview.
20. Interviews.
21. U.S. Emb. telegram, Apr. 15, 1970.
22. *Listín*, Aug. 5, 1971, 1.
23. *Listín*, Jan. 18, 1973, 6A; interviews.
24. Frederick M. Nunn, "Professional Militarism in Twentieth-Century Peru: Historical and Theoretical Background to the *Golpe de Estado* of 1968," *Hispanic American Historical Review*, Vol. 59, No. 3 (1979), 416 (hereafter cited as Nunn, *Militarism, Peru*).
25. Peru, Comando Conjunto de la Fuerza Armada, *Centro de Altos Estudios Militares* (1972), 2.
26. George W. Grayson Jr., "Peru's Military Government," *Current History*, Vol. 58, No. 342 (Feb. 1970), 71; George L. Vásquez, "Peru," in *The Political Role of the Military: An International Handbook*, edited by Constantine P. Danopoulos and Cynthia Watson (Westport, Connecticut: Greenwood Press, 1966), 346.
27. Nunn, *Militarism, Peru*, 391.
28. Stepan, *Brazil*, 175–177.
29. Stepan, *Brazil*, 176.
30. Stepan, *Brazil*, 179; *Time*, Jan. 5, 1970, 27.
31. Inter-American Defense College, *Revista del Colegio Interamericano*, Vol. XIII, No. 1 (1986), 151, 153, 155, 157, 161, 163, 171.
32 Inter-American Defense College, *Inter-American Defense College* (n.d), 2.
33. Interviews; U.S. Emb. airgram, Sep. 11, 1966, 6.
34. Interviews.
35. Bosch, *Professionalism*, 7–8.

Chapter VIII

1. *Onda Musical*, Feb. 12, 1969.
2. *Testimony, Wessin y Wessin*, 109–110; *Revista* (Jan.-Jun. 1988), 8–9; *Radio Caribe*, Nov. 23, 1961.
3. *AFP*, Jan. 19, 1962; *Testimony, Wessin y Wessin*, 112.
4. Martin, *Events*, 484; Kurzman, *Revolt*, 87, 95; Gleijeses, *Crisis*, 104; *Time*, May 7, 1965, 30; James A. Clark, *The Church and the Crisis in the Dominican Republic* (Westminster, Maryland: The Newman Press, 1967), 177–178.

5. Martin, *Events*, 127.
6. Kurzman, *Revolt*, 95.
7. *Revista* (May-Jun. 1963), 13.
8. Atkins, *Arms and Politics*, 58; Martin, *Events*, 484; interviews.
9. Martin, *Events*, 113–114; Kurzman, *Revolt*, 101; *Radio Caribe*, Apr. 18, 1962.
10. Martin, *Events*, 233, 254–255, 264–265, 280.
11. Martin, *Events*, 284–290.
12. Martin, *Events*, 277.
13. *Testimony, Wessin y Wessin*, 114.
14. *Testimony, Wessin y Wessin*, 116; Martin, *Events*, 438.
15. *Testimony, Wessin y Wessin*, 117.
16. *Testimony, Wessin y Wessin*, 119, 124.
17. Martin, *Events*, 481–484, 489–490; U.S. Library of Congress (DRD), *1961–1966 Chronology for the Dominican Republic* (1967), entry for Jul. 16, 1963.
18. Martin, *Events*, 483, 487, 491.
19. *Testimony, Wessin y Wessin*, 118, 122, 125.
20. Gleijeses, *Crisis*, 104–105.
21. Martin, *Events*, 521.
22. Kurzman, *Revolt*, 104.
23. Martin, *Events*, 561.
24. Kurzman, *Revolt*, 104–105; *Revista* (Sep.-Oct. 1963), 4.
25. *Revista* (Jan.-Jun. 1988), 8
26. Lowenthal, *Intervention*, 43.
27. U.S. Emb. airgram, Sep. 30, 1964, 6.
28. *Listín*, Oct. 3, 1964, 4; U.S. Emb. airgram, Oct. 7, 1964, 2–3.
29. Gleijeses, *Crisis*, 131.
30. U.S. Emb. airgram, Jan. 20, 1965, 2; *Radio Comercial*, Jan. 19, 1965.
31. *Radio Comercial*, Jan. 27, 1965; U.S. Emb. airgram, Feb. 3, 1965, 2.
32. *Radio Comercial*, Jan. 27, 1965; U.S. Emb. airgram, Jan. 27, 1965, 2; U.S. Emb. airgram, Feb. 3, 1965, 2.
33. Gleijeses, *Crisis*, 131; SDDS, Feb. 17, 1965.
34. Kurzman, *Revolt*, 88.
35. *Testimony, Wessin y Wessin*, 175.
36. General Elías Wessin y Wessin, "Bitter Salt of a Stranger's Bread," *National Review*, Vol. XVII, No. 42 (Oct. 19, 1965), 911.
37. *Testimony, Wessin y Wessin*, passim; *Listín*, Dec. 17, 1969, 14.
38. U.S. Emb. telegram, Sep. 7, 1966; U.S. Emb. telegram, Jan. 25, 1966; *Washington Post*, Sep. 3, 1966, A14.
39. SDDS, Sep. 6, 1966.
40. Atkins, *Arms and Politics*, 60; *AFP*, Feb. 25, 1968.
41. *Radio Comercial*, Jul. 3, 1967; *Radio Comercial*, Oct. 13, 1967; SDDS, Nov. 29, 1967; *Radio Comercial*, Oct. 24, 1968.
42. U.S. Emb. airgram, Aug. 20, 1967, 1–2; U.S. Emb. telegram, Sep. 7, 1967.

43. Atkins, *Arms and Politics*, 64; *Reuters,* Jan. 20, 1968; *AFP,* Feb. 25, 1968; *Radio Comercial,* Apr. 25, 1968.

44. *Radio Continental,* Apr. 26, 1968; *Listín,* Apr. 26, 1968, 1.

45. SDDS, May 16, 1968.

46. *Listín,* May 17, 1968, 13; *AFP,* May 17, 1968.

47. *Radio Comercial,* May 27, 1968; *Radio Comercial,* Jul. 19, 1968; *Radio Comercial,* Sep. 18, 1968; *Radio Comercial,* Sep. 27, 1968.

48. *Radio Comercial,* Mar. 18, 1968.

49. *Radio Comercial,* Apr. 25, 1968.

50. *Listín,* Sep. 11, 1968, 1.

51. *Ahora.* Sep. 23, 1968, 7; *Listín,* Sep. 14, 1968, 1; *Listín,* Apr. 25, 1968, 1; *Listín,* Oct. 30, 1969, 12.

52. *Radio Comercial,* Sep. 27, 1968.

53. SDDS, Dec. 11, 1968.

54. *Onda Musica,* Jan. 12, 1969; *Radio Comercial,* Jan. 13, 1969.

55. *Radio Comercial,* Jan. 6, 1969.

56. *Onda Musical,* Feb. 12, 1969; *Onda Musical,* Feb. 15, 1969.

57. *Radio Continental,* Mar. 23, 1969; *Radio Comercial,* Apr. 30, 1969.

58. *Listín,* May 1, 1969, 1.

59. *Listín,* May 5, 1969, 1; SDDS, May 7, 1969.

60. *Radio Comercial,* Oct. 17, 1969.

61. *Radio Comercial,* Aug. 29, 1969; *Listín,* Sep. 2, 1969, 1, 4.

62. *Radio Comercial,* Aug. 29, 1969; *Revista* (Sep. 1960), 41.

63. U.S. Emb. airgram, Sep. 22, 1969, 2.

64. U.S. Emb. airgram, Sep. 22, 1969, 1.

65. U.S. Emb. telegram, Oct. 3, 1969.

66. Interview.

67. *Listín,* Jan. 1, 1970, 2; *Radio Comercial,* Jan. 5, 1970; *Radio Comercial,* Jan. 7, 1970.

68. Atkins, *Arms and Politics*, 64; U.S. Embassy, Santo Domingo, *Briefing Paper, Dominican Republic, 1961–1971,* 4.

69. *Reuters,* Aug. 13, 1970.

70. *Listín,* Jul. 31, 1970, 1, 14.

71. *LATIN,* Jul. 4, 1971.

72. *LATIN,* Jul. 4, 1971; SDDS, Jul. 1, 1971.

73. *Revista* (May- Jun.-Jul. 1970), 10, 13; *Listín,* May 18, 1970, 10; *Radio Comercial,* May 15, 1968; interviews.

74. Interviews.

75. Peguero, "Trujillo and the Military," 192.

76. *Listín,* Feb. 2, 1970, 11; interview.

77. *Listín,* Jul. 31, 1971, 15; *Listín,* Nov. 15, 1971, 1,4; *Listín,* Dec. 23, 1971, 1; *Listín,* Aug. 23, 1971, 6A; *Radio Comercial,* Jul. 16, 1971.

78. *AFP,* Jun. 8, 1971; *Radio Mil,* Jul. 1, 1971.

79. U.S. Emb. telegram, Jun. 30, 1971; *Listín,* Jun. 30, 1971, 1,4; *Reuters,* Jun. 30, 1971.

80. *Listín,* Jul. 1, 1971, 4; *Radio Clarín,* Jun. 30, 1971; *Radio Mil,* Jul. 1, 1971.

81. SDDS, Jul. 1, 1971.

82. SDDS, Jul. 1, 1971.

83. *El Caribe,* Jul. 1, 1971, 6.

84. *Listín,* Jul. 2, 1971, 1; *Radio Mil,* Jul. 1, 1971.

85. *Revista* (Jul. 1971), 31–34.

86. *Radio Comercial,* Jul. 7, 1971.

87. *Listín,* Jul. 10, 1971, 1.

88. SDDS, Jul. 14, 1971.

89. *Radio Comercial,* Jul. 14, 1971.

90. Bosch, *Professionalism,* 8.

91. U.S. Emb. telegram, Jul. 9, 1971; *Radio Continental,* Jul. 18, 1971; *Radio Cristal,* Jul. 4, 1971; *Listín,* Jul. 5, 1971, 1.

92. *AFP,* Jun. 8, 1971; *Radio Clarín,* Jun. 9, 1971; O'Leary, "Strongman," A10.

CHAPTER IX

1. U. S. Emb. airgram, Oct. 7, 1971, 11; interviews.

2. Interviews.

3. U.S. Emb. airgram, Oct. 7, 1971, 12; U.S. Emb. telegram, Jul. 16, 1970; *Reuters,* Jul. 16, 1970; *Radio Comercial,* Jul. 18, 1970; interviews.

4. Interviews.

5. U.S. Emb. telegram, Jul. 2, 1970.

6. Interview.

7. *Radio Comercial,* Nov. 19, 1970.

8. *Listín,* Jan. 1, 1971, 1.

9. SDDS, Jan. 5, 1971; SDDS, Jan. 7, 1971; *Listín,* Jan. 20, 1971, 1; interview.

10. *Radio Clarín,* Jan. 19, 1971.

11. *Listín,* Jan. 20, 1971, 1; *Listín,* Jan. 16, 1971, 12.

12. SDDS, Jan. 20, 1971.

13. *Listín,* Feb. 4, 1971, 1.

14. *Listín,* Jan. 7, 1971, 4; *Listín,* Jan. 16, 1971, 12.

15. Interview.

16. *Listín,* Jan. 27, 1971, 15.

17. Gutiérrez, *Repression,* 19; *Listín,* Jun. 30, 1972, 4.

18. Norman Gall, "The Only Logical Answer," *Fieldstaff Reports,* American Universities Field Staff, Inc., Vol. VI, No. 1 (Jun. 1971), 4 (hereafter cited as Gall, *Reports*); *Listín,* Jun. 30, 1972, 4.

19. *NY Times,* Aug. 28, 1971, 2; *Washington Post,* Sep. 7, 1971, A1; Gall, *Reports,* 4.

20. *Washington Post,* Sep. 7, 1971, A1.

21. *Listín,* May 11, 1971, 1; *Listín,* Sep. 13, 1971, 1; *Listín,* Oct. 25, 1972, 3B; *Listín,* Nov. 11, 1972, 14.

22. *Radio Comercial,* Apr. 20, 1971; *Washington Post,* Sep. 7, 1971, A16.

23. Gall, *Reports,* 4.

24. *Washington Post*, Sep. 7, 1971, A16; *Listín*, Apr. 20, 1971, 5; *Listín*, Apr. 22, 1971, 1, 6.

25. *Radio Comercial*, Apr. 19, 1971; *Radio Comercial*, Apr. 20, 1971; *Radio Comercial*, May 4, 1971; *Radio Comercial*, May 8, 1971.

26. *Radio Comercial*, May 5, 1971; *Radio Comercial*, May 8, 1971; *Radio Comercial*, May 10, 1971; *Radio Comercial*, May 12, 1971.

27. *AFP*, May 13, 1971.

28. *Radio Comercial*, May 15, 1971; *Radio Clarín*, May 13, 1971.

29. *Radio Comercial*, May 31, 1971.

30. *Radio Comercial*, May 27, 1971.

31. *Radio Clarín*, May 17, 1971; *Radio Comercial*, May 15, 1971.

32. *Radio Clarín*, May 14, 1971; *Radio Clarín*, Jun. 3, 1971.

33. U.S. Emb. telegram, May 26, 1971.

34. *Radio Comercial*, Jun. 7, 1971; *Radio Clarín*, Jun. 14, 1971; *Radio Continental*, Jun. 13, 1971; *Radio Comercial*, Jun. 16, 1971.

35. *Radio Comercial*, Jun. 8, 1971.

36. Gall, *Reports*, 4; *Radio Comercial*, Jun. 8, 1971.

37. *Radio Comercial*, Jul. 17, 1971; *Radio Comercial*, Jul. 22, 1971; *Radio Continental*, Jul. 25, 1971.

38. *Radio Comercial*, Aug. 2, 1971.

39. *Listín*, Jul. 26, 1971, 6.

40. SDDS, Jul. 28, 1971.

41. U.S. Emb. telegram, Jul. 31, 1971.

42. *Radio Comercial*, Jul. 22, 1971; *Radio Comercial*, Jul. 26, 1971; *Radio Continental*, Jul. 25, 1971.

43. *Listín*, Jul. 27, 1971, 5; *Listín*, Jul. 31, 1971, 2.

44. Interview.

45. *Radio Continental*, Jul. 25, 1971.

46. *Listín*, Jul. 31, 1971, 6A.

47. *Radio Comercial*, Aug. 2, 1971; *Listín*, Jul. 31, 1971, 2.

48. *Revista* (Aug. 1971), 23–24.

49. U.S. Emb. telegram, Aug. 9, 1971.

50. *Listín*, Aug. 5, 1971, 1.

51. U.S. Emb. telegram, Aug. 5, 1971.

52. Interview.

53. Peguero, "Trujillo and the Military," 323–334.

54. U.S. Emb. telegram, Aug. 9, 1971.

55. U.S. Emb. telegram, Aug. 10, 1971.

56. U.S. Emb. telegram, Aug. 10, 1971.

57. *Radio Comercial*, Aug. 10, 1971; U.S. Emb. telegram, Aug. 10, 1971.

58. *NY Times*, Aug. 28, 1971, 2.

59. *Radio Continental*, Aug. 8, 1971; *NY Times*, Aug. 28, 1971, 2.

60. *Radio Comercial*, Aug. 9, 1971.

61. *Radio Continental*, Aug. 15, 1971.

62. *Radio Continental*, Aug. 29, 1971.

63. *Washington Post*, Sep. 7, 1971, A1.

64. *Radio Comercial*, Sep. 11, 1971.

65. *Radio Clarín*, May 26, 1971; *Radio Comercial*, Jun. 8, 1971; *Radio Clarín*, Jun. 8, 1971; *Radio Comercial*, Jun. 17, 1971; *Radio Comercial*, Jul. 29, 1971.

66. *NY Times*, Aug. 28, 1971, 2; interview.

67. *Washington Post*, Sep. 7, 1971, A1, A16; *The Wall Street Journal*, Sep. 9, 1971, 1, 21.

68. *Listín*, Sep. 11, 1971, 1, 4; SDDS, Sep. 11, 1971.

69. *AFP*, Sep. 12, 1971; *Listín*, Sep. 13, 1971, 1, 4.

70. U.S. Emb. airgram, Oct. 1, 1971, 5.

71. Interviews.

72. O'Leary, "Strongman," A10; interview.

73. Bosch, *Professionalism*, 10; interviews.

74. *Listín*, Oct. 11, 1971, 1,4.

75. *AFP*, Oct. 12, 1971; *Radio Clarín*, Oct. 12, 1971; *Radio Clarín*, Oct. 13, 1971.

76. U.S. Emb. telegram, Oct. 14, 1971; *Radio Clarín*, Oct. 14, 1971.

77. Interview.

78. *Listín*, Sep. 22, 1971, 8A.

79. Interviews.

80. Interview.

81. U.S. Emb. telegram, Oct. 14, 1971; interview.

82. U.S. Department of State, Bureau of Intelligence and Research, Intelligence Note, Subject: *Dominican Republic: President Balaguer Outflanks his Critics* (Nov. 8, 1971), 1.

83. U.S. Emb. airgram, Dec. 10, 1971, 2.

CHAPTER X

1. Interviews; O'Leary, "Strongman," A10.

2. SDDS, Oct. 15, 1971; *Revista* (Oct. 1971), 6–7; *Listín*, Oct. 16, 1971, 2.

3. *Listín*, Oct. 18, 1971, 1.

4. *Listín*, Oct. 18, 1971, 1, 4; *Listín*, Oct. 19, 1971, 12.

5. *Listín*, Oct. 22, 1971, 1, 4.

6. SDDS, Oct. 21, 1971.

7. *Listín*, Oct. 22, 1971, 1; U.S. Emb. airgram, Oct. 22, 1971, 4.

8. Interview.

9. *Radio Comercial*, Oct. 19, 1971; *Listín*, Oct. 19, 1971, 1; *Listín*, Oct. 25, 1971, 13; *Listín*, Oct. 26, 1971, 13; *Radio Clarín*, Oct. 22, 1971.

10. Interviews.

11. Interviews.

12. *Listín*, Jan. 1, 1972, 15; *Revista* (Oct. 1971), 7; interview.

13. *Listín*, Oct. 19, 1971, 4; *Listín*, Aug. 2, 1972, 13.

14. *Listín*, Oct. 18, 1971, 1.

15. *Radio Comercial*, Oct. 21, 1971.

16. SDDS, Oct. 27, 1971; *Radio Cristal.* Oct. 30, 1971.

17. *Radio Comercial,* Nov. 4, 1971.

18. Atkins, *Arms and Politics,* 74.

19. *Listín,* Oct. 25, 1971, 13; *LATIN,* Oct. 23, 1971; interviews.

20. *Listín,* Jun. 30, 1972, 1, 4; *Radio Comercial,* Apr. 22, 1972.

21. Interview.

22. Official notation updating U.S. Department of the Army, U.S. Army South, *Biographic Data, Neit Nivar Seijas,* Mar. 1972, 4; interviews.

23. *Listín,* Oct. 7, 1972, 12.

24. O'Leary, "Strongman," A10.

25. SDDS, Oct. 21, 1971; *Radio Comercial,* Oct. 21, 1971; SDDS, Oct. 28, 1971; *Radio Comercial,* Oct. 29, 1971; U.S. Emb. airgram, Oct. 22, 1971, 1, 4.

26. *Radio Clarín,* Nov. 3, 1971; *Radio Clarín,* Nov. 30, 1971.

27. *Radio Clarín,* Oct. 26, 1971; *Radio Comercial,* Oct. 21, 1971.

28. *Radio Continental,* Oct. 31, 1971.

29. *Revista* (Sep.-Oct. 1956), 45.

30. USARSA Letter; interviews.

31. O'Leary, "Strongman," A10; Atkins, *Arms and Politics,* 74–75; DIA *Bio Sketch, Pérez y Pérez,* Sep. 1978, 1; interviews.

32. *Listín,* Nov. 9, 1971, 1.

33. *Listín,* Nov. 22, 1971, 1.

34. Interview.

35. *Listín,* Dec. 3, 1971, 12A.

36. *LATIN,* Jan. 5, 1972; *Radio Comercial,* Jan. 6, 1972; *Radio Continental,* Jan. 9, 1972.

37. *LATIN,* Jan. 9, 1972; *Radio Continental,* Jan. 9, 1972; *Listín,* Jan. 10, 1972, 1.

38. *Listín,* Jan. 13, 1972, 1, 4; *Listín,* Jan. 14, 1972, 1, 4; *El Caribe,* Jan. 14, 1972, 12.

39. *Listín,* Jan. 14, 1972, 14; *El Caribe,* Jan. 14, 1972, 12, 16.

40. *Listín,* Jan. 13, 1972, 1, 4; *El Caribe,* Jan. 13, 1972, 12; *Washington Post,* Jan. 13, 1972, A17.

41. *Listín,* Jan. 13, 1972, 4; *NY Times,* Jan. 13, 1972, 3; *Washington Post,* Jan. 13, 1972, A17; *El Caribe,* Jan. 13, 1972, 12, 14; interview.

42. *Listín,* Jan. 13, 1972, 4; *El Caribe,* Jan. 14, 1972, 16; interviews.

43. *Radio Clarín,* Jan. 12, 1972.

44. *Radio Clarín,* Jan. 12, 1972; *Listín,* Jan. 13, 1972, 4; *Listín,* Jan. 14, 1972, 14; *El Caribe,* Jan. 13, 1972, 12, 14; *El Caribe,* Jan. 14, 1972, 16.

45. Interview.

46. *Listín,* Jan. 13, 1972, 14.

47. Interviews.

48. *NY Times,* Jan. 13, 1972, 3.

49. *NY Times,* Jan. 13, 1972, 3; *Radio Comercial,* Jan. 12, 1972.

50. *Listín,* Jan. 13, 1972, 14; *Listín,* Jan. 14, 1972, 1; *El Caribe,* Jan. 14, 1972, 8.

51. U.S. Emb. airgram, Nov. 19, 1971, 3–4; SDDS, Nov. 15, 1971.

52. *Listín,* Nov. 15, 1971, 1.

53. Interviews.

54. U.S. Emb. airgram, Dec. 10, 1971, 3.

55. U.S. Emb. telegram, Apr. 21, 1972; *Radio Comercial,* Feb. 12, 1972; *Listín,* Feb. 22, 1972, 3; *Listín,* Mar. 8, 1972, 6; U.S. Emb. telegram, Apr. 24, 1972.

56. *Radio Comercial,* Apr. 4, 1972; *Radio Comercial,* Apr. 5, 1972.

57. *Listín,* Apr. 6, 1972, 1; *Listín,* Apr. 12, 1972, 3; *Radio Clarín,* Apr. 11, 1972; *Radio Comercial,* Apr. 12, 1972; *Radio Comercial,* Apr. 14, 1972; *Radio Cristal,* Apr. 15, 1972; SDDS, May 5, 1972.

58. U.S. Emb. telegram, Apr. 21, 1972.

59. *Radio Comercial,* Apr. 12, 1972.

60. *Radio Comercial,* Apr. 12, 1972.

61. *Radio Comercial,* Apr. 12, 1972.

62. *Revista* (Apr. 1972), 26–27.

63. *El Caribe,* Apr. 12, 1972, 1.

64. U.S. Emb. telegram, Jul. 25, 1972; interview.

65. U.S. Emb. airgram, May 5, 1972, 3; U.S. Emb. telegram, Jul. 25, 1972.

66. U.S. Emb. airgram, May 5, 1972, 3; *AFP,* Aug. 22, 1972.

67. U.S. Emb. telegram, Jul. 25, 1972.

68. U.S. Emb. telegram, Apr. 24, 1972.

69. U.S. Emb. airgram, May 5, 1972, 2–3; *Radio Comercial,* Apr. 27, 1972; *Radio Comercial,* Apr. 28, 1972.

70. U.S. Emb. airgram, May 5, 1972, 3.

71. *Listín,* Apr. 28, 1972, 13; *Listín,* Apr. 29, 1972, 13.

72. Interview.

73. *Listín,* May 23, 1972, 1; *Radio Clarín,* May 22, 1972.

74. *Revista* (Jan. 1972), 9–14; *Revista* (Aug. 1972), 13–15.

75. U.S. Emb. telegram, Jul. 25, 1972.

76. O'Leary, "Strongman," A10; interview.

77. *Listín,* Mar. 10, 1972, 13.

78. *Radio Clarín,* Mar. 9, 1972.

79. *Listín,* Sep. 11, 1972, 3.

80. *Listín,* Sep. 9, 1972, 9A.

81. U.S. Emb. telegram, Jan. 16, 1973; DIA *Bio Sketch, Nivar,* Apr. 1979, 2.

82. *Listín,* Oct. 17, 1972, 14; *Listín,* Oct. 18, 1972, 1; *Listín,* Oct. 19, 1972, 1, 14–15; *Radio Comercial,* Oct. 18, 1972; interview.

83. U.S. Emb. airgram, Jul. 29, 1972, 3; *Radio Continental,* Nov. 26, 1972.

84. U.S. Emb. telegram, Jan. 16, 1973.

85. *Radio Comercial,* Jul. 17, 1972.

86. *Radio Mil,* Dec. 26, 1972; *Listín,* Dec. 27, 1972, 1, 14; *Latin America* (Latin American Newsletters, Ltd., Jan. 19, 1973), LA VII, 18.

87. *Radio Mil,* Dec. 30, 1972; *Listín,* Dec. 30, 1972, 1.

CHAPTER XI

1. *AFP,* Jan. 5, 1973.
2. Juan Ventura, *Presidentes, Juntas, Consejos, Triunviratos, y Gabinetes de la República Dominicana, 1844–1984* (Santo Domingo: Publicaciones ONAP, 1985), 92 (hereafter cited as Ventura, *Presidentes*).
3. U.S. Emb. telegram, Jan. 16, 1973.
4. *Listín,* Jan. 5, 1973, 4.
5. "Presidencia de la República, 16 de enero 1968," in *Listín,* Jan. 16, 1968, 10–11.
6. Interview.
7. *Listín,* Jan. 11, 1973, 13; *Listín,* Feb. 6, 1973, 1; U.S. Emb. airgram, Jan. 30, 1973, 3–4; interviews.
8. Interviews.
9. *El Nacional,* Dec. 26, 1972, 1.
10. *Listín,* Apr. 5, 1972, 15; interviews.
11. *Listín,* Jan. 17, 1973, 12.
12. *Radio Continental,* May 28, 1972.
13. *Radio Comercial,* Jan. 12, 1970; *Listín,* Jan. 22, 1973, 10A; interviews.
14. Interviews.
15. U.S. Emb. telegram, Apr. 19, 1969.
16. U.S. Department of Defense message, Nov. 6, 1969.
17. U.S. Emb. telegram, Dec. 19, 1969; U.S. Emb. telegram, Sep. 30, 1970; U.S. Emb. telegram, Oct. 7, 1970; U.S. Emb. telegram, Oct. 14, 1970; U.S. Emb. telegram, Oct. 23, 1970.
18. U.S. Emb. telegram, Dec. 11, 1970.
19. *Revista* (Mar.-Apr. 1963), 28–32.
20. Tte. Coronel Piloto Rafael Antonio Reyes Jorge, "Una Exposición Beneficiosa," *Revista* (Oct.-Dec. 1966), 50.
21. *Revista* (Dec. 1972), 55–59; interview.

CHAPTER XII

1. Hermann, *Caamaño,* 24–32; Palmer, *Crisis of 1965,* 201-fn. 15; Alejandro Ovalles, *Caamaño, El Gobierno y las Guerrillas del 1973* (Santo Domingo: Taller de Impresiones, n.d), 65 (hereafter cited as Ovalles, *Guerrillas*).
2. *Revista* (Aug. 1961), 28.
3. Hermann, *Caamaño,* 79–80; U.S. Emb. telegram, Jul. 27, 1965.
4. Hermann, *Caamaño,* 83–91; Martin, *Events,* 303–305; *El Caribe,* Dec. 29, 1962, 1, 13; U.S. Emb. telegram, Jul. 26, 1965.
5. U.S. Emb. telegram, Jul. 27, 1965; *Listín,* Sep. 26, 1963, 8.
6. *Latin America* (Latin American Newsletters, Ltd., Feb. 23, 1973), LA VII, 57; Martin, *Events,* 594.
7. Fred Goff and Michael Klare, "How U.S. AID Shapes the Dominican Police,"

NACLA Newsletter, Vol. V, No. 2 (Apr. 1971), 19–28.
8. Hermann, *Caamaño,* 131; *El Caribe,* Nov. 26, 1965, 10; *Listín,* Jan. 14, 1965, 1, 4.
9. Martin, *Events,* 667; *Listín,* Jan. 14, 1965, 1; *El Caribe,* Feb. 9, 1966, 10.
10. Hermann, *Caamaño,* 131–132; *Emisoras Nacionales,* Jan. 19, 1965; *Listín,* Jan. 19, 1965, 1; *El Caribe,* Feb. 9, 1966, 10; Lowenthal, *Intervention,* 196-fn. 24; Martin, *Events,* 667; *Listín,* Feb. 17, 1965, 1, 4.
11. Martin, *Events,* 667.
12. U.S. Emb. telegram, Jul. 26, 1965; U.S. Emb. telegram, Jan. 31, 1966; Szulc, *Diary,* 170.
13. Palmer, *Crisis of 1965,* 112, 201-fn. 15.
14. Martin, *Events,* 670.
15. Palmer, *Crisis of 1965,* 91.
16. Martin, *Events,* 676.
17. *Testimony, Wessin y Wessin,* 189.
18. Palmer, *Crisis of 1965,* 80.
19. David Atlee Phillips, *The Night Watch* (New York: Ballantine Books, 1977), 191.
20. Szulc, *Diary,* 40–41, 135–136.
21. Yates, *Power Pack,* 46.
22. Gleijeses, *Crisis,* 252, 401-fn. 68.
23. Moreno, *Barrios,* 153–157.
24. Palmer, *Crisis of 1965,* 83–84.
25. Dominican Republic, "Act of Dominican Reconciliation," in *Testimony, Wessin y Wessin,* Appendix VI, 265–266; *Listín,* Jan. 24, 1966, 1.
26. Hermann, *Caamaño,* 345, 350; U.S. Emb., London, telegram, Mar. 23, 1966; U.S. Emb. airgram, Jun. 2, 1966, 11.
27. Interviews.
28. Hermann, *Caamaño,* 353–357; U.S. Emb., London, telegram, May 17, 1966; U.S. Emb., Madrid, airgram, Mar. 9, 1967, 1.
29. Hermann, *Caamaño,* 349-fn.; *Prensa Latina.* Mar. 25, 1966.
30. *Listín,* Aug. 22, 1968, 13.
31. *Radio Comercial,* Mar. 19, 1966.
32. *Radio Continental,* May 18, 1966; Hermann, *Caamaño,* 350; U.S. Emb., London, telegram, May 17, 1966.
33. U.S. Emb., London, telegram, May 17, 1966.
34. U.S. Emb., London, telegram, Jun. 8, 1966.
35. U.S. Emb. telegram, Jun. 1, 1966.
36. *Radio Continental,* Jul. 12, 1966.
37. Hermann, *Caamaño,* 359.
38. *Prensa Latina,* Jan. 24, 1967.
39. U.S. Emb., Paris, airgram, Dec. 13, 1967, 1.
40. *Radio HIN,* Apr. 25, 1967.
41. *Radio Comercial,* Jul. 3, 1967.
42. Hermann, *Caamaño,* 361–363.
43. *Onda Musical,* Aug. 15, 1967.
44. *Radio Comercial,* Nov. 23, 1967.

45. *Radio HIN,* Nov. 27, 1967.
46. U.S. Department of State, Bureau of Intelligence and Research, Intelligence Note, Subject: *Missing Dominican Rebel Leader May Be in Cuba* (Dec. 8, 1967), 2–3 (hereafter cited as State, INR, *Rebel Leader*).
47. *The Christian Science Monitor.* Aug. 1, 1969, 2.
48. Hermann, *Caamaño,* 368–369.
49. U.S. Emb., The Hague, telegram, Dec. 29, 1967.
50. State, INR, *Rebel Leader,* 2.
51. *Listín,* Nov. 23, 1967, 1, 4; *Radio Comercial,* Nov. 23, 1967; *Onda Musical,* Nov. 23, 1967.
52. Havana Domestic Service, Nov. 29, 1967.
53. *Radio HIN,* Nov. 27, 1967; *Listín,* Nov. 24, 1967, 1, 4.
54. *Radio HIN,* Nov. 27, 1967; *AFP,* Nov. 29, 1967; U.S. Emb., Paris, airgram, Dec. 13, 1967, 1, 3.
55. *Listín,* Nov. 24, 1967, 1.
56. *Radio HIN,* Nov. 27, 1967; *Radio Comercial,* Nov. 30, 1967; *Onda Musical,* Dec. 8, 1967.
57. *Radio HIN,* Nov. 27, 1967.
58. SDDS, Nov. 30, 1967.
59. *Radio Comercial,* Nov. 30, 1967.
60. *AFP,* Dec. 6, 1967.
61. *Radio HIN,* Dec. 19, 1967.
62. *Radio Continental,* Dec. 5, 1967.
63. State, INR, *Rebel Leader,* 2.
64. SDDS, Feb. 29, 1968; *AFP,* Mar. 4, 1968; *Radio Continental,* Mar. 4, 1968; *Reuters,* Mar. 5, 1968; *Radio Comercial,* Mar. 8, 1968; *Listín,* Mar. 5, 1968, 4.
65. SDDS, Mar. 5, 1968.
66. *Reuters,* Jan. 20, 1968.
67. *Radio Comercial,* Feb. 19, 1968.
68. SDDS, Feb. 26, 1968.
69. *Radio HIN,* Feb. 29, 1968.
70. *Listín,* Mar. 12, 1968, 4.
71. U.S. Emb. telegram, Mar. 12, 1968; *Radio Comercial,* Mar. 11, 1968.
72. *Radio Comercial,* Mar. 11, 1968.
73. *Radio Comercial,* Mar. 11, 1968.
74. *Listín,* Mar. 12, 1968, 4.
75. *AFP,* Apr. 12, 1968; *Listín,* Feb. 17, 1973, 14.
76. *Listín,* May 6, 1968, 11; *NY Times,* May 7, 1968, 17; *NY Times,* May 8, 1968, 3.
77. *Radio Comercial,* May 9, 1968.
78. *Radio HIN,* May 8, 1968.
79. SDDS, May 16, 1968.
80. *AFP,* May 17, 1968.
81. *La República,* Jun. 20, 1968, 20; *Radio Comercial,* Sep. 11, 1968; *Radio Comercial,* Nov. 11, 1968; *Listín,* Feb. 17, 1973, 14.
82. U.S. Congress, House of Representatives, Committee on Foreign Affairs, *The New Strategy of Communism in the Caribbean: Report of a Special Study Mission,* by the Hon. Armistead I. Selden, Jr., Chairman, Subcommittee on Inter-American Affairs, 90th Congress, 2nd Session, Nov. 2, 1968 (Washington, D.C.: Government Printing Office, 1968), 23.
83. *Radio Comercial,* Jan. 11, 1969; *Radio Comercial,* Jan. 13, 1969.
84. U.S. Emb. telegram, Jan. 15, 1969.
85. *El Tiempo,* Feb. 7, 1969, 1, 6.
86. *Radio Comercial,* Feb. 25, 1969.
87. *Radio HIN,* Jul. 28, 1969.
88. *Radio Comercial,* Apr. 10, 1969.
89. *Radio Comercial,* May 23, 1969.
90. *Listín,* Aug. 15, 1969, 1.
91. *Listín,* Aug. 15, 1969, 1, 4; *Listín,* Sep. 1, 1969, 14; *Listín,* Sep. 8, 1969, 12.
92. *The Christian Science Monitor.* Aug. 1, 1969, 2.
93. *Punto Final,* Mar. 17, 1970, 18.
94. Interview.
95. *AFP,* Jan. 24, 1971.
96. *Radio Comercial,* Jan. 30, 1971.
97. *Radio Continental,* Feb. 7, 1971.
98. *AFP,* Jan. 24, 1971.
99. *LATIN,* Jan. 19, 1973; *Listín,* Jan. 20, 1973, 1, 4.
100. *Radio Continental,* Jan. 21, 1973.
101. Hermann, *Caamaño,* 371–428; Emma Tavarez Justo, "La Vida de Caamaño en Cuba," *Ahora,* Jun. 4, 1973, 27–35.

CHAPTER XIII

1. Hamlet Hermann, *Caracoles: La Guerrilla de Caamaño* (Santo Domingo: Editora Alfa y Omega, 1980), 67–81 (hereafter cited as Hermann, *Caracoles*); *Ultima Hora,* Jun. 7, 1973, 4–5.
2. U.S. Defense Attaché Office, Santo Domingo, intelligence information message, IR68270038 73 (hereafter cited as DAO IR).
3. DAO IR6827003873; *El Caribe,* Feb. 6, 1973, 15.
4. DAO IR6827003873.
5. DAO IR6827003873.; *Radio Comercial,* Feb. 5, 1973; Hermann, *Caracoles,* 88–99, 107–109.
6. DAO IR6827003873.
7. DAO IR6827003873.
8. Major Brian J. Bosch, "The Caamano Expedition of 1973: Twilight of the Cuban Insurgency Doctrine?" *MI Magazine,* Vol. 1, N0.4 (Jan.-Feb.-Mar. 1975), 9 (hereafter cited as Bosch, "Caamaño Expedition").
9. U.S. Emb. telegram, Feb. 5, 1973.
10. U.S. Emb. telegram, Feb. 6, 1973.

11. *Radio Comercial,* Feb. 5, 1973.
12. *El Caribe,* Feb. 6, 1973, 15; SDDS, Feb. 6, 1973.
13. *Listín,* Dec. 13, 1963, 4; SDDS, Dec. 3, 1963; SDDS, Dec. 19, 1963.
14. *Listín,* Feb. 13, 1967, 1, 4; *Listín,* Feb. 16, 1967, 10; Major Brian J. Bosch, *Dominican Rural and Urban Ground Force Counterinsurgency Operations—A Military Assessment* (U.S. Embassy, Santo Domingo: U.S. Department of Defense Intelligence Information Report, DD Form 1396, Apr. 11, 1973), 5 (hereafter cited as Bosch, *Counterinsurgency Operations*).
15. DAO IR6827004473; Bosch, "Caamaño Expedition,"10.
16. *Listín,* Dec. 5, 1963, 1; *Listín,* May 22, 1967, 5; interviews.
17. DAO IR6827004473; DAO IR6827005073; Bosch, "Caamaño Expedition," 10.
18. U.S. Department of State telegram, Feb. 7, 1973.
19. DAO IR6827004473; DAO IR6827004973; Bosch, "Caamaño Expedition," 10.
20. DAO IR6827004673.
21. DAO IR6827004973.
22. U.S. Emb. telegram, Feb. 7, 1973; *Listín,* Feb. 7, 1973, 15.
23. Ovalles, *Guerrillas,* 103, 107–108.
24. *AFP,* Feb. 7, 1973.
25. DAO IR6827004673; DAO IR6827004973.
26. *Revista* (May 1972), 5–7.
27. DAO IR6827005573.
28. DAO IR6827005073.
29. *Listín,* Feb. 8, 1973, 1.
30. *Listín,* Dec. 11, 1963, 1; Hermann, *Caamaño,* 448; interview.
31. *Prensa Latina,* Jul. 15, 1968.
32. *Listín,* Dec. 16, 1968, 4, 10.
33. DAO IR6827020173.
34. Bosch, *Counterinsurgency Operations,* 4, 8; *Listín,* Feb. 8, 1973, 1.
35. Bosch, "Caamaño Expedition," 10.
36. DAO IR6827004973; DAO IR6827005073.
37. DAO IR6827005373; *El Caribe,* Feb. 17, 1973, 12.
38. SDDS, Feb. 8, 1973; U.S. Emb. telegram, Feb. 8, 1973.
39. U.S. Emb. telegram, Feb. 6, 1973.
40. U.S. Emb. telegram, Feb. 7, 1973; *Radio Mil,* Feb. 7, 1973.
41. U.S. Emb. telegram, Feb. 7, 1973.
42. Interview.
43. Bosch, *Counterinsurgency Operations,* 4, 6; U.S. Emb. telegram, Feb. 8, 1973; U.S. Emb. airgram, Feb. 9, 1973, 2; *Listín,* Feb. 9, 1973, 1, 4; *LATIN,* Feb. 8, 1973.

44. Major Brian J. Bosch, Memorandum, Subject: *Assessment* (Defense Attaché Office, Santo Domingo, Feb. 8, 1973).
45. *Listín,* Feb. 8, 1973, 15; *Radio Mil,* Feb. 8, 1973.
46. Interview.
47. *AFP,* Feb. 7, 1973; *Listín,* Feb. 7, 1973, 15; Hermann, *Caracoles,* 7.
48. U.S. Emb. telegram, Feb. 8, 1973.
49. Hermann, *Caracoles,* 8.
50. *Listín,* Feb. 13, 1967, 1, 4.
51. DAO IR6827004673.
52. *Listín,* Feb. 6, 1973, 15.
53. *Listín,* Feb. 8, 1973, 1.
54. DAO IR6827005173.
55. DAO IR6827005573.
56. U.S. Emb. telegram, Feb. 9, 1973.
57. DAO IR6827005173.
58. U.S. Emb. telegram, Feb. 9, 1973; *El Caribe,* Feb. 8, 1973, 17; *Listín,* Feb. 9, 1973, 14.
59. DAO IR6827005573.
60. DAO IR6827005173; DAO IR6827005573; U.S. Emb. telegram, Feb. 9, 1973.
61. SDDS, Feb. 8, 1973; *Listín,* Feb. 9, 1973, 1.
62. DAO IR6827005173.
63. Bosch, *Counterinsurgency Operations,* 3, 6.
64. Major Brian J. Bosch, *Captured Material of Guerrillas* (U.S. Embassy, Santo Domingo: U.S. Department of Defense Intelligence Information Report, DD Form 1396, Feb. 13, 1973), 1–2 (hereafter cited as Bosch, *Captured Material*); interview.
65. DAO IR6827006073; Bosch, *Captured Material,* 2.
66. Bosch, *Captured Material,* 3.
67. Bosch, *Captured Material,* 2.
68. *Listín,* Feb. 10, 1973, 1, 15; *AFP,* Feb. 10, 1973; Ovalles, *Guerrillas,* 123–125.
69. DAO IR6827005973.
70. DAO IR6827006173.
71. DAO IR6827006273.
72. DAO IR6827006273; DAO IR6827006373.
73. DAO IR6827006373; DAO IR6827006773; Hermann, *Caracoles,* 135.
74. U.S. Department of Defense, U.S. Southern Command message, Feb. 12, 1973 (hereafter cited as USSOUTHCOM, message).
75. USSOUTHCOM, message, Feb. 12, 1973.
76. USSOUTHCOM, message, Feb. 13, 1973; USSOUTHCOM, message, Feb. 12, 1973; U.S. Emb. telegram, Mar. 2, 1973.
77. *Listín,* Feb. 13, 1973, 1, 4, 14.
78. U.S. Emb. telegram, Feb. 13, 1973.
79. DAO IR6827006373.
80. DAO IR6827007173.
81. Bosch, "Caamaño Expedition," 10; Bosch, *Counterinsurgency Operations,* 4.

82. DAO IR6827006773; Bosch, "Caamaño Expedition," 10.
83. DAO IR6827004473.
84. DAO IR6827005573; *Listín*, Feb. 10, 1973, 14.
85. *Listín*, Feb. 15, 1973, 1,4; *Listín*, Feb. 16, 1973, 14; *Washington Post*, Feb. 16, 1973, A24; *LATIN*, Feb. 15, 1973.
86. *Radio Comercial*, Feb. 6, 1973.
87. DAO IR6827006873.
88. *La Noticia*, Jul. 1, 1973, 1,4.
89. Interview.
90. *Radio Comercial*, Feb. 7, 1973; *El Caribe*, Feb. 8, 1973, 8.
91. *AFP*, Feb. 7, 1973.
92. *Listín*, Feb. 8, 1973, 14.
93. *Radio Cristal.* Jun. 1, 1973.
94. *Listín*, Dec. 29, 1971, 14; *Listín*, Dec. 28, 1972, 4; U.S. Emb. telegram, Feb. 12, 1973; *LATIN*, Feb. 10, 1973.
95. Interview.
96. *Listín*, Feb. 12, 1973, 9A; *Radio Mil*, Feb. 12, 1973.
97. DAO IR6827006773; U.S. Emb. telegram, Feb. 13, 1973.
98. U.S. Emb. telegram, Feb. 14, 1973.
99. DAO IR6827006773; DAO IR6827007173.
100. DAO IR6827006773; DAO IR6827007373.
101. *Listín*, Feb. 15, 1973, 14.
102. DAO IR6827006373.
103. DAO IR6827007173; DAO IR6827007473.
104. Hermann, *Caracoles*, 147–150.
105. *Listín*, Feb. 19, 1973, 1.
106. U.S. Emb. telegram, Feb. 12, 1973; *AFP*, Feb. 13, 1973; Ovalles, *Guerrillas*, 133.

Chapter XIV

1. Hermann, *Caracoles*, 152.
2. *Ultima Hora*, Jun. 11, 1973, 5; *Listín*, Feb. 19, 1973, 15.
3. *Listín*, Feb. 19, 1973, 15; Ovalles, *Guerrillas*, 153.
4. *La Noticia*, Dec. 23, 1973, 13-C.
5. *Listín*, Feb. 19, 1973, 15.
6. Hermann, *Caracoles*, 150, 154; *Listín*, Feb. 19, 1973, 14.
7. *El Caribe*, Feb. 19, 1973, 1; Ovalles, *Guerrillas*, 81.
8. Hermann, *Caracoles*, 155.
9. Hermann, *Caracoles*, 155–156; DAO IR6827007873.
10. Hermann, *Caracoles*, 156–157, 160.
11. *Listín*, Feb. 17, 1973, 14.
12. SDDS, Feb. 17, 1973; *Listín*, Feb. 17, 1973, 14.
13. Interview.
14. *El Caribe*, Feb. 17, 1973, 1; *Listín*, Feb. 19, 1973, 1; *El Caribe*, Feb. 19, 1973, 12.
15. *El Caribe*, Feb. 19, 1973, 1; *LATIN*, Feb. 17, 1973; *The Miami Herald*, Feb. 18, 1973, 1.
16. *Listín*, Feb. 19, 1973, 1, 15.
17. DAO IR6827008173.
18. Bosch, *Counterinsurgency Operations*, 3.
19. Bosch, *Counterinsurgency Operations*, 3; interviews.
20. Bosch, *Counterinsurgency Operations*, 4; interviews.
21. DAO IR6827007973; DAO IR6827008273.
22. DAO IR6827007373; DAO IR6827008273.
23. DAO IR6827008173; DAO IR6827008273; interviews.
24. DAO IR6827008273.
25. U.S. Emb. telegram, Feb. 20, 1973; DAO IR6827007973; *EFE*, Feb. 17, 1973.
26. DAO IR6827008373; DAO IR6827008573; U.S. Emb. telegram, Feb. 22, 1973; *Listín*, Feb. 22, 1973, 1, 4.
27. *Listín*, Feb. 21, 1973, 1, 4, 14; U.S. Emb. telegram, Feb. 22, 1973; DAO IR6827008573; *LATIN*, Feb. 21, 1973.
28. Hermann, *Caracoles*, 7.
29. U.S. Emb. telegram, Feb. 20, 1973.
30. DAO IR6827008273; DAO IR6827008373; DAO IR6827008573; DAO IR6827008773; DAO IR6827009373.
31. DAO IR6827008373; DAO IR6827008773; DAO IR6827009673; DAO IR6827010273.
32. DAO IR6827008773.
33. DAO IR6827008773; DAO IR6827009373.
34. DAO IR6827008773.
35. DAO IR6827009373.
36. *Listín*, Feb. 24, 1973, 1, 14; *LATIN*, Feb. 23, 1973.
37. Ovalles, *Guerrillas*, 150–153; *Listín*, Feb. 24, 1973, 1.
38. *Listín*, Feb. 24, 1973, 12.
39. DAO IR6827009573; Hermann, *Caracoles*, 182–183.
40. DAO IR6827009573.
41. DAO IR6827009573; DAO IR6827010173.
42. DAO IR6827010173; *Listín*, Mar. 1, 1973, 1; *Listín*, Mar. 2, 1973, 1; *AFP*, Mar. 2, 1973; *LATIN*, Feb. 28, 1973.
43. Hermann, *Caracoles*, 184–185.
44. DAO IR6827010573.
45. Interview.
46. Bosch, *Counterinsurgency Operations*, 5; DAO IR6827010573.
47. Bosch, *Counterinsurgency Operations*, 4, 5; DAO IR6827010573.
48. Interviews.

49. DAO IR6827010273; DAO IR6827010673.
50. DAO IR6827010273.
51. DAO IR6827010573.
52. DAO IR6827010573.
53. DAO IR6827010773; *AFP,* Mar. 3, 1973; *LATIN,* Mar. 5, 1973; *Listín,* Mar. 5, 1973, 14; Ovalles, *Guerrillas,* 30.
54. *Listín,* Mar. 5, 1973, 14; Hermann, *Caracoles,* 8.
55. DAO IR6827010773.
56. DAO IR6827011773.
57. *Listín,* Mar. 6, 1973, 1, 2, 4; *Radio Mil,* Mar. 6, 1973.
58. Hermann, *Caracoles,* 7–8.
59. *Radio Cristal,* Mar. 8, 1973.
60. DAO IR6827010973.
61. *Listín,* Mar. 6, 1973, 1, 4.
62. DAO IR6827010273; *Radio Comercial,* Mar. 1, 1973.
63. DAO IR6827010673; interview.
64. U.S. Emb. telegram, Feb. 22, 1973; DAO IR6827008773; leaflet presumably distributed by the extreme left.
65. DAO IR6827010873; DAO IR6827011173; DAO IR6827011873; DAO IR6827012872.
66. DAO IR6827011573.
67. Interviews.
68. DAO IR6827011573.
69. DAO IR6827011573.
70. DAO IR6827011973.
71. Hermann, *Caracoles,* 197.
72. DAO IR6827012573.
73. Bosch, *Counterinsurgency Operations,* 3; DAO IR6827008973; DAO IR6827011373; DAO IR6827012573; DAO IR6827014273.
74. Major Brian J. Bosch, *The 10th Battalion During the Government Reaction to the Guerrilla Landing—An Example of Operations of a Dominican Army Unit in the Interior* (U.S. Embassy, Santo Domingo: U.S. Department of Defense Intelligence Information Report, DD Form 1396, Mar. 28, 1973), 1–2 (hereafter cited as Bosch, *10th Battalion*).
75. Bosch, *10th Battalion,* 2–3.
76. Bosch, *10th Battalion,* 3.
77. Bosch, *10th Battalion,* 3.
78. Bosch, *10th Battalion,* 4; DAO IR6827014273.
79. *Radio Mil,* Mar. 7, 1973.
80. *Revista* (Mar. 1973), 88–89.
81. *Listín,* Mar. 12, 1973, 2.
82. *AFP,* Mar. 13, 1973; *Radio Mil,* Mar. 13, 1973.
83. DAO IR6827012873.
84. *Listín,* Mar. 16, 1973, 1.
85. U.S. Emb. telegram, Mar. 16, 1973.
86. DAO IR6827011873.
87. DAO IR6827012873; DAO IR6827013573; *Listín,* Mar. 21, 1973, 3; *El Caribe,* Mar. 21, 1973, 9.
88. DAO IR6827010573; DAO IR6827010673; DAO IR6827012873; DAO IR6827013573; Bosch, *Counterinsurgency Operations,* 6.
89. Interview.
90. DAO IR6827012873.
91. DAO IR6827013573.
92. DAO IR6827013673.
93. DAO IR6827013173.
94. U.S. Emb. telegram, Feb. 13, 1973.
95. *Latin America* (Latin American Newsletters, Ltd., Apr. 20, 1973), LA VII, 121.
96. DAO IR6827013873; interview.
97. *El Caribe,* Mar. 21, 1973, 9.
98. *El Caribe,* Mar. 24, 1973, 19.
99. DAO IR6827010973.
100. DAO IR6827013873; DAO IR6827013173.

CHAPTER XV

1. DAO IR6827014173; Bosch, "Caamaño Expedition," 11; U.S. Emb. telegram, Mar. 23, 1973.
2. Hermann, *Caracoles,* 204, 217.
3. U.S. Emb. telegram, Mar. 26, 1973.
4. *Listín,* Mar. 24, 1973, 1, 14; *El Caribe,* Mar. 24, 1973, 19.
5. DAO IR6827014173.
6. *El Caribe,* Mar. 24, 1973, 19.
7. *El Caribe,* Mar. 24, 1973, 1; *Listín,* Mar. 24, 1973, 1, 4.
8. U.S. Emb. telegram, Mar. 26, 1973.
9. Hermann, *Caracoles,* 7.
10. Hermann, *Caracoles,* 8.
11. Hermann, *Caracoles,* 7; U.S. Emb. telegram, Mar. 26, 1973; *Listín,* Mar. 26, 1973, 15.
12. DAO IR6827014173.
13. DAO IR6827014173; DAO IR6827013573.
14. DAO IR6827015273.
15. DAO IR6827011573; DAO IR6827014673;DAO IR6827014973.
16. Hermann, *Caracoles,* 227–228; *Listín,* Mar. 26, 1973, 14; *El Caribe,* Mar. 26, 1973, 1.
17. Herman, *Caracoles,* 228–229; DAO IR6827014673.
18. Interviews.
19. Hermann, *Caracoles,* 230–231; *Listín,* Mar. 27, 1973,14; *El Caribe,* Mar. 27, 1973, 15.
20. *Listín,* Mar. 27, 1973, 14; *El Caribe,* Mar. 27, 1973, 15.
21. *El Caribe,* Mar. 27, 1973, 15.
22. U.S. Emb. telegram, Mar. 27, 1973.
23. *Listín,* Mar. 27, 1973, 1, 14; U.S. Emb. telegram, Mar. 27, 1973.

24. Hermann, *Caracoles*, 173, 176–177, 233.

25. Hermann, *Caracoles*, 233; *Listín*, Mar. 29, 1973, 1; *El Caribe*, Mar. 29, 1973, 1, 12.

26. Hermann, *Caracoles*, 8.

27. Hermann, *Caracoles*, 233–234.

28. DAO   IR6827014673;   DAO IR6827014973.

29. DAO   IR6827014673;   DAO IR6827014973; DAO IR6827015873; *Listín*, Mar. 27, 1973, 4.

30. U.S. Emb. airgram, Apr. 6, 1973, 2; *El Caribe*, Mar. 28, 1973, 1.

31. U.S. Emb. telegram, Mar. 27, 1973; *Listín*, Mar. 28, 1973, 1.

32. DAO IR6827010973.

33. DAO IR6827015273.

34. U.S. Emb. airgram, Apr. 6, 1973, 2.

35. Balaguer, *Memorias*, 281.

36. *Listín*, Mar. 29, 1973, 14; *El Caribe*, Mar. 29, 1973, 12.

37. *Listín*, Mar. 30, 1973, 1, 2.

38. *El Caribe*, Mar. 30, 1973, 20.

39. Interviews.

40. *Latin America* (Latin American Newsletters, Ltd., Apr. 20, 1973), LA VII, 121.

41. *Listín*, Apr. 3, 1973, 1; Atkins, *Arms and Politics*, 77.

42. *Listín*, Apr. 4, 1973, 1, 2, 4, 11.

43. *Listín*, Apr. 6, 1973, 1, 14; *Radio Comercial*, Apr. 6, 1973.

44. U.S. Emb. airgram, Apr. 6, 1973, 1–3.

45. *Listín*, Apr. 10, 1973, 1.

46. U.S. Emb. airgram, Apr. 20, 1973, 2.

47. *La Noticia*. Dec. 23, 1973, 14C; *AFP*, Apr. 11, 1973.

48. U.S. Emb. airgram, Apr. 20, 1973, 2.

49. *Listín*, Apr. 17, 1973, 1, 2.

50. *Listín*, Apr. 17, 1973, 4; interview.

51. U.S. Emb. airgram, Apr. 6, 1973, 3; *Listín*, May 29, 1973, 15; *Listín*, May 31, 1973, 7A.

52. DAO IR6827014973; *AFP*, Mar. 31, 1973; *Listín*, Mar. 29, 1973, 4; *Listín*, Mar. 31, 1973, 12; *El Caribe*, Mar. 30, 1973, 1.

53. *Listín*, Apr. 3, 1973, 1; *Radio Comercial*, Apr. 3, 1973.

54. DAO IR6827016773.

55. Interview.

56. *Ultima Hora*, Jun. 8, 1973, 3.

57. U.S. Emb. telegram, Apr. 18, 1973; *Listín*, Apr. 18, 1973, 1.

58. Hermann, *Caracoles*, 236–237.

59. Interview.

60. Hermann, *Caracoles*, 237.

61. DAO IR6827020273.

62. U.S. Emb. telegram, Apr. 26, 1973.

63. U.S. Emb. telegram, May 9, 1973; *Listín*, May 8, 1973, 12–13.

64. U.S. Emb. telegram, May 9, 1973.

65. U.S. Emb. telegram, May 9, 1973.

66. U.S. Emb. telegram, Apr. 18, 1973.

67. *El Caribe*, Apr. 24, 1973, 1.

68. *Listín*, Apr. 28, 1973, 1,13.

69. *Radio Continental*, Apr. 29, 1973.

70. U.S. Emb. telegram, May 9, 1973.

71. Interviews.

72. *El Caribe*, May 19, 1973, 1.

73. Extract of G-1, Army General Staff, document.

74. *El Caribe*, May 19, 1973, 8.

75. *El Caribe*, May 19, 1973, 1, 8.

76. *El Caribe*, May 19, 1973, 8; *Revista* (Jun. 1973), 91–93.

77. DAO IR6827020273.

78. *AFP*, Apr. 19, 1973.

79. *Radio Mil*, May 18, 1973; *Listín*, May 18, 1973, 15.

80. *Listín*, May 28, 1973, 1.

81. *El Nacional*, May 28, 1973, 1.

82. *Listín*, Jun. 4, 1973, 1, 4.

83. *Ultima Hora*, Jun. 6, 1973, 2.

84. *Listín*, Jun. 5, 1973, 4; *Prensa Latina*, Jun. 5, 1973; *El Nacional*, Jun. 14, 1974, 2.

85. *Radio Comercial*, Mar. 27, 1973.

86. U.S. Emb. telegram, May 9, 1973.

87. *Ultima Hora*, Jun. 4, 1973, 4.

88. *Listín*, May 19, 1973, 12.

89. *Listín*, May 26, 1973, 13B.

90. *Radio HIN*, Jun. 8, 1973.

91. *Ultima Hora*, Jun. 8, 1973, 7; SDDS, Jun. 9, 1973.

92. *Listín*, Jul. 3, 1973, 13; *Listín*, Jul. 4, 1973, 1, 4.

93. *Radio Mil*, Jul. 5, 1973.

94. *El Nacional*, Sep. 18, 1973, 1–2.

95. Carmelo Mesa-Lago, *Cuba in the 1970s: Pragmatism and Institutionalization*, 2nd ed. (Albuquerque: University of New Mexico Press, 1978), 116–117.

96. Gleijeses, *Crisis*, 415-fn. 34.

97. Interviews.

98. *The Christian Science Monitor*, Aug. 1, 1969, 2.

99. Georges Fauriol, Editor, *Latin American Insurgencies* (Washington, D.C.: The Center for Strategic and International Studies, Georgetown University, 1985), 132–133 (hereafter cited as Fauriol, *Latin American*).

100. Fauriol, *Latin American*, 14–15.

101. *Revolutionary Nationalism Network*, Jan. 13, 1972.

102. *AFP*, Apr. 19, 1973.

103. *Ultima Hora*, Jun. 6, 1973, 2.

104. Interview.

105. Robert Taber, *The War of the Flea: A Study of Guerrilla Warfare, Theory and Practice* (London: Paladin, 1970), 27–44.

106. *Listín*, Feb. 7, 1973, 15; *Ultima Hora*, Jun. 7, 1973, 4, 12.

107. *Ultima Hora,* Jun. 6, 1973, 2; *Ultima Hora,* Jun. 11, 1973, 4; *La Noticia,* Jul. 29, 1974, 1, 11.

108. *Ultima Hora,* Jun. 8, 1973, 2.

109. Bosch, *Counterinsurgency Operations.*

110. Bosch, *Counterinsurgency Operations,* 1–9.

111. Bosch, *Counterinsurgency Operations,* 1.

112. Bosch, *Counterinsurgency Operations,* 2–3.

113. Bosch, *Counterinsurgency Operations,* 8–9.

114. Bosch, *Counterinsurgency Operations,* 3.

115. Bosch, *Counterinsurgency Operations,* 4.

116. Bosch, *Counterinsurgency Operations,* 5.

117. Bosch, *Counterinsurgency Operations,* 6–7.

118. Bosch, *Counterinsurgency Operations,* 5–6, 9.

119. Bosch, *Counterinsurgency Operations,* 7.

120. *La Noticia.* Mar. 1, 1974, 1, 4.

CHAPTER XVI

1. *Listín,* Apr. 18, 1973, 11A.

2. *Listín,* Apr. 24, 1973, 4.

3. Bosch, *Counterinsurgency Operations,* 8.

4. Interview.

5. *La Noticia,* Jul. 1, 1973, 1, 4.

6. See Chapters II and V.

7. Interview.

8. DAO IR6827015873.

9. Interview; *El Nacional,* Oct. 18, 1973, 1, 12.

10. Atkins, *Arms and Politics,* 78, 82; *Revista* (Jun. 1974), 96–97; *Revista* (Jan. 1974), 90; *Listín,* Apr. 23, 1974, 1.

11. USSOUTHCOM *Bio Data, Nivar,* Sep. 1974, 3; interviews.

12. Hartlyn, *Democratic Politics,* 113.

13. Atkins, *Arms and Politics,* 79–80; interviews.

14. *Latin America* (Latin American Newsletters, Ltd., May 16, 1975), LA IX, 149.

15. Atkins, *Arms and Politics,* 82.

16. *Listín,* May 8, 1975, 1; Atkins, *Arms and Politics,* 82.

17. *Listín,* May 9, 1975, 1, 4; *El Caribe,* May 9, 1975, 15.

18. *El Caribe,* May 12, 1975, 1.

19. Atkins, *Arms and Politics,* 83.

20. Atkins, *Arms and Politics,* 83; *LATIN,* May 10, 1975; *El Caribe,* May 12, 1975, 1; *Listín,* May 12, 1975, 3, 14.

21. *Revista* (Jul. 1973), 70.

22. *Revista* (Jul. 1971), 39.

23. *El Caribe,* May 12, 1975, 1.

24. *Revista* (May 1975), 45–46.

25. *Listín,* May 12, 1975, 14.

26. *Listín,* May 12, 1975, 14; *El Caribe,* May 12, 1975, 1, 12.

27. *LATIN,* May 10, 1975; Atkins, *Arms and Politics,* 84.

28. *Listín,* May 12, 1975, 14; *El Caribe,* May 12, 1975, 12; Atkins, *Arms and Politics,* 84.

29. *Listín,* May 12, 1975, 14; *El Caribe,* May 12, 1975, 12.

30. SDDS, May 12, 1975.

31. *Listín,* May 12, 1975, 8A.

32. *El Caribe,* May 12, 1975, 1; *Listín,* May 12, 1975, 14.

33. *Listín,* May 12, 1975, 15.

34. *Revista* (May 1975), 45–47; *Listín,* May 13, 1975, 1; *El Caribe,* May 13, 1975, 1.

35. *Listín,* Jun. 3, 1975, 1, 4.

36. *Listín,* Jun. 4, 1975, 1.

37. Atkins, *Arms and Politics,* 84; *Listín,* May 15, 1975, 3; interviews.

38. *Radio Clarín,* May 13, 1975; *El Caribe,* May 14, 1975, 9.

39. *Latin America* (Latin American Newsletters, Ltd., May 16, 1975), LA IX, 149.

40. Atkins, *Arms and Politics,* 102–103.

41. Balaguer, *Memorias,* 273–274.

42. Atkins, *Arms and Politics,* 87, 109–110.

43. *Latin American Political Report* (Latin American Newsletters, Ltd., Jun. 2, 1978), LAPR XII, 166; Atkins, *Arms and Politics,* 111.

44. Atkins, *Arms and Politics,* 107.

45. Atkins, *Arms and Politics,* 119.

46. Atkins, *Arms and Politics,* 120.

47. Atkins, *Arms and Politics,* 120–121, 141–142.

48. *Revista* (Aug.-Nov. 1978), 58–61; Hartlyn, *Democratic Politics,* 127.

49. *Revista* (Aug.-Nov. 1978), 65–70.

50. *Revista* (Feb.-Mar. 1979), 106–107; Atkins, *Arms and Politics,* 137, 142.

51. *Facts on File World News Digest* (Facts on File, Inc., Oct. 13, 1978), 774; *Revista* (Aug.-Nov. 1978), 58.

52. *Latin American Political Report* (Latin American Newsletters, Ltd., Oct. 13, 1978), LAPR XII, 319.

53. *Latin American Political Report* (Latin American Newsletters, Ltd., Nov. 17, 1978), LAPR XII, 354.

54. *Latin American Political Report* (Latin American Newsletters, Ltd., Nov. 24, 1978), LAPR XII, 363.

55. *Latin American Political Report* (Latin American Newsletters, Ltd., Nov. 24, 1978), LAPR XII, 363; interview.

56. Atkins, *Arms and Politics,* 139.

CHAPTER XVII

1. Atkins, *Arms and Politics*, 110.
2. Interviews.
3. DIA *Bio Sketch, Nivar*. Apr. 1979, 5.
4. Interview.
5. Atkins, *Arms and Politics*, 137.
6. *Listín*, Feb. 28, 1980, 1–2.
7. *Listín*, Feb. 8, 1982, 1, 13; *El Caribe*, Feb. 9, 1982, 1, 4A-5A.
8. Interview.
9. *Latin American Political Report* (Latin American Newsletters, Ltd., Nov. 17, 1978), LAPR XII, 354.
10. *Washington Post*, Aug. 5, 2000, A14.
11. *BBC Summary of World Broadcasts* (The British Broadcasting Corporation, Jun. 19, 1993), Part 4.
12. *United Press International* (UPI International Section, Jun. 11, 1996).
13. *BBC Summary of World Broadcasts* (The British Broadcasting Corporation, Oct. 31, 1996), Part 5.
14. *Noticias Dominicanas* (Santo Domingo: Servicio informativo con noticias de la República Dominicana, Nov. 12, 1996), 1; *D.R. Week in Review* (Mar. 21–27, 1997).
15. *Listín*, Feb. 28, 1980, 1.
16. *Revista* (Feb.-Mar. 1979), 102.
17. Castleman, Letter, Oct. 26, 1998, 1.
18. Atkins, *Arms and Politics*, 140.
19. Interview.
20. *El Caribe*, May 13, 1975, 1; *Latin American Political Report* (Latin American Newsletters, Ltd., Nov. 17, 1978), LAPR XII, 354; *Listín*, Dec. 31, 1977, 1, 13.
21. See Chapter II.
22. *Revista* (Jun.-Jul. 1977), 77–79.
23. *Revista* (Aug.-Nov. 1978), 73–75; *Revista* (Sep.-Oct. 1983), 66; *Revista* (Jul.-Sep. 1984), 71; *Listín*, Aug. 18, 1984, 1.
24. Atkins, *Arms and Politics*, 138.
25. Atkins, *Arms and Politics*, 139; interviews.
26. Atkins, *Arms and Politics*, 70–71.
27. *Listín*, Aug. 17, 1978, 15.
28. *El Nacional*, Apr. 24, 1983, 5-B; *Listín*, Aug. 18, 1984, 15; interview.
29. Ventura, *Presidentes*, 112–113; *El Nacional*, Apr. 24, 1983, 5-B.
30. *El Nacional*, Apr. 24, 1983, 5-B.
31. Wiarda, *Control*, 34.
32. See Chapter III.
33. Balaguer, *Memorias*, 273.
34. Balaguer, *Memorias*, 412.
35. Balaguer, *Memorias*, 411.
36. U.S. Emb. telegram, May 4, 1967, paragraph 2.
37. U.S. Emb. telegram, May 4, 1967, paragraph 9.
38. U.S. Emb. telegram, May 4, 1967, paragraph 10.

Bibliography

BOOKS, ARTICLES, AND REPORTS

Ameringer, Charles D., *The Caribbean Legion: Patriots, Politicians, Soldiers of Fortune, 1946–1950.* University Park: The Pennsylvania State University Press, 1996.

Angulo, Liliano. "Escuela para Oficiales Celebra 3ra Promoción." *Revista de las Fuerzas Armadas.* Dec. 1968.

_____. "Marina de Guerra, Una Profesión Honorable." *Revista de las Fuerzas Armadas.* Sep. 1972.

Arciniegas, Nelson. "La Escuela Naval y su Historia." *Revista de las Fuerzas Armadas.* May 1974.

_____. "Ingeniero Naval Contreras Peña Ofrece Declaraciones a Revista Militar." *Revista de las Fuerzas Armadas.* Mar. 1971.

_____. "Trayectoria de la Fuerza Aérea Dominicana." *Revista de las Fuerzas Armadas.* Jun. 1974.

Atkins, G. Pope. *Arms and Politics in the Dominican Republic.* Boulder, Colorado: Westview Press, 1981.

Atkins, G. Pope, and Larman C. Wilson. *The United States and the Trujillo Regime.* New Brunswick, New Jersey: Rutgers University Press, 1972.

Báez Berg, Fidel, Tte. Coronel. "Progreso en las Fuerzas Armadas." *Revista de las Fuerzas Armadas.* Dec. 1973.

Balaguer, Joaquín. *Memorias de un Cortesano de la "Era de Trujillo."* Madrid: G. del Toro, 1989.

Barquín, Ramón M., Coronel. *Las Luchas Guerrilleras en Cuba: De la Colonia a la Sierra Maestra.* 2 Vols. Madrid: Editorial Playor, S.A., 1975.

BBC Summary of World Broadcasts. The British Broadcasting Corporation. Part 4, Jun. 19, 1993.

Beaulac, Willard L., et al. *Dominican Action–1965: Intervention or Cooperation?* The Center for Strategic Studies. Washington, D.C.: Georgetown University, Jul. 1966.

Bell, Ian. *The Dominican Republic.* Boulder, Colorado: Westview Press, 1981.

Bosch, Brian J. Major. "The Caamano Expedition of 1973: Twilight of the Cuban Insurgency Doctrine?" *MI Magazine.* Vol. 1, No. 4, Jan.-Feb.-Mar. 1975.

_____. *Captured Material of Guerrillas.* U.S. Department of Defense Intelligence Information Report (DD Form 1396). U.S.Embassy, Santo Domingo, Feb. 13, 1973.

_____. *Dominican Rural and Urban Ground Force Counterinsurgency Operations—A Military Assessment.* U.S. Department of Defense Intelligence Information Report (DD Form 1396). U.S. Embassy, Santo Domingo, Apr. 11, 1973.

_____. Memorandum, Subject: *Assessment.* Defense Attaché Office, Santo Domingo, Feb. 8, 1973.

_____. Memorandum, Subject: *The Plight of Military Professionalism in the Dominican Republic.* Defense Attaché Office, Santo Domingo, Jan. 9, 1973.

_____. *New Armor Order of Battle and Political Significance.* U.S. Department of Defense Intelligence Information Report (DD Form 1396). U.S. Embassy, Santo Domingo, Feb. 22, 1971.

_____. *Order of Battle Summary, Foreign Ground Forces.* U.S. Department of Defense Intelligence Information Report (DD Form 1396). U.S. Embassy, Santo Domingo, Jul. 28, 1971.

_____. *The Salvadoran Officer Corps and the Final Offensive of 1981.* Jefferson, North Carolina: McFarland, 1999.

_____. *The 10th Battalion During the Government Reaction to the Guerrilla Landing—An Example of Operations of a Dominican Army Unit in the Interior.* U.S. Department of Defense Intelligence Information Report (DD Form 1396). U.S. Embassy, Santo Domingo, Mar. 28, 1973.

Bosch, Juan. *The Unfinished Experiment: Democracy in the Dominican Republic.* New York: Frederick A. Praeger, 1965.

Brugal Alfau, Danilo. *Tragedia en Santo Domingo (Documentos para la Historia).* Santo Domingo: Editora del Caribe, 1966.

Caamaño Grullón, Claudio. Interview. *Ultima Hora.* Jun. 6, 7, 8, 1973.

Calder, Bruce J. *The Impact of Intervention: The Dominican Republic during the U.S. Occupation of 1916–1924.* Austin: University of Texas Press, 1984.

Camper, William C., Lt. Col. (ret). Letter. Apr. 24, 1999.

Castillo Pimentel, Carlos Antonio, Capitán. "Escuela para Oficiales y sus Proyecciones Futuras." *Revista de las Fuerzas Armadas.* Sep. 1968.

Castleman, Stanley A., Lt. Col. (ret). Letters. Oct. 26, 1998, Dec. 16, 1999, and Sep. 14, 2000.

Clark, James A. *The Church and the Crisis in the Dominican Republic.* Westminster, Maryland: Newman, 1967.

Crassweller, Robert D. *Trujillo: The Life and Times of a Caribbean Dictator.* New York: Macmillan, 1966.

Cruz Brea, José Ernesto, Tte. Coronel. "Las Unidades Blindadas en la Segunda Guerra Mundial." *Revista de las Fuerzas Armadas.* Jan. 1969.

Cuervo Gómez, Manuel Antonio, Coronel, "Breves Comentarios Sobre el Estado Mayor." *Revista de las Fuerzas Armadas.* Jun. 1972.

_____.Coronel. "Características y Misiones de la Caballería Blindada." *Revista de las Fuerzas Armadas.* Sep. 1972.

_____, Coronel. "Razonamiento Sobre el Problema de la Justicia." *Revista de las Fuerzas Armadas.* Jul. 1973.

_____, Coronel de Estado Mayor. "La Artillería es por Excelencia, El Arma del Fuego, Constituyendo en la Batalla un Medio Esencial de Destrucción." *Revista de las Fuerzas Armadas.* Oct. 1968.

_____, General de Brigada. "Guerra Subversiva y Revolucionaria." *Revista de las Fuerzas Armadas.* Dec. 1973.

_____, Tte. Coronel de Blindados. "Estado Mayor y Proceso de la Decisión." *Revista de las Fuerzas Armadas.* Oct.-Dec. 1966.

Díaz, Porfirio Alejandro, Mayor. "Que es el Comando de Escuelas, Ejército Nacional." *Revista de las Fuerzas Armadas.* Jul. 1971.

Diederich, Bernard. *Trujillo: The Death of the Goat.* Boston: Little, Brown, 1978.

Dominican Republic. "Act of Dominican Reconciliation." In U.S. Congress, Senate, Committee on the Judiciary, Subcommittee to Investigate the Administration of the Internal Security Act and Other Internal Security Laws. *Communist Threat to the U.S. Through the Caribbean: Testimony of Brigadier General Elias Wessin y Wessin.* Appendix VI, 89th Congress, 1st Session, Oct. 1, 1965. Washington, D.C.: Government Printing Office, 1965.

Dominican Republic. "Institutional Act." In U.S. Congress, Senate, Committee on the Judiciary, Subcommittee to Investigate the Administration of the Internal Security Act and Other Internal Security Laws. *Communist Threat to the U.S. Through the Caribbean: Testimony of Brigadier General Elias Wessin y Wessin.* Appendix VI, 89th Congress, 1st Session, Oct. 1, 1965. Washington, D.C.: Government Printing Office, 1965.

Dominican Republic. *Reglamento de Uniformes.* Ciudad Trujillo: Roques Román, C. por A., n.d.

Dominican Republic. Centro de Enseñanza de las Fuerzas Armadas (CEFA). *Libro Blanco de las Fuerzas Armadas y de la Policía Nacional de la República Dominicana.* Santo Domingo: Editora del Caribe, C. por A., 1964.

Dominican Republic. Secretaría de Estado de las Fuerzas Armadas Dominicanas. *Revista de las Fuerzas Armadas.* 1952–1988. (Formerly *Revista Militar.*)

Dominican Republic Week in Review. Mar. 21–27, 1997.

Draper, Theodore. *The Dominican Revolt: A Case Study in American Policy.* New York: Commentary, 1968.

El Salvador. Estado Mayor General de la Fuerza Armada. "Historia del Estado Mayor General de la Fuerza Armada." *Revista de la Fuerza Armada.* Jan.-Feb.-Mar. 1979.

English, Adrian J. *Armed Forces of Latin America: Their Histories, Development, Present Strength and Military Potential.* London: Jane's, 1984.

Espaillat, Arturo R. *Trujillo: The Last Caesar.* Chicago: Regnery, 1963.

Facts on File World News Digest. Facts on File, Oct. 13, 1978.

Fauriol, Georges, editor. *Latin American Insurgencies.* The Center for Strategic and International Studies. Washington, D.C.: Georgetown University, 1985.

Ferreras, Ramón Alberto. *Guerra Patria.* n.p., 1966.

Floyd, Troy S. *The Columbus Dynasty in the Caribbean, 1492–1526.* Albuquerque: University of New Mexico Press, 1973.

Fuller, Stephen M., Captain, USMCR, and Graham A. Cosmas. *Marines in the Dominican Republic, 1916–1924.* History and Museums Division. Washington, D.C.: Headquarters, U.S. Marine Corps, 1974.

Gall, Norman. "The Only Logical Answer." *Fieldstaff Reports.* Vol. VI, No. 1, Jun. 1971.

García Recio, Luis Ney, Tte. Coronel. "La Academia Militar 'Batalla de las Carreras' y su Aporte al Ejército Nacional." *Revista de las Fuerzas Armadas.* Oct. 1968.

Gleijeses, Piero. *The Dominican Crisis: The 1965 Constitutionalist Revolt and American Intervention.* Translated by Lawrence Lipson. Baltimore: Johns Hopkins University Press, 1978.

Goff, Fred, and Michael Klare. "How U.S. AID Shapes the Dominican Police." *NACLA Newsletter.* Vol. V, No. 2, Apr. 1971.

Goldwert, Marvin. *The Constabulary in the Dominican Republic and Nicaragua: Progeny and Legacy of United States Intervention.* Gainesville: University of Florida Press, 1962.

Grayson, George W., Jr. "Peru's Military Government." *Current History.* Vol. 58, No. 342, Feb. 1970.

Greenberg, Lawrence M., Major. *United States Army Unilateral and Coalition Operations in the 1965 Dominican Republic Intervention.* Washington, D.C.: U.S. Army Center of Military History, Analysis Branch, 1987.

Grimaldi, Víctor. "Fidel Habla de Caamaño." *La Noticia.* Jul. 29, 1974.

Gutiérrez, Carlos María. *The Dominican Republic: Rebellion and Repression.* Translated by Richard E. Edwards. New York: Monthly Review Press, 1972.

Halle, Armin. *Tanks: An Illustrated History of Fighting Vehicles.* Greenwich, Connecticut: New York Graphic Society, 1971.

Hartlyn, Jonathan. *The Struggle for Democratic Politics in the Dominican Republic.* Chapel Hill: The University of North Carolina Press, 1998.

Hermann, Hamlet. *Caracoles: La Guerrilla de Caamaño.* Santo Domingo: Editora Alfa y Omega, 1980.

_____.*Francis Caamaño.* Santo Domingo: Editora Alfa y Omega, 1983.

_____.Interview. *Ultima Hora.* Jun. 6, 11, 1973.

Hicks, Albert C. *Blood in the Streets: The Life and Rule of Trujillo.* New York: Creative Age, 1946.

Hogg, Ian V. *British and American Artillery of World War 2.* London: Arms and Armour, 1978.

Icks, Robert J., Lt. Col. *Tanks and Armored Vehicles.* New York: Duell, Sloan and Pearce, 1945.

Inter-American Defense College. *Inter-American Defense College.* Pamphlet, n.d.

Inter-American Defense College. *Revista del Colegio Interamericano.* Vol. XIII, No. 1, 1986.

Jane's Armour and Artillery, 1979–1980. Edited by Christopher F. Foss. London: Jane's, 1979.

Jane's Fighting Ships, 1972–1973. Edited by Raymond V.B. Blackman. New York: McGraw-Hill, 1972.

Johnson, Robert Erwin. *Guardians of the Sea: History of the United States Coast Guard, 1915 to the Present.* Annapolis: Naval Institute Press, 1987.

Kurzman, Dan. *Santo Domingo: Revolt of the Damned.* New York: Putnam, 1965.

Latin America. Latin American Newsletters, Ltd. (after Jan. 1977, *Latin America Political Report.*)

Lombraña, Ildefonso, Jr., Lt. Col. (ret). Personal papers. Four sections, 1962–1965.

Lowenthal, Abraham F. *The Dominican Intervention.* Cambridge: Harvard University Press, 1972.

_____. "The Dominican Republic: The Politics of Chaos." In *Reform and Revolution: Readings in Latin American Politics.* Edited by Arpad von Lazar and Robert R. Kaufman. Boston: Allyn and Bacon, 1969.

_____. "The Political Role of the Dominican Armed Forces: A Note on the 1963 Overthrow of Juan Bosch and on the 1965 Dominican 'Revolution.'" *Journal of Interamerican Studies and World Affairs.* Vol. 15, No. 3, Aug. 1973.

Macaulay, Neill. *The Prestes Column: Revolution in Brazil.* New York: New Viewpoints, 1974.

MacDougall, A. Kent. "Caribbean Terror." *The Wall Street Journal.* Sep. 9, 1971.

Martin, John Bartlow. *Overtaken by Events: The Dominican Crisis from the Fall of Trujillo to the Civil War.* Garden City, New York: Doubleday, 1966.

Matos González, Ramiro, Coronel. "Curso Elemental de Lectura de Cartas." *Revista de las Fuerzas Armadas.* Aug.-Sep.-Oct. 1970.

McAlister, Lyle N. *The "Fuero Militar" in New Spain, 1764–1800.* Gainesville: University of Florida Press, 1957.

Medrano Ubiera, Pedro. Coronel DEM. "Don de Mando." *Revista de las Fuerzas Armadas.* May-Jun.-Jul.-Aug. 1969.

Mendoza Morales, Eduardo Ernesto, Mayor. "Reseña Histórica, Escuela de Comando y Estado Mayor 'Dr. Manuel Enrique Araujo.'" *Revista Docente.* No. II, Sep. 1995.

Mesa-Lago, Carmelo. *Cuba in the 1970s: Pragmatism and Institutionalization.* 2nd ed. Albuquerque: University of New Mexico Press, 1978.

Meza Gallont, Rafael. *El Ejército de El Salvador.* San Salvador: Imprenta Nacional, 1964.

The Military Balance, 1973–1974. London: International Institute for Strategic Studies, 1974.

Moreno, José A. *Barrios in Arms: Revolution in Santo Domingo.* Pittsburgh: University of Pittsburgh Press, 1970.

Noboa Leyba, Diógenes. Segundo Teniente. "El Soldado, Futuro Oficial." *Revista Militar.* Oct. 1948.

Noticias Dominicanas. Servicio informativo con noticias de la República Dominicana. Santo Domingo, Nov. 12, 1996.

Nunn, Frederick M. "Professional Militarism in Twentieth-Century Peru: Historical and Theoretical Background to the *Golpe de Estado* of 1968." *Hispanic American Historical Review.* Vol. 59, No. 3, 1979.

O'Leary, Jeremiah. "Dominican Politics. Police Strongman Follows Trujillo's Path to Power." *The Evening Star.* Feb. 16, 1972.

Ornes, Germán E. *Trujillo: Little Caesar of the Caribbean.* New York: Thomas Nelson, 1958.

Ortega, Manuel. *The Political and Socio-Economic Role of the Military in Latin America.* Appendix F: "Dominican Republic." Carol Gables, Florida: University of Miami, Division of Research. Center for Advanced International Studies, 1969.

Ovalles, Alejandro. *Caamaño, El Gobierno y las Guerrillas del 1973.* Santo Domingo: Taller de Impresiones, n.d.

Palmer, Bruce, Jr. General. *Intervention in the Caribbean: The Dominican Crisis of 1965.* Lexington: The University Press of Kentucky, 1989.

Paulino, Aliro, Jr. *La Noche que Trujillo Volvio.* 4th ed. Santo Domingo: Mundo Diplomático Internacional, 1986.

Peguero, Valentina. "Trujillo and the Military: Organization, Modernization and Control of the Dominican Armed Forces, 1916–1961." Ph.D. diss. Columbia University, 1993.

Pérez, Louis A., Jr. *Army Politics in Cuba, 1898–1958.* Pittsburgh: University of Pittsburgh Press, 1976.

Peru. Comando Conjunto de la Fuerza Armada. *Centro de Altos Estudios Militares.* 1972.

Phillips, David Atlee. *The Night Watch.* New York: Ballantine, 1977.

Reyes Jorge, Rafael Antonio, Tte. Coronel Piloto. "Una Exposición Beneficiosa." *Revista de las Fuerzas Armadas.* Oct.-Dec. 1966.

Roberts, T.D., et al. *Area Handbook for the Dominican Republic.* Washington, D.C.: The American University, Foreign Area Studies, 1966.

Rodman, Selden. "Why Balaguer Won." *The New Republic.* Vol. 154, No. 25, Jun. 18, 1966.

Romero Pumarol, Teófilo Ramón, Coronel. "El Estado Mayor de la Unidad y Funciones del Oficial de Enlace." *Revista de las Fuerzas Armadas.* Jul. 1972.

_____. "En las Fuerzas Armadas Dominicanas, Esto fué lo Primero." *Revista de las Fuerzas Armadas.* Jun. 1972.

_____. "Temas de Comando y Estado Mayor. Sequencia de Acciones Para Llegar a Decisiones Lógicas y Ejecutarlas con Exito." *Revista de las Fuerzas Armadas.* Sep. 1972.

_____, Coronel Diplomado de Estado Mayor. "Estudio de Estado Mayor." *Revista de las Fuerzas Armadas.* Dec. 1972.

Saldaña Jiménez, Rafael, Coronel Abogado. "Las Fuerzas Armadas en 1971." *Revista de las Fuerzas Armadas.* Jan. 1972.

SOA Graduates. Jul. 16-Nov. 30, 1962. Washington, D.C.: School of the Americas Watch, n.d.

Stepan, Alfred. *The Military in Politics: Changing Patterns in Brazil.* Princeton, New Jersey: Princeton University Press, 1971.

Szulc, Tad. *Dominican Diary.* New York: Delacorte, 1965.

Taber, Robert. *The War of the Flea: A Study of Guerrilla Warfare, Theory and Practice.* London: Paladin, 1970.

Tavarez Justo, Emma. "La Vida de Caamaño en Cuba." *Ahora.* Jun. 4, 1973.

Thomas, Hugh. *The Spanish Civil War.* New York: Harper and Brothers, 1961.

United Press International. UPI International Section, Jun. 11, 1996.

U.S. Agency for International Development. Office of Public Safety. *Weekly Progress Report, Dominican Republic.* Mar. 4 and May 27, 1966.

U.S. Congress, House of Representatives, Committee on Foreign Affairs. *The New Strategy of Communism in the Caribbean: Report of a Special Study Mission,* by the Hon. Armistead I. Selden, Jr., Chairman, Subcommittee on Inter-American Affairs. 90th Congress, 2nd Session, Nov. 2, 1968. Washington, D.C.: Government Printing Office, 1968.

U.S. Congress, Senate, Committee on the Judiciary, Subcommittee to Investigate the Administration of the Internal Security Act and Other Internal Security Laws. *Communist Threat to the U.S. Through the Caribbean: Testimony of Brigadier General Elias Wessin y Wessin.* 89th Congress, 1st Session, Oct. 1, 1965. Washington, D.C.: Government Printing Office, 1965.

U.S. Defense Attaché Office, Santo Domingo. Intelligence information messages. 1973.

U.S. Defense Intelligence Agency. *Biographic Data.* 1967, 1969, 1970, 1973.

U.S. Defense Intelligence Agency. *Biographic Sketch.* 1966, 1969, 1978, 1979.

U.S. Department of the Army. U.S. Army School of the Americas. "Diagrama Histórico de la Escuela de las Américas." *Adelante.* Summer, 1988.

U.S. Department of the Army. U.S. Army School of the Americas. Letter. Subject: *Freedom of Information Act Report—Command and Staff Course Graduates.* Dec. 9, 1998.

U.S. Department of the Army. U.S. Army South. *Biographic Data.* 1972.

U.S. Department of Defense. Messages. 1966, 1969.

U.S. Department of Defense. U.S. Southern Command. *Biographic Data.* 1974.

U.S. Department of Defense. U.S. Southern Command. Messages. 1973.

U.S. Department of State. "Military Assistance Agreement Between the United States of America and the Dominican Republic. Mar. 8, 1962."Vol. XV. *United States Treaties And Other International Agreements*. Washington, D.C.: Government Printing Office, 1950–1996.

_____. Telegrams and airgrams. 1964–1973.

U.S. Department of State. Bureau of Intelligence and Research. Intelligence Note. Subject: *Dominican Republic: President Balaguer Outflanks his Critics*. Nov. 8, 1971.

_____. _____. Intelligence Note. Subject: *Missing Dominican Rebel Leader May be in Cuba*. Dec. 8, 1967.

U.S. Embassy, Santo Domingo. *Briefing Paper, Dominican Republic, 1961–1971*.

U.S. Foreign Broadcast Information Service. *Daily Report: Latin America*. Washington, D.C. 1962–1975.

U.S. Library of Congress (DRD). *1961–1966 Chronology for the Dominican Republic*, 1967.

Vásquez, George L. "Peru." In *The Political Role of the Military: An International Handbook*. Edited by Constantine P. Danopoulos and Cynthia Watson. Westport, Connecticut: Greenwood, 1996.

Vega y Pagán, Ernesto, Teniente de Navío. *Biografía Militar del Generalísimo Doctor Rafael Leonidas Trujillo Molina, Benefactor de la Patria y Padre de la Patria Nueva, Comandante en Jefe de las Fuerzas Armadas de la Nación*. Ciudad Trujillo: Editorial Atenas, 1956.

Ventura, Juan. *Presidentes, Juntas, Consejos, Triunviratos, y Gabinetes de la República Dominicana, 1844–1984*. Santo Domingo: Publicaciones ONAP, 1985.

Weil, Thomas E., et al. *Area Handbook for the Dominican Republic*. Washington, D.C.: The American University, Foreign Area Studies, 1973.

Welles, Sumner. *Naboth's Vineyard: The Dominican Republic, 1844–1924*. 2 Vols. Mamaroneck, New York: Paul P. Appel, 1966.

Wessin y Wessin, Elías. Coronel. "A Todos Mis Hermanos de Armas." *Revista de las Fuerzas Armadas*. May-Jun. 1963.

_____, General. "Bitter Salt of a Stranger's Bread." *National Review*. Vol. XVII, No. 42, Oct. 19, 1965.

Wiarda, Howard J. *Dictatorship and Development: The Methods of Control in Trujillo's Dominican Republic*. Gainesville: University of Florida Press, 1968.

_____. "The Dominican Fuse." *The Nation*. Vol. 206, No. 8, Feb. 19, 1968.

_____. *The Dominican Republic: Nation in Transition*. New York: Frederick A. Praeger, 1969.

_____, editor. *Materials for the Study of Politics and Government in the Dominican Republic, 1930–1966*. Santiago, Dominican Republic: Universidad Católica Madre y Maestra, 1968.

Wiarda, Howard J., and Michael J. Kryzanek. "Dominican Dictatorship Revisited: The Caudillo Tradition and the Regimes of Trujillo and Balaguer." *Revista/Review Interamericana*. Vol. 7, No. 3, Fall 1977.

Wilson, Larman C. *United States Military Assistance to the Dominican Republic, 1916–1967*. (Paper prepared for delivery before the Seminar on the Dominican Republic, Center for International Affairs, Harvard University, April 20, 1967.) n.p., 1967.

Yates, Lawrence A. *Power Pack: U.S. Intervention in the Dominican Republic, 1965–1966*. Fort Leavenworth, Kansas: U.S. Army Command and General Staff College, Combat Studies Institute. 1988.

NEWSPAPERS AND NEWSMAGAZINES

Ahora (Dominican Republic)
El Caribe (Dominican Republic)
The Christian Science Monitor (U.S.)
The Evening Star (U.S.)
Listín Diario (Dominican Republic)
The Miami Herald (U.S.)

El Nacional (Dominican Republic)
The New York Times (U.S.)
La Noticia (Dominican Republic)
Punto Final (Chile)
Renovación (Dominican Republic)
La República (Venezuela)

El Tiempo (Dominican Republic)   *The Wall Street Journal* (U.S.)
Time (U.S.)   *The Washington Post* (U.S.)
Ultima Hora (Dominican Republic)

BROADCASTS

All non-U.S. broadcasts were acquired from the Foreign Broadcast Information Service *Daily Report: Latin America.*

Agence France-Presse-AFP (France)
Dominican Armed Forces Radio-San Isidro (Dominican Republic)
EFE (Spain)
Emisoras Nacionales (Dominican Republic)
Havana Domestic Service ("Havana Domestic Service" is a U.S. Foreign Broadcast Information Service term for a government-owned Cuban news outlet.)
LATIN (Argentina)
National Reconstruction Government Radio (Dominican Republic)
Onda Musical (Dominican Republic)
Prensa Latina (Cuba)
Radio Caribe (Dominican Republic)
Radio Clarín (Dominican Republic)
Radio Comercial (Dominican Republic)
Radio Continental (Dominican Republic)
Radio Cristal (Dominican Republic)
Radio HIN (Dominican Republic)
Radio Mil (Dominican Republic)
Radio Pueblo (Dominican Republic)
Radio Universal (Dominican Republic)
Reuters (U.K.)
Revolutionary Nationalism Network (Dominican Republic)
Santo Domingo Domestic Service-SDDS ("Santo Domingo Domestic Service" is a U.S. Foreign Broadcast Information Service term for a government-owned Dominican news outlet.)

INTERVIEWS

This work contains information obtained during numerous personal interviews conducted by the author when he was the army attaché in the U.S. Embassy, Santo Domingo, from 1971 to 1974. During 1998–2002, former U.S. Army advisers orally contributed facts and insights concerning the Dominican Armed Forces. These ex–U.S. MAAG officers were the then Majors Mario Burdick, Orlando Rodriguez, Juan Armando Montes, and Ildefonso Lombraña, and Captain Rodolfo Roberts. In addition, Lieutenant Colonels William Camper, U.S. Army, and Stanley Castleman, U.S. Air Force, provided written responses to a series of questions.

Index